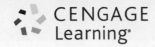

COMM3
Kathleen S. Verderber
Deanna D. Sellnow
Rudolph F. Verderber

Product Director: Monica Eckman

Product Manager: Nicole Morinon

Content Developer:
  Kathy Sands-Boehmer

Content Coordinator: Alicia Landsberg

Product Assistant: Colin Solan

Product Director, 4LTR Press:
  Steven E. Joos

Media Developer: Jessica Badiner

Marketing Manager: Lydia Lestar

Content Project Manager:
  Corinna Dibble

Art Director: Linda May

Manufacturing Planner: Doug Bertke

Rights Acquisition Specialist:
  Ann Hoffman

Design and Production Service:
  B-books, Ltd.

Cover Designer: Studio Montage

Compositor: B-books, Ltd.

For product information and technology assistance, contact us at
Cengage Learning Customer & Sales Support, 1-800-354-9706.

For permission to use material from this text or product,
submit all requests online at **www.cengage.com/permissions**.
Further permissions questions can be emailed to
permissionrequest@cengage.com.

Library of Congress Control Number: 2013947732

ISBN-13: 978-1-285-44558-8
ISBN-10: 1-285-44558-9

Cengage Learning
200 First Stamford Place, 4th Floor
Stamford, CT 06902
USA

Cengage Learning is a leading provider of customized learning solutions with office locations around the globe, including Singapore, the United Kingdom, Australia, Mexico, Brazil and Japan. Locate your local office at **international.cengage.com/region**.

Cengage Learning products are represented in Canada by Nelson Education, Ltd.

For your course and learning solutions, visit **www.cengage.com**. Purchase any of our products at your local college store or at our preferred online store **www.CengageBrain.com**.
Instructors: Please visit **login.cengage.com** and log in to access instructor-specific resources.

Printed in the United States of America
1 2 3 4 5 6 7 17 16 15 14 13

COMM3 Brief Contents

© Creatas Images/Thinkstock.com

Contents

COMM3

©iStockphoto/Thinkstock.com

4 Verbal Messages 48

5 Nonverbal Messages 60

6 Listening 72

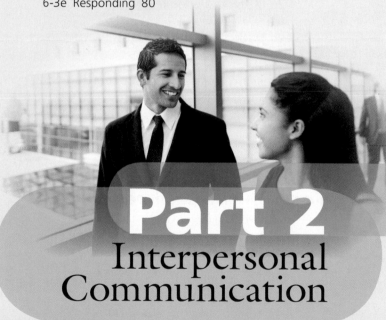

Part 2
Interpersonal Communication

7 Interpersonal Relationships 84

© aldomurillo/iStockphoto.com

Part 3
Group Communication

© GlobalStock/iStockphoto.com

© Sheff/Shutterstock.com

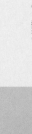

Part 4
Public Speaking

10 Group Leadership and Problem Solving 132

11 Topic Selection and Development 150

16 Informative Speaking 242

17 Persuasive Speaking 262

Appendix: Interviewing 290

References 298

Index 305

HEY!
WATSUP
N2M, U?
N2M, IN CLASS :(
R WE STILL ON 4 L8R?
4 SURE, 8 RIGHT?
YUP :) CU L8R!

Communication Perspectives

Learning Outcomes

1-1 Describe the nature of communication

1-2 Explain the communication process

1-3 Identify the characteristics of communication

1-4 Use the major tenets of ethical communication to create and evaluate messages

1-5 Create a plan to increase communication competence

What do you think?
I prefer to share my ideas in a group setting.

1	2	3	4	5	6	7	8	9	10
STRONGLY DISAGREE									STRONGLY AGREE

Numerous studies done over the years have shown that for almost any job, employers seek oral communication skills, teamwork skills, and interpersonal abilities (College learning for the new global century, 2007; Hansen & Hansen,(n.d.); Young, 2003). For example, an article on the role of communication in the workplace reported that in engineering, a highly technical field, speaking skills were very important for 72 percent of the employers surveyed (Darling & Dannels, 2003). A survey by the National Association of Colleges and Employers (Hart Research Associates, 2006) reported the top 10 personal qualities and skills that employers seek from college graduates. The number one skill was communication, including face-to-face speaking, presentational speaking, and writing. Other "Top 10" skills, which you will learn about and practice in this course, include teamwork skills (number three), analytical skills (number five), interpersonal skills (number eight), and problem-solving skills (number nine). The employers also said that these very skills are, unfortunately, the ones many new graduates lack (Hart Research Associates, 2010). Taking this course to heart can significantly increase your ability to get a job and be successful in your chosen career.

How effectively you communicate with others is important not only to your career but also to your personal relationships. Your ability to make and keep friends, to be a good family member, to have satisfying intimate relationships, to participate in or lead groups, and to prepare and present speeches depends on your communication skills. During this course, you will learn about the communication process and have an opportunity to practice basic communication skills that will help you improve your relationships.

We begin this chapter by describing the nature of communication and the communication process. From there, we will discuss several principles of communication and five tenets of ethical communication. Finally, we explain how to develop a personal communication improvement plan to hone your skills based on what you learn throughout the semester.

1-1 The Nature of Communication

Communication is a complex process through which we express, interpret, and coordinate messages with others to create shared meaning, meet social goals, manage personal identity, and carry out our relationships. At its core, communication is about messages.

Messages are the verbal utterances, visual images, and nonverbal behaviors used to convey thoughts and feelings. We refer to the process of creating messages as **encoding** and the process of interpreting them as **decoding**. So when the toddler points to her bottle and cries out "Ba-ba," her message (consisting of a nonverbal gesture—pointing—and a verbal utterance—"Ba-ba") expresses her desire to have her father hand her the bottle of milk she sees on the table. How her father responds, however, depends on how he decodes it. He might respond by handing her the bottle or by saying, "Sorry, cutie, the bottle is empty." Or he may just look at her with a puzzled expression on his face. Either response is also a message. **Feedback** is a reaction and response to a message that indicates how the message was interpreted.

1-1a Canned Plans and Scripts

How do we form and interpret messages? We do so, in part, based on our canned plans and scripts. A **canned plan** is a "mental library" of scripts each of us draws from to create messages based on what worked for us or others in the past (Berger, 1997). A **script** is an actual text of what to say and do in a specific situation. We have canned plans and scripts for a wide variety of typical interactions, such as greeting people, making small talk, giving advice, complimenting or criticizing someone, or persuading others.

↘ Great apes, such as gorillas, are known for their complex communication system and for their ability to learn sign language to communicate with humans. This rehabilitator works and communicates with gorillas to help them learn to form sustainable social groups in the wild as part of a project aiming to save the species from extinction. Both the gorillas and the rehabilitator use scripts to communicate.

© Michael Nichols/National Geographic/Getty Images

We develop canned plans and scripts from our own previous experiences and by observing what appears to work for other people (even fictitious people we see on TV or in movies) (Pajares, Prestin, Chen, & Nabi, 2009). Think about the first time you asked someone out on a date. In all likelihood you pulled your method from your canned plan of "ask for a date" scripts. We draw on scripts from our canned plans as we form a message and usually customize what we say based on the person and the situation. For example, you might have several canned "greeting" plan scripts to draw from when addressing a close friend, a parent, a supervisor, or a stranger.

The point is that we don't usually start from scratch to form messages. Instead, we recognize what type of message we want to form, search our mental canned plan library for an appropriate script, and then customize it to fit the unique parts of the current situation. All of this mental choosing happens in nanoseconds and somewhat automatically. We also use our canned plans and scripts when we interpret messages from others.

communication
the process through which we express, interpret, and coordinate messages with others

messages
the verbal utterances, visual images, and nonverbal behaviors used to convey thoughts and feelings

encoding
the process of putting our thoughts and feelings into words and nonverbal behaviors

decoding
the process of interpreting another's message

feedback
reactions and responses to messages

canned plan
a "mental library" of scripts each of us draws from to create messages based on what worked for us in the past or that we have heard or used numerous times in similar situations

script
an actual text of what to say and do in a specific situation

Obviously, the larger your canned plan library and the more scripts you have for each canned plan, the more likely you will be to form appropriate and effective messages, as well as to understand and respond appropriately to the messages of others.

1-1b Communication Contexts

According to noted German philosopher Jürgen Habermas, the ideal communication situation is impossible to achieve, but considering its contexts as we communicate can move us closer to that goal (Littlejohn & Foss, 2011). The context in which a message is embedded affects the expectations of the participants, the meaning these participants derive, and their subsequent behavior. The **communication context** is made up of the physical, social, historical, psychological, and cultural situations that surround a communication event.

The **physical context** includes the location of a communication encounter, the environmental conditions surrounding it (temperature, lighting, noise level), and the physical proximity of participants to each other. Increasingly, however, communication occurs via smartphones and over the Internet. And while e-communication allows us to interact at a distance, our ability to share meaning may be affected by the media we use. For instance, when you telephone a friend, you lose nonverbal cues such as posture, gestures, eye contact, and facial expressions that are part of a face-to-face message. Without these cues, you have less information on which to base your interpretation of your friend's message. E-mail and text messages are missing even more of the nonverbal cues that help us interpret messages accurately.

The **social context** is the nature of the relationship that already exists between the participants. The better you know someone and the better relationship you have with him or her, the more likely you are to accurately interpret the messages.

The **historical context** is the background provided by previous communication between the participants. For instance, suppose Chas texts Anna saying he will pick up the draft of the report they had left for their manager. When Anna sees Chas at lunch later that day, she asks, "Did you get it?" Another person listening to the conversation would have no idea what "it" is. Yet Chas may well reply, "It's on my desk." Anna and Chas understand one another because of their earlier exchange.

The **psychological context** includes the moods and feelings each person brings to the communication encounter. For instance, suppose Corinne is under a great deal of stress. While she is studying for an exam, a friend stops by and asks her to take a break to go to the gym. Corinne, who is normally good-natured, may respond with irritation, which her friend may misinterpret as Corinne being mad at him.

The **cultural context** includes the beliefs, values, orientations, underlying assumptions, and rituals that belong to a specific culture (Samovar, Porter, & McDaniel, 2010). Everyone is part of one or more cultural groups (e.g., ethnicity, religion, age, gender, sexual orientation, physical ability). When two people from different cultures interact, misunderstandings may occur because of their different cultural values, beliefs, orientations, and rituals.

1-1c Communication Settings

The setting in which communication occurs also affects how we form and interpret messages. **Communication settings** differ based on the number of participants and the level of formality in the interactions (Littlejohn & Foss, 2008). These settings are intrapersonal, interpersonal, small group, public, and mass.

Intrapersonal communication refers to the interactions that occur in our minds when we are talking to ourselves. We usually don't verbalize our intrapersonal communication. When you think about what you'll do later today or when you send yourself e-mail reminders, you are communicating intrapersonally. Much of our intrapersonal communication occurs subconsciously (Kellerman, 1992). When you drive to school every day "without

communication context
the physical, social, historical, psychological, and cultural situations that surround a communication event

physical context
the location of a communication encounter, the environmental conditions surrounding it (temperature, lighting, noise level), and the physical proximity of participants to each other

social context
the nature of the relationship that exists between participants

historical context
the background provided by previous communication episodes between the participants that influence understandings in the current encounter

psychological context
the mood and feelings each person brings to a communication encounter

cultural context
the beliefs, values, orientations, underlying assumptions, and rituals that belong to a specific culture

communication setting
the different communication environments within which people interact, characterized by the number of participants and the extent to which the interaction is formal or informal

intrapersonal communication
the interactions that occur in our minds when we are talking to ourselves

thinking" about each turn you make along the way, you are communicating intrapersonally on a subconscious level. The study of intrapersonal communication often focuses on its role in shaping self-perceptions and in managing communication apprehension—that is, the fear associated with communicating with others (Richmond & McCroskey, 1997). In this book, our study of intrapersonal communication focuses on self-talk as a means to improve self-concept and self-esteem and, ultimately, communication competence in a variety of situations.

Interpersonal communication is characterized by informal interaction between two people who have an identifiable relationship with each other (Knapp & Daly, 2002). Talking to a friend between classes, visiting on the phone with your mother, and texting or chatting online with your brother are all examples of interpersonal communication. In chapters 7 and 8, we will study how interpersonal communication helps us develop, maintain, improve, and end interpersonal relationships.

Small-group communication typically involves three to 20 people who come together to communicate with one another (Beebe & Masterson, 2006; Hirokawa, Cathcart, Samovar, & Henman, 2003). Examples of small groups include a family, a group of friends, a group of classmates working on a project, and a workplace management team. Small-group communication can occur in face-to-face settings as well as online through electronic mailing lists, discussion boards, virtual meetings, and blogs. In chapters 9 and 10, our study of small groups focuses on the characteristics of effective groups, ethical and effective communication in groups, leadership, problem-solving, conflict, and group presentations.

Public communication is delivered to audiences of more than 20 people. Examples include public speeches, presentations, and forums we may experience in person or via mediated or

technology-driven channels. For example, when President Barack Obama delivered his inaugural address some people were there in person, others watched on TV or the Internet as he spoke, and still others viewed it later in the form of televised snippets or an online video such as

Intrapersonal Communication

Interpersonal Communication

Small-Group Communication

Public Communication

Mass Communication

YouTube. The Internet is also becoming the medium of choice for posting job ads and résumés, for advertising and buying products, and for political activism. In chapters 11 through 17, our study of public communication focuses on preparing, practicing, and delivering effective oral presentations in both face-to-face and virtual environments.

Mass communication is delivered by individuals and entities through mass media to large segments of the population at the same time. Some examples include newspaper and magazine articles and advertisements, as well as radio and television programs and advertisements.

© Chris Tobin/Lifesize/Getty Images

Messages are not always interpreted as the sender expects, which can be clarified by feedback.

<u>1-2</u> The Communication Process

The **communication process** is a complex set of three different and interrelated activities intended to result in shared meaning (Burleson, 2009). These sub-processes are affected by the channels used and by interference/noise.

1-2a Sub-Processes of Communication

Three sub-processes that must be performed to achieve shared meaning are message production, message interpretation, and interaction coordination.

First, **message production** is what you do when you *encode* a message. You begin by forming goals based on your understanding of the situation and your values, ethics, and needs. Based on these goals, you recall a canned plan and script that was effective in achieving similar goals and adapt it to the current situation. Then you share your message.

Second, **message interpretation** is what you do when you *decode* a message. The process begins when you notice someone is trying to communicate with you. You read or listen to her words, observe her nonverbal behavior, and take note of other visuals. You then interpret the message based on the canned plan scripts you remember that seem similar. Based on this interpretation, you prepare a feedback message, which leads into the third sub-process.

Interaction coordination consists of the behavioral adjustments each participant makes in an attempt to create shared meaning (Burgoon et. al., 2002). For example, if your partner's message is more positive than you expected, you might adjust your behavior by mirroring that positive behavior. If your partner's message is more negative than you expected, you might respond in kind with a negative message of your own, or you might behave in a more positive manner to encourage your partner to reciprocate.

Shared meaning occurs when the receiver's interpretation is similar to what the speaker intended. We can usually gauge the extent to which shared meaning is achieved by the sender's response to the feedback message. For example, Sarah says to Nick, "I dropped my phone and it broke." Nick replies, "Cool, now you can get a Droid." Sarah responds, "No, you don't understand, I can't afford to buy a new phone." Sarah's

mass communication
communication that is delivered by individuals and entities through mass media to large segments of the population at the same time

communication process
a complex set of three different and interrelated activities intended to result in shared meaning

message production
the steps you take when you encode a message

message interpretation
the steps you take when you decode a message.

interaction coordination
the behavioral adjustments each participant makes in an attempt to create shared meaning

response to Nick's feedback message lets Nick know he misunderstood her. The extent to which we achieve shared meaning can be affected by the channels we use and by the interference/noise that compete with our messages.

1-2b Channels

Channels are both the route traveled by the message and the means of transportation. Face-to-face communication has three basic channels: verbal symbols, nonverbal cues, and visual images. Technologically mediated communication uses these same channels, though nonverbal cues such as movements, touch, and gestures are represented by visual symbols like **emoticons** (textual images that symbolize the sender's mood, emotion, or facial expressions) and **acronyms** (abbreviations that stand in for common phrases). For example, in a face-to-face interaction, Barry might express his frustration about a poor grade verbally by noting why he thought the grade was unfair, visually by showing the assignment along with the grading criteria for it, and nonverbally by raising his voice and shaking his fist. In an online interaction, however, he might need to insert a frowning-face emoticon (☹) or the acronym "POed" to represent those nonverbal behaviors.

1-2c Interference/Noise

Interference or **noise** is any stimulus that interferes with the process of sharing meaning. Noise can be external, internal, or semantic. **External noises** are sights, sounds, and other stimuli that draw people's attention away from the message. For instance, a pop-up advertisement may draw your attention away from a Web page or blog, the sound of a fire engine may distract you from a professor's lecture, or the smell of donuts may interfere with your train of thought during a conversation with a friend.

Internal noises are thoughts and feelings that draw people's attention away from the message. For example, you might lose track of a message because you are daydreaming or thinking about something you need to do later. **Semantic noises** are emotional distractions aroused by specific word choices. For instance, if a coworker describes a forty-year-old secretary as "the girl in the office," you may think "girl" is a condescending term for a forty-year-old woman and not hear the rest of what your co-worker has to say.

1-2d A Model of the Communication Process

In summary, let's look at a graphic model of a message exchange between two people presented in Figure 1.1. The process begins when one person, who we will call

channel
the route traveled by the message and the means of transportation

emoticons
textual images that symbolize the sender's mood, emotion, or facial expressions

acronyms
abbreviations that stand in for common phrases

interference (noise)
any stimulus that interferes with the process of sharing meaning

external noise
sights, sounds, and other stimuli that draw people's attention away from the message

internal noise
thoughts and feelings that compete for attention and interfere with the communication process

semantic noise
distractions aroused by certain word choices that take our attention away from the main message

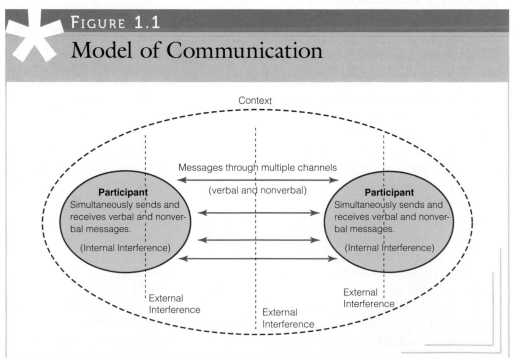

FIGURE 1.1

Model of Communication

© Cengage Learning

Modern Mourning

Mourning is a universal human communication process of celebrating the life of someone while grieving his or her death. Mourning rituals and traditions vary by culture and religion and change over time. So it is not surprising that mourning in the United States in the 21st century is adapting past practices to modern life.

Web sites such as Legacy.com, MyDeathSpace.com, and Memory-Of.com facilitate the creation of these interactive online memorials. Users can create slide shows to "talk" about their deceased loved one and mourners can "visit" with the departed and connect with other mourners. T-shirts have become a new type of mourning clothes, often featuring pictures of the deceased. This is particularly common when commemorating a young person or a violent death. Another sign of mourning in the 21st century is the use of decals on cars and bikes. Decals are visual markers that can not only memorialize a loved one who died but can also connect mourners to others who have suffered a similar loss.

Andy, is motivated to share his thoughts with another person, Taylor. Andy reviews the communication situation, including the communication context, and sorts through the scripts in his canned plan library to find one he thinks will be appropriate. Based on this script, he encodes a customized message and shares it with Taylor.

Taylor decodes the message using her understanding of the situation and matching it to scripts in her canned plan library. She might misinterpret Andy's intended meaning because she is distracted by external, internal, or semantic interference/noise, or because her scripts don't match Andy's. Taylor encodes a feedback message using a script from her canned plan library as a guide. She then shares her feedback message and Andy decodes it. If Taylor understood what Andy was saying, he will extend the conversation. If, on the other hand, Andy believes Taylor misunderstood his meaning, he will try to clarify what he meant before extending the conversation. Finally, the communication process is not linear. In other words, both Andy and Taylor simultaneously encode and decode verbal and nonverbal messages throughout the message exchange.

1-2e Mediated Communication

Thanks to smartphone and Internet technology, we can now communicate 24/7 without conversing face-to-face—this is communication that is "mediated" through a device of some sort, including both social media and any digital communication. Yet, these very technologies that allow us to communicate anytime and nearly anywhere can also lead to greater chances for misunderstandings.

In these mediated communication sections throughout the text, we will look at the ways technology affects our communication in general, the development of interpersonal relationships, dynamics of group communication, and technological advances in public speaking. In chapters 1, 2, and 5 we will explore three important ways in which the channel affects our ability to achieve mutual understanding and, ultimately, how these mediated exchanges can affect our relationships.

Channels and Synchronicity

We can talk face-to-face or through a variety of technology-mediated channels (MC), many of which are computer mediated (CMC). So if we can't or prefer not to talk with someone in person, we might:

- call them on the phone (MC),
- send a text message (MC),
- talk with them through Skype (CMC),
- e-mail them (CMC),
- send them a fax (MC), or
- post on their Facebook page (CMC).

Because each of these channels has different potential benefits and drawbacks, understanding how they function can help us make informed choices about which one to use at a particular time. Three characteristics that differentiate these communication channels are synchronicity, social presence, and media richness, (see Figure 1.2). In this chapter, we will discuss synchronicity. Chapter 2 covers social presence, and chapter 5 covers richness.

synchronicity
the extent to which a channel allows you to get immediate feedback

synchronous channels
allow communicators to exchange messages in "real time"

asynchronous channels
message exchanges are separated by both time and space

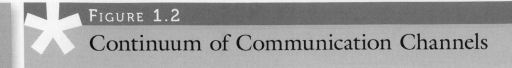

FIGURE 1.2

Continuum of Communication Channels

ASYNCHRONOUS					SYNCHRONOUS	
Bulk letters	Posted letters	Facebook	Interactive	Telephone	Skype	Face-to-Face
Posters	E-mail	Twitter	chat		iChat	
E-mail spam	Text	Other social			Other video	
	messages	media Web sites			conferencing	
LEAN						RICH
LOW SOCIAL PRESENCE					HIGH SOCIAL PRESENCE	

Synchronicity is the extent to which a channel allows you to get immediate feedback (Kiesler, Zubrow, Moses, & Geller, 1985). **Synchronous channels** (like telephone calls, conference calls, and video chats) allow communicators to exchange messages in "real time." Although communicators are physically separated from one another when communicating via any mediated channel, synchronous channels allow all to be "present" in virtual time and space with little or no lag between sending, receiving, and responding to messages. Messages conveyed through synchronous channels allow for immediate feedback to clarify potential misunderstandings before they are acted upon or damage the relationship (Condon & Cech, 2010).

In **asynchronous channels** (such as e-mails and letters), message exchanges are separated by both time and space. When you e-mail your friend, for example, there is usually lag time between sending a message and receiving a response. With the exception of voicemail recordings, asynchronous channels rely only on written verbal messages. However, most messages delivered via asynchronous channels replace the careful composition process normally associated with written communication with "talking by writing." In other words, language choices are similar to those used in oral, synchronous conversations even though the messages are actually written (Spitzer, 1986). Unfortunately, however, when "talking by writing," we often fail to consider emotional tone and the possible ways our partner may interpret that tone. Thus, the chances for misunderstanding are high. For example, a message we intend to be clear and direct might be interpreted as intimidating, cold, or angry because the nonverbal cues that would soften the tone if conveyed orally are missing. To account for this limitation, we have developed acronyms like "LOL" and emoticons like ☺ to represent the emotional tone that is more readily conveyed in synchronous channels. Figure 1.2 illustrates how face-to-face communication is high in synchronicity, and as you scan back to the left, the messages are more and more asynchronous.

1-3 Characteristics of Communication

Several communication characteristics provide a foundation for practicing and improving communication skills. In this section, we discuss eight of them.

1-3a Communication Has Purpose

Whenever we communicate, we have a purpose for doing so. The purpose may be serious or trivial, and we may or may not be aware of it at the time. There are five basic purposes for communication.

1. We communicate to develop and maintain our sense of self. Through our interactions, we learn who we are and what we are good at.

2. We communicate to meet our social needs. Just as we need food, water, and shelter, we also need contact with other people.

3. We communicate to develop and maintain relationships. We communicate not only to meet simple social needs but also to develop relationships.

4. We communicate to exchange information. We exchange information through observation, reading, and direct communication with others, whether face-to-face, via text messaging, or online.

5. We communicate to influence others. We may communicate to try to convince friends to go to a particular restaurant or to see a certain movie, encourage a supervisor to alter the work schedule, or talk an instructor into changing a grade.

1-3b Communication Is Continuous

We are always sending and interpreting messages. Even silence communicates if another person infers meaning from it. Why? Because our nonverbal behavior represents reactions to our environment and to the people around us. If we are cold, we might shiver; if we are hot or nervous, we might perspire; if we are bored, happy, or confused, our nonverbal language will probably show it.

1-3c Communication Is Irreversible

Once an exchange takes place, we can never go back in time and erase the communication. We might be able to repair damage we have done, but the message has been communicated. When you participate in an online discussion or leave a post on a blog, you are leaving an electronic "footprint" that others can follow and read. E-mails, IMs, and text messages are not always completely private either. Once you push the "send" button, not only can't you take it back, but you have little control over who the receiver might forward it to or how it might be used publicly.

1-3d
Communication Is Situated

When we say that communication is *situated* we mean that it occurs within a specific communication setting that affects how the messages are produced, interpreted, and coordinated (Burleson, 2009). The interpretation of the statement "I love you" varies depending on the setting. During a candlelit anniversary dinner, it may be interpreted as a statement of romantic feelings. If a mother says it as she greets her daughter, it may be interpreted as motherly love. If it is made in response to a joke delivered by someone in a group of friends gathered to watch a football game, it may be interpreted as a complement for being clever. So what is said and what is meant depends on the situation.

1-3e Communication Is Indexical

How we communicate is also an **index** or measure of the emotional temperature of our relationship at the time. For instance, when they are getting in the car to leave for a holiday, Laura says to Darryl, "I remembered to bring the map." She is not just reporting information. Through her tone of voice and other nonverbal cues, she is also communicating something about the relationship, such as, "You can always depend on me" or "You never remember to think of these things."

> **index**
> a measure of the emotional temperature of our relationship at the time

This couple's position suggests trust and intimacy in their relationship.

© Chris Schmidt/iStockphoto.com

trust
the extent to which partners rely on, depend on, and have faith that their partners will not intentionally do anything to harm them

control
the degree to which one participant in the communication encounter is perceived to be more dominant or powerful

complementary feedback
a message that signals agreement about who is in control

symmetrical feedback
a message that signals disagreement about who is in control

intimacy
the degree of emotional closeness, acceptance, and disclosure in a relationship

spontaneous expressions
messages spoken without much conscious thought

constructed messages
messages that are formed carefully and thoughtfully when our known scripts are inadequate for the situation

culture
a system of shared beliefs, values, symbols, and behaviors

A message exchange can also signal the level of trust, control, and intimacy in a relationship (Millar & Rogers, 1987).

Trust is the extent to which partners rely on, depend on, and have faith that their partners will not intentionally do anything to harm them. For instance, Mark says, "I'll do the final edits and turn in the paper." Sandy replies, "Never mind, I'll do it so that it won't be late." Sandy's response may signal that she doesn't trust Mark to get the group's paper in on time.

Control is the degree to which one participant in the communication encounter is perceived to be more dominant or powerful than the other. When Tom says to Sue, "I know you're concerned about the budget, but I'll see to it that we have enough money to cover everything," through his words, tone of voice, and nonverbal behavior, he is signaling that he is "in charge" of the finances. In turn, Sue may respond by either verbally responding or nonverbally showing that she agrees with him or by challenging him and asserting her desire to control the budget. In other words, control is communicated with either complementary or symmetrical feedback. **Complementary feedback** signals agreement about who is in control, whereas **symmetrical feedback** signals disagreement. If Sue says, "Great, I'm glad you're looking after it," her feedback complements his message. But if Sue responds, "Wait a minute, you're the one who overdrew our checking account last month," she is challenging his control with a symmetrical response. Relational control is not negotiated in a single exchange, but through many message exchanges over time. The point, however, is that control is negotiated through communication.

Intimacy is the degree of emotional closeness, acceptance, and disclosure in a relationship. When Cody asks Madison what she is thinking about, and Madison begins to pour out her problems, she is revealing the degree of intimacy she feels in the relationship. Or, should she reply, "Oh I'm not really thinking about anything important. Did you hear the news this morning about . . . ," her subject change signals that the relationship is not intimate enough to share her problems.

1-3f Communication Is Learned

Just as we learn to walk, so do we learn to communicate. Because communication is learned, we can always improve our ability to communicate.

1-3g Communication Messages Vary in Conscious Thought

Recall that creating shared meaning involves encoding and decoding verbal messages, nonverbal cues, and even visual images. Our messages may (1) occur spontaneously, (2) be based on a "script," or (3) be carefully constructed.

Many messages are **spontaneous expressions**, spoken without much conscious thought. For example, when you burn your finger, you may blurt out, "Ouch!" When something goes right, you may break into a broad smile. Some messages are *scripted* and drawn from our canned plan libraries. Finally, some are **constructed messages** that are formed carefully and thoughtfully when our known scripts are inadequate for the situation.

1-3h Communication Is Guided by Cultural Norms

Culture is a system of shared beliefs, values, symbols, and behaviors. How messages are formed and interpreted depends on the cultural background of the participants. We need to be mindful of our communication behavior as we interact with others from different cultures, so we don't unintentionally communicate in ways that are culturally inappropriate or insensitive.

The United States has become more culturally diverse than ever before. According to the U.S. Census Bureau (Humes, Jones, & Ramirez, 2011), using data from the 2010 census, people of Latin and Asian decent constituted 16.3 percent and 5.6 percent, respectively, of the total U.S. population. African-Americans make up about 13 percent of the U.S. population, and another 2.9 percent regards itself as multiracial. These four groups account for nearly 49 percent of the total U.S. population. The cultural influences of all these groups are profoundly changing our nation's demographics.

According to Samovar, Porter, and McDaniel (2007), "a number of cultural components are particularly relevant to the student of intercultural communication. These include (1) perception, (2) patterns of cognition, (3) verbal behaviors, (4) nonverbal behaviors, and (5) the influence of context" (p. 13). Because cultural concerns permeate all of communication, each chapter of this book points out when certain concepts and skills may be viewed differently by members of various cultural groups.

1-4 Communication and Ethics

Can people depend on you to tell the truth? Do you do what you say you will do? Can people count on you to be respectful? In any encounter, we choose whether to behave in a way others view as ethical. **Ethics** is a set of moral principles that may be held by a society, a group, or an individual. An ethical standard does not tell us exactly what to do in any given situation, but it can tell us what general principles to consider when deciding how to behave.

1-4a Ethical Principles

Every field of study—from psychology and biology to sociology and history—has a set of ethical principles designed to guide the practice of that field.

Communication is no exception. Every time we communicate, we make choices with ethical implications. The general principles that guide ethical communication include:

1. Ethical communicators are truthful and honest. We should not intentionally try to deceive others.

2. Ethical communicators act with integrity. Integrity is maintaining consistency between what we say we believe and what we do. The person who says "Do what I say, not what I do" lacks integrity, while the person who "practices what he or she preaches" acts with integrity. Integrity is basically the opposite of hypocrisy.

3. Ethical communicators behave fairly. A fair person is impartial. To be fair to someone is to gather all of the relevant facts, consider only circumstances relevant to the decision at hand, and not be swayed by

> ## " An honest person is widely regarded as a moral person, and honesty is a central concept to ethics as the foundation for a moral life . . . "
>
> *(Terkel & Duval, 1999, p. 122).*

prejudice or irrelevancies. For example, if two siblings are fighting, their mother exercises fairness if she allows both children to explain "their side" before she decides what to do.

4. Ethical communicators demonstrate respect. Respect is showing regard for others, their points of view, and their rights. We demonstrate respect through listening and understanding others' points of view, even when they differ from our own.

5. Ethical communicators are responsible. Responsible communicators recognize the power of words. Our messages can hurt others and their reputations. So we act responsibly when we refrain from gossiping, spreading rumors, bullying, and so forth.

1-4b Dark Side Messages

The "dark side" is a metaphor for inappropriate and/or unethical communication (Spitzberg & Cupach, 2011). It follows, then, that **dark side messages** are ones that are not ethical and/or appropriate (see Figure 1.3).

When Liz, who just spent a fortune having her hair cut and colored asks, "Do you like my new hairstyle?" and you think it is awful, how do you answer? The bright side answer would be one that is both ethical (honest, respectful, empathetic, etc.) and appropriate (sensitive to Liz's feelings and maintaining a good relationship). The hard side answer would be ethical, but it will likely hurt Liz and damage your relationship with her. The easy side

ethics
a set of moral principles that may be held by a society, a group, or an individual

dark side messages
messages that are not ethical and/or appropriate

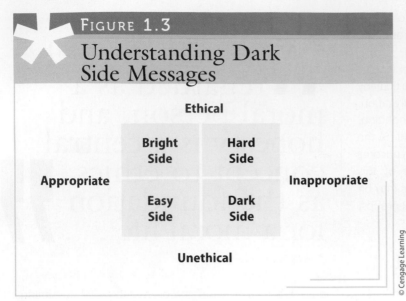

FIGURE 1.3

Understanding Dark Side Messages

Ethical

	Bright Side	Hard Side	
Appropriate			Inappropriate
	Easy Side	Dark Side	

Unethical

would be unethical but would spare Liz's feelings. The evil dark side would be both unethical and inappropriate. The box "Look on the Bright Side" offers some examples of the different ways you could respond to Liz.

As you can see, relationships may benefit from bright, hard, and easy side responses depending on the situation. But dark side responses damage people and relationships.

1-5 Increasing Your Communication Competence

When we communicate effectively and ethically, it feels good. And when we experience the opposite, we may get frustrated and even angry. So let's look what it means to be a competent communicator, how communication anxiety can affect competence, and how to develop and use your own communication improvement plan to improve chances for success in your interactions with others.

1-5a Communication Competence

Communication competence is the impression that communicative behavior is both appropriate and effective in a given situation (Spitzberg, 2000). Communication is *effective* when it achieves its goals and *appropriate* when it conforms to what is expected in a situation. Competence is a judgment people make about others. Our goal is to communicate in ways that increase the likelihood that others will judge us as competent.

Communication competence is achieved through personal motivation, knowledge acquisition, and skills practice (Spitzberg, 2000). Motivation is important because we will be able to improve our communication only if we are *motivated*—that is, if we want to improve. Knowledge is important because we must know what to do to increase competence. The more knowledge we have about how to behave in a given situation, the more likely we are to convey competence. Skill is important because we must act in ways that are consistent with our communication knowledge. The more skills we have, the more likely we are to structure our messages effectively and appropriately.

In addition to motivation, knowledge, and skills, credibility and social ease also influence whether others perceive us to be competent communicators. **Credibility** is a perception of a speaker's knowledge, trustworthiness, and warmth. Listeners are more likely to be attentive to and influenced by speakers they perceive as credible. **Social ease** means managing communication apprehension so we do not appear nervous or anxious.

communication competence
the impression that communicative behavior is both appropriate and effective in a given situation

credibility
a perception of a speaker's knowledge, trustworthiness, and warmth

social ease
communicating without appearing to be anxious or nervous

Look on the Bright Side

Bright side response: "Liz, it doesn't matter what I think. I can see that you really like how it looks and that makes me happy."

Hard side response: "Wow Liz, it's a dramatic change. I liked your hair long and I'd always admired the red highlights you had. But I'm sure it will grow on me."

Easy side response: "It looks great."

Evil dark side response: "It doesn't matter what you do to your hair, you're still fat and ugly."

This man may experience trait-based apprehension and feel nervous even when faced with making small talk while waiting with co-workers for a meeting.

To be perceived as a competent communicator, we must speak in ways that convey confidence and poise. Communicators that appear apprehensive are not likely to be regarded as competent, despite their motivation or knowledge.

1-5b Communication Apprehension

Communication apprehension is "the fear or anxiety associated with real or anticipated communication with others" (McCroskey, 1977, p. 78). Although most people think of public speaking anxiety when they hear the term *communication apprehension* (CA), there are actually four different types of CA. These are traitlike CA, audience-based CA, situational CA, and context-based CA. People who experience *traitlike communication apprehension* feel anxious in most speaking situations. About 20 percent of all people experience traitlike CA (Richmond & McCroskey, 1997). People who experience *audience-based communication apprehension* feel anxious about speaking only with a certain person or group of people. *Situational communication apprehension* is a short-lived feeling of anxiety that occurs during a specific encounter—for example, during a job interview. Finally, *context-based communication apprehension* is anxiety only in a particular situation—for example, when speaking to a large group of people.

All these forms of communication apprehension can be managed effectively in ways that help convey social ease. Throughout this book, we offer strategies for managing communication apprehension in various settings.

The combination of motivation, knowledge, skills, perceived credibility, and social ease make up competent communication. The goal of this book is to help you become a competent communicator in interpersonal, group, and public speaking situations.

1-5c Communication Improvement Plans

A communication improvement plan consists of setting a new goal to resolve a communication problem, identifying procedures to reach the goal, and determining a way to measure progress.

Before you can write a goal statement, you must first analyze your current communication skills repertoire. After you read each chapter and practice the skills described, select one or two skills to work on. Then write down your plan in four steps.

1. Identify the problem. For example: "*Problem: Even though some of the members of my class project

> **communication apprehension**
> the fear or anxiety associated with real or anticipated communication with others

group have not produced the work they promised, I haven't spoken up because I'm not very good at describing my feelings."

2. State the specific goal. A specific goal identifies a measurable outcome. For example, to deal with the problem just identified, you might write: "*Goal:* To describe my disappointment to other group members about their failure to meet deadlines."

3. Outline a specific procedure for reaching the goal. To develop a plan for reaching your goal, first consult the chapter that covers the skill you wish to hone. Then translate the general steps recommended in the chapter to your specific situation. For example: "*Procedure:* I will practice the steps of describing feelings. (1) I will identify the specific feeling I am experiencing. (2) I will encode the emotion I am feeling accurately. (3) I will include what

has triggered the feeling. (4) I will own the feeling as mine. (5) I will then put that procedure into operation when I am talking with my group members."

4. Devise a method for measuring progress. A good method points to minimum requirements for determining positive progress. For example: "*Test for Making Progress Toward Goal Achievement:* I will have made progress each time I describe my feelings to my group members about missed deadlines."

Figure 1.4 provides another example of a communication improvement plan, this one relating to a public speaking problem.

iStockphoto/Thinkstock.com

Figure 1.4

Sample Communication Improvement Plan

Problem: When I speak in class or in the student senate, I often find myself burying my head in my notes or looking at the ceiling or walls.

Goal: To look at people more directly when I'm giving a speech.

Procedure: I will take the time to practice oral presentations aloud in my room.

(1) I will stand up just as I do in class.

(2) I will pretend various objects in the room are people, and I will consciously attempt to look at those objects as I am talking.

(3) When giving a speech, I will try to be aware of when I am looking at my audience and when I am not.

Test for Achieving Goal: I will have achieved this goal when I am maintaining eye contact with my audience most of the time.

© Cengage Learning

Quick Quiz

T F 1. A participant in a communication interaction can either be the sender or receiver of a message.

T F 2. The context of a message is the organizational aspect of the message.

T F 3. Meaning shared in a communication can be affected by the physical context in which the message is delivered.

T F 4. Competence is the perception by others that our communication behavior is appropriate as well as effective.

T F 5. When you show regard or consideration for others and their ideas, even if you don't agree with them, you are demonstrating the ethical standard of fairness.

6. What are the three sub-processes that must be performed to achieve shared meaning?

a. message production, message interpretation, and interaction coordination
b. nonverbal coding, acronym depiction, and feeling coordination
c. canned plan access, spontaneous construction, and symmetrical feedback
d. recipient selection, message production, interaction method
e. channel selection, feedback decoding, response construction

7. An example of intrapersonal communication is

a. chatting around the dinner table with your family and friends.
b. recounting a past experience during a speech to an audience.
c. thinking to yourself about what you are going to make for dinner that evening.
d. texting a message to a friend.
e. entering into a discussion in a chatroom.

8. Why do we communicate?

a. to meet our social needs
b. to develop and maintain our sense of self
c. to develop relationships
d. to exchange information and influence others
e. All of these answers are correct.

9. Which of the following is NOT one of the guidelines for ethical communication?

a. Ethical communicators are truthful and honest.
b. Ethical communicators act spontaneously.
c. Ethical communicators behave fairly.
d. Ethical communicators demonstrate respect.
e. Ethical communicators are responsible.

10. If you feel anxious about speaking with a certain person or group of people, you are experiencing

a. situational communication apprehension.
b. audience-based communication apprehension.
c. traitlike communication apprehension.
d. general communication apprehension.
e. context-based communication apprehension.

Answers: 1. T, 2. F, 3. T, 4. T, 5. F, 6. A, 7. C, 8. E, 9. B, 10. B

Perception
of Self and Others

What do you think?
My self-perception usually matches other people's descriptions of me.

1	2	3	4	5	6	7	8	9	10
STRONGLY DISAGREE									STRONGLY AGREE

Learning Outcomes

2-1 Understand how the perception process works

2-2 Explain how self-perception is formed and maintained

2-3 Discuss how others can impact self-perception

2-4 Understand how self-perception affects communication

2-5 Discuss the ways we form perceptions of others

2-6 Know how to increase the accuracy of perceptions

Social perception—who we believe ourselves and others to be—influences how we communicate. To explain how, we begin this chapter by reviewing the basics of sensory perception. Then we explore how social perception influences self-concept and self-esteem and how these self-perceptions in turn influence communication. From there we offer suggestions for improving self-perceptions, explain how and why we perceive others as we do, and offer guidelines for improving our perceptions of others.

2-1 The Perception Process

Perception is the process of selectively attending and assigning meaning to information (Gibson, 1966). At times, our perceptions of the world, other people, and ourselves agree with the perceptions of others. At other times, our perceptions are significantly different from the perceptions of other people. For each of us, however, our perception becomes our reality. What one person sees, hears, and interprets is real and considered true to that person. Another person may see, hear, and interpret something entirely different from the same situation and also regard his or her different perception as real and true. When our perceptions differ from those with whom we interact, sharing meaning becomes more challenging. So how does perception work? Essentially, the brain selects some of the information it receives from the senses (sensory stimuli), organizes the information, and then interprets it.

social perception
who we believe ourselves and others to be

perception
the process of selectively attending and assigning meaning to information

2-1a Attention and Selection

Although we are constantly exposed to a barrage of sensory stimuli, we focus our attention on relatively little of it. Just think about how many TV channels you watch regularly compared to the number of channels offered. Or consider how many Web sites pop up when you do an Internet search. Can you imagine visiting all of them? Because we cannot focus on everything we see and hear all the time, we choose what stimuli to concentrate on based on our needs, interests, and expectations.

Needs

We choose to pay attention to information that meets our biological and psychological needs. When you go to class, how well you pay attention usually depends on whether you believe the information is relevant. Your brain communicates intrapersonally by asking such questions as "Will what I learn here help me in school, in the work world, in my personal life?"

Interests

We are likely to pay attention to information that piques our interest. For instance, you may not notice music playing in the background while dining at a restaurant until you suddenly find yourself hearing an old favorite. Similarly, when you are really attracted to a person, you are more likely to pay attention to what that person is saying. Likewise, when you get an e-mail from someone you don't like or don't recognize, you might simply delete it.

Out of 50 e-mails, you will only read the ones pertaining to your interests.

Expectations

Finally, we are likely to see what we expect to see and miss what violates our expectations. Take a quick look at the phrases in the triangles in Figure 2.1. If you have never seen these triangles, you probably read "Paris in the springtime," "Once in a lifetime," and "Bird in the hand." But if you reexamine the words, you will see that what you perceived was not exactly what is written. Do you now see the repeated words? They are easy to miss because we don't *expect* to see the words repeated.

2-1b Organization

Through the process of attention and selection, we reduce the number of stimuli our brains must process. Still, the number of stimuli we attend to at any moment is substantial. So our brains organize these stimuli using the principles of simplicity and pattern.

Simplicity

If the stimuli we attend to are complex, the brain simplifies them into some commonly recognized form. Based on a quick

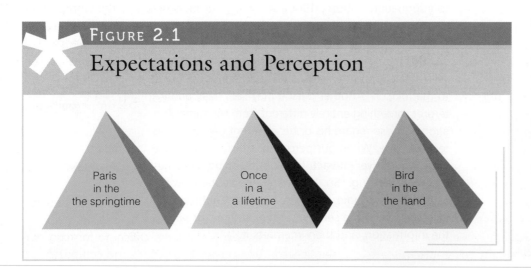

FIGURE 2.1

Expectations and Perception

Paris in the the springtime

Once in a a lifetime

Bird in the the hand

look at what someone is wearing, how she is standing, and the expression on her face, we may perceive her as a business executive, a doctor, or a soccer mom. We simplify the verbal messages we receive in a similar way. For example, after an hour-long performance review in which his boss described four of Tony's strengths and two areas for improvement, Tony might say to Jerry, his coworker, "Well, I'd better shape up or I'm going to get fired!"

Pattern

The brain also makes sense of complex stimuli by relating them to things it already recognizes. For example, when you see a crowd of people, instead of perceiving each individual, you may focus on sex and "see" men and women. Alternatively, you may focus on age and "see" children, teens, and adults.

2-1c Interpretation

As the brain selects and organizes information, it also assigns meaning to it. Look at these three sets of numbers. What are they?

A. 631 7348

B. 285 37 5632

C. 4632 7364 2596 2174

If you are used to seeing similar sets of numbers every day, you might interpret A as a telephone number, B as a Social Security number, and C as a credit card number. But your ability to interpret these numbers depends on your familiarity with the patterns. A French person may not recognize *631 7348* as a phone number since the pattern for phone numbers in France is: *0x xx xx xx xx*.

2-1d Dual Processing

You may be thinking, "Hey, I don't go through all of these steps. I just automatically 'understand' what's going on." If so, you are right. Most of the perceptual processing we do happens subconsciously (Baumeister, 2005). This **automatic processing** is a fast, top-down subconscious approach of making sense of what we are encountering. In other words, we use **heuristics**, which are our short-cut rules of thumb for understanding how to perceive something based on past experience with similar stimuli. Consider, for example, sitting at a red light. When it turns green, you go. You probably don't consciously think about taking your foot off the brake and applying it to the gas pedal.

But what happens when we encounter things that are out of the realm of our normal experiences or expectations? Then we must exert conscious effort to make sense of what is going on. **Conscious processing** is a slow, deliberative approach where we examine and reflect about the stimuli. Remember when you were first learning to drive? It took a lot of concentration to figure out what was happening on the road and how you were supposed to react. You probably thought carefully about doing things like taking your foot off the brake and applying it to the gas pedal when the light turned green.

Whether we engage in automatic or conscious processing, perception influences and is influenced by communication in a number of ways. The rest of this chapter is devoted to how we form our perceptions of self and others and the role communication plays in each.

automatic processing
a fast, top-down subconscious approach that draws on previous experience to make sense of what we are encountering

heuristics
short-cut rules of thumb for understanding how to perceive something based on past experience with similar stimuli

conscious processing
a slow, deliberative approach to perceiving where we examine and reflect about the stimuli

self-perception
the overall view we have of ourselves, which includes both our self-concept and self-esteem

self-concept
the perception we have of our skills, abilities, knowledge, competencies, and personality traits

self-esteem
the evaluation we make about our personal worthiness based on our self-concept

2-2 Perception of Self

Self-perception is the overall view we have of ourselves, which includes both self-concept and self-esteem. **Self-concept** is the perception we have of our skills, abilities, knowledge, competencies, and personality traits (Baron, Byrne, & Branscombe, 2006). It is how we describe ourselves. **Self-esteem** is the evaluation we make about our personal worthiness based on our self-concept (based on Mruk, 2006). In this section, we explain how self-concept and self-esteem are formed and describe guidelines to improve self-perception.

2-2a Self-Concept

How do we decide what our skills, abilities, competencies, and personality traits are? We do so based on the interpretations we make about our personal experiences and how others react and respond to us.

Our personal experiences are critical to forming our self-concept. We cannot know if we are competent at

Alanna perceives that she has
strength
(self-concept), and
evaluates that strength
is a **positive
competency,**
giving her high self-esteem.

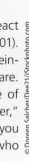

Our self-concept is also shaped by how others react and respond to us in two important ways (Rayner, 2001). First, we use other people's comments to validate, reinforce, or alter our perceptions of who we think we are. For example, if during a brainstorming session, one of your coworkers says, "You're really a creative thinker," you may decide this comment fits your image of who you are, thus reinforcing your self-concept as someone who can think "outside the box."

Second, the feedback we receive from others may reveal abilities and personality characteristics we had never before associated with ourselves. For example, after Michael receives several compliments about being good with children, he decides to pursue a career in early childhood education. The feedback (compliments) helped him recognize his natural ability to connect with preschoolers.

Not all reactions and responses we receive have the same effect on our self-concept. For instance, reactions and responses coming from someone we respect or someone we are close to tend to be more powerful (Aron, Mashek, & Aron, 2004; Rayner, 2001). This is especially important in families. Since self-concept begins to form early in life, information we receive from our family deeply shapes our self-concept (Demo, Small, & Savin-Williams, 1987). Thus, one major ethical responsibility of family members is to notice and comment on traits and abilities that help develop accurate and positive self-concepts in other family members. When Jeff's dad compliments him for keeping his bedroom clean because he is "so organized" or Carla's brother tells her she did a great job on her science project because she is "really smart," they are encouraging positive self-concepts.

As we interact with others, we also form an **ideal self-concept**, which is what we would like to be. For example, although Jim may know he is not naturally athletic, in his ideal self-concept he wants to be. So he plays on an intramural basketball team, works out at the gym daily, and regularly runs in local 5k and 10k races.

ideal self-concept
what we would like to be

something until we've tried doing it, and we cannot discover our personality traits until we uncover them through experience.

We place a great deal of emphasis on our first experiences with particular phenomena (Centi, 1981). When we have a positive first experience, we are likely to believe we possess the competencies and personality traits associated with that experience. So if Sonya discovers at an early age that she does well on math problems and exams, she is likely to incorporate "competent mathematician" into her self-concept. If Sonya continues to excel at math throughout her life, that part of her self-concept will be reinforced and maintained.

Similarly, when our first experience is negative, we are likely to conclude we do not possess that particular skill or trait. For instance, if you get anxious and draw a blank while giving a speech for the first time, you might conclude that you are a poor public speaker. Even when a negative first experience is not repeated, however, it is likely to take more than one contradictory additional experience to change our original perception. So even if you succeed the second time you give a speech, it will probably take several more positive public speaking experiences for you to change your original conclusion about not being a good public speaker.

2-2b Self-Esteem

Self-concept and self-esteem are two different but related components of self-perception. Whereas self-concept is our perception of our competencies and personality traits, self-esteem is our positive or negative evaluation of those competencies and traits. So self-esteem is not just our perception of how well or poorly we do things (self-concept), but also the importance we place on what we do well or poorly (Mruk, 2006). For instance, Eduardo believes he is an excellent piano player, a faithful friend, and good with kids. But if he doesn't believe that these competencies and traits are valuable to have, then he will have low self-esteem. It takes both the perception of having a competency or personality trait and a belief that it is valuable to produce high self-esteem (Mruk, 2006). When we use our skills to achieve worthwhile endeavors, we raise our self-esteem. When we are unsuccessful in doing so, and/or when we use them in unworthy endeavors, we lower our self-esteem.

As is the case with self-concept, self-esteem depends not only on what each individual views as worthwhile but also on the ideas, morals, and values of the family and cultural group(s) to which the individual belongs. So

© Sylvie Bouchard/Shutterstock.com

⬂ Media attention on cyber-bullying has increased awareness about the seriousness of the effects on children. More than "kids being kids," cyberbullying has effects such as dropping out of school and even suicide.

if Eduardo comes from a family where athletic success is valued but artistic talents are not, if he hangs out with friends who don't appreciate his piano playing, and if he lives in a society where rock guitarists (not piano players) are the superstars, then his piano-playing ability may not raise his self-esteem and might actually lower it.

We've already noted that families are critically important to developing one's self-concept, but they are even more central to developing positive self-esteem. For example, when Jeff's dad pointed out that Jeff's room is always tidy, he also said he was proud of Jeff, which raised Jeff's self-esteem about being organized. And when Carla's brother said she did a great job on her science project, he reinforced the value their family places on being smart, which raised her self-esteem about that attribute of her self-concept. Unfortunately, in some families, negative messages repeatedly sent can create an inaccurate self-concept and damage self-esteem. Communicating blame, name-calling, and constantly pointing out shortcomings are particularly damaging to self-esteem and some people never fully overcome the damage done to them by members of their families.

Our self-esteem can affect the types of relationships we form and with whom. Individuals with high self-esteem tend to form relationships with others who reinforce their positive self-perception; similarly, individuals with low self-esteem tend to form relationships with those who reinforce their negative self-perception (Leary, 2002). This phenomenon plays out in unfortunate ways when a person perpetually goes from one abusive relationship to another (Engel, 2005).

Bullying and cyberbullying, which are aggressive behaviors designed to intimidate others, also damage self-esteem. Children who are just forming their self-concepts and self-esteem, and adolescents whose self-concepts and self-esteem are in transition, are particularly sensitive to bullying messages. The effects of bullying can have long-lasting effects on self-esteem. In fact, many years after childhood bullying incidents, victims may still have inaccurate self-perceptions (Hinduja & Patchin, 2010).

2-3 Culture and Self-Perceptions

Cultural norms play a critical role in shaping both our self-concept and self-esteem (Chen & Starosta, 1998). Two important ways they do so are in terms of independence/interdependence and masculinity/femininity.

In individualist cultures, such as Western Europe and the United States, people tend to form and value

independent self-perceptions perceptions based on the belief that traits and abilities are internal to the person and are universally applicable to all situations

interdependent self-perceptions perceptions based on the belief that traits and abilities are specific to a particular context or relationship

incongruence a gap between self-perception and reality

independent self-perceptions. In collectivist cultures, such as Japan and China, people form and value interdependent self-perceptions (Markus & Kitayama, 1991). **Independent self-perceptions** are based on the belief that traits and abilities are internal to the person and are universally applicable to all situations. The goal for people with independent self-perceptions is to demonstrate their abilities, competencies, characteristics, and personalities during interactions with others. For example, if you have an independent self-concept and believe that one of your competencies is your ability to persuade others, you gain self-esteem by demonstrating your skill, convincing others, and having others praise you for it.

Interdependent self-perceptions are based on the belief that traits and abilities are specific to a particular context or relationship. The goal of people with interdependent self-perceptions is to maintain or enhance the relationship by demonstrating the appropriate abilities and personality characteristics for the situation. People with interdependent self-perceptions don't think, "I'm really persuasive," but rather, "When I am with my friends I am able to convince them to do what is good for all of us. When I am with my father I do what he believes is best for the good of our family." High self-esteem comes from knowing when to be persuasive and when to be compliant.

Cultural norms also play a role in shaping self-perception around masculinity and femininity. In the dominant culture of the United States, for instance, many people continue to expect boys to behave in "masculine" ways and girls to behave in "feminine" ways (Wood, 2007). In the past, boys in the United States were taught to base their self-esteem on their achievements, status, and income, and girls learned that their culture valued their appearance and their relationship skills. So boys and girls developed high or low self-esteem based on how well they met these criteria (Wood, 2007).

Today these cultural norms about "appropriate" characteristics and behaviors for males and females are becoming less rigid, but they do still exist and are promoted incessantly in popular culture and entertainment media. Consider just about any television sitcom (e.g., *Two and a Half Men* and even *Modern Family*). Such programs continue to portray women as the "natural" caregivers for the family, and when men attempt to perform a caregiver behavior, they often make a mess of the situation.

Some people are intimately involved in more than one cultural group. If one of the cultures encourages interdependent and/or gendered self-perceptions and the other encourages independent and/or gender neutral self-perceptions, these people may develop both types of self-perception and actually switch "cultural frames" based on the cultural group they are interacting within at a given time. They are more likely to do this well when they see themselves as part of and appreciate the strengths of both cultures (Benet-Martínez & Haritatos, 2005).

2-3a Accuracy and Distortion of Self-Perceptions

The accuracy of our self-concept and self-esteem depends on the accuracy of our perceptions of our own experiences and observations, as well as how we interpret others' reactions and responses to us. All of us experience successes and failures, and all of us hear praise and criticism. Since our perceptions are more likely than our true abilities to influence our behavior (Weiten, 1998), accurate self-perception is critical to competent communication. Self-perception may suffer from **incongruence** when there is a gap between self-perception and reality. For example, Sean may actually possess all of the competencies and personality traits needed for effective leadership, but if he doesn't perceive himself to have these skills and characteristics, he won't step forward when leadership is needed. Unfortunately, individuals tend to reinforce these incongruent self-perceptions by behaving in ways that conform to them rather than attempting to break free from them.

If we are overly attentive to successful experiences and positive responses, our self-perception may become inflated. We tend to describe such individuals as "arrogant," "pompous," "haughty," or "snobbish." On the other hand, if we dwell on our failures and not our successes, remember only the criticism we receive, or focus on how we don't measure up to our ideal self-concept, we may have a deflated self-perception. We tend to describe such individuals as "depressed," "despondent," "sullen," or "gloomy." Neither the person with the inflated nor deflated self-perception accurately reflects who they are. These incongruent and distorted self-perceptions are magnified through self-fulfilling prophecies, filtering messages, and media images.

IF PAUL EXPECTS PEOPLE TO IGNORE HIM AT HIS NEW SCHOOL, HE IS LESS LIKELY TO TRY AND ENGAGE THEM—ULTIMATELY ENDING UP SPENDING THE WHOLE DAY NOT TALKING TO ANYONE NEW.

self-fulfilling prophecy
an inaccurate perception of a skill, characteristic, or situation that leads to behaviors that perpetuate that false perception as true

Self-Fulfilling Prophecies

A **self-fulfilling prophecy** is an inaccurate perception of a skill, characteristic, or situation that leads to behaviors that perpetuate that false perception as *true* (Merton, 1968). Self-fulfilling prophesies may be self-created or other-imposed.

Self-created prophecies are predictions you make about yourself. We often talk ourselves into success or failure. For example, when people expect rejection, they are more likely to behave in ways that lead others to reject them (Downey, Freitas, Michaelis, & Khouri, 2004). By contrast, if Stefan sees himself as quite social and able to get to know people easily, he looks forward to attending a friend's party and, just as he predicted, makes several new acquaintances and enjoys himself.

Sometimes a self-fulfilling prophecy is other-imposed and is based on what others say about us. When teachers act as if their students are bright, students buy into this expectation and learn more as a result. Likewise, when teachers act as if students are not bright, students may "live down" to these imposed prophecies and fail to achieve. A good example takes place in the popular book *Harry Potter and the Order of the Phoenix*. A prophecy was made that suggested Harry Potter would vanquish

the Dark Lord (Voldemort). So the Dark Lord sets out to kill Harry Potter. Dumbledore explains to Harry that the prophecy is true only because the Dark Lord believes it. Still, because the Dark Lord will not rest until he kills Harry, it becomes inevitable that Harry will, in fact, have to kill Voldemort (or vice versa).

Filtering Messages

Our self-perceptions can also become distorted through the way we filter what others say to us. We tend to pay attention to messages that reinforce our self-perception, and downplay or ignore messages that contradict this image. For example, suppose Tien prepares an agenda for her study group. Someone comments that Tien is a good organizer. If Tien spent her childhood hearing how disorganized she was, she may downplay or even ignore this comment. If, however, Tien thinks she is good at organizing, she will pay attention to the compliment and may even reinforce it by responding, "Thanks, I AM a pretty organized person. I learned it from my mom."

Media Images

Another way self-perception can become distorted is through our interpretation of what we see on television, in the movies, and in popular magazines. Social cognitive learning theory suggests that we strive to copy the characteristics and behaviors of the characters portrayed as perfect examples or "ideal types" (Bandura, 1977). Persistent media messages of violence, promiscuity, use of profanity, bulked-up males, and pencil-thin females have all been linked to distorted self-perceptions among viewers. One particularly disturbing study found that before television was widely introduced on the Pacific island of Fiji, only 3 percent of girls reported vomiting to lose weight or being unhappy with their body image. Three years after the introduction of television, that percentage had risen to 15 percent, and an alarming 74 percent reported thinking of themselves as too big or too fat (Becker, 2004). Unfortunately, distorted body image perceptions lead to low self-esteem and, sometimes, to self-destructive behaviors such as anorexia and bulimia.

2-4 Self-Perception and Communication

Self-perception influences how we talk to ourselves, how we talk about ourselves with others, how we talk about others to ourselves, the self we present to others, and our ability to communicate with others.

Self-talk (or intrapersonal communication) is the internal conversation we have with ourselves in our thoughts. People who have a positive self-perception are more likely to engage in positive self-talk, such as "I know I can do it" or "I did a really good job." People who have a negative self-perception are more likely to engage in negative self-talk, such as "There's no way I can do

that" or "I really blew it." Not surprisingly, a high level of speech anxiety (the fear of public speaking) is often rooted in negative self-talk.

Self-perception also influences how we talk about ourselves with others. If we have a positive self-perception, we are likely to convey a positive attitude and take credit for our successes. If we have a negative self-perception, we are likely to convey a negative attitude and downplay our accomplishments. Some research suggests that the Internet can influence how we communicate about ourselves with others in unique ways. Some Internet discussion groups, for example, are designed to be online journals where the user engages in reflection and introspection. These users are actually communicating with themselves while imagining a reader. On the Internet, people can be more aware of themselves and less aware of the people to whom they are talking (Shedletsky & Aitken, 2004).

Self-perception also influences how we talk about others to ourselves. First, the more accurate our self-perception is, the more likely we are to perceive others accurately. Second, the more positive our self-perception is, the more likely we are to see others favorably. Studies show that people who accept themselves as they are tend to be more accepting of others; similarly, those with

Girl's Day Out Self

Work-at-Home Self

Professional Self

Socialite Self

Four social constructs, one woman, all real.

Born This Way?

From the moment she burst onto the pop music scene in 2009, Lady Gaga has been synonymous with outrageous performances and heavily stylized celebrity personas. For Lady Gaga, her "behind-the-scenes self" appears to be just as constructed as her public celebrity persona. At the same time, however, she consistently frames this self as "real" in her songs and media appearances. Her celebrity persona is completely rooted in the idea that she is being her true self, even though that self is glamorous, constructed, extreme, over-the-top, and all the things that we already associate with her public image. Like all personas, what you see is constructed, but it is not necessarily "fake" or "inauthentic."

Gaga's "real" self remains self-consciously constructed in her physical appearance and how she behaves in public, but it is not intended to be an act or something distinct from her "authentic" self. Her constant message is that individuals should be themselves no matter what, even if that self does not fit into dominant social expectations. Indeed, Gaga further supported her message after being lambasted in the popular media for gaining weight. She posted images of herself online in just her underwear—no make-up, no wigs, no platform shoes—along with the caption "Bulimia and anorexia since I was 15." The photos became the first in a series of posts by Gaga and her fans supporting a "body revolution" of self-acceptance and rejection of media-imposed ideals. In some ways, this would seem to contradict her well-constructed media image, but in fact it functions as another persona, consistent with her presentation of public and private self, icon of outsiders, supporter of real self-image.

SOURCE: Haiken, M. (2012, September 26). Lady Gaga puts bulimia and body image on the table in a big way. Forbes. Retrieved from http://www.forbes.com/sites/melaniehaiken/2012/09/26/lady-gaga-puts-bulimia-and-body-image-on-the-table-in-a-big-way.

a negative self-perception are more likely to be critical of others. Third, our own personal characteristics influence the types of characteristics we are likely to perceive in others. For example, people who are secure tend to see others as equally secure. If you recall that we respond to the world as we perceive it to be (and not necessarily as it is), you can readily see how negative self-perception can account for misunderstandings and communication breakdowns.

Our self-perceptions are the complete picture of how we view ourselves. When we communicate with others, however, most of us share only the parts we believe are appropriate to the situation. This phenomenon is known as the **social construction of self**. For example, Damon presents his "manager self" at work where he is a serious, task-oriented leader. When he is with his good friends, however, he is laid back, jovial, and more than happy to follow what the group wants to do. Which is the "real" Damon? Both are. Social networking sites such as Facebook have added a new twist to the social construction of self because once we have posted information on our page, others can co-opt our identity and actually reconstruct us in ways we never intended to do.

How effective we are at constructing different social selves depends on how actively we self-monitor. **Self-monitoring** is the internal process of being aware of how we are coming across to others and adjusting our behavior accordingly. It involves being sensitive to other people's feedback and using that information to determine how we will respond (Gangestad & Snyder, 2000). If you have ever been in a situation where you made a remark and did not get the response you expected, you may have thought to yourself, "Ooh, I wish I hadn't said that. I wonder how to fix it." This is an example of self-monitoring. Some people are naturally high self-monitors, constantly aware of how they are coming across to others. But even low self-monitors are likely to self-monitor when they are in a new situation or relationship.

We all use self-monitoring to determine which "self" we choose to display in different situations and with different people.

social construction of self
the phenomenon of sharing different aspects of our self-concept based on the situation and people involved

self-monitoring
the internal process of being aware of how we are coming across to others and adjusting our behavior accordingly

uncertainty reduction
communication theory that explains how individuals monitor their social environment to know more about themselves and others

impression formation
processes we use to form perceptions of others

attributions
reasons we give for our own and others' behavior

situational attribution
attributing behavior to a cause that is beyond someone's control

dispositional attribution
attributing behavior to a cause that is under someone's control

2-4a Changing Self-Perceptions

Self-concept and self-esteem are fairly enduring characteristics, but they can be changed. Comments that contradict your current self-perception may lead you to slowly change it. Certain situations, such as experiencing a profound change in your social environment, can expedite this process. When children begin school or go to sleep-away camp; when teens start part-time jobs; when young adults go to college; or when people begin or end jobs or relationships, become parents, or grieve the loss of someone they love, they are more likely to absorb messages that contradict their current self-perceptions.

Therapy and self-help techniques can help alter our self-concept and improve our self-esteem. In his analysis of numerous research studies, Christopher Mruk (1999) found that self-esteem is increased through "hard work and practice, practice, practice—there is simply no escaping this basic existential fact" (p. 112).

So why is this important to communication? Because our self-perception affects who we choose to form relationships with, how we interact with others, and how comfortable we feel when we are called on to share our opinions or present a speech. Essentially, improving self-perception improves how we interact with others, and improving how we interact with others improves self-perception.

2-5 Perceptions of Others

Now that you have a basic understanding of self-perception, let's look at how we perceive others and the role communication plays in that process. When you meet someone for the first time, you may ask yourself questions such as "What is this person like?" or "What is this person likely to do, and why?" You might wonder whether you have anything in common, whether he or she will like you, whether you will get along, and whether you will enjoy the experience or feel uncomfortable. The natural reaction to such feelings is to say and do things that will reduce these uncertainties (Littlejohn & Foss, 2011).

2-5a Uncertainty Reduction

Uncertainty reduction (Berger & Bradac, 1982) is a communication theory that explains how individuals monitor their social environment in order to know more about themselves and others (Littlejohn & Foss, 2011). When people interact, they look for information to help them understand who their partner is and predict what their partner is likely to do. As we reduce uncertainty, we usually become more comfortable communicating (Guerrero, Andersen, & Afifi, 2007). To reduce uncertainty, we form impressions and make judgments about others as we interact with them.

Forming Impressions

We engage in a variety of processes to form our perceptions about others. Researchers call these processes **impression formation**. Three of the most important ways we form impressions are based on physical appearance, perceived personality, and assumed similarity.

Making Attributions

At the center of our quest to reduce uncertainty is the need to predict how others will behave. By its nature, predicting something depends on understanding the cause and effect relationship between two things. When we see someone acting a certain way, we try to figure out why. Then we use this explanation to predict how that person will act in similar situations in the future. **Attributions** are reasons we give for our own and others' behavior. For instance, suppose a coworker with whom you had a noon lunch date has not arrived by 12:30. How do you explain her tardiness? One way you might explain it is to make a **situational attribution**, a reason that is beyond your coworker's control. You might assume, for instance, that your coworker must have had an accident on the way to the restaurant. On the other hand, you may make a **dispositional attribution**, attributing behavior to a cause that is under your coworker's control. In this case, you may perceive your coworker to be forgetful, self-absorbed, or insensitive to others. In any case, your attribution reduces your uncertainty by answering the question, "Why is my coworker late?" But the type of attribution you make influences how you interact with

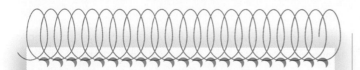

Forming Impressions

☐ Physical appearance

The first thing we notice about other people is how they look. Although it may seem superficial, we form these first impressions very quickly. In fact, one study found that we assess how attractive, likeable, trustworthy, competent, and aggressive we think people are after looking at their faces for only 100 milliseconds (Willis & Todorov, 2006).

☐ Implicit personality theory

We also form impressions based on assumptions we make about another's personality. **Implicit personality theory** is our tendency to assume that two or more personality characteristics go together. So if we see someone displaying one trait, we assume she has the other traits we associate with it. For example, if you meet someone who is multilingual you might assume she is also intelligent. Or if you meet someone who volunteers at a homeless shelter, you might assume that he is compassionate.

☐ Assumed similarity

We also form impressions about others by assuming that someone who shares one characteristic with us also shares others. Researchers call this **assumed similarity**. We assume someone is similar to us in a variety of ways until we get information that contradicts this assumption. For instance, when Ian attended a campaign event for a city council candidate who belonged to his political party, he expected the candidate's views on locating a new prison in the city to be the same as his. Ian was pleased to hear that the candidate agreed with his viewpoint, but he was shocked to hear the candidate's racist reasoning.

your coworker once she shows up. If you believe it is not her fault, you are likely to be concerned, understanding, and supportive. On the other hand, if you made a dispositional attribution, you are likely to be annoyed or hurt.

2-5b Mediated Communication and Social Presence

Have you ever "talked back" to someone on the TV or radio or "coached" your favorite team while watching a televised game? If so, you perceived yourself as in some way "present" with those on the screen, even though you knew they could not actually see or hear you. **Social presence** is the sense of being "there" with another person in a particular moment in time. Social presence is also the extent to which you believe you can sense what another person is thinking and feeling and the extent to which you believe your partner also knows that you are "there." When we interact face-to-face, we are fully aware of the social presence of one another.

When we interact with others through a mediated channel, however, social presence is filtered through technology. So instead of experiencing another's physical presence, we experience their "mediated presence." In other words, we sense that someone is immediately available to us in a particular moment—even if they are not (Biocca & Harms, 2002). Experiencing someone's social presence is easier through some mediated channels (such as phone calls and text messages) than others (e-mails, blogs, and Facebook posts). When we communicate through mediated channels, we usually realize that our partner is not really physically present; however, when we communicate through richer and more synchronous channels, we are more likely to perceive others as socially present. For example, when we read an e-mail message, we may be able to conjure up a mental image of the person that wrote it, but we don't generally perceive them to be present with us as we read. In fact, the time stamp may indicate that the message was written hours, days, or weeks earlier. However, when we Skype with someone, we experience them as more socially present since we can talk back and forth and interpret nonverbal cues to understand their emotional tone.

Refer back to Figure 1-2 in chapter 1, which displays common forms of social media by degrees of richness, synchronicity, and social presence. Notice the position of face-to-face communication along the right side of

implicit personality theory
the tendency to assume that two or more personality characteristics go together

assumed similarity
assuming someone is similar to us in a variety of ways until we get information that contradicts this assumption

social presence
the sense of being "there" with another person in a particular moment in time

selective perception
the perceptual distortion that arises from paying attention only to what we expect to see or hear and ignoring what we don't expect

forced consistency
the inaccurate attempt to make several perceptions about another person agree with each other

prejudice
judging a person based on the characteristics of a group to which the person belongs without regard to how the person may vary from the group characteristic

stereotypes
exaggerated or oversimplified generalizations used to describe a group

discrimination
acting differently toward a person based on prejudice

racism, ethnocentrism, sexism, heterosexism, ageism, and ableism
various form of prejudice in which members of one group believe that the behaviors and characteristics of their group are inherently superior to those of another group

the continuum and how mediated messages demonstrate a lower social presence as you scan further and further to the left.

2-5c Inaccurate and Distorted Perceptions of Others

As we work to reduce uncertainty, we also must be careful to reduce perceptual inaccuracies. Because perception is a complex process, we use shortcuts to help us focus attention, interpret information, and make predictions about others. Selective perceptions, faulty attributions, forced consistency, and prejudice are shortcuts that can lead to perceptual inaccuracies.

Selective perception is the perceptual distortion that arises from paying attention only to what we expect to see or hear and ignoring what we don't expect. For instance, if Lily sees Mason as a man with whom she would like to develop a strong relationship, she will tend to see the positive side of Mason's personality and ignore the negative side. Similarly, if Artrell thinks that his landlord is mean and unfair, he may ignore any acts of kindness or generosity offered by the landlord.

Forced consistency is the inaccurate attempt to make several perceptions about another person agree with each other. It arises from our need to eliminate contradictions. Imagine that Leah does not like her coworker, Jill. If Jill supplies some information Leah missed on a form, Leah is likely to perceive Jill's behavior as interference, even if Jill's intention was to be helpful. If Leah likes Jill, however, she might perceive the very same behavior as helpful—even if Jill's intention was to interfere. In each case, the perception of "supplying missing information" is shaped by the need for consistency. It is consistent to regard someone we like as doing favors for us. It is

inconsistent to regard people we don't like as doing favors for us. However, consistent perceptions of others are not necessarily accurate.

Prejudice is judging a person based on the characteristics of a group to which the person belongs without regard to how the person may vary from the group characteristic (Jones, 2002). Prejudices are based on **stereotypes**, which are exaggerated or oversimplified generalizations used to describe a group. A professor may see a student's spiked purple hair and numerous tattoos and assume the student is a rebel who will defy authority, slack off on classroom assignments, and seek attention. In reality, this person may be a polite, quiet, serious honor student who aspires to go to graduate school. Prejudice can lead to **discrimination**, which is acting differently toward a person based on prejudice (Jones, 2002). Prejudice deals with perception and attitudes, while discrimination involves actions. For instance, when Laura meets Wasif and learns that he is Muslim, she may use her knowledge of women's roles in Islamic countries to inform her perception of Wasif and conclude that he is a chauvinist without really talking to him. This is prejudice. If based on this prejudice she refuses to be in a class project group with him, she would be discriminating. Wasif may actually be a feminist, but Laura's use of the perceptual shortcut may prevent her from getting to know Wasif for the person he really is, and she may have

© El Greco/Shutterstock.com

cost herself the opportunity of working with the best student in class.

Racism, **ethnocentrism**, **sexism**, **heterosexism**, **ageism**, and **ableism** are various forms of prejudice in which members of one group believe that the behaviors and characteristics of their group are inherently superior to those of another group. All people can be

> ## *Prejudices of groups with power are farther reaching in their consequences than others.*

perception check
a message that reflects your understanding of the meaning of another person's behavior

prejudiced and act on their prejudices by discriminating against others. Nevertheless, "prejudices of groups with power are farther reaching in their consequences than others" (Sampson, 1999, p. 131). Because such attitudes can be deeply ingrained and are often subtle, it is easy to overlook behaviors we engage in that in some way meet this definition. Prejudicial perceptions may be unintentional, or they may seem insignificant or innocuous, but even seemingly unimportant prejudices rob others of their humanity and severely impede competent communication.

2-6 Improving Our Perceptions of Others

Because perceptual distortions of others and their messages are common and because they influence how we communicate, improving perceptual accuracy is an important first step in becoming a competent communicator. The following guidelines can help you construct accurate impressions of others and assess your perceptions of others' messages.

1. Question the accuracy of your perceptions. Questioning accuracy begins by saying, "I know what I think I saw, heard, tasted, smelled, or felt, but I could be wrong. What other information should I be aware of?" By accepting the possibility that you have overlooked something, you will stop automatic processing and begin to consciously search out information that should increase your accuracy.

2. Choose to use conscious processing as you get to know people. When you mindfully pay attention to someone, you are more likely to understand that person's uniqueness. Doing so can increase the accuracy of your perceptions.

3. Seek more information to verify perceptions. If your perception is based on only one or two pieces of information, try to collect additional information. Note that your perception is tentative—that is, subject to change. The best way to get additional information about people is to talk with them. It's OK to be unsure about how to treat someone from another group. But rather than letting your uncertainty cause you to make mistakes, talk with the person and tell him you want to be respectful. Then ask him for the information you need to become more comfortable about interacting appropriately and respectfully with him.

4. Realize that your perceptions of a person will change over time. People often base their opinions, assumptions, and behaviors on perceptions that are outdated. So when you encounter someone you haven't seen for a while, let the person's current behavior rather than her past actions or reputation inform your perceptions. For example, a former classmate who was wild in high school may well have changed and become a mature, responsible adult.

5. Seek clarification respectfully by perception checking. One way to assess the accuracy of a perception is to verbalize it and see whether others agree with what you see, hear, and interpret. A **perception check** is a message that reflects your understanding of the meaning of another person's behavior. It is a process of describing what you have seen and heard and then asking for feedback from the other person. A perception check consists of three parts. First, you describe what you observed. Second, you offer two possible interpretations of it. Third, you ask for clarification.

Let's look at an example. Isabel's boyfriend, Liam, has not responded to her texts all day and was very quiet at dinner the night before. Isabel has jumped to the conclusion that Liam is going to break up with her. Rather than use this assumption and cause a defensive reaction when she does talk to Liam, Isabel could employ a perception-checking message—something like this:

> *"When you didn't respond to my texts today" (nonjudgmental description of the observed behavior), "I thought you were mad at me" (first interpretation), "or maybe you were really busy at work" (second interpretation). "Is everything ok? Is it something else?" (request for clarification).*

Perception checking is simply a tool to respectfully check for understanding of another's behavior without assuming your interpretation is correct. It helps you seek mutual understanding without directly threatening or attacking the other person.

Quick Quiz

T F 1. The process of selectively attending to information and assigning meaning to it is called perception.

T F 2. A person's culture has a strong influence on the self-perception process.

T F 3. Self-created prophecies are predictions that you make about other people.

T F 4. Implicit personality theories are assumptions about which physical characteristics and personality traits or behaviors are associated with each other.

T F 5. A reality check is a message that reflects your understanding of the meaning of another person's nonverbal communication.

6. The phenomenon of presenting different aspects of self-concept based on the social context (people and situations involved) is called

a. social construction.
b. self-concept.
c. personality.
d. temperament.
e. persona.

7. Suppose you expect to be rejected when you ask someone out and then behave in ways that lead the person to reject you. This would be an example of

a. high self-esteem.
b. incongruence.
c. a self-fulfilling prophecy.
d. filtering messages.
e. a perception.

8. The process of monitoring the social environment to learn more about self and others is called

a. observing others.
b. uncertainty reduction.
c. the halo effect.
d. stereotyping.
e. social construction.

9. If you grew up hearing that you were a "slow learner" and then a professor praised you for being a quick study, you might downplay the comment, not really hear it, or discount it entirely. This is an example of

a. incongruence.
b. filtering messages.
c. poor self-perception.
d. delayed reaction.
e. a self-fulfilling prophecy.

10. Which of the following is performed during a perception check?

a. watching the behavior of another person
b. describing the behavior
c. considering what the behavior means
d. putting your interpretation into words
e. all of the above

Answers: 1. T, 2. T, 3. F, 4. T, 5. F, 6. A, 7. C, 8. B, 9. B, 10. E

THE  IN-CROWD

Share your 4LTR Press story on Facebook at
www.facebook.com/4ltrpress for a chance to win.

To learn more about the
In-Crowd opportunity 'like'
us on Facebook.

NANDI

BRISBANE

ROME 2365km

SINGAPORE 18083km

HONOLU

LONDON 8161km

PAGA

BANGKOK 18939km

SA

ANGEL 9614km

HONG KONG 9297km

MON

NORFOLK ISLAND 1345km

TOKYO 9057km

Intercultural
Communication

Because culture has a profound impact on perception and communication, in this chapter we examine the relationship between culture and communication. We begin by explaining some basic concepts of culture and several ways cultures are unique. We end by proposing how to improve intercultural communication competence.

Learning Outcomes

3-1 Define culture and the role of communication in it

3-2 Explain the relationship between dominant and co-cultures

3-3 Understand the seven dimensions in which cultures differ

3-4 Describe the inherent barriers in intercultural communication and the methods to develop competent intercultural communication

> **What do you think?**
> I feel very comfortable communicating with people of different genders, ages, and ethnicities.
>
> **1 2 3 4 5 6 7 8 9 10**
> STRONGLY DISAGREE   STRONGLY AGREE

3-1 Culture and Communication

Culture is the system of shared values, beliefs, attitudes, and norms that guides what is considered appropriate among an identifiable group of people (Samovar, Porter, & McDaniel, 2009). In a real sense, culture is a way of life. It's the structure of taken-for-granted *rules* for how and why we believe and behave as we do.

At the heart of any culture are its values. **Values** are the commonly accepted standards of what is considered right and wrong, good and evil, fair and unfair, just and unjust, and so on. Cultures have both ideal and real values. **Ideal values** are the ones that members profess to hold, whereas **real values** are the ones that guide actual behavior. For example, Israel is a democratic state whose constitution offers protections for members of religious minorities (ideal value). But the legal system's treatment of minorities

culture
the system of shared values, beliefs, attitudes, and norms that guides what is considered appropriate among an identifiable group of people

values
the commonly accepted standards of what is considered right and wrong, good and evil, fair and unfair, etc.

ideal values
values that members of a culture profess to hold

real values
values that guide actual behavior

(e.g., Muslims, Christians) sometimes falls short of this ideal. In other words, religious minorities are sometimes subject to legal hassles that their fellow Jewish citizens don't experience (real value in action). Similarly, the United States Constitution professes equal rights and opportunities for all (ideal value), yet some people are treated unfairly based on sex, race, ethnicity, age, disability, or sexual orientation (real value in action).

Intercultural communication refers to the interactions that occur between people whose cultures are so different that the communication between them is altered (Samovar, Porter, & McDaniel, 2009). To become effective intercultural communicators, we must begin by understanding what a culture is, then identifying how cultures differ from one another, and finally realizing how those differences influence communication.

We do not need to visit other countries to meet people of different cultures. The United States is a multicultural society. Our population includes not only recent immigrants from other countries, but also descendents of earlier immigrants and of native peoples. So understanding how communication varies among cultural groups can help us as we interact with the people we encounter every day right here in the United States.

Because each of us is so familiar with our own customs, norms, and values, we may feel anxious when they are disrupted. We call this psychological discomfort when engaging in a new cultural situation **culture shock** (Klyukanov, 2005). We are likely to feel culture shock most profoundly when thrust into an unfamiliar culture through travel, business, or studying abroad. In the film *Lost in Translation*, for example, Bill Murray's character struggles with culture shock while filming a commercial on location in Japan. Culture shock can also occur when interacting with others within our own country. For instance, city-dwellers may experience culture shock when visiting a small, rural town, or vice versa.

Culture is both transmitted and modified through communication. In Western cultures, for example, most people eat using forks, knives, spoons, individual plates, and bowls. In many Eastern cultures, people may eat with chopsticks. In some countries, people use bread as a utensil, and in others, people use their fingers and share a common bowl. All of these dining rituals are culturally based and taught by one generation to the next through communication.

© Jessicaphoto/iStockphoto.com

Traditional South Asian wedding ceremonies are one example of how cultures differ. Ceremonies can last for days and are highly intricate. For example, the bride always sits on the right side of the groom (a place reserved for acquaintances) until they exchange their vows, when she sits on the left, becoming the Vamangi, or one-who-sits-on-the-left, signifying the couple's unity.

Communication is also the mechanism through which culture is modified. For example, several generations ago most American children were taught to show respect by addressing adult family friends using a title and last name (e.g., Mr. Jones, Miss Smith). Today, children often address adult family friends by their first names.

3-2 Dominant Cultures, Co-Cultures, and Cultural Identity

Dominant culture refers to the learned system of norms held by the majority group of empowered people in a society. The dominant culture of the United States has evolved over time. It once strictly reflected and privileged the values of white, western European, English-speaking, Protestant, heterosexual men. Before the 1960s, people immigrating to the United States were expected to embrace and adapt to this dominant culture in place of the culture of their native country. Immigrants even changed their names to sound more "American." They were expected to learn English as quickly as possible and use it instead of their native language. Since the 1960s, however, dominant American culture has slowly begun to respect and honor the diversity of cultures that co-exist in the United States.

In addition to embracing the dominant American culture, then, many people also identify with one or more co-cultures. A **co-culture** is a group consisting of a smaller number of people who hold common values, beliefs, attitudes, and customs that differ from those of the dominant culture.

Co-culture also influences communication behavior. For example, co-cultural group members sometimes **code switch**, altering their linguistic and nonverbal patterns to conform to the dominant culture or co-culture depending on the circumstances (Bonvillain, 2003). So Linh may speak Vietnamese and defer to her older relatives while conversing at the dinner table. She may speak English and question her teachers openly during class discussions at school. And she may speak a mixture of Vietnamese and English (as well as slang and other accepted in-group jargon) when hanging out with friends. If you are familiar with the movie *Windtalkers,* you might know that the film is based on the real-life role Navajo code switchers played in Saipan during World War II (Jackson, 2004).

Cultural identity is the part of our self-concept that is based on how closely we associate with both the dominant culture and various co-cultures (Ting-Toomey et al., 2000). For example,

you may be proud to be a third-generation Polish-American who embraces the co-culture of your heritage through communication patterns, religion, food choices, and so on. Or you might identify more with the dominant American culture and rarely think about being Polish. If the dominant culture stigmatizes your co-culture, you might downplay this part of your identity to fit into the dominant culture. Conversely, you may choose to identify even more closely with the co-culture and become a vocal activist for it.

Some of the co-cultures that exist in the United States today are formed around shared beliefs and values related to, for example, race, ethnicity, sex and gender, sexual orientation, religion, socioeconomic status, age or generation, and disability.

dominant culture
the learned system of norms held by the majority group of empowered people in a society

co-culture
a group consisting of a smaller number of people who hold common values, beliefs, attitudes, and customs that differ from those of the dominant culture

code switch
altering linguistic and nonverbal patterns to conform to the dominant or co-culture

cultural identity
the part of our self-concept that is based on how closely we associate with both the dominant culture and various co-cultures

3-2a Race

Traditionally, the term *race* was used to classify people based on biological characteristics (e.g., skin and eye color, hair texture, body shape). However, scientific justifications for such divisions have proven elusive (Hotz, 1995). Nevertheless, people do experience the social effects of *perceived* race and form co-cultures based on similar experiences with respect to it.

3-2b Ethnicity

Ethnicity is a classification of people based on combinations of shared characteristics such as nationality, geographic origin, language, religion, ancestral customs, and tradition. The degree to which people identify with their ethnic heritage can vary greatly. Generally, the further removed you are from your family's immigrant experience, the less likely you are to be influenced by your ethnic co-culture. For example, Maria and Juan are both Mexican-Americans. Juan, who immigrated with his parents to the United States, identifies more with his ethnic heritage than does Maria, who is a fourth-generation Mexican-American.

Native language (sometimes referred to as **mother tongue**) is the language of one's ethnic heritage and is typically the language a person learns from birth. Native language obviously influences communication. Even after learning English, many immigrants choose to speak their native language at home and to live in close proximity to others from their home country. Although the United States is considered an English-speaking country, it now has the second-largest Spanish-speaking population of any country in the world (Mantilla, 2008).

3-2c Sex and Gender

In the dominant American culture, **sex** (which consists of biologically determined physical traits) and **gender** (which consists of the learned roles and communication patterns deemed "appropriate" for males and females in the dominant culture) tend to be intertwined. In other words, the dominant American culture expects men to communicate in masculine ways and women to communicate in feminine ways. If you have ever heard someone tell an outspoken young girl to "hush up and act like a lady," or a weeping boy to "buck up and act like a man," you have witnessed young people *learning gender* based on their sex. Obviously, people differ in the extent to which they identify with these gendered co-cultures, and those who do not strongly identify with them may not behave in accord with expectations at all.

3-2d Sexual Orientation

The dominant American culture has historically valued and privileged heterosexuality. People who deviated from the heterosexual norm were severely mistreated. Although laws that reflect a change in attitude toward sexuality are gaining popularity, people who are not heterosexual still face discrimination, as well as legal and physical threats. Thus, co-cultures exist across the country based on the collective experiences of those who embrace a sexual orientation that is not heterosexual. Although many people are working hard to modify the dominant American culture with regard to sexual orientation, and some progress has been made, much remains to be done.

3-2e Religion

A **religion** is a belief system with a set of rituals and ethical standards based on a common perception of what is sacred or holy. Although the dominant culture in the United States values religious freedom, historically it has reflected monotheistic Judeo-Christian values and practices. However, many religious co-cultures exist harmoniously across the country today. Unfortunately, some people in the United States have become prejudiced against Muslims based on a misunderstanding that inaccurately equates Muslims with Al-Qaeda, the militant group responsible for the 9/11 terrorist attacks. Did you know that one-fifth of the world's population—that is, 1.6 billion people—is Muslim and that some of the core values of this religion are peace, mercy, and forgiveness (Lugo, Cooperman, O'Connell, & Stencel, 2011)?

3-2f Socioeconomic Status (SES)

Socioeconomic status (SES) is the position of a person or family in the power hierarchy of a society based on income, education, and occupation. SES is typically divided into three categories: high, middle, and low. Most Americans identify with the middle class even though they may really be members of a higher or lower class (Ellis, 1999). People develop co-cultures that reinforce distinct values, rituals, and communication practices based on SES. Although not true in all cases, parents in

ethnicity
a classification of people based on combinations of shared characteristics such as nationality, geographic origin, language, religion, ancestral customs, and tradition

native language (mother tongue)
the language of one's ethnic heritage; typically the language learned at birth

sex
biologically determined physical traits

gender
the learned roles and communication patterns deemed "appropriate" for males and females in the dominant culture

religion
a belief system with a set of rituals and ethical standards based on a common perception of what is sacred or holy

socioeconomic status (SES)
the position of a person or family in the power hierarchy of a society based on income, education, and occupation

low-SES groups tend to emphasize obedience, acceptance of what others think, and hesitancy in expressing desires to authority figures. Middle-class parents tend to emphasize intellectual curiosity. Such differences based on SES may lead those from middle-class backgrounds to speak more directly and assertively than people from lower-class backgrounds. And, in terms of nonverbal communication, people of high SES backgrounds tend to perform more disengagement cues (e.g., doodling) and fewer engagement cues (e.g., head nods, laughs) than people from low SES backgrounds (Bornstein & Bradley, 2003; Kraus & Keltner, 2009). Finally, SES is at the heart of the American dream. Even in tough economic times, a nationwide poll conducted by the *New York Times* revealed that nearly 80 percent of Americans believe their chances to move up to a higher class are the same or greater than they were 30 years ago (Leonhardt, 2005).

3-2g Age/Generation

People born and raised in the same generation may identify with a co-culture distinct to it. Although not all people identify with their generational co-culture, generally speaking, people who grew up during the Great Depression tend to be frugal, and those who grew up during World War II tend to value sacrifice of self for cause and country. Baby Boomers who came of age during the turbulent 1960s are likely to question authority. Many Generation Xers, who grew up as *latch-key kids* (with parents at work when they got home from school), are likely to be self-sufficient and adaptable. Millennials (a.k.a. Generation Y and Generation NeXt), who grew up during the 1990s and came of age after 9/11, have never known life without computers, became aware of the realities of school and world violence at an early age, and experienced globalization. They tend to be adept at using technology to multitask, are cautious about safety issues, and appreciate diversity (Pew Research Center, 2007). Finally, Generation Z (a.k.a. the Internet Generation or Digital Natives) were born after the Cold War era and the fall of the Soviet Union. They have never known a world without instant access to information via Internet searches on computers and smartphones, nor access to others via text messaging and social media sites like Facebook. They are adept at multitasking as well as learning and using new technologies (Prensky, 2001; Wallis, 2006).

When people from different generations interact, their co-cultural orientations can cause communication challenges. For example, when people from earlier generations interact with people who came of age after the 1960s, different expectations about how to demonstrate respect might cause misunderstandings and even conflict (Zemke, Raines, & Filipczak, 2000).

3-2h Disability

A **disability** is any physical, emotional, mental, or cognitive impairment that impacts how a person functions in society. A disability co-culture is a group of people who share a distinct set of shared values, beliefs, and attitudes based on their common experiences of living with a disability. Physically disabled veterans who may have lost a limb in a war, for example, sometimes form co-cultures where they share inside jokes and draw on common experiences to support each other during rehabilitation and afterward.

Recently, a number of feature films and documentaries have been produced to help

disability
any physical, emotional, mental, or cognitive impairment that impacts how a person functions in society

STRIVING TO DEMONSTRATE RESPECT FOR ALL PEOPLE OF ALL AGES IS ONE WAY TO WORK TOWARD INTERCULTURAL HARMONY.

© Yuri Arcurs/Shutterstock.com

people who do not live with a disability to both understand and respect various disability co-cultures. For example, in 2010 HBO produced a film about the real life of Temple Grandin, a professor of animal science who improved the ethical treatment of animals, and who is also autistic.

3-3 How Cultures Differ

Understanding how cultures differ becomes critical when we interact with people whose cultural norms differ from ours, because it helps us empathize and adapt our communication patterns accordingly (Kim, 2001; 2005). Consequently, we end up demonstrating the ethical principles of respect and integrity.

Understanding to which cultural groups people identify with can be challenging. The early work of Edward T. Hall and, more recently, Gerard Henrik (Geert) Hofstede give us a way to understand how cultures are similar to and different from one another and to understand how these cultural variations may affect communication. Based on their work, we offer several dimensions for consideration: (1) individualism/collectivism, (2) context, (3) chronemics, (4) uncertainty avoidance, (5) power distance, (6) masculinity/femininity, and (7) long-term/short-term orientation.

3-3a Individualism/Collectivism

Cultures differ in the extent to which individualism or collectivism is valued. Highly **individualistic cultures** value personal rights and responsibilities, privacy, voicing one's opinion, freedom, innovation, and self-expression (Andersen, Hecht, Hoobler, & Smallwood, 2003). People in highly individualistic cultures place primary value on the self and personal achievement. Competition is considered both desirable and useful, and the interests of others are considered primarily as they affect personal interests. If you come from an individualistic culture, you may consider your family and close friends when you make decisions, but only because your personal interests align with theirs. Cultures in the United States, Australia, Canada, and Northern and Western European countries are considered to be highly individualistic.

© Joan Vicent Cantó Roig/SensorSpot/iStockphoto.com

In contrast, highly **collectivist cultures** value community, collaboration, shared interests, harmony, the public good, and avoiding embarrassment (Andersen, et al., 2003). Highly collectivist cultures place primary value on the interests of the group and group harmony. Decisions are shaped by what is considered best for the group, regardless of whether they serve an individual's personal interests. Maintaining harmony and cooperation is valued over competition and personal achievement. A variety of cultures throughout South and Central America, East and Southeast Asia, and Africa are considered to be highly collectivist.

Individualism and collectivism influence many aspects of communication (Samovar, Porter, & McDaniel, 2009). First, individualism and collectivism affect self-concept and self-esteem. People in individualist cultures form independent self-concepts and base their self-esteem on individual accomplishments. People in collectivist cultures form interdependent self-concepts and base their self-esteem on how well they work in a group.

Second, emphasis on the individual leads members of highly individualistic cultures to be assertive and confront conflict directly, whereas members of highly collectivist cultures are more likely to engage in collaboration or to avoid conflict. In the United States, assertiveness and argumentation are skills used in personal relationships, small group situations, politics, and business. In Japan, a highly collectivist culture, common business practices are based on an elaborate process called *nemawashii* (a term that also means "binding the roots of a plant before pulling it out"). To maintain harmony and avoid confrontational argument, any subject that might cause conflict should be discussed among individuals before

individualistic cultures cultures that value personal rights and responsibilities, privacy, voicing one's opinion, freedom, innovation, and self-expression

collectivist cultures cultures that value community, collaboration, shared interests, harmony, the public good, and avoiding embarrassment

the group meets to ensure that interactions during the meeting will not seem rude or impolite (Samovar, Porter, & McDaniel, 2009).

Finally, individualism and collectivism influence how people make group decisions. In highly collectivist cultures, group members strive for consensus and may sacrifice optimal outcomes for the sake of group harmony. In highly individualistic cultures, optimal outcomes are paramount, even at the expense of disharmony. Groups consisting of members who come from both highly individualistic and highly collectivist cultures may experience difficulties because of these different cultural values related to individualism and collectivism.

3-3b Context

Another cultural distinction that affects intercultural communication is the extent to which members rely on contextual cues to convey the meaning of a message (Hall, 1976). In **low-context cultures**, speakers use words to convey most of the meaning. In low-context cultures such as those of the United States, Germany, and Scandinavia, verbal messages are direct, specific, and detailed. Speakers are expected to say exactly what they mean and get to the point. In **high-context cultures**, much of the speaker's message is understood from the context. Much of the meaning is conveyed indirectly and can be accurately interpreted only by referring to unwritten cultural rules and subtle nonverbal behaviors. So in high-context cultures such as those of American Indian, Latin American, and Asian communities, verbal messages are ambiguous and understood by "reading between the lines" (Chen & Starosta, 1998).

Effective communication between members of high- and low-context cultures can be challenging. When low-context communicators interact with high-context communicators, they should be mindful that building a good relationship first is important for long-term effectiveness. Also, nonverbal messages and gestures will probably be more important than what is actually said. When high-context communicators interact with low-context communicators, they should recognize that the verbal message should be taken at face value and direct questions, assertions, and observations are not meant to be offensive. Finally, they need to recognize that low-context communicators might not notice or understand indirect contextual cues.

3-3c Chronemics

Chronemics is the study of how the perception of time differs among cultures (Hall, 1976). **Monochronic**

cultures view time as a series of small units that occur sequentially. Monochronic cultures value punctuality, uninterrupted task completion, meeting deadlines, following plans, and doing things one at a time. For instance, when Margarite (who values a monochronic time orientation) is interrupted by her roommate, who wants to share some good news about her day, Margarite may respond, "I can't talk now. It's my study time!" The dominant culture of the United States values a monochronic orientation to time.

Polychronic cultures, for example, Latin American, Arab, and Southern European cultures, view time as a continuous flow. Thus, appointment times and schedules are perceived as approximate and fluid. People who abide by a polychronic orientation to time are comfortable doing several things at once, having a flexible schedule or none at all, and disregarding deadlines to satisfy other needs (Chen & Starosta, 1998). Interruptions are not perceived as annoying but as natural occurrences.

Differences in time orientation can make intercultural communication challenging. In polychronic cultures, relationships are more important than schedules. So when Dante, who is polychronic, shows up for a noon lunch with Sean at 12:47 because a coworker had needed some help, he doesn't perceive this as a problem. But Sean, who is monochronic, is annoyed because Dante arrived so "late," and quickly moves the discussion to the business they need to complete. Sean's attitude and immediate discussion of business seems rude to Dante.

3-3d Uncertainty Avoidance

Cultures differ in their attitudes toward **uncertainty avoidance**, which is the extent to which people desire to predict what is going to happen. **Low uncertainty-avoidance cultures** such as those of the United States, Sweden, and Denmark tolerate uncertainty and are less driven to control unpredictable people, relationships, or events. People tend to accept unpredictability,

low-context cultures
cultures in which speakers use words to convey most of the meaning; verbal messages are direct, specific, and detailed

high-context cultures
cultures in which much of a speaker's message is understood from the context

chronemics
the study of how the perception of time differs among cultures.

monochronic cultures
cultures that view time as a series of small units that occur sequentially

polychronic cultures
cultures that view time as a continuous flow

uncertainty avoidance
the extent to which people desire to predict what is going to happen

low uncertainty-avoidance cultures
cultures that tolerate uncertainty and are less driven to control unpredictable people, relationships, or events

high uncertainty-avoidance cultures
cultures with a low tolerance for uncertainty and a high need to control unpredictable people, relationships, or events

power distance
the extent to which members of a culture expect and accept that power will be equally or unequally shared

high power-distance cultures
cultures that view unequal power distribution as normal

low power-distance cultures
cultures in which members prefer power to be more equally distributed

Needing to control unpredictable events may create systems of formal rules and stems from high-uncertainty avoidance.

tolerate the unusual, prize creative initiative, take risks, and think there should be as few rules as possible.

High uncertainty-avoidance cultures such as those of Germany, Portugal, Greece, Peru, and Belgium have a low tolerance for uncertainty and a high need to control unpredictable people, relationships, or events. These cultures often create systems of formal rules as a way to provide more security and reduce risk. They also tend to be less tolerant of people or groups with deviant ideas or behaviors. People in these cultures often experience anxiety when confronted with unpredictable people, relationships, or situations (Samovar, Porter, & McDaniel, 2009).

How our culture teaches us to view uncertainty impacts communication. People from high uncertainty-avoidance cultures tend to value and use precise language to be more certain of what a person's message means. Students from high uncertainty-avoidance cultures would probably ask a lot of questions about school assignments and would probably welcome a specific checklist of the exact criteria by which an assignment would be graded. By contrast, students from low uncertainty-avoidance cultures might be annoyed if given such a specific list of rules, viewing them as a barrier to creativity.

Uncertainty avoidance also influences how people communicate in new and developing relationships. People from high uncertainty-avoidance cultures tend to be wary of strangers and may not seek out new relationships with people they perceive as different and, thus, unpredictable. They might prefer meeting people through friends and family. And in the early stages of a developing relationship, they might guard their privacy and refrain from self-disclosure. People from low uncertainty-avoidance cultures, on the other hand, are likely to initiate new relationships with people who seem unusual and unique, and might enjoy the excitement of disclosing personal information as a way to get to know one another earlier in the relationship.

3-3e Power Distance

Power distance is the extent to which members of a culture expect and accept that power will be equally or unequally shared. In **high power-distance cultures**, unequal distribution of power is accepted by both high and low power holders. Although no culture distributes power equally, people in high power-distance cultures (like many countries in the Middle East, Malaysia, Guatemala, Venezuela, and Singapore) view unequal power distribution as normal.

In **low power-distance cultures**, members prefer power to be more equally distributed. In the cultures of Austria, Finland, Denmark, Norway, and the United

States, inequalities in power and status are muted. People know that some individuals have more clout, authority, and influence, but lower-ranking people are not in awe of or more respectful toward people in higher positions of power. Even though power differences exist, people value democracy and egalitarian behavior.

Our cultural beliefs about power distance naturally affect how we interact with others in authority positions. If you are a student or employee living in a high power-distance culture, you are not likely to argue with your teacher, supervisor, or boss. Rather, you will probably do what is ordered without question. In contrast, if you come from a low power-distance culture where status differences are muted, you might be more comfortable questioning or even arguing with those in authority.

3-3f Masculinity/Femininity

Cultures differ in how strongly they value traditional gender role distinctions. In highly **masculine cultures**, men and women are expected to adhere to traditional gender roles and behaviors. These cultures also value masculine roles more highly than feminine ones. If you come from a highly masculine culture (like those of Mexico, Italy, and Japan), you are likely to expect men to act in assertive and dominant ways and to expect women to be nurturing, caring, and service-oriented. You are likely to feel uncomfortable when you encounter people who don't meet these expectations. You are also likely to view masculine behaviors as more valuable, regardless of your sex. As a result, even though women are not supposed to enact such behaviors, you are likely to value the traditionally masculine characteristics of performance, ambition, assertiveness, competitiveness, and material success enacted by men more than you value traditionally

feminine traits such as service, nurturing, relationships, and helping behaviors enacted by women embracing traditional gender roles and behaviors. (Hofstede, 2000).

In highly **feminine cultures**, people assume a variety of roles and are valued for doing so regardless of sex. In feminine cultures (like those of Sweden, Norway, and Denmark), both men and women are accustomed to being nurturing, caring, and service oriented and value those traits as much as performance, ambition, and competitiveness depending on the circumstances of a situation (Hofstede, 1998).

Whether you come from a highly masculine or feminine culture influences how you communicate with others. People from masculine cultures have strict definitions of what are appropriate behaviors for males and females and are rewarded for adhering to them. Men in these cultures tend to be unprepared to engage in nurturing and caring behaviors and women tend to be unprepared to be assertive or to argue persuasively. Both women and men in feminine cultures learn to nurture, empathize, assert, and argue, and are rewarded for doing so.

3-3g Long-Term/Short-Term Orientation

Long-term and short-term orientations deal with how a culture values patience in arriving at rewards in the future or immediately in the here and now. **Short-term oriented cultures** tend to value rewards in the here and now and, thus, emphasize quick results, fulfilling social obligations, and getting to the bottom line efficiently. People in cultures with a short-term orientation, such as those found in the United States, Pakistan, Russia, Canada, Norway, and the United Kingdom, tend to determine what result is desired at the outset of an experience and then do whatever it takes to achieve it. People in short-term oriented cultures also value keeping leisure time distinctly separate from working time. **Long-term oriented cultures**, such as those of China, Japan, Hong Kong,

masculine cultures
cultures in which men and women are expected to adhere to traditional gender roles

feminine cultures
cultures in which people assume a variety of roles and are valued for doing so regardless of sex

short-term oriented cultures
cultures that tend to value static rewards in the here and now and emphasizes quick results

long-term oriented cultures
cultures that emphasize potential future rewards that will eventually be realized after slow and steady perseverance toward achieving a mutually acceptable result

© Joan Vicent Cantó Roig/Vetta Collection/iStockphoto.com

and Taiwan, emphasize potential future rewards that will be realized after slow and steady perseverance toward achieving a mutually acceptable result. Adaptability and honoring relationships are more important than quickly achieving the bottom line. And leisure time is not expected to be separate from working time.

Misunderstandings may arise when people from cultures with a long-term orientation interact with people from cultures with a short-term orientation. One of your authors experienced this on a business trip to Shanghai, China. Coming from a short-term oriented culture, when her hosts began discussing business ideas at dinner, she lightheartedly said, "No talking business at the dinner table." While this remark would have been quite appropriate in the United States, where a short-term orientation values leisure time as separate from working time, her hosts politely reminded her that they always talk business at the dinner table.

3-4 Developing Intercultural Communication Competence

We can develop intercultural communication competence by first acknowledging potential barriers and then by employing several strategies to overcome them.

3-4a Potential Barriers

Several of the most common barriers to effective intercultural communication include anxiety, assuming similarity or difference, ethnocentrism, stereotyping, incompatible communication codes, and incompatible norms and values.

Anxiety

It is normal to feel some level of discomfort when entering a cultural setting with unfamiliar norms and customs. Most people experience fear, dislike, and distrust when first interacting with someone from a different culture (Luckmann, 1999).

Assumed Similarity or Difference

When we cross into an unfamiliar cultural environment, we might assume that the norms that apply to our culture will also apply in the new one. When traveling internationally

ethnocentrism
the belief that one's own culture is superior to others

↘ Respecting other cultures is one way to avoid ethnocentricity and to experience different cultures than your own.

from the United States, for example, many people expect to eat their familiar hamburgers and fries and to be provided with rapid service when ordering. Likewise, they may be annoyed when shops and restaurants close during the early afternoon in countries that observe the custom of a siesta.

It can be just as great a mistake to assume that *everything* about an unfamiliar culture will be different. For example, a Mexican-American student from California studying at a small private college in Vermont may assume that everyone is different from her. However, her *quinceañera* party is very similar to Jewish bat/bar mitzvah celebrations and confirmation parties, all three celebrating coming of age.

Ethnocentrism

Ethnocentrism is the belief that one's own culture is superior to others. The stereotype of the tourist in the host country, loudly complaining about how much better everything is back home, is the classic example of ethnocentrism. Ethnocentrism exists in every culture to some degree (Haviland, 1993) and can occur in co-cultures, as well. An ethnocentric view of the world leads to attitudes of superiority and messages that are condescending in content and tone.

Stereotyping

Recall that stereotyping is a perceptual shortcut in which people assume that everyone in a cultural group is the same. When we interact based on stereotypes, we risk engaging in inaccurate and even unethical communication that is likely to damage our relationships.

Incompatible Communication Codes

When others speak a different language than we do, it is easy to see that we have incompatible communication codes. But even when people speak the same language, cultural variations can result from belonging to different co-cultures. For example, people from Great Britain take a "lift" to reach a higher floor and eat "chips" with their fish. Americans ride an "elevator" and eat "French fries" with their burgers. Within the United States, many Midwesterners drink "pop" rather than "soda." Co-cultural groups will often purposefully develop in-group codes that are easily understood by co-culture members but are unintelligible to those from the outside.

Incompatible Norms and Values

Sometimes what is considered normal or highly valued in one culture is offensive in another. To the Vietnamese, dog meat is considered a delicacy. Many Americans might find the practice of eating dog meat disgusting but think nothing of eating beef. However, practicing Hindus may not eat beef because the cow is sacred to their religion. Different norms and values can cause serious problems when communicating unless we are aware of and respect differences.

3-4b Competent Communication Strategies

Unfortunately, there is no "silver bullet" strategy for communicating effectively across cultures. However, competent intercultural communicators work to overcome potential cultural barriers by acquiring accurate information about other cultures' values and practices, adopting an appropriate attitude, and developing culture-centered skills.

Acquire Accurate Knowledge

The more we know about other cultures before we attempt to interact with people in them, the more likely we are to be competent intercultural communicators (Neuliep, 2006). There are several ways to learn about other cultures.

© Carmen Martinez Banus/E+/Getty Images

1. Formal study. You can learn about other cultures by reading books, periodicals, and Web sites about them. You can read personal accounts and ethnographic research studies, take courses, and interview members of the group.

2. Observation. You can learn about a culture or co-culture by watching as members interact with each other. We call this form of watching **nonparticipant observation**. As you watch, you can notice how certain values, rituals, and communication styles are similar to and different from your own.

3. Immersion. You can learn a great deal about another culture by actively participating in it. When you live or work with people whose cultural assumptions are different from yours, you not only acquire obvious cultural information, you also learn nuances that escape passive observers and are not accessible through formal study alone. We call this form of immersion **participant observation**. One reason study-abroad programs often include home stays is to ensure that students become immersed in the culture of the host country.

nonparticipant observation
learning about a culture or co-culture by watching as members interact with each other

participant observation
learning about a culture or co-culture by living or working with people whose cultural assumptions are different from yours

Adopt an Appropriate Attitude

The right attitude involves one's motivations and flexibility in interacting with others (Neuliep, 2006). In other words, we must be willing to try and must have a genuine desire to succeed when communicating across cultures. We must be willing to adapt rather than expect the other person to adjust to our communication style. We can begin to adopt an appropriate attitude by tolerating ambiguity, being open-minded, and acting altruistically.

1. Tolerate ambiguity. Communicating with strangers usually creates uncertainty; when the stranger also comes from a different culture, we often become even more anxious about what he or she will expect of us. When communicating, we must be prepared to tolerate a high degree of uncertainty about the other person and to tolerate it for a long time. If you enter an intercultural interaction believing that it is OK to be unsure about how

altruism
a display of genuine and unselfish concern for the welfare of others

egocentricity
a selfish interest in one's own needs to the exclusion of everything else

intercultural empathy
imaginatively placing yourself in another person's cultural world and attempting to experience what he or she is experiencing

flexibility
the ability to adjust your communication to fit the other person and the situation

to proceed, you are likely to pay closer attention to the feedback you receive. You can then work to adjust your communication to demonstrate respect and to achieve mutual understanding.

2. Be open-minded. Open-minded people are aware of their own cultural norms and values and recognize that other people's norms and values may be different, but not wrong. Resist the impulse to judge the values of other cultures in terms of your own culture. Also avoid jumping to conclusions about what you think others mean by something they say or do. Instead, seek to learn from those you interact with by assuming their intentions are honorable and asking sincere questions about what they say and do differently and why.

3. Be altruistic. Altruism is a display of genuine and unselfish concern for the welfare of others. The opposite of altruism is **egocentricity**, a selfish interest in one's own needs to the exclusion of everything else. Egocentric people are focused on themselves, whereas altruistic people are focused on others. Altruistic communicators do not neglect their own needs, but they recognize that for a conversation to be successful, both parties must be able to contribute what they want and take what they need from the exchange. One way to demonstrate this is to learn some basic phrases in the language of your peer's culture and try to use them when possible. When people hear you say "please" and "thank you" in their native language, even if your pronunciation is imperfect, they are likely to perceive you as respectful and are likely to engage more openly with you as a result.

Develop Culture-Centered Skills

To be effective in intercultural situations, you may need to adapt the basic communication skills you learn in this course to a particular culture. Three very useful skills are listening, empathy, and flexibility.

1. Practice listening. There are cultural differences in how people value and engage in listening. In the dominant culture of the United States, people listen closely for concrete facts and information and often ask questions

while listening. In other cultures, such as those in Japan, Finland, and Sweden, listeners are more reserved and do not ask as many questions (Samovar, Porter, & McDaniel, 2009). Many cultures in East Asian countries value listening more than speaking.

2. Practice intercultural empathy. Intercultural empathy means imaginatively placing yourself in the other person's cultural world and attempting to experience what he or she is experiencing (Ting-Toomey et al., 2000). Conveying intercultural empathy demonstrates that we sincerely respect the other person and his or her cultural norms even though those norms may not be upheld in our culture. Try to honor the practices of the host culture. If you are in an East Asian country, for example, try to use chopsticks rather than asking for a knife and fork.

3. Develop flexibility. We discussed the concept of flexibility as part of an appropriate attitude toward intercultural encounters, but we can also provide concrete strategies for becoming more flexible while communicating. **Flexibility** is the ability to adjust your communication to fit the other person and the situation. With flexibility, you can use a wide variety of communication skills during an interaction and modify your behavior within and across situations. Being flexible means analyzing a situation, making good decisions about how to communicate in that situation, and then modifying your communication when necessary as you go along.

Practice Makes... for Smoother Communication

When visiting with college students at Shanghai University, one of your authors asked each student his or her name. Although each student first introduced himself or herself with an "English" name, your author also asked students to offer their Chinese names, which she repeated back to them. When the students heard her make this genuine attempt to honor them and their given Chinese names, they began to trust her and opened up more during the classroom discussion. People who make a sincere effort to listen attentively and respond in an other-centered way find the most success when interacting with people from cultures that differ from their own.

Quick Quiz

T F 1. Intercultural communication can be defined as the psychological discomfort of adjusting to a new cultural situation.

T F 2. Once immigrants to the United States have learned English, they often speak it at home so they can learn to better fit in with their neighbors.

T F 3. People who come from high uncertainty-avoidance cultures have a high tolerance for unpredictable people, relationships, and events.

T F 4. People from masculine cultures expect that individuals will assume a variety of roles depending on the circumstances and their own choices, regardless of sex; they do not have any sex-role expectations.

T F 5. An ethnocentric view of the world leads to attitudes of superiority and messages that are directly and subtly condescending in content and tone.

6. Which of the following is not one of the major contributors to co-cultures in U.S. society today, as listed by the text?
   a. gender
   b. ethnicity
   c. race
   d. political beliefs
   e. sexual orientation

7. Which of the following is the most obvious influence of ethnicity on communication?
   a. the foods you prefer
   b. your religion
   c. the language of your original country
   d. traditions handed down from your ancestors
   e. distinguishable physical characteristics

8. Based on the discussion in the text, when parents place emphasis on intellectual curiosity, they are likely to be associated with which social class?
   a. upper class
   b. lower class
   c. elite
   d. middle class
   e. impoverished

9. Geert Hofstede identified major dimensions of culture that affect communication. Which of the following is NOT one of them?
   a. individualism-collectivism
   b. religious beliefs
   c. uncertainty avoidance
   d. power distance
   e. masculinity-femininity

10. In cultures characterized by _____, inequalities in power, status, and rank are underplayed and muted.
   a. high power distance
   b. low power distance
   c. masculinity
   d. femininity
   e. individualism

Answers: 1. F, 2. F, 3. F, 4. F, 5. T, 6. D, 7. C, 8. D, 9. B, 10. B

Verbal Messages

What do you think?

It is more important to communicate precise details rather than general ideas.

1 2 3 4 5 6 7 8 9 10
STRONGLY DISAGREE   STRONGLY AGREE

Learning Outcomes

4-1 Define a language, a dialect, and an idiolect

4-2 List the characteristics of language

4-3 Explain how conversational, social, and cultural contexts shape meaning and know-how to shape messages that accurately convey your meaning

In this chapter, you'll learn that there are many reasons why people can interpret the same message in a wide variety of ways, which can lead to serious misunderstandings that affect our relationships. We begin by explaining the nature of language. Then we describe the relationship between language and meaning and offer suggestions for improving your ability to communicate both face-to-face and online.

4-1 The Nature of Language

When you hear the word "language," what comes to mind? If you're like most people, you probably think of English, Spanish, French, Chinese, Hindi, Swahili, and so forth. While each language is certainly different from the others in some ways, their purposes and fundamentals are the same.

In terms of purposes, we use language to label, compare, and define. So when we label some music as hip hop, we do so to differentiate it from other musical genres such as rock, pop, country, and classical. We also use language to compare and judge things as better or worse. Television programs such as *What Not to Wear* and *American Idol* are based on this very principle. We also use language to discuss and learn from the experiences of others. We might do so by taking a course, attending a lecture, visiting with a friend, watching a TV program, or surfing the Internet.

In terms of fundamentals, all languages are based on the exchange of utterances. An **utterance** is a complete unit of talk bounded by the speaker's

utterance
a complete unit of talk bounded by the speaker's literal or figurative silence

turn-taking
the exchange of utterances

language
a system of symbols used by people to communicate

lexicon
the collection of words and expressions in a language

phonology
the sounds used to pronounce words

syntax and grammar
rules for combining words to form sentences and larger units of expression

language community
all people who can speak or understand a particular language

dialect
a unique form of a more general language spoken by a specific culture or co-culture

speech communities
smaller groups that speak a common dialect

idiolect
our own personal symbol system that includes our active vocabularies and our unique pronunciations, grammar, and syntax

silence (Arnoff & Rees-Miller, 2001). "Silence" can be either literal (e.g., during a face-to-face or telephone conversation) or figurative (e.g., waiting for a response to a text message). Exchanging utterances is known as **turn-taking**. With these purposes and fundamentals in mind, let's turn now to a more specific discussion about what a language is and what its characteristics are.

4-1a What Is a Language?

A **language** is a system of symbols used by people to communicate. Verbal languages communicate thoughts and feelings. Each verbal language consists of a **lexicon**, the collection of words and expressions; a **phonology**, the sounds used to pronounce words; and **syntax and grammar**, the rules for combining words to form sentences and larger units of expression.

All people who understand a particular language are part of a **language community**. For example, the English language is spoken by people who live in Australia, Scotland, Ireland, Canada, India, and the United States, among others. The five largest language communities in the world are Chinese, Spanish, English, Arabic, and Hindi (Lewis, 2009).

If all people in a particular language community knew all the words, pronounced them the same way, and used the same rules of grammar and syntax, communication would be easy. Unfortunately, this is not the case. The English spoken in England is not the same as the English spoken in the United States. And the English spoken in Boston is not the same as the English spoken in Biloxi, Mississippi, or in Fargo, North Dakota.

Languages are really collections of dialects. A **dialect** is a unique form of a more general language spoken by a specific culture or co-culture (O'Grady, Archibald, Aronoff, & Rees-Miller, 2001). These smaller groups that speak a common dialect are known as **speech communities**. Dialects exist on a continuum. The more commonalities shared by two dialects, the closer they are on the continuum. This is why Americans can generally understand Canadians more easily than they can understand Scots or Aussies.

No one dialect is better or worse than another. Each simply uses different lexicons, phonologies, grammars, and syntaxes. However, some dialects are *perceived* to be "better" than others because they are spoken by the power elite of a language community. This dialect tends to be promoted as the "proper" form.

As is demonstrated in the cases of the former Yugoslavia and China, what is called a *language* and what is called a *dialect* is usually rooted in politics. When Yugoslavia was a country, its official language (Serbian-Croatian) consisted of many similar dialects among various regions. Since the collapse of Yugoslavia in the 1990s, however, each region is now a separate country and many of these regional dialects are considered the official languages of each country. Serbian is spoken in Serbia, Croatian in Croatia, Bosnian in Bosnia, and Montenegrin in Montenegro (Cvetkovic, 2009).

On the other hand, the official language of China is Chinese and all literate people use this same written symbol system. Thus, people from one part of the country can easily read compositions written by someone in other parts of the country. But the written symbols do not have commonly shared pronunciations. So although the regional tongues of Mandarin, Wu, Cantonese, and Min are dialects of Chinese, speakers of one dialect often can't understand someone speaking another (Wright, 2010).

In addition to language and dialect, each of us uses our own personal symbol system called an **idiolect**, which includes our active vocabularies and our unique pronunciations, grammar, and syntax (Higginbotham, 2006). We may have words in our personal lexicon that are understood by very few people as well as words understood by large numbers of people. Likewise, we may pronounce some words or use grammar or syntax in idiosyncratic ways. Those with whom we talk frequently understand our idiolect best. That's why parents can understand their toddlers' speech even though it is unrecognizable to others.

4-2 Characteristics of Language

Sharing meaning can be difficult because we speak different languages and use different dialects and idiolects than those with whom we are communicating. Sharing meaning can also be difficult because language is arbitrary, abstract, and constantly changing.

4-2a Language Is Arbitrary

In any language, the **words** used to represent things are arbitrary symbols. There is not necessarily a literal connection between a word and the thing it represents. For a word to have meaning, it must be recognized by members of the language or speech community as standing for a particular object, idea, or feeling. The word *dog* is nothing more than three letters used together unless members of a community agree that it stands for a certain four-legged animal. Different language communities use different word symbols to represent the same phenomenon. In Spanish, for instance, *el perro* represents the same thing that *dog* represents in English. Different speech communities within a language community may also use different words to represent the same phenomenon. For example, the storage compartment of an automobile is called a *trunk* in the United States, but it is called a *boot* in England.

words
arbitrarily chosen symbols used to represent thoughts and feelings

4-2b Language Is Abstract

Not only is language arbitrary, but it is also abstract. For example, in the United States, the word *pet* is commonly understood to be an animal kept for companionship. Still, if Rema refers simply to her "pet," Margi may think of a dog, cat, snake, bird, or hamster. Even if Rema specifically mentions her cat, Margi still might think of cats of various breeds, sizes, colors, and temperaments.

4-2c Language Changes over Time

New words are constantly being invented and existing words abandoned or assigned new meanings. Just think, for example, of the words that have been invented to represent new technologies, such as *texting, Googling, cyberbullying, sexting, tweeting, retweeting, netiquette, webinar, emoticon,* and *blogging*. Some of the new words most recently added to English dictionaries include *vanity sizing* (the deliberate undersizing of clothes), *twirt* (flirt via Twitter), *mankle* (the male ankle), and *cougar* (an older woman in a romantic relationship with a younger man). Did you know that the *Oxford English Dictionary* now also includes *OMG, LOL,* and *<3* as actual words?

Some words become obsolete because the thing they represent is no longer used. For example, today we use *photocopiers* and *computers* to make multiple copies of print documents rather than

The characteristics of language demonstrate why sharing meaning can be challenging.

mimeographs (low-cost printing presses) and *stencils.* We record audio and video data using *smartphones* rather than using *tape recorders, cassette tapes,* and *videotapes.* And we take notes on *iPads* and *laptops* rather than on paper that we organize in a *Trapper Keeper* (a loose-leaf binder used by school children in the United States during the 1970s and 1980s).

Sometimes the meanings of existing words change. For example, in the United States, *gay* once meant *happy* and only that. Today, its more common usage references one's sexual orientation. In some communities, *bad* might mean *not good,* in others it might mean *naughty,* and in others it might mean *really great* (e.g., "That movie was really bad."). And language can change when aspects of multiple languages blend together. For instance, phrases in *Tex-Mex* and *Spanglish* both blend English and Spanish, and we don't think twice about children going to *kindergarten,* a word introduced into the United States by German immigrants.

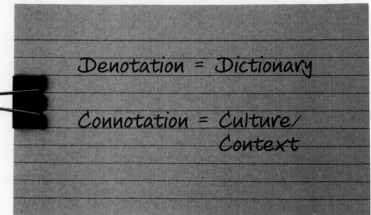

Denotation = Dictionary

Connotation = Culture/ Context

4-3 The Relationship between Language and Meaning

As you saw in the previous section, language is an imprecise and complex way to transfer meaning from one person to another. That is why we must consider not only the words themselves, but also the conversational, social, and cultural contexts in which they are used.

On the surface, the relationship between language and meaning seems pretty simple. If we select words and structure them using the grammar and syntax rules of a language community, people in that language community should understand what we mean when we say them. As you undoubtedly know, however, communicating verbally is much more complicated than that. Therefore, in this section we focus specifically on the relationship between language and meaning in terms of semantics (meanings derived from the words themselves), pragmatics (meanings derived from the conversational context), and sociolinguistics (meanings derived from social and cultural contexts).

semantic meaning
meaning derived from the words themselves and how they are arranged into sentences

denotation
the direct, explicit meaning of a word found in the dictionary of a language community

connotation
feelings or evaluations associated with a word

4-3a Semantics

Semantic meaning is derived from the words themselves and how they are arranged into sentences. Recall that *words* are the arbitrarily chosen symbols used to represent thoughts and feelings (Saeid, 2003). Although we learn new words every day, our ability to express our thoughts and feelings and to understand others is limited by the size and accuracy of our vocabulary.

Identifying the meaning of a word is tricky because words have two types of meanings. **Denotation** is the direct, explicit meaning of a word found in the dictionary of a language community. However, different dictionaries may define words in slightly different ways and many words have multiple denotative definitions. For instance, the *Random House Dictionary of the English Language* lists 23 definitions for the word *great.* Not only that, the lexicon of our personal idiolect rarely corresponds precisely to the definitions found in formal dictionary definitions. Thus, your definition of a word may be different from mine. So when your friend says your performance was *great*, he might mean it was very good, exceptional, powerful, or that it lasted a long time. All are denotative dictionary definitions of *great.*

Connotation, the feelings or evaluations we associate with a word, also influences meaning. For example, think of the different meanings people might associate with the word *family* based on their experiences growing up. To one person, a "family" may connote a safe place where one is loved unconditionally. To another, it might connote a dangerous place where people must fend for and protect themselves. Word denotation and connotation are important because the only message that counts is the message that is understood, regardless of whether it is the one you intended.

Semantic meaning is based on both the words themselves and how they are combined into meaningful phrases, sentences, and larger units of expression For example, you might communicate the same message by saying:

"When he went to the pound, he adopted a three-pound puppy."

"He went to the pound and adopted a three-pound puppy."

"Upon arriving at the pound, he adopted a three-pound puppy."

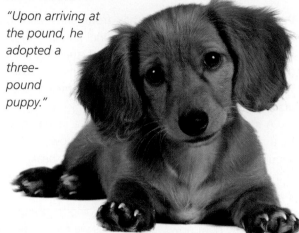

These three sentences use slightly different syntax and grammar to convey the same semantic meaning. But notice how the semantic meaning can change through subtle modification:

"He went to the pound, the adopted three-pound puppy."

By changing "and" to "the" and adding a comma to the second example above, the semantic meaning is that an adopted three-pound premature canine went to the place where unclaimed animals are kept. Next consider how the semantic meaning can change based on its position in a sentence. The word *pound* is used twice in each sentence, but in one instance it signifies a unit of weight, and in the other it signifies a place. We knew which meaning to apply based on syntax. With this in mind, let's consider several semantics guidelines for forming effective verbal messages.

Guidelines for Improving Semantics

To improve semantics, choose words and arrange them in ways that both improve clarity and demonstrate respect. You can do so by using specific, concrete, and familiar words; by embellishing them with descriptive details and examples; and by demonstrating linguistic sensitivity. In terms of clarity, compare the language used in the following two descriptions of the same incident:

"Some nut almost got me a while ago."

"About 1:00 p.m. last Saturday afternoon, an older man in a banged-up Honda Civic ran through the red light at Calhoun and Clifton and came within inches of hitting my car while I was in the intersection waiting to turn left."

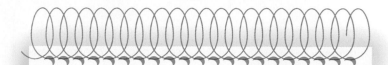

Improving Semantics

1. **Use specific language. Specific language** refers to precise words that clarify semantic meaning by narrowing what is understood from a general category to a particular item or group within that category. The first words that come to mind are often general, abstract, and imprecise. The ambiguity of these words forces the receiver to choose from many possible images rather than the precise one we have in mind. To improve semantics, use specific language. For example, saying "a banged-up Honda Civic" is more specific than saying "a car."

2. **Use concrete language. Concrete language** clarifies semantic meaning by appealing to the senses (e.g., seeing, hearing, feeling, tasting, smelling). Instead of saying Jill "speaks in a weird way," we might say Jill "mumbles," "whispers," "blusters," or "drones." Each of these words provides a more concrete description of the sound of Jill's voice.

3. **Use familiar language.** We also need to use words our receivers will understand. For example, we should use jargon and slang only when we are certain the meaning will be clear or by defining it clearly the first time we use it. Overusing and misusing abbreviations and acronyms can also hinder understanding.

4. **Use descriptive details and examples.** Sometimes semantic meaning can be improved by using descriptive details or examples. Suppose Lucy says, "Rashad is very loyal." Since the meaning of *loyal* (faithful to an idea, person, company, and so on) is abstract, Lucy might add, "I mean, he never criticizes friends behind their backs." By following up the abstract concept of loyalty with an example, Lucy clarifies what she means as it applies to Rashad.

5. **Demonstrate linguistic sensitivity. Linguistic sensitivity** is achieved by using language that is inclusive and demonstrates respect for others.

specific language
precise words that clarify semantic meaning by narrowing what is understood from a general category to a particular item or group within it

concrete language
words that clarify semantic meaning by appealing to the senses

linguistic sensitivity
inclusive word choices that demonstrate respect for others

inclusive language
use of words that do not apply only to one sex, race, or other group

pragmatic meaning
understanding a message related to its conversational context

speech act
the utterance of a verbal message by a speaker and what it implies about how the listener should respond

In the second description, the speaker used specific, concrete language, as well as descriptive details and examples, to improve semantic clarity. Let's look closer at each one.

Inclusive language does not use words that apply only to one sex, race, or other group as though they represent everyone. In the past, English speakers used the masculine pronoun *he* to represent all humans regardless of sex. This approach is not inclusive because it excludes half of the population. Instead, use plurals or both male and female pronouns (Stewart, Cooper, Stewart, & Friedley, 1998). So rather than saying, "When *a person* shops, *he* should have a clear idea of what *he* wants to buy," say "When *people* shop, *they* should have a clear idea of what *they* want to buy."

To be inclusive, we also need to avoid words that indicate a sex, race, age, or other group distinction. For example, rather than saying *fireman, mailman, stewardess,* or *mankind,* saying *firefighter, postal carrier, server,* and *humankind* is more inclusive and semantically accurate.

Demonstrating linguistic sensitivity also means avoiding potentially offensive humor, profanity, and vulgarity. Dirty jokes and racist, sexist, or other "-ist" remarks may not be intended to be offensive, but if someone perceives them to be offensive, then that person will likely lose sight of your intended meaning and focus on the offensive remark instead. The same thing can happen when you pepper your message with profanity and vulgar expressions. Listeners may be offended and focus on those words rather than on the semantic meaning of your intended message.

4-3b Pragmatics

Pragmatic meaning comes from understanding a message related to its conversational context. Whereas semantic meaning focuses on what the *words* mean (Korta & Perry, 2008), pragmatic meaning focuses on what *people* mean. So, pragmatic meaning changes across speakers and situations.

A **speech act** is the utterance of a verbal message by a speaker and what it implies about how the listener should respond. In other words, when we *speak,* we *do.* Although our speech acts are usually explicit, what we are doing is often implied. To discover pragmatic meaning, we ask ourselves, "What is the speaker *doing* by saying these words to me right now?" Similarly, as we form a message we choose language intended to evoke a certain response. For example, if I say, "Karen, pass me the bowl of potatoes," I have directly ordered Karen to pick up the bowl of potatoes and hand them to me. Instead, suppose I ask, "Karen, would you mind passing me the potatoes?" At the semantic level, this question appears to give Karen a choice. At the pragmatic level, however, what I am doing is the same. I am directing her to pass the bowl of potatoes to me. As you can see, then, we can accomplish the same pragmatic goal with either a direct/explicit or indirect/implicit speech act.

What is meant by a speech act also depends on the

© Rick Lord/Shutterstock.com

A doctor asking "How are you feeling" is a speech act— his words invite you to explain your ailment or reason for visiting the doctor's office.

Mainstream Media: Rumor Mill or Reliable Source?

The tabloids that line the checkout aisles claim to bring us the latest juicy details about the private lives of our favorite celebrities. Headlines pasted over photos of famous women like Angelina Jolie, Jennifer Aniston, and Catherine Duchess of Cambridge (Kate Middleton) often proclaim: "I'm having a baby!," "Yes, I'm pregnant!," or "Countdown to baby!" Yet more often than not, the featured celebrity isn't pregnant (though, this year, Kate was, as proclaimed by the tabloid featured in this box). Most of us understand that what is shouted in the headline of a tabloid will be a far cry from what is reported in the actual article. Because of the context, we question the accuracy of the headline and become curious about the "real story."

Though we may expect such gossip-oriented reporting from tabloids and take their stories with a grain of salt, there is increasing concern about the "tabloidization of the mainstream press" and biased reporting from sources we have historically turned to for facts and evidence. Driven in part by financial considerations, traditional media sources are reporting more sensational stories and using the same sorts of embedded sensationalism as the tabloids (Slattery, Doremus, & Marcus, 2001). Celebrity stories were once largely confined to the tabloids, but in this hyper-competitive media market, the so-called "serious" news outlets now spend more time reporting on celebrity deeds and misdeeds than in the past, and articles and stories in general focus more on rumors and innuendos. For example, mainstream media frequently

© George Rose/Getty Images News/Getty Images

"report" stories that appear in tabloids without confirming the information reported in the original article ("The Star reports that Jen is pregnant"). Meanwhile, stories about political candidates increasingly use "facts" to speculate about the underlying motivation for a candidate's position rather than digging up the facts that would reveal the validity of the position itself (e.g., speculating that Mitt Romney's wealth puts him "out of touch" with middle-class Americans rather than examining his position and arguments or focusing on rumors about President Obama's place of birth instead of his policy initiatives).

---

context. Let's look at a simple example. When Harry's car wouldn't start one morning, he made three phone calls:

Phone Call 1:

Harry: The car won't start.
Katie: Sorry about that. I'll just take the bus.

Phone Call 2:

Harry: The car won't start.
AAA Customer Service Representative: Where is the car, sir? I'll send a tow truck right away.

Phone Call 3:

Harry: The car won't start.
Previous owner who recently sold the car to Harry: Wow, that never happened to me. But I told you I was selling the car "as is."

In all three cases, the verbal utterance and the semantic meaning of Harry's message is the same. In terms of pragmatic meaning, however, Harry performed three different speech acts. What he was *doing* when he was talking to Katie was different from what he was *doing* when he was talking with the AAA customer service representative and different still from what he was *doing* when he made the statement to the person who sold him the car. He expressed his feelings by apologizing to Katie and implied that Katie should understand and release him from his obligation to take her to school. With the AAA representative, Harry's speech act was a demand for assistance. When Harry called the previous owner of the car, he was complaining and implying that the previous owner should accept responsibility. In each case, Harry used the same words and syntax, but performed three different speech acts.

The feedback from each person illustrates that each understood Harry's pragmatic meaning. Katie's response showed that she understood she would need to find another way to get to school. The AAA representative expected the call to be about car trouble so she responded by asking where the car was located. The previous owner also understood Harry's speech act when he responded by refusing to accept responsibility for the problem.

Sometimes the media use the principles of pragmatics to get the attention of and even mislead us about what the facts are in a given situation. For example, tabloids do so to entice potential readers to buy magazines. The practice is even being adopted by mainstream media outlets today.

As you can imagine, accurately conveying and interpreting the pragmatic meaning and what is being implied in verbal messages can be challenging. Let's consider several guidelines to improve your use of pragmatics in verbal messages.

Guidelines for Improving Pragmatics

We understand pragmatic meaning based on an assumption that both partners want to achieve mutual understanding (Grice, 1975). With this in mind, we suggest the following guidelines.

1. Tell the truth. This guideline seems pretty self-explanatory. Fully disclose all that you know about something. Say only what you believe to be true based on evidence to support your position. Sometimes we tell partial truths and rationalize that we are "protecting" our listeners or ourselves. For example, when your friend asks you what you think of her new boyfriend, you may offer a noncommittal response that masks your immediate dislike for the guy. You might say, "Well, he certainly appears to like you." Your friend may interpret your remark as approval rather than an attempt to spare her feelings. Obviously, this makes it more difficult to correctly understand what you truly believe. You can tell the truth by adding a comment about something you don't particularly like about him.

2. Provide the right amount of information. Include all the information needed to fully answer the

> We understand pragmatic meaning based on an assumption that both partners want to achieve mutual understanding.

question and refrain from adding irrelevant information. For instance, when Sam is getting ready to leave for work, he asks Randy where he parked the car. Randy answers "down the street." In this case, Randy does not provide enough information because Sam needs to know exactly where to find the car. On the other hand, if Randy responds with, "You just wouldn't believe the trouble I had finding a parking space . . ." followed by a five-minute monologue about trying to find a parking space after midnight, he would be providing too much irrelevant information.

3. Relate what you say to the topic being discussed. Link your messages to the purpose of the conversation and interpret the messages of others in line with the topic at hand. For example, Barry asks, "Who's going to pick up Mom from work today?" His brother answers, "I've got a big test tomorrow." Barry assumes that his brother's remark is relevant to the topic at hand and interprets it as, "I can't. I have to study." Barry was able to correctly understand the pragmatic meaning of his brother's answer because he assumed that it was relevant to figuring out how to get their mother home.

4. Acknowledge when your message violates a guideline. When you violate one of these guidelines, you should tell your partner that you are breaking it. Doing so will help your partner interpret what you are saying accurately. For example:

- If you violate guideline #1, you might say "I don't know if this is true, but my sister said. . . ."

- If you violate guideline #2, you might say "If I told you, I'd have to kill you. . . ."

- If you violate guideline #3, you might say "This may be beside the point, but. . . ."

5. Assume the best first. At times, you or your partner may intentionally break one of these guidelines and not signal beforehand. In these instances, rather than take offense, employ perception checking in an attempt to come to mutual understanding.

4-3c Sociolinguistics

Sociolinguistic meaning varies according to the norms of a particular culture or co-culture. Sociolinguistic misunderstandings occur when we interact with someone who operates using different norms regarding how words are combined, how and when to say what to whom, and verbal style.

↘ The saying "his head was in the clouds" could be confusing to non-native speakers of English, since it is used to say a person is daydreaming and has nothing to do with clouds.

© Brian Jackson/iStockphotos.com

First, cultures have norms that assign meaning to specific words and combinations of words that may be different from their semantic meaning. For example, in English we associate the word *pretty* with women and *handsome* with men, even though both refer to physical beauty. So choosing to say "She is a pretty woman" sends a different message than saying "She is a handsome woman" (Chaika, 2008). All cultures also use **idioms**, which are expressions whose meanings are different from the literal meanings associated with the words used in them. So imagine how confusing it is to someone learning English when we say, "That test was *a piece of cake*." Similarly, when Janelle attempted to impress the new guy in her life by asking her seven-year-old sister to "Bring me the trophy on my dresser," Janelle expected her sister to return with the award she won at a recent swim meet. Instead, her sister returned with an 8" × 10" picture of Janelle's last boyfriend, whom her father jokingly referred to as her "trophy."

Second, cultures develop different norms about what is appropriate to say to whom, by whom, when, and about what. For example, the "appropriate" way to compliment others and accept compliments can vary from culture to culture. In the dominant culture of the United States, you might compliment your Japanese friend by saying, "Miki, this is the *best* miso soup I have ever tasted." To Miki, however, your compliment might sound insincere because in Japanese culture the language of compliments is more humble. So she might reply, "Oh, it's nice of you to say that, but I am sure that you have had better miso soup at sushi restaurants in the city." Similarly, mid-westerners often smile and say "Hi" to strangers on the street as a sign of being friendly. In China, acknowledging a stranger in this way typically assumes an unwarranted familiarity and is likely to be considered rude.

Third, preferred verbal style differs from culture to culture, particularly in terms of how

sociolinguistic meaning
meaning that varies according to the norms of a particular culture or co-culture

idioms
expressions whose meanings are different from the literal meanings associated with the words used in them

direct verbal style
language that openly states the speaker's intention in a straightforward and unambiguous way

indirect verbal style
language that masks the speaker's true intentions in a roundabout and ambiguous way

mindfulness
paying attention to what is happening at any given moment during a conversation

direct or indirect one ought to be (Ting-Toomey & Chung, 2005). A **direct verbal style** is characterized by language that openly states the speaker's intention in a straightforward and unambiguous way. An **indirect verbal style** is characterized by language that masks the speaker's true intentions in a roundabout and ambiguous way. Consider the following example of how these different styles can create communication challenges.

Jorge and Kevin are roommates at college. They come from the same hometown as Sam, who lives across the hall and owns a car. Thanksgiving is fast approaching and both Jorge and Kevin need to find a ride home. One night while watching a football game in Sam's room, the following conversation occurs:

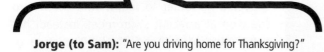

> **Jorge (to Sam):** "Are you driving home for Thanksgiving?" [Maybe he'll give me a ride.]
>
> **Sam:** "Yep." [If he wanted a ride he'd ask.]
>
> **Kevin:** "Well, I'd like a ride home."
>
> **Sam:** "Sure, no problem."
>
> **Jorge:** "Are you taking anyone else?" [I wonder if he still has room for me.]
>
> **Sam:** "Nope. I'm leaving after my last class on Tuesday and not coming back until late Sunday evening." [I guess Jorge already has a ride home.]
>
> **Jorge:** "Well, enjoy Thanksgiving!" [If he wanted to give me a ride I gave him plenty of opportunities to offer. I guess I'll take the bus.]

In this conversation, Jorge used an indirect style he learned from his parents and relatives, who are all from Nicaragua. His questions were meant to prompt Sam to offer him a ride home. But Sam, whose family is from New York, used a direct style and completely missed Jorge's intent. As a result, Jorge rode the bus even though Sam would have gladly given him a ride if

their preferred verbal styles had not gotten in the way of mutual understanding.

Guidelines for Improving Sociolinguistic Understanding

1. Develop intercultural competence. The more you learn about other cultures, the better you will be able to convey and interpret messages when communicating with those whose sociolinguistic verbal styles differ from yours.

2. Practice mindfulness. Mindfulness is the practice of paying attention to what is happening at any given moment during a conversation (Langer & Moldoveanu, 2000). If we are mindful when we interact with others, we will constantly attend to how our cultural norms, idioms, scripts, and verbal styles are similar to and different from our conversational partners'.

3. Respect and adapt to the sociolinguistic practices of others. The old saying, "When in Rome, do as the Romans do" captures the essence of this guideline. For example, if you are invited to your Indonesian-American friend's home for the weekend, you should adapt your verbal style to that of your hosts. Or if you are from a low-context culture and are talking with someone from a high-context culture, be sensitive to the indirect meanings in their verbal messages. If you are fluent in more than one language or dialect, you can even codeswitch and converse in the language or use the dialect of your conversational partner.

© Vadym Drobot/Shutterstock.com

Quick Quiz

T F 1. Waiting for a response to an e-mail is an example of silence.

T F 2. If you are confused when your friend asks you to put something in the boot, it is because you are not from the same language community.

T F 3. We can improve our messages by choosing words that make our meaning clear and language that makes a message memorable and demonstrates sensitivity.

T F 4. Inclusive sensitivity means choosing language and symbols that are adapted to the needs, interests, knowledge, and attitudes of the listeners and avoiding language that alienates them.

T F 5. Saying, "Kalpana, would you text Daphne and see if she is bringing a salad?" is an example of an idiolect.

6. What term or terms clarify meaning by narrowing what is understood from a general category to a particular item or group within that category?

   a. general responses
   b. correct words
   c. specific language
   d. descriptive words
   e. metaphors

7. Your friend says, "My mom told me my room smells like gym socks. I think she wants me to clean it." Your friend's mom is using

   a. concrete language.
   b. specific language.
   c. a dialect.
   d. sociolinguistics.
   e. metaphors.

8. Saying "Ralphie borrowed my phone" instead of, "Ralphie took my phone" is choosing a word based on

   a. sociolinguistics.
   b. denotation.
   c. connotation.
   d. pragmatics.
   e. idiolects.

9. Which of the following is an example of an idiolect?

   a. You say "Ouch!" when you stub your toe.
   b. Your dad says "out of the frying pan into the fire" when your sister gets a new (apparently not great) boyfriend.
   c. Your best friend says "Geesh-a-la-momma!" when excited or surprised.
   d. Your teacher instructs the class to "hit the books" after passing back a low-scoring test.
   e. All of the above.

10. Which of the following is NOT an example of linguistic sensitivity?

   a. If you are an industrial engineer and are talking to the teenager who cuts your grass, you use jargon to help him understand what it is that you do.
   b. If you are communicating with someone whose vocabulary is not as vast as yours, you adjust your words accordingly without talking down to the person.
   c. You're visiting with your grandmother and avoid using slang because she won't understand what you are saying.
   d. You see a police car speed down your street and say, "Wow, I wonder where that police officer is heading in such a hurry!"
   e. During class, you refrain from using offensive language that you normally use when hanging out with friends.

Answers: 1. T, 2. F, 3. T, 4. F, 5. F, 6. C, 7. A, 8. C, 9. E, 10. A

Nonverbal
Messages

Learning Outcomes

5-1 Identify characteristics of nonverbal communication

5-2 Identify the different types of nonverbal communication

5-3 Understand guidelines for improving nonverbal communication

What do you think?

I don't like it when people stand too close when they're talking to me.

1	2	3	4	5	6	7	8	9	10
STRONGLY DISAGREE									STRONGLY AGREE

Communication exchanges are more than verbal messages, such as those covered in chapter 4. Communication is also rich in nonverbal communication, to which this chapter is devoted. **Nonverbal communication** consists of all the messages we send in ways that transcend spoken or written words (Knapp & Hall, 2006). More specifically, **nonverbal messages** are cues we send with our body, voice, space, time, and appearance to support, modify, contradict, or even replace a verbal message.

Nonverbal messages play an important role in communication. In fact, nonverbal messages convey as much as 65 percent of the meaning communicated in face-to-face interactions (Burgoon and Bacue, 2003). In other words, the meaning we assign to any utterance is based on our interpretation of both the verbal message and the nonverbal messages that accompany it. Interpreting nonverbal messages accurately is critical to understanding and responding appropriately to what our partner is "saying."

The widespread use of social media (e.g., e-mail, Facebook, texting) emphasizes the important role of nonverbal messages in communication. Because we cannot communicate nonverbally via social media, chances for misunderstanding skyrocket (Olaniran, 2002–2003). So we often use emoticons, all capital letters, and acronyms such as LOL to communicate the feelings and emotions that nonverbal messages communicate in face-to-face encounters.

We begin this chapter by briefly describing the characteristics of nonverbal communication. Next, we identify the types of nonverbal messages we use to

nonverbal communication
all the messages we send in ways that transcend spoken or written words

nonverbal messages
cues we send with our body, voice, space, time, and appearance to support, modify, contradict, or even replace a verbal message

communicate with others, including use of body (kinesics), use of voice (paralanguage/vocalics), use of space (proxemics), use of time (chronemics), and appearance (including clothing and grooming). Finally, we offer suggestions for improving clarity when sending nonverbal messages and accuracy when interpreting the nonverbal messages we receive from others.

5-1 Characteristics of Nonverbal Communication

We use nonverbal messages to provide unique information by emphasizing, substituting for, or contradicting a verbal message. Nonverbal messages can also regulate our interactions. In other words, we can cue a sender to continue, repeat, elaborate, or hurry up and finish what he or she is saying through shifts in eye contact, slight head movements, posture changes, and raised eyebrows. And nonverbal messages can convey a particular image of ourselves to others through our choice of clothing, grooming, jewelry, and body art. Even when we don't consciously choose to do so, our nonverbal messages give people an impression of who we are. Sometimes we use nonverbal messages to express our status in a situation or a relationship. For example, managers may dress more formally than their employees. The challenge of conveying and interpreting nonverbal messages accurately is rooted in four fundamental characteristics.

1. Nonverbal communication is inevitable. The phrase "We cannot NOT communicate" (Watzlawick, Bavelas, & Jackson, 1967) captures the essence of this characteristic. If you are in the presence of someone else, your nonverbal messages (whether intentional or not) are communicating. When Austin yawns and stares off into the distance during class, his classmates may notice this behavior and assign meaning to it. One classmate may interpret it as a sign of boredom, another might see it as a sign of fatigue, and yet another

may view it as a message of disrespect. Meanwhile, Austin may be oblivious to all of the messages his behavior is sending.

2. Nonverbal communication is the primary conveyer of emotions. We interpret how others feel about what they are communicating based almost entirely on their nonverbal messages. In fact, some research suggests that an overwhelming 93 percent of the emotional meaning of messages is conveyed nonverbally (Mehrabian, 1972). So, when Janelle frowns, clenches her fists, and forcefully says, "I am NOT angry!" her sister Renée ignores the verbal message and believes the contradicting nonverbal messages, which communicate that Janelle is actually very angry.

3. Nonverbal communication is *multi-channeled*. We perceive meaning from a combination of different nonverbal behaviors including, for example, posture, gestures, facial expressions, vocal pitch and rate, and appearance. So, when Anna observes her daughter Mimi's failure to sustain eye contact, her bowed head, and her repetitive toe-stubbing in the dirt, she may decide that Mimi is lying when she says she did not hit her brother. The fact that nonverbal communication is multi-channeled is one reason people are more likely to believe nonverbal communication when nonverbal behaviors contradict the verbal message (Burgoon, Blair, & Strom, 2008).

4. Nonverbal communication is *ambiguous*. Very few nonverbal messages mean the same thing to everyone. The meaning of one nonverbal behavior can vary based on culture, sex, gender, and even context or situation. For example, in the dominant American culture, direct eye contact tends to be understood as a sign of respect. That's why parents often tell their children, "Look at me when I'm talking to you." In other cultures, however, direct eye contact from a listener might be interpreted as disrespectful if the speaker is a superior, whereas averting one's eyes might signal respect. Not only can the meaning of nonverbal messages vary among different cultures, but the meaning of the same nonverbal message also can differ

© Hyunsuss/Shutterstock.com

based on the situation. For example, a furrowed brow might convey Byron's confusion when he did not understand his professor's explanation of the assignment, or Monica's anger when she discovered she did not get the internship she had worked so hard for, or Max's disgust when he was dissecting a frog during biology lab.

5-2 Types of Nonverbal Communication

We use various types of nonverbal messages to communicate. These include the use of body (kinesics), voice (paralanguage/vocalics), space (proxemics), and time (chronemics), as well as physical appearance.

5-2a Use of Body: Kinesics

Of all the research on nonverbal behavior, you are probably most familiar with **kinesics**, the technical name for the interpretation of what and how body motions communicate (Birdwhistell, 1970). These motions include gestures, eye contact, facial expression, posture, and touch.

Gestures

Gestures are the movements of our hands, arms, and fingers to replace or accompany a verbal message. Some people gesture more than others. Unfortunately, "talking with our hands" too much can actually distract listeners from the message we are trying to convey. **Emblems** are gestures that substitute entirely for a word or words. For example, when you raise your finger and place it vertically across your lips, it signifies "Be quiet." Other gestures, called **illustrators**, clarify a verbal message. When you say "about this high" or "nearly this round," your listeners expect to see a gesture accompanying your verbal description. Sometimes, these gestures augment the verbal message by conveying the emotional stance of the sender. Still other gestures, called **adaptors**, are unconscious responses to physical or psychological needs. For example, you may scratch an itch, adjust your glasses, or rub your hands together when they are cold. You do not mean to communicate a message with these gestures, but others may notice and attach meaning to them.

The use and meaning of gestures can vary greatly across cultures. For example, the American hand sign for "OK" has an obscene sexual meaning in some European countries, means "worthless" in France, is a symbol for money in Japan, and stands for "I'll kill you" in Tunisia (Axtell, 1998). When communicating with people who come from different cultures, be especially careful about the gestures you use; their meaning is not necessarily universal.

Eye Contact

The technical term for **eye contact** is oculesics. It has to do with how and how much we look at others when communicating. Eye contact can signal that you are paying attention and that you respect the person you are speaking with, as well as a variety of different emotions. Intense eye contact may be an attempt to dominate (Pearson, West, & Turner, 1995). That's why we sometimes say things like "if looks could kill" when we see someone glare at someone else.

What is considered appropriate eye contact varies across cultures. Studies show that in Western cultures, talkers hold eye contact about 40 percent of the time and listeners nearly 70 percent of the time (Knapp & Hall, 2006). In Western cultures, people also generally maintain more eye contact when discussing topics they are comfortable with, when they are genuinely interested in what another person is saying, and when they are trying to persuade others. Conversely, they tend to avoid eye contact when discussing topics that make them feel uncomfortable, when they aren't interested in the topic or the person talking, or when they are embarrassed, ashamed, or trying to hide something.

A majority of people in the United States and other Western cultures expect those with whom they are communicating to "look them in the eye." But direct eye contact is not universally considered appropriate (Samovar, Porter, & McDaniel, 2009). For instance, in Japan, prolonged eye contact is considered rude, disrespectful, and threatening. Similarly, in China and Indonesia, too much direct eye contact is a sign of bad manners. In many Middle Eastern countries, people tend to use continuous and direct eye contact with others to demonstrate keen interest.

Various co-cultural groups within the United States use eye contact differently as well. For instance, African Americans tend to use more continuous eye contact than European Americans when they are speaking, but less when they are listening (Samovar, Porter, & McDaniel,

kinesics
the interpretation of what and how body motions communicate

gestures
movements of our hands, arms, and fingers to replace or accompany a verbal message

emblems
gestures that substitute entirely for a word or words

illustrators
gestures that clarify a verbal message

adaptors
unconscious responses to physical or psychological needs

eye contact (oculesics)
how and how much we look at others when communicating

2009). Native Americans tend to avoid eye contact when communicating with superiors as a sign of respect for their authority. And women tend to use more eye contact during conversations than men do (Wood, 2007).

Facial Expression

Facial expression is arranging facial muscles to communicate. Facial expressions are especially important in conveying the six basic emotions of happiness, sadness, surprise, fear, anger, and disgust. For example, we may furrow our brows and squint our eyes when we are confused, or purse our lips and raise one eyebrow to convey skepticism. Facial expressions are so important for communicating emotional intent that we often use emoticons to represent emotions when texting, sending e-mail, or posting comments on Facebook (Walther & Parks, 2002).

Studies show that there are many similarities across cultures with regard to the meaning of certain facial expressions (Samovar, Porter, & McDaniel, 2009). For instance, a slight raising of the eyebrow communicates

recognition and wrinkling one's nose conveys repulsion (Martin & Nakayama, 2012). However, whether or not doing so is appropriate varies across cultures and co-cultures. For instance, in some Eastern cultures people downplay facial expressions like frowning and smiling; members of other cultures, by contrast, amplify their displays of emotion through facial expressions. For example, in the United States, women who identify with the feminine co-culture tend to smile more frequently when communicating than do men who identify with the masculine co-culture.

Posture

Posture is how we position and move our body. Posture can communicate attentiveness, respect, and dominance. **Body orientation** refers to how we position our body in relation to other people. *Direct body orientation* is when two people face each other squarely; *indirect body orientation* is when two people sit or stand side-by-side. In many situations, direct body orientation signals attentiveness and respect while indirect body orientation shows inattentiveness and disrespect. In a job interview, for example, you are likely to sit up straight and face the interviewer directly because you want to communicate your interest, attentiveness, and respect. Yet in other situations, such as talking with friends, a slouched posture and indirect body orientation may be appropriate and may not carry messages about attention or respect. **Body movement** is changing body position. It can be motivated (movement that helps clarify meaning) or unmotivated (movement that distracts listeners from the point being made). When you make a speech, an upright stance and squared shoulders communicates poise and confidence. Taking a few steps to the left or right can signal a transition from one main point to the next, but pacing actually distracts listeners from the message.

Touch

Haptics is the technical term for the interpretation of what and how touch communicates. We use our hands, arms, and other body parts to pat, hug, slap, kiss, pinch, stroke, hold, embrace, and tickle others.

© Konstantin Chagin/Shutterstock.com /
© Viktor Gladkov/Shutterstock.com

Direct Body Orientation

Indirect Body Orientation

There are three types of touch: spontaneous touch, ritualized touch, and task-related touch. *Spontaneous touch* is automatic and subconscious. Patting someone on the back when you hear that he or she has won an award is an example of spontaneous touch. *Ritualized touch* is scripted rather than spontaneous. Handshakes and high-fives are examples of ritualized touch. *Task-related touch* is used to perform a certain unemotional function. For instance, a doctor may touch a patient during a physical examination or a personal trainer may touch a client during a gym workout. There is also a type of touch that combines spontaneity and task-related touch to convey messages of closeness. For example, when someone adjusts your coat collar or removes some lint from your clothing in a public place, the person may not only be doing a task-related favor for you but also may be signaling a degree of closeness between the two of you.

People differ in their touching behavior and in their reactions to unsolicited touch from others. Some people like to touch and be touched; other people do not. Although American culture is relatively non–contact oriented, the kinds and amounts of touching behavior within our society vary widely. Touching behavior that seems innocuous to one person may be perceived as overly intimate or threatening to another. Moreover, the perceived appropriateness of touch differs with the context. Touch that is considered appropriate in private may embarrass a person when done in public.

Differences in touching behavior are highly correlated with culture (Gudykunst & Kim, 1997). In some cultures, frequent touching is considered normal; in other cultures, it is considered inappropriate. Some countries in South and Central America, as well as many in southern Europe, encourage contact and engage in frequent touching (Neuliep, 2006). In many Arabic countries, for example,

two grown men walking down the street holding hands is a sign of friendship. In the United States, however, it might be interpreted as a sign of an intimate relationship. Because the United States is a country of immigrants, however, the degree of touching behavior considered appropriate varies widely from individual to individual based on family heritage and norms.

5-2b Use of Voice: Paralanguage

Paralanguage (also known as *vocalics*) is the voiced part of a spoken message that goes beyond the actual words. Six vocal characteristics of paralanguage are pitch, volume, rate, voice quality, intonation, and vocalized pauses.

Pitch
Pitch is the highness or lowness of vocal tone. People raise and lower vocal pitch to emphasize ideas and emotion, as well as to signal a question. We sometimes raise our pitch when feeling nervous or afraid. We may lower our pitch to convey peacefulness or sadness (as in a speech given at a funeral) or when we are trying to be forceful.

Volume
Volume is the loudness or softness of vocal tone. Whereas some people have booming voices that carry long distances, others are normally soft-spoken. Regardless of our normal volume level, however, we also tend to vary our volume depending on the situation, the topic of discussion, and

paralanguage (vocalics)
the voiced part of a spoken message that goes beyond the actual words

pitch
the highness or lowness of vocal tone

volume
the loudness or softness of vocal tone

emotional intent. For example, we might talk more loudly when we wish to be heard in noisy settings and when we are angry. We might speak more softly when we are being reflective or romantic. There are also some cultural variations in the meanings attached to volume. For example, Arabs tend to speak with a great deal of volume to convey strength and sincerity; whereas soft voices are preferred in Britain, Japan, and Thailand (Samovar, Porter, & McDaniel, 2009).

Rate

Rate is the speed at which a person speaks. Most people in the USA naturally speak between 100 and 200 words per minute. People tend to talk more rapidly when they are happy, frightened, nervous, or excited and more slowly when they are problem-solving out loud or are trying to emphasize a point. People who speak too slowly run the risk of boring listeners, and those who speak too quickly may not be intelligible.

SPEAK EXPRESSIVELY!

Voice Quality (Timbre)

Voice quality (or **timbre**) is the sound of a person's voice that distinguishes it from others. Voice quality may be breathy (Marilyn Monroe or Kathleen Turner), strident (Joan Rivers or Marge Simpson), throaty (Nick Nolte or Jack Nicholson), or nasal (Fran Drescher in *The Nanny*). Although each person's voice has a distinct quality, too much breathiness can make people sound frail, too much stridence can make them seem overly tense, too much throatiness can make them seem cold and unsympathetic, and too much nasality can make them sound immature or unintelligent.

Intonation

Intonation is the variety, melody, or inflection in one's voice. Voices that use very little or no intonation are described as monotone and tend to bore listeners. If you've ever seen the movie *Ferris Bueller's Day Off,* you may recall the teacher (played by Ben Stein) who is portrayed as boring via a monotone voice as he questions the class: "Anyone? Anyone? Bueller? Bueller?" Other voices that use a lot of intonation may be perceived as ditzy, singsongy, or childish. People prefer to listen to voices that use a moderate amount of intonation.

In the United States, there are stereotypes about masculine and feminine voices. Masculine voices are expected to be low-pitched and loud, with moderate to low intonation; feminine voices are expected to be higher-pitched, softer in volume, and more expressive. Although both sexes have the option to portray a range of masculine and feminine paralanguage, most people usually conform to the expectations for their sex (Wood, 2007).

Vocalized Pauses

Vocalized pauses are extraneous sounds or words that interrupt fluent speech. They are essentially "place markers" designed to fill in momentary gaps while we search for the right word or idea. The most common vocalized pauses that creep into our speech include "uh," "er," "well," "OK," "you know," and "like."

Occasional vocalized pauses are generally ignored by listeners. However, when used excessively, vocalized pauses can give others the impression that we are unsure of ourselves or that our ideas are not well thought out. Sometimes speakers use so many vocalized pauses that listeners are distracted by them to the point of not being able to concentrate on the meaning of the message.

We can interpret the paralinguistic part of a message as complementing, supplementing, or contradicting the meaning conveyed by a verbal message. So when Joan says, "Well, isn't that an interesting story," how we interpret her meaning will depend on her paralanguage. If she alters her normal voice so that "Well" is varied both in pitch and tone and the rest of her words are spoken in a staccato monotone, we might perceive her message as sarcasm because we interpret the paralanguage to contradict the words. But if her pitch rises with each word, we might perceive the paralanguage as supplementing the message and understand that she is asking a question.

5-2c **Use of Space: Proxemics**

Proxemics is the formal term for the study of how space and distance communicate (Hall, 1968). Some of the ways we communicate via proxemics include our use of personal space, territorial space, acoustic space, and artifacts.

rate
the speed at which a person speaks

voice quality (timbre)
the sound of a person's voice that distinguishes it from others

intonation
the variety, melody, or inflection in one's voice

vocalized pauses
extraneous sounds or words that interrupt fluent speech

proxemics
the study of how space and distance communicate

© Kasiutek/Shutterstock.com

Personal Space

Personal space is the distance we try to maintain when interacting with others. How much space we perceive as appropriate depends on our individual preference, the nature of our relationship to the other person or people, and our cultural norms. With these variations in mind, the amount of personal space we view as appropriate generally decreases as the intimacy of our relationship increases. For example, in the dominant U.S. culture, four distinct distances are generally perceived as appropriate and comfortable, depending on the nature of the conversation and relationship. *Intimate distance* is defined as up to 18 inches and is appropriate for private conversations between close friends. *Personal distance*, from 18 inches to 4 feet, is the space in which casual conversation occurs. *Social distance*, from 4 to 12 feet, is where impersonal business such as a job interview is conducted. *Public distance* is anything more than 12 feet (Hall, 1968). Figure 5.1 illustrates the concept of personal space.

Of greatest concern to us is intimate distance—that which we regard as appropriate for intimate conversation with close friends and family. Americans usually become uncomfortable when "outsiders" violate this intimate distance. For instance, in a movie theater that is less than one-quarter full, people will tend to leave one or more seats empty between themselves and others they do not know. If a stranger sits right next to us in such a setting, we are likely to feel uncomfortable and may even move to another seat. Intrusions into our intimate space are acceptable only in certain settings and then only when all involved follow the unwritten rules. So, we tolerate being packed into a crowded elevator or subway and even touching others we do not know by following unwritten rules, such as standing rigidly, looking at the floor or above the door, and not making eye contact or talking with others.

Territorial Space

Territorial space is the physical space over which we claim ownership. As with personal space, we expect others to respect our territory and may feel annoyed or even violated when they do not. Sometimes we do not realize how we are claiming or "marking" our territory. For example, Graham may have subconsciously marked "his chair" in the family room and others just "know" not to sit in it when Graham is around. Other times we mark our territory quite consciously. People consciously mark territory, for example, by using locks, signs, and fences.

personal space
the distance we try to maintain when we interact with other people

territorial space
the physical space over which we claim ownership

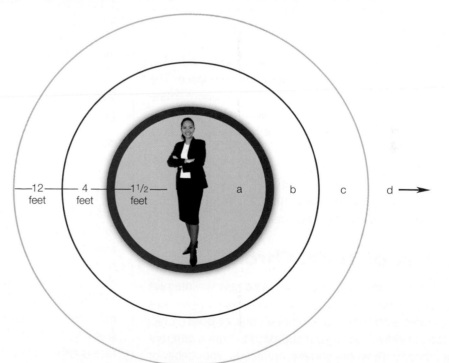

FIGURE 5.1
Personal Space

12 feet — 4 feet — 1½ feet — a — b — c — d →

Zone a, **intimate distance:** spouses, significant others, family members, and others with whom we have an intimate relationship
Zone b, **personal distance:** friends
Zone c, **social distance:** business associates and acquaintances
Zone d, **public distance:** strangers

acoustic space
the area over which your voice can be comfortably heard

artifacts
the objects we use to adorn our territory

physical appearance
how we look to others

media richness
how much and what kinds of information can be transmitted via a particular channel

Not only can we understand someone's ownership of space by the territorial markers they use, but also their status. For instance, higher-status people generally claim larger and more prestigious territory (Knapp & Hall, 2006). In business, for example, the supervisor is likely to have the largest and nicest office in the unit.

Acoustic Space

Acoustic space is the area over which your voice can be comfortably heard. Competent communicators protect acoustic space by adjusting the volume of their voices to be easily heard by their conversational partners and not overheard by others. Loud cell phone conversations occurring in public places violate acoustic space.

Artifacts

Artifacts are the objects we use to adorn our territory. We display things on our desks and in our offices and homes, not just for their function but also because we find them pleasing in some way. Other people observe these artifacts to make interpretations about us.

We use artifacts to achieve certain effects, including signaling what we expect to happen in the space. The chairs and couch in your living room may approximate a circle that invites people to sit down and talk. A manager's office with a chair facing the manager across the desk encourages formal conversation and signals status. It says, "Let's talk business—I'm the boss and you're the employee." Another manager's office with a chair placed at the side of her desk encourages more informal conversation. It says, "Don't be nervous—let's just chat."

5-2d Use of Time: Chronemics

Recall from chapter 3 that chronemics is how we interpret the use of time; it is largely based on cultural norms. Just as cultures tend to be more monochronic or polychronic, so too are individuals. If your approach to time is different from those with whom you are interacting, your behavior could be viewed as inappropriate and put strains on your relationship.

5-2e Physical Appearance

Physical appearance is how we look to others and is one of the first things others notice and judge. American society places so much emphasis on physical appearance that entire industries are devoted to changing it. Options for changing our physical appearance range from surgical procedures to weight loss programs and products to cosmetics and clothing lines.

Today, more than ever, people use clothing choices, body art, and other personal grooming to communicate who they are and what they stand for. Likewise, when we meet new people, we are likely to form our first impression of them based on how they are dressed and groomed. Because clothing and grooming can be altered to suit the occasion, we can influence how others are likely to perceive us by our clothing and grooming choices. For example, Marcus, a successful sales representative, typically wears dress slacks and a collared shirt to the office, a suit and tie when giving a formal presentation, and a graphic T-shirt and jeans when hanging out with friends. Body art (such as piercings and tattoos) has become quite popular in the United States today. Although body art can be an important means of self-expression, we often make choices about how much of it to display based on the situation and how others are likely to judge us based on it. For example, when Tiffany is at work she dresses conservatively and covers the tattoo on her arm by wearing long-sleeved blouses. But on evenings and weekends, she does not.

5-2f Mediated Communication and Media Richness

Media richness refers to how much and what kinds of information can be transmitted via a particular channel. Media richness theory suggests that some media are better suited than others for communicating the meaning of different types of messages (Daft & Lengel, 1984). Face-to-face is generally the richest channel and the standard against which other channels are measured. When we communicate face-to-face, we not only hear the verbal message content, but we also observe the nonverbal cues and physical context to interpret a speaker's meaning. We can touch each other, hear pitch, and interact spatially. Sometimes, however, communicating face-to-face is either impossible or not a good use of time. Other times, we may want time to carefully compose and revise our message, as well as time to carefully ponder the feedback we receive, even at the expense of physical interaction.

Although mediated channels allow us to communicate across distances, they often cannot do so as richly as in face-to-face interaction. The less information

The New Age of Old Body Art

Did you know that every culture has used body art to signal status, to mark a special occasion, or just to make a fashion statement (American Museum of Natural History, 1999)? There are many different types of body art, all stemming from ancient practices and adapted to modern definitions of status, ritual, and beauty.

- Body painting is a temporary means of creating a different identity or celebrating a particular occasion. For centuries, Eastern cultures have used henna to dye hands and other body parts to celebrate rites of passage such as marriages. Today, women use cosmetics, sports fans decorate their faces and bodies before big games, and children have their faces painted at community festivals.

- Piercing has a long history. Some tribal cultures had a rite of passage calling for a person to hang from large piercings in the limbs or body trunk, other societies used piercings as a sign of slavery, and still others viewed them as signs of beauty or royalty (Schurman, n.d.). Today piercing is voluntary and ranges from nose, ear, and genital piercing to stretching and gauging.

- Scarification is the deliberate and controlled cutting or burning of the skin to create a pattern or picture. Scarification has been widely practiced in Africa, where facial scars identify a person's ethnic group or family or can just be an individual statement of beauty. Today, scarification may be part of a fraternity or gang initiation rite; cutting is also sometimes used to escape from feeling trapped in an intolerable psychological and emotional situation (Jacobs, 2005). Such application is generally considered unacceptable by United States society.

- Tattooing is the oldest form of body art; tattooed mummies have been found in various parts of the world. Tattoos are permanent alterations to the body using inks or dyes, and they are symbolic in nature. Historically, tattoos have been used to mark people who were considered property or inferior in some other way, such as African-American slaves or Jews and

© Bonnie Schupp/Vetta Collection/iStockphoto.com

other "undesirables" in World War II concentration camps. Today, tattoos are losing their outsider status. Celebrities, soccer moms, corporate executives, star athletes, and high school students sport tattoos as statements of individuality and personal aesthetic.

- Shaping, another type of body art, is altering the silhouette or shape of the body based on a culturally validated aesthetic (Australian Museum, 2009). Cranial shaping, neck stretching, foot binding, and corsetry have been practiced in various cultures at various times. The Spanx undergarments that many women wear today have their origins in body shaping.

offered via a given channel, the leaner it is. The leaner the channel, the greater the chances become for misunderstanding. For example, text messages are very lean since they do not include nonverbal cues and context information and because they use as few characters as possible to convey a single message. On the other hand, videoconferencing channels such as Skype are richer than text messaging because we can observe nonverbal cues and contextual information almost as much as in a face-to-face setting. However, sending a composed email may offer more benefits than calling a person. The situation dictates the proper channel for mediated communication. Chapter 6 offers guidelines on how to choose the best channel.

5-3 Guidelines for Improving Nonverbal Communication

Because nonverbal messages are inevitable, multi-channeled, ambiguous, and sometimes unintentional, interpreting them accurately can be tricky. Add to this the fact that the meaning of any nonverbal behavior can vary by situation, culture, and gender, and the reasons we so often misinterpret the behavior of others become clear. The following guidelines can help improve the likelihood that your nonverbal messages will be perceived accurately and that you will accurately interpret others' nonverbal messages.

5-3a Sending Nonverbal Messages

1. Consciously monitor your nonverbal messages. Try to be more consciously aware of the nonverbal messages you send through your use of body, voice, space, time, and appearance. If you have difficulty doing this, ask a friend to point them out to you.

2. Align your nonverbal messages with your purpose. When nonverbal messages contradict verbal messages, people are more likely to believe the nonverbal messages, so it is important to align your nonverbal messages with your purpose. For instance, if you want to be persuasive, you should use direct eye contact, a serious facial expression, an upright posture, a commanding vocal tone with no vocalized pauses, and professional clothing and grooming. If you want to be supportive and convey empathy, you might use less direct eye contact, a more relaxed facial expression, a softer voice, a nonthreatening touch, and a lean inward towards your partner.

3. Adapt your nonverbal messages to the situation. Just as you make language choices to suit different situations, you should vary your nonverbal messages depending on the circumstances. Assess what the situation calls for. For example, you would not dress the same way for a wedding as you would for a workout.

4. Reduce or eliminate distracting nonverbal messages. Fidgeting, tapping your fingers on a table, pacing, mumbling, using lots of pauses, and checking your phone often for texts and e-mails can distract others from the message you are trying to convey. Make a conscious effort to learn which distracting nonverbal messages have become habits and work to eliminate them from your communication with others.

5-3b Interpreting Nonverbal Messages

1. Remember that the same nonverbal message may mean different things to different people. Most nonverbal messages have multiple meanings that vary from person to person and culture to culture. Just because you fidget when you are bored doesn't mean that others are bored when they fidget. What you perceive as an angry vocal tone might not be intended as such by the person talking. So always try to consider multiple interpretations of the nonverbal messages you receive, particularly when your first interpretation is negative. As you interact more with someone, you will learn to "read" his or her nonverbal messages accurately.

2. Consider each nonverbal message in context. Because any one nonverbal message can mean different things in different contexts, take the time to consider how it is intended in a given situation. Also realize that you might not understand all the details of the situation. For example, if you see a classmate sleeping during your speech, you might interpret the nonverbal message as boredom or disrespect. What the message might be communicating, however, is utter exhaustion because your classmate just finished back-to-back 12-hour shifts at work while trying to keep up with homework for a full load of courses.

3. Pay attention to the multiple nonverbal messages being sent and their relationship to the verbal message. In any one interaction, you are likely to receive simultaneous messages from a person's appearance, eye contact, facial expressions, gestures, posture, voice, and use of space and touch. By considering *all* nonverbal messages together with the verbal message, you are more likely to interpret others' messages accurately.

4. Use perception checking. The skill of perception checking lets you see if your interpretation of another person's message is accurate. By describing the nonverbal message you notice, sharing your interpretation of it, and asking for clarification, you can get confirmation or correction of your interpretation.

Quick Quiz

T F 1. Studies show that talkers hold eye contact about 70 percent of the time and listeners only 40 percent of the time.

T F 2. While talking quietly to a friend at a restaurant, you realize you have attracted the attention of other diners. You need to adjust your rate to decrease your territorial space.

T F 3. Nonverbal messages convey as much as 65 percent of the meaning in face-to-face interactions.

T F 4. Some societies used body painting as a sign of slavery.

T F 5. Fidgeting, tapping your fingers on a table, pacing, mumbling, and using vocal interferences and adaptors can hinder another person's interpretation of your message.

6. Which of the following is NOT a characteristic of nonverbal communication?
   a. It is continuous.
   b. It is multi-channeled.
   c. It is intentional.
   d. It is unintentional.
   e. It is unambiguous.

7. Gestures that augment a verbal message are called
   a. emphasizers.
   b. illustrators.
   c. emblems.
   d. symbols.
   e. adaptors.

8. Which of the following is an interrupter of fluent speech?
   a. the variety or melody, or inflections in one's voice
   b. pauses like "uh," "er," and "um"
   c. the loudness or softness of a person's tone
   d. too much stridence in a person's voice
   e. the speed at which a person speaks

9. Your boss asks you to lead a meeting regarding a new client and tells you he has booked the conference room and arranged for the projector to be on hand. Your boss is
   a. giving you permission to increase your acoustic space.
   b. using artifacts to indicate he would like a visual presentation.
   c. demonstrating his ownership of the space.
   d. using task-related touch to show the conference room.
   e. using posture to indicate he isn't very interested in what happens.

10. In interpreting nonverbal messages, you should
   a. consider the situation before making assumptions.
   b. not assume that another person will interpret a particular behavior the same way you do.
   c. pay attention to the relationship of the verbal message and the multiple nonverbal cues being sent.
   d. check in with someone else to see if your interpretation of what you think you are seeing is accurate or inaccurate.
   e. All of the above.

Answers: 1. F, 2. F, 3. T, 4. F, 5. T, 6. E, 7. B, 8. B, 9. B, 10. D

Listening

What do you think?
I find it easy to identify
with the feelings of the
person I am talking to.

1 2 3 4 5 6 7 8 9 10
STRONGLY DISAGREE   STRONGLY AGREE

Learning Outcomes

6-1 Define listening

6-2 Identify the three challenges
of listening

6-3 List the steps involved in
active listening

Are you a good listener? Or do you occasionally find yourself jumping to conclusions before hearing others out, particularly when you're under pressure? We shouldn't underestimate the importance of listening; it can provide clarification, help us understand and remember material, improve our personal and professional relationships, and increase our ability to evaluate information effectively (Donoghue & Siegel, 2005).

We begin this chapter with a discussion of what listening is and some of the challenges we must overcome to listen effectively. Then we describe the steps involved in the active listening process and propose some specific guidelines you can follow to improve your listening skills during each step. Finally, we suggest strategies for responding appropriately in different listening situations.

6-1 What Is Listening?

People sometimes make the mistake of thinking listening and hearing are the same, but they're not. Hearing is a physiological process, whereas listening is a cognitive one. In other words, listening occurs only when we choose to focus on and attach meaning to what we hear. According to the International Listening Association, **listening** is the process of receiving, constructing meaning from, and responding to spoken and/or nonverbal messages (International Listening Association, 1996).

Of the basic communication skills (reading, writing, speaking, and listening), we use listening the most. In fact, although we spend more than 50 percent of our communication time listening, many

listening
the process of receiving, constructing meaning from, and responding to spoken and/or nonverbal messages

listening style
our favored and usually unconscious approach to listening

content-oriented listeners
listeners who focus on and evaluate the facts and evidence

people-oriented listeners
listeners who focus on the feelings their conversational partners may have about what they're saying

action-oriented listeners
listeners who focus on the ultimate point the speaker is trying to make

time-oriented listeners
listeners who prefer brief and hurried conversations and use nonverbal and verbal cues to signal that their partner needs to be more concise

of us can remember only about 25 percent of what we hear 48 hours later (Janusik & Wolvin, 2006). A survey of Fortune 500 firms conducted jointly by the American Society for Training and Development and the U.S. Department of Labor showed listening to be one of the five most important basic workplace skills expected of employees. What is somewhat troubling, however, is the fact that fewer than 2 percent of us have had any formal listening training (Listening Factoid, 2003). So the skills you learn and apply from this chapter will set you apart in ways that will benefit you both personally and professionally.

We choose to listen for various reasons depending on the situation. For example, sometimes we listen to learn about something new. Other times we might listen to provide support as others work through their feelings about an emotionally charged experience. Still other times we listen to make discerning inferences beyond the surface message by "listening between the lines," so to speak. And we sometimes listen not only to understand but also to evaluate and assign worth to a message. To become effective listeners, we must first consciously overcome three key challenges.

6-2 Challenges to Effective Listening

The three challenges to effective listening are rooted in listening style, apprehension, and processing approach.

6-2a Listening Style

Listening style is our favored and usually unconscious approach to listening (Watson, Barker, & Weaver, 1995). Each of us favors one of four listening styles. Few people can switch effectively between styles based on the situation (Weaver & Kirtley, 1995).

Content-oriented listeners focus on and evaluate the facts and evidence. Content-oriented listeners appreciate details and enjoy processing complex messages that may include a good deal of technical information. Content-oriented listeners are likely to ask questions to get even more information.

People-oriented listeners focus on the feelings their conversational partners may have about what they are saying. For example, people-oriented listeners tend to notice whether their partners are pleased or upset and will encourage them to continue speaking based on nonverbal cues like head nods, eye contact, and smiles.

Action-oriented listeners focus on the ultimate point the speaker is trying to make. Action-oriented listeners tend to get frustrated when ideas are disorganized and when people ramble. Action-oriented listeners also often anticipate what the speaker is going to say and may even finish the speaker's sentences.

Finally, **time-oriented listeners** prefer brief and hurried conversations and often use nonverbal and verbal cues to signal that their partner needs to be more concise. Time-oriented listeners may tell others exactly how much time they have to listen, interrupt when feeling time pressures, regularly check the time during a conversation, and may even nod their heads rapidly to encourage others to pick up the pace.

Each of these styles has advantages and disadvantages. Content-oriented listeners are likely to understand and remember details but may miss the overall point of the message and be unaware of the speaker's feelings. People-oriented listeners are likely to understand how the speaker feels, empathize, and offer comfort and support. However, they might become so focused on

© Ameng Wu/iStockphoto.com

Visiting a doctor can create apprehension and negatively affect listening.

© Monkey Business Images/Shutterstock.com

the speaker's feelings that they miss important details or fail to evaluate the facts offered as evidence. Action-oriented listeners may notice inconsistencies but, because they tend to anticipate what will be said rather than hearing the speaker out, may miss important details. Finally, time-oriented listeners are prone to only partially listen to messages while also thinking about their time constraints; thus, they might miss important details and be insensitive to their partner's emotional needs.

Preferred listening style may also be influenced by cultural and co-cultural identity. For example, women who identify with the feminine co-culture are more likely to describe themselves as person-oriented. Similarly, men who identify with the masculine co-culture are more likely to be time-oriented (Salisbury & Chen, 2007). People from collectivist cultures, where maintaining group harmony is highly valued, are more likely to have a people-oriented listening style; conversely, people from individualistic cultures often have an action-oriented listening style (Kiewitz, Weaver, Brosius, & Weimann, 1997). People from high-context cultures tend to favor a person-oriented listening style; people from low-context cultures tend to prefer an action-oriented style (Harris, 2003).

6-2b Listening Apprehension

Listening apprehension is the anxiety we feel about listening. Listening apprehension may increase when we are worried about misinterpreting the message or when we are concerned about how the message may affect us psychologically (Brownell, 2006). For example, if you are

in an important meeting or job training session, you may worry about trying to absorb all the important technical information needed to do your job well. Or you might feel anxiety when the material you need to absorb is difficult or confusing. Likewise, your anxiety may increase when you feel ill, tired, or stressed about something else going on in your life at the time. Listening apprehension makes it difficult to focus on the message.

6-2c Processing Approach

We use one of two approaches to process information. The approach we use depends, in part, on how we listen. **Passive listening** is the habitual and unconscious process of receiving messages. When we listen passively, we are on automatic pilot. We may attend only to certain parts of a message and assume the rest. We tend to listen passively when we aren't really interested or when we are multitasking. By contrast, **active listening** is the deliberate and conscious process of attending to, understanding, remembering, evaluating, and responding to messages. Active listening requires practice. The rest of this chapter focuses on helping you become a better active listener.

6-3 Active Listening

Active listening is a complex process made up of five steps: attending, understanding, remembering, evaluating, and responding to the messages we receive.

6-3a Attending

Active listening begins with attending. **Attending** is the process of willfully perceiving selected sounds (O'Shaughnessey, 2003).

listening apprehension
the anxiety felt about listening

passive listening
the habitual and unconscious process of receiving messages

active listening
the deliberate and conscious process of attending to, understanding, remembering, evaluating, and responding to messages

attending
the process of willfully perceiving selected sounds

Presidential Debates, Freedom of Speech, and Democratic Discourse

Political debates are, ideally, moments of civil discourse intended to enhance a listener's understanding of a topic or viewpoint. However, debates in the most recent presidential election mattered more for what they revealed about the continuing decline of civil discourse in political culture.

There are several examples of crowd noise moving the dialogue away from policy, such as the cheers that erupted when reporter Brian Williams asked Texas Governor Rick Perry about "the 234 executions of death row inmates over which Perry has presided" (Greenwald, 2011). Though the cheers were clearly an instance of partisan support for Perry's position on the death penalty, many criticized this response as inappropriate, saying it shut down any meaningful public conversation about this difficult issue.

The candidates themselves also used emotionally charged language during the debates and cut one another off mid-sentence. In their second debate, former Massachusetts Governor Mitt Romney and President Barack Obama both found themselves reprimanding the other, Obama saying at one point, "I'm used to being interrupted" as Romney attempted to take the floor. At another point in the debate, Romney held off the president by saying, "You'll get your chance in a moment. I'm still speaking." These demonstrations of control became the object of media attention, rather than the policies the candidates were discussing. How do these interruptions and power struggles impact how we hear the candidates?

© Win McNamee/Staff/Getty Images News/Getty Images

One research study showed that, in debates that are less than civil, viewers are less likely to remember the actual arguments underlying the positions than in more civil debates (Mutz, Reeves, & Wise, 2003). The National Institute for Civil Discourse, a bipartisan organization chaired by former presidents George H. W. Bush and Bill Clinton, suggests that the decline of civil discourse in politics and the media's focus on the loudest and most extreme voices over rational and substantive debate "impairs the development of sound policy, making government less effective" and ignores "the multiplicity of opinions and approaches" needed to address the complex political problems facing our nation. Indeed, Mitt Romney's "binders full of women," a phrase from the second debate to which the Internet and media gave full coverage (both mocking and serious), will be remembered much longer than his concern over cutting Medicare or drive to cut taxes.

Poor listeners have difficulty exercising control over what they attend to, often letting their minds drift to thoughts unrelated to the topic. One reason for this is that people typically speak at a rate of about 120–150 words per minute, but our brains can process between 400 and 800 words per minute (Wolvin & Coakley, 1996). This means we usually assume we know what a speaker is going to say before he or she finishes saying it. So our minds tend to wander from the message.

The first step to becoming a good active listener, then, is to train ourselves to focus on or attend to what people are saying regardless of potential distractions. Let's consider five techniques that can help improve attending skills.

1. Get physically ready to listen. Good listeners create a physical environment conducive to listening and adopt a listening posture. It is easier to pay attention when we eliminate possible sources of distraction. For example, you can turn music down or off. You can silence your cell phone and even put it away so you won't be tempted to check messages when you are supposed to be listening. Good listeners also adopt a listening posture by sitting upright or moving closer to the speaker and by making direct eye contact. You have probably noticed that when a professor tells the class that the next bit of information will be on the test, students often sit upright in their chairs, lean forward slightly, and look directly at the professor.

2. Resist mental distractions. Work consciously to block out wandering thoughts that might come from a visual distraction (e.g., a classmate who enters the room while the professor is lecturing), an auditory distraction (e.g., coworkers chatting beside you while your supervisor is giving instructions), or a physical distraction (e.g., wondering what you'll eat for lunch because your stomach is growling).

3. Make the shift fully from speaker to listener. In conversation, we may find it difficult to completely make the shift from speaker to listener. When we fail to do so, we might rehearse what we plan to say next or even interrupt the speaker rather than attending to her. This is especially true when engaged in a heated conversation. During such exchanges, consciously stop yourself from preparing a response or interrupting the speaker. Shifting completely from the role of speaker to listener requires constant conscious effort.

4. Observe nonverbal cues. We interpret messages more accurately when we observe the nonverbal behaviors that accompany the words. For instance, when your friend says, "Don't worry about me. I'm fine, really," actively attend to nonverbal cues such as tone of voice, body actions, and facial expression to tell whether she is really fine or whether she is upset but reluctant to tell you about it.

5. Hear a person out. Far too often, we stop listening before the person has finished speaking because, relying on our scripts library, we think we "know" what he is going to say. But what we think he is going to say is only a guess. Active listeners cultivate the habit of hearing the speaker out.

6-3b Understanding

Understanding results from accurately decoding a message. We offer four sets of guidelines to help you make sense of the messages you receive.

1. Identify the main point. As you listen ask yourself, "What does the speaker want me to understand?" and "What is the point being made?" In addition to the surface message, you might also need to consider the pragmatic meaning couched within it. For example, when Makayla, who is running for city council, asks Joanna what she thinks about the plans for the new arts center and begins to talk about some of its pros and cons, Joanna understands that, beneath the surface, Makayla is also attempting to persuade Joanna to vote for her.

2. Ask questions. A **question** is a statement designed to clarify information or get additional details.

Effective questioning begins by identifying the kind of information you need to increase your understanding. Suppose Chris says to you, "I am totally frustrated. Would you stop at the store on the way home and buy me some more paper?" You may be a bit confused by his request and need more information to understand. Yet if you simply respond, "What do you mean?" Chris—who is already frustrated—may become defensive. Instead, you might think about what type of information you need and form a question to meet that need. To increase your understanding, you can ask one of these three types of questions:

- *To get details*: "What kind of paper would you like me to get, and how much will you need?"

- *To clarify word meanings*: "Could you tell me what you mean by *frustrated*?"

- *To clarify feelings*: "What's frustrating you?"

3. Paraphrase. **Paraphrasing** is the process of putting your interpretation of a message into words. For example, during an argument with her sister, Midori paraphrased what she thought she heard her sister saying: "You say that you are tired of me talking about work and that you feel that I'm trying to act like I'm better than you when I talk about my successes." Paraphrases may focus on content, on feelings underlying the content, or on both. A **content paraphrase** focuses on the

By paraphrasing, you give the speaker a chance to verify your understanding.

understanding
the process of accurately decoding a message

question
a statement designed to clarify information or get additional details

paraphrasing
the process of putting your interpretation of a message into words

content paraphrase
a paraphrase that focuses on the denotative meaning of the message

© Mehmet Salih Guler/iStockphoto.com

feelings paraphrase
a paraphrase that captures the emotions attached to the message

empathy
the ability to identify with or vicariously experience another's feelings or attitudes

empathic responsiveness
occurs when you experience an emotional response parallel to another person's actual or anticipated display of emotion

perspective taking
occurs when you use everything you know about a sender and his or her circumstances to understand their feelings

sympathetic responsiveness
occurs when you feel concern, compassion, or sorrow for another's situation

remembering
the process of moving information from short-term to long-term memory

denotative meaning of the message. The first part of Midori's response ("You say that you are tired of me talking about work") is a content paraphrase. A **feelings paraphrase** is a response that captures the emotions attached to the message. The second part of Midori's statement ("you feel that I'm trying to act like I'm better than you") is a feelings paraphrase.

By paraphrasing, you give the speaker a chance to verify your understanding. The longer and more complex the message, the more important it is to paraphrase. When the speaker appears to be emotional or when the speaker is not using his or her native language, paraphrasing is essential to understanding.

To paraphrase effectively, (1) listen carefully to the message, (2) notice what images and feelings you have experienced from the message, (3) determine what the message means to you, and (4) create a message that conveys these images or feelings.

4. Empathize. Empathy is the ability to identify with or vicariously experience another's feelings or attitudes. Three approaches are empathic responsiveness, perspective taking, and sympathetic responsiveness (Weaver & Kirtley, 1995).

- **Empathic responsiveness** occurs when you experience an emotional response parallel to, and as a result of observing, another person's actual or anticipated display of emotion (Omdahl, 1995; Stiff, Dillard, Somera, Kim, & Sleight, 1988). For instance, when Jackson tells Janis that he is in real trouble financially, and Janis senses the stress and anxiety that Jackson is feeling, we would say that Janis has demonstrated empathic responsiveness.

- **Perspective taking** occurs when you use everything you know about the sender and his or her circumstances to understand their feelings. For example, suppose that Jackson tells Janis that he is

in serious financial trouble. Janis, who has known Jackson since grade school, understands that Jackson was raised by parents who were very frugal and paid their bills on time. Because of what she knows about Jackson, Janis understands that Jackson must be very worried about his rising debts.

- **Sympathetic responsiveness** occurs when you feel concern, compassion, or sorrow for another's situation. Sympathy differs from the other two approaches. Rather than attempting to experience the feelings of the other, we translate our intellectual understanding of what the speaker has experienced into feelings of concern, compassion, and sorrow for that person. In our previous example, Janis has sympathy for Jackson when she understands that Jackson is embarrassed and worried, but instead of trying to feel those same emotions herself, she feels concern and compassion for her friend.

How well we empathize also depends on how observant we are of others' behavior and how clearly we read their nonverbal messages. To improve these skills, develop the habit of silently posing two questions to yourself: "What emotions do I believe the person is experiencing right now?" and "On what cues from the person am I basing this conclusion?"

To further increase the accuracy of reading emotions, you can also use perception checking. This is especially helpful when the other person's culture is different from yours. Let's consider an example. Atsuko, who was raised in rural Japan and is now studying at a university in Rhode Island, may feel embarrassed when her professor publicly compliments her work. Her friend Meredith might notice Atsuko's reddened cheeks and downcast eyes and comment, "Atsuko, I noticed that you looked down when Professor Shank praised you. Did the compliment embarrass you, make you feel uncomfortable, or was it something else?"

6-3c **Remembering**

Remembering is the process of moving information from short-term to long-term memory. Several things can make remembering difficult. For example, we filter out information that doesn't fit our listening style, our listening anxiety prevents us from recalling what we have heard, we engage in passive listening, we practice selective listening and remember only what supports our position, and we fall victim to the primacy-recency effect of remembering only what is said at the beginning and end of a message. Let's look at three techniques to improve our ability to remember information.

Three techniques to improve our ability to remember information

1. **Repeat the information. Repetition**— saying something aloud or mentally rehearsing it two, three, or four times—helps store information in long-term memory (Estes, 1989). If information is not reinforced, it will be held in short-term memory for as little as 20 seconds and then forgotten. So when you are introduced to a stranger named Jon McNeil, you will increase the chances that you will remember his name if you mentally think, "Jon McNeil, Jon McNeil, Jon McNeil." Likewise, when a person gives you directions to "go two blocks east, turn left, turn right at the next light, and it's the second apartment building on the right," you should immediately repeat the directions to yourself to help remember them.

2. **Construct mnemonics.** A **mnemonic device** is a learning technique that associates a special word or very short statement with new and longer information. One of the most common mnemonic techniques is to form a word with the first letters of a list of items you are trying to remember. For example, a popular mnemonic for the five Great Lakes is HOMES (*H*uron, *O*ntario, *M*ichigan, *E*rie, *S*uperior). Most beginning music students learn the mnemonic "*every good boy does fine*" for the notes on the lines of the treble clef (E, G, B, D, F) and the word *face* (F, A, C, E) for the notes on the spaces.

3. **Take notes.** Although note taking may not be an appropriate way to remember information when you are engaged in casual interpersonal encounters, it is a powerful tool for increasing recall during lectures, business meetings, and briefing sessions. Note taking provides a written record that you can go back to later. It also allows you to take an active role in the listening process (Wolvin & Coakley, 1996).

© CREATISTA/Shutterstock.com

What constitutes "good notes" varies depending on the situation. Useful notes may consist of a brief list of main points or key ideas plus a few of the most significant details. Or they may be a short summary of the entire concept (a type of paraphrase). For lengthy and detailed information, however, good notes are likely to consist of a brief outline, including the overall idea, the main points, and key developmental material. Good notes are not necessarily long. In fact, many classroom lectures can be reduced to a one-page or shorter outline.

6-3d Evaluating

Evaluating is the process of critically analyzing what you hear to determine how truthful, authentic, or believable you judge the message to be. This may involve ascertaining the accuracy of facts, the amount and type of evidence used, and how a position relates to your personal values. Here are some suggestions to help you evaluate messages effectively.

1. **Separate facts from inferences. Facts** are statements whose accuracy can be verified as true. If a statement is offered as a fact, you need to determine if it is true. Doing so often requires asking questions that probe the evidence. For example, if Raoul says, "It's going to rain tomorrow," you might ask, "Oh, did you see the weather report this morning?" **Inferences** are assertions based on the facts presented. When a speaker makes an inference, you need to determine whether the inference is valid. You can ask: (1) What are the facts that support this inference? (2) Is this information really central to the inference? (3) Is there other information that would contradict this inference? For example,

repetition
saying something aloud or mentally rehearsing it two, three, or more times

mnemonic device
a learning technique that associates a special word or very short statement with new and longer information

evaluating
the process of critically analyzing what you hear

facts
statements whose accuracy can be verified as true

inferences
assertions based on the facts presented

responding
the process of providing feedback

feedback cues
verbal and nonverbal signals used to indicate to the speaker that you are attending to and understanding the message

if someone says, "Better watch it—Katie's in a really bad mood today. Did you catch the look on her face?" you should stop and ask yourself if Katie *is* really in a bad mood. The support for this inference is her facial expression. Is this inference accurate? Is Katie's expression one of anger, unhappiness, or something else? Is the look on her face enough to conclude that she's in a bad mood? Is there anything else about Katie's behavior that could lead us to believe that she's not in a bad mood? Separating facts from inferences helps us realize the difference between a verifiable observation and an opinion related to that observation. Separating facts from inferences is important because inferences may be false, even if they are based on verifiable facts.

2. Probe for information. Sometimes we need to encourage the speaker to delve deeper into a topic in order to truly evaluate the message critically. For example, suppose that Jerrod's prospective landlord asked him to sign a lease. Before signing it, Jerrod should probe for more information. He might ask about the term of the lease and the consequences for breaking the lease early. He might also ask about a deposit and what he will need to do to get the deposit back when the lease is up. He may have noticed inconsistencies between the rental ad on Craigslist and something the landlord says. In that case he might say, "Your ad said that utilities would be paid by the landlord, but just now you said the tenant pays the utility bill. Which one is correct?" With questions like these, Jerrod is probing to accurately evaluate the message.

6-3e **Responding**

The final step in active listening is **responding**, the process of providing feedback. When we respond to a friend or family member who appears emotionally upset, to a colleague's ideas, or to a public speech, we need to do so in ways that demonstrate respect for the speaker even when we disagree with him or her. Let's take a look at some general guidelines for responding effectively and then some specific guidelines to follow when offering emotional support, when critiquing others, and when evaluating public speeches.

General Response Guidelines

Regardless of the situation, you should respond to a message by providing appropriate feedback cues—but only

THE LISTENER IN THIS PHOTO PROVIDES ATTENTIVE FEEDBACK CUES TO HIS PARTNER, WHO IS FRUSTRATED.

after the speaker has finished. You should also provide feedback to the speaker's message before changing the subject.

- **Provide feedback cues. Feedback cues** are the verbal and nonverbal signals you use to indicate to the speaker that you are attending to and understanding the message. These cues include nodding, smiling, laughing, head cocking, frowning, eyebrow furrowing, or even saying "huh?," "uh huh," or "yeah." Feedback cues are appropriate when they communicate to the speaker without becoming distractions.

- **Respond only after the speaker has finished.** Except for feedback cues, respond only after the speaker has finished. One of the most common signs of poor listening is interrupting (Halone & Pecchioni, 2001). Learning to wait can be especially challenging for those of us with a time-oriented listening style, when a group of people is talking, when we are in a heated conversation, or when we are excited and enthusiastic about what we have just heard.

- **Respond to the message before changing the subject.** Abrupt topic changes are inappropriate because they don't acknowledge what the speaker has said. Acknowledge your partner's message before changing the subject by asking questions, paraphrasing, offering emotional support, or critiquing.

Emotional Support Response Guidelines

Sometimes the appropriate response is to reassure, encourage, soothe, console, or cheer up the speaker. **Supportive responses** create an environment that encourages the other person to talk about and make sense of a distressing situation. Supporting does not mean making false statements or telling someone only what he or she wants to hear. Figure 6.1 summarizes research-based guidelines for forming supportive messages (Burleson, 2003).

Critique Response Guidelines

When you cannot agree with what a speaker has said, or when it is appropriate for you to offer a critique, your messages will be most effective if they clearly demonstrate respect for the speaker. Figure 6.2 provides some guidelines to help

supportive responses feedback that creates an environment that encourages the other person to talk about and make sense of a distressing situation

---

FIGURE 6.1
Guidelines for Supportive Responses

Guideline	Example
1. Clearly state that your aim is to help.	*I'd like to help you, what can I do?*
2. Express acceptance or affection; do not condemn or criticize.	*I understand that you just can't seem to accept this.*
3. Demonstrate care, concern, and interest in the speaker's situation; do not give a lengthy recount of a similar situation.	*What are you planning to do now? OR Gosh, tell me more! What happened then?*
4. Indicate that you are available to listen and support the speaker without intruding.	*I know that we've not been that close, but sometimes it helps to have someone to listen and I'd like to do that for you.*
5. State that you are an ally.	*I'm with you on this. OR Well, I'm on your side. This isn't right.*
6. Acknowledge the speaker's feelings and situation, and express your sincere sympathy.	*I'm so sorry to see you feeling so bad. I can see that you're devastated by what has happened.*
7. Assure the speaker that his or her feelings are legitimate; do not tell the speaker how to feel or to ignore those feelings.	*Hey, it's OK, man. With all that has happened to you, you have a right to be angry.*
8. Use prompting comments to encourage elaboration.	*Uh-huh, yeah. OR I see. How did you feel about that? OR Tell me more.*

© Cengage Learning

FIGURE 6.2
Guidelines for Critiquing Others

Guidelines	Example
1. Use "I" language to clearly own the comments you make. Do not ascribe them to others.	*Carla, I really like the way you cited the references for your opening quotation.*
2. Use specific language and specific examples to point out areas of disagreement and areas for improvement.	*I can't agree to this plan because I cannot afford a 15% reduction in my personnel budget. I could probably live with a 10% decrease.*
3. Find a point to agree with or something positive to say before expressing your disagreement or offering a negative critique.	*I really appreciate what you have to say on this topic and agree that we need to support our coworkers who need after-school care for their children. I wonder, though, if we should brainstorm additional potential solutions before settling on one.*

© Cengage Learning

you demonstrate respect when disagreeing with or critiquing others.

Public Speech Evaluation Response Guidelines

You may be asked to respond to a speech given by one of your classmates in this course or by a colleague in the workplace. If so, you will want to remember that your goal is to be respectful, honest, and helpful. Since you will be critiquing, you will want to use "I" language, be specific and use examples, and make statements about what was done well before offering suggestions for improvement. Good speech critiques also address each primary element of an effective speech—the content, structure, and delivery—as well as the construction and integration of presentational aids if used.

- When critiquing content, you can comment on the appropriateness of the speech for that particular audience and the use of facts and inferences. You can also analyze the logic of the arguments and the evidence used to support ideas.

- When critiquing structure, you can focus on the introduction, the use of transitions, the choice of organizational pattern, and the concluding remarks.

- When critiquing delivery, you can comment on the use of voice, face, and gestures, as well as whether the tone was appropriately conversational or formal.

- When critiquing presentational aids, you can talk about whether they were easy to see, were professional in appearance, and enhanced the verbal message by using a visual symbol system such as charts, graphs, or photos. You can also mention how the speaker referenced them during the speech.

When you critique a speech, remember that it is important to point out things you thought the speaker did particularly well and why, as well as specific things you believe they could do differently to improve the content, structure, delivery, and presentational aids. Figure 6.3 provides examples of ineffective and effective speech critique statements.

FIGURE 6.3

Examples of Effective and Ineffective Speech Critiques

	Ineffective Critique	Effective Critique
Content	The sources you cited are old and no longer represent current thinking on the topic.	I noticed you relied heavily on Johnson's 1969 essay about global warming. For me, your argument would be more compelling if you cited research that has been published in the last five years.
Structure	You were really hard to follow.	I really appreciate what you had to say on this topic. I would have been able to follow your main points better if I had heard clear transitions between each one. Transitions would have helped me notice the switch from one topic to the next.
Delivery	You talk too fast!	I was fascinated by the evidence you offered to support the first main point. It would have been even more compelling for me if you had spoken just a bit more slowly while explaining that information. That would have given me time to understand the material more fully before we moved on to the next main point.
Presentational Aids	Your PowerPoint was ugly.	The content you chose to put on your PowerPoint presentation really highlighted what you were saying. I would have had an easier time reading the slides if the text were shorter and the background was a dark color with light text, or a light color with dark text. This would have made your point even clearer to me.

© Cengage Learning

Quick Quiz

T F 1. A biology professor is leading an advanced team as they work on some genetic coding. When one student explains a problem with the experiment, the professor quickly grasps the student's meaning and finishes her sentence for her with enthusiasm. This professor is an action-oriented listener.

T F 2. The five steps in the active listening process are: attending, understanding, remembering, evaluating, and responding.

T F 3. Studies show that our brains can process between 400 and 800 words per minute, which gives us the ability to listen effectively while at the same time we rehearse what we are going to say in response.

T F 4. Empathy is putting into words the ideas or feelings you have perceived from the message.

T F 5. A mnemonic device is any artificial technique used as a memory aid.

6. The process of receiving, constructing meaning from, and responding to spoken and/or nonverbal messages is
   a. remembering.
   b. understanding.
   c. attending.
   d. evaluating.
   e. listening.

7. Ansel's puppy has been missing all day, and he is very upset, worried, and constantly trying to find her. When he tells you about this, which is the appropriate response?
   a. You express concern for the puppy and offer to do whatever you can to help track her down.
   b. You look at your watch and tell Ansel you can't help, you have a casserole in the oven.
   c. You want to verify the fact that the puppy is missing so you ask if your friend is telling the truth.
   d. You think to yourself, "Wow, Ansel doesn't even care that I have a basketball game. He's a bad friend."
   e. You say, "Oh man, good luck with that."

8. During the response phase, which of the following should NOT occur?
   a. You offer supportive phrases that encourage a person to feel less stressed.
   b. You laugh at your friend's explanation of a humorous but slightly embarrassing event.
   c. You change the subject as soon as your sister finishes speaking.
   d. You offer suggestions for changing a presentation when a colleague requests help.
   e. Your mom insists that squid is shellfish, and you explain that you understand how it's tricky, but the squid is not a shellfish.

9. The process of selecting and focusing on specific stimuli from the countless ones that we receive is called
   a. listening.
   b. attending.
   c. understanding.
   d. remembering.
   e. evaluating.

10. _____ is the process of decoding a message so that the meaning accurately reflects that intended by the speaker.
   a. Listening
   b. Attending
   c. Understanding
   d. Empathizing
   e. Responding

Answers: 1. T, 2. T, 3. F, 4. F, 5. F, 6. E, 7. A, 8. C, 9. B, 10. C

Interpersonal
Relationships

Learning Outcomes

7-1 Identify the major types
of relationships

7-2 Explain how disclosure and
feedback affect relationships

7-3 Examine levels of
communication at various
stages in relationships

7-4 Identify the sources of tension
in relationships

Interpersonal communication is all the interactions that occur between two people to help start, build, maintain, and sometimes end or redefine our interpersonal relationships.

Interpersonal relationships are defined by the sets of expectations two people have for each other based on their previous interactions (Littlejohn & Foss, 2011). We form interpersonal relationships as we communicate overtly and covertly through face-to-face and online interactions. Interpersonal relationships help satisfy our innate human need to feel connected with others and run the gamut from impersonal acquaintances to intimate friends. Regardless of the level of intimacy, we want to be involved in **healthy relationships**, ones in which the interactions are satisfying and beneficial to all those involved. How we communicate is central to achieving that goal.

We begin this chapter by describing three types of interpersonal relationships and providing guidelines for healthy communication in each of them. Next, we explain the role of disclosure in the stages of relationship life cycles. Finally, we talk about the dialectical tensions that exist in any interpersonal relationship and ways to manage them.

7-1 Types of Relationships

We communicate differently based on the level of intimacy we feel toward our partner. Moving on a continuum from impersonal to personal (Dindia &

interpersonal communication
all the interactions that occur between two people to help start, build, maintain, and sometimes end or redefine the relationship

interpersonal relationship
a relationship that is defined by sets of expectations two people have for each other based on their previous interactions

healthy relationship
a relationship in which the interactions are satisfying and beneficial to all those involved

Timmerman, 2003), we can classify our relationships as acquaintances, friends, and intimates.

7-1a **Acquaintances**

Acquaintances are people we know by name and talk with when the opportunity arises, but with whom our interactions are limited. For example, we become acquainted with those who live in our apartment building or dorm or the house next door, sit next to us in class, go to our church, or belong to our club. Thus Whitney and Paige, who meet in calculus class, may talk with each other about class-related issues but make no effort to share personal ideas or to see each other outside of class. Most conversations with acquaintances can be defined as **impersonal communication**, which is essentially interchangeable chit-chat (Buber, 1970). In other words, I may talk about the same thing—for instance, the weather—with the grocery clerk, the sales associate, the bank teller, and the restaurant server. If you have an online social networking profile on Facebook, Twitter, or LinkedIn, many of your online "friends" are probably acquaintances if your online conversations with them are primarily superficial.

Our goals when communicating with acquaintances are usually to reduce uncertainty and maintain face. We attempt to reduce uncertainty by seeking information that may reveal similar beliefs, attitudes, and

values (Berger, 1987). In doing so, however, we may say or do something that offends the other person or is taken the wrong way. So our second goal is to help one another save face. **Saving face** is the process of attempting to maintain a positive self-image in a relational situation (Ting-Toomey, 2004).

Acquaintanceship Guidelines

To meet other people and develop acquaintance relationships, it helps to be good at starting and developing conversations. The following guidelines can help you develop scripts to become more competent in doing so:

- **Initiate a conversation** by introducing yourself, referring to the physical context, referring to your thoughts or feelings, referring to another person, or making a joke. For example:

  Whitney: "Do you think it's hot in here, or is it just me? By the way, I'm Whitney."

- **Make your comments relevant** to what has previously been said before you change subjects:

  Paige: "My name's Paige. Yes, I'm burning up. I wonder if the air conditioner is broken. Do you know if this class meets for 75 or 90 minutes today?"

- **Develop an other-centered focus** by asking questions, listening carefully, and following up on what has been said. For example:

  Whitney: "I'm pretty sure it's only a 75-minute session. Have you ever taken a class from this professor?"
  Paige: "Yeah, I took algebra from her."
  Whitney: "What was she like?"
  Paige: "She was pretty good. Her tests were hard, but they were fair. I learned a lot."
  Whitney: "Did she offer study guides?"
  Paige: "Yes, and we reviewed as a class by playing what she called 'algebra *Jeopardy*.' That worked well for me."
  Whitney: "Sounds like I'm going to like this class and this instructor!"

- **Engage in appropriate turn-taking** by balancing talking with listening and not interrupting.

- **Be polite.** Consider how your conversational partner will feel about what you say and work to phrase your comments in a way that allows your partner to save face. For example:

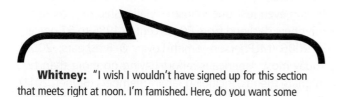

Whitney: "I wish I wouldn't have signed up for this section that meets right at noon. I'm famished. Here, do you want some M&Ms?"
Paige: "No thanks."
Whitney: "Are you sure? I don't mind sharing. A little sugar never hurt anyone."
Paige: "I'm diabetic."
Whitney: "Oh, I'm so sorry. I'll save these for later."

7-1b **Friends**

Over time, some acquaintances become friends. **Friends** are people with whom we have voluntarily negotiated more personal relationships (Patterson, Bettini, & Nussbaum, 1993). As friendships develop, people move toward interactions that are more interpersonally satisfying. For example, Whitney and Paige, who are acquaintances, may decide to get together after class to work out at the gym. If they find that they enjoy each other's company, they may continue to meet outside of class and eventually become friends.

We often refer to friends according to the context in which we interact with them. For example, we may have tennis friends, office friends, or neighborhood friends. These context friendships may fade if the context changes. For instance, your friendship with a person at the office may fade if you or your friend takes a job with a different company.

Friendship Guidelines

Several key communication behaviors will help you maintain your friendships whether you live close to one another or are separated by a distance and can only communicate remotely via e-mail, Facebook, Skype, or mobile phone (Sampter, 2003; Walther & Parks, 2002).

- **Initiation.** Be proactive in setting up times to spend together. One person must get in touch with the other. A friendship is not likely to form or endure between people who rarely interact.

friends
people with whom we have voluntarily negotiated more personal relationships

- **Responsiveness.** Each person must listen. Listen to others and respond to what they say. It is difficult to form or maintain friendships with people who focus only on themselves or their issues, and it is equally difficult to maintain relationships with people who are uncommunicative altogether.

- **Self-disclosure.** Friends share thoughts and feelings with each other. Although acquaintances can be maintained by conversations that discuss surface issues, a friendship is based on the exchange of more personal and specific information including personal history, opinions, and feelings. For example, after Paige and Whitney start to spend more time together outside of class, they might have this conversation:

Paige: "Can I tell you something and trust you to keep it between us?"
Whitney: "Of course."
Paige: "Well, you know I've been seeing David for a while now."
Whitney: "Yeah, he seems like a nice guy."
Paige: "Well, the other night we got into a little fight and he pushed me onto the couch. I actually have a bruise here on my arm from it."

- **Emotional support.** Provide comfort and support when needed. When we are emotionally or psychologically vulnerable, we expect to be helped by those we consider our friends. When your friends are hurting, they need you to support them by clarifying your supportive intentions, confirming their feelings, helping them make sense of what has happened, and giving advice (Burleson, 2003; Burleson & Goldsmith, 1998).

Whitney: "Oh, no. I'm here to help in any way I can."

Paige: "He said he was sorry and I believe him, but I just don't feel comfortable around him now."

Whitney: "I understand. I'm not sure I would feel comfortable either. Is there anything I can do?"

Paige: "No, not really. I guess I just wanted someone to confirm that I'm not overreacting."

Whitney: "Well, I don't think you're overreacting at all. Please let me know what I can do to help, OK?"

Paige: "OK. I'm so lucky to have you for a friend."

- **Conflict management.** Friends will sometimes disagree about ideas or behaviors. Healthy friendships handle these disagreements effectively through conversation.

Whitney: "Maybe you should talk to a campus counselor about this."

Paige: "No, I don't want to make a big deal out of it."

Whitney: "Paige, you got a bruise. That seems like a big deal to me."

Paige: "Actually, I bruise really easily. I don't want to see a counselor. Maybe I shouldn't have even told you about it."

Whitney: "Oh, Paige. I'm so glad you did and I totally respect your decision. If anything like this happens again, though, will you please talk to someone?"

Paige: "OK, if something happens again, I promise I will."

intimates
people with whom we share a high degree of interdependence, commitment, disclosure, understanding, affection, and trust

platonic relationship
an intimate relationship in which the partners are not sexually attracted to each other or do not act on an attraction they feel

romantic relationship
an intimate relationship in which the partners act on their sexual attraction

trust
placing confidence in another in a way that almost always involves some risk

7-1c Intimates

Intimates are those close, personal friends with whom we share a high degree of interdependence, commitment, disclosure, understanding, affection, and trust. We may have countless acquaintances and many friends, but we are likely to have only a few truly intimate relationships. Unfortunately, the percentage of Americans who identify having even just one intimate relationship beyond family members declined from 80 percent in 1985 to 57 percent in 2006 (McPherson, Smith-Lovin, & Brashears, 2006). Today most Americans report having no more than two intimate friends, including family members (Bryner, 2011). This dramatic decline is particularly troubling given that these close personal relationships help define who we are (Aron, Aron, Tudor, & Nelson, 2004; Moore, 2003; Fiske, Gilbert, & Lindzey, 2010). Empirical research reports a direct relationship between intimate relationships and a strong self-concept and positive self-esteem (Prager & Buhrmester, 1998). And many studies suggest that intimate relationships are the most important predictor of life satisfaction and emotional well being (Moore, 2003; Peterson, 2006).

Intimacy is not synonymous with "love" or exclusivity, and intimate relationships can be platonic or romantic. A **platonic relationship** is one in which the partners are not sexually attracted to each other or do not act on an attraction they feel. If you're familiar with the television series *Will and Grace*, the relationship between the title characters is platonic. Although Will and Grace live together and are intimate friends, Will is a homosexual man and Grace is a heterosexual woman. Other examples include the relationship between Leslie and Ron on *Parks and Recreation* and Alex and Meredith on *Grey's Anatomy*. Conversely, a **romantic relationship** is one in which the partners act on their sexual attraction.

Regardless of whether the relationship is platonic or romantic, both partners must trust each other for it to become and remain intimate. **Trust** is placing confidence in another in a way that almost always involves some risk. As we share private information and feelings, we monitor how well our partner keeps our confidence. If our partner keeps our confidence, we share more and the relationship becomes more intimate. If our

Who Are You IRL?

Throughout history—in life, literature, and the media—people hoping to find love have solicited help from others. Today we've expanded our search for love to online dating services, but advanced technologies don't eliminate the need some of us have to seek outside help in expressing ourselves. A quick Amazon search produces several results promising online dating success, and personal coaching for online dating is also on the rise. Online services such as Dating-Profile.com, ProfileHelper.com, and E-Cyrano.com help singles write their profiles for a fee ranging from $29 to $2,000 (Alsever, 2007). Dating coaches claim their services are not aimed at helping clients lie but, rather, to more effectively communicate their true, in-real-life (IRL) identities in a virtual dating world.

Opinions vary on the ethics of using such ghostwriting services on dating profile sites. One Match.com user says hiring someone to help write her profile would obscure who she truly is. "I'm not a person who is put together or always knows the right thing to say," she says. "I would feel like if I went out on a date with someone, I would have to be what they read instead of myself" (Alsever, 2007). Another online dater sings the praises of ProfileHelper.com, where he learned to be more specific and inquisitive when communicating on online dating sites (Alsever, 2007). In his case, a profile-writing coach stressed basic communication principles that helped him more accurately convey the

kind of person he is, pinpointing the types of things he enjoys, and what he is looking for in a potential partner.

However you feel about profile-writing coaches, most would agree that communication on online dating sites is tricky. An article in *Skeptic* explores the pros and cons of self-disclosing when dating online (King, Austin-Oden, & Lohr, 2009): On one hand, information presented online is easy to manipulate and control, so people can present themselves in any way they like—even if what they present isn't 100 percent accurate. On the other hand, the relative anonymity of online communication "accelerates intimacy through increased openness about aspects of the self." When what we disclose about ourselves is true, self-disclosure is an important step in making a successful relationship.

partner proves untrustworthy, we share less and, as a result, over time intimacy decreases. When there is a severe breach of trust, we may even abruptly end the relationship altogether.

Cultural and Co-cultural Influences on Intimacy

Research shows that intimate relationships are based on at least one of four types of interactions. The first comes from physical touch, which may include holding hands, hugging, being held, kissing, and engaging in sexual relations. The second comes from the intellectual sharing of important ideas and opinions. The third comes from sharing important feelings. The final type comes from participating in shared activities. Such activities can include anything from working together on the job or on a class project to participating on a sports team or in a civic club, getting together regularly for coffee or lunch, going to a movie or dinner, or going shopping.

Research suggests that our cultural identity may influence which type of interactions we are most likely to engage in to foster intimacy. For example, women who identify with the feminine co-culture tend to be more willing to share their thoughts and feelings than men (Dindia, 2000). Men who identify with the masculine co-culture tend to foster intimate relationships by participating in shared activities (Bowman, 2008; Morman & Floyd, 1999; Stafford, Dainton, & Haas, 2000; Swain, 1989). Of course, since masculine and feminine co-cultural norms are socialized, these generalizations may not be true for all men or for all women. Frankly, research suggests that such differences are increasingly becoming less prominent (Morman & Floyd, 2002).

Intimacy development norms also vary across cultures. In collectivist cultures such as China, Taiwan, and Japan, for example, people do not typically reach out to acquaintances until properly introduced and then take care to keep private information about close friends and family to themselves. In individualistic cultures such as the United States, people are likely to share more private information and personal feelings with acquaintances (Triandis, 1994). As with gender differences, however, such cultural differences are becoming increasingly less pronounced as the world becomes more connected through travel, media, and technology (Hatfield & Rapson, 2006).

Intimacy Guidelines

Regardless of the type(s) of interaction you rely on to foster intimacy, the following guidelines can help you establish and maintain affection, understanding, trust, and commitment in your intimate relationships (Boon, 1994):

- **Be dependable** so your partner learns that he or she can rely on you. Of course, nobody is perfect. But striving to be dependable will provide a foundation for understanding when something does come up.

- **Be responsive** in meeting your partner's needs. At times, this will require you to put your partner's needs before your own.

- **Be collaborative** in managing conflict. Doing so includes saying you're sorry for something you've done or said, agreeing to disagree, and letting go of the need to be "right."

- **Be faithful** by maintaining your partner's confidential information and by abiding by sexual or other exclusivity agreements between you and your partner. If your partner tells you something in confidence, honor that request.

- **Be transparent** by honestly sharing your real ideas and feelings with your partner.

- **Be willing** to put your relationship first. This is not to say you should give up all other activities and relationships. Rather, healthy, intimate relationships are characterized by a balance between doing things together and doing things apart (Baxter & Montgomery, 1996).

7-2 Disclosure in Relationship Life Cycles

Relationships are not something we *have,* but rather are something we *make* as we communicate with others (Parks, 2007). Even though no two relationships develop in exactly the same manner, all relationships tend to move through identifiable and overlapping phases of coming together and coming apart (Knapp & Vangelisti, 2009). This moving back and forth among the phases is known as the **relationship life cycle**.

How we move among the phases depends on how we communicate with one another (Duck, 2007). We do so through **disclosure**, which is the process of revealing confidential information, and feedback, which includes the verbal and nonverbal responses to such information. Disclosure can come in the form of **self-disclosure**, which is the confidential information we deliberately choose to share about ourselves, and **other-disclosure**, which is the confidential information shared about someone by a third party (Petronio, 2002). **Social penetration theory** describes the different kinds of self-disclosure we use in our relationships, and the **Johari window**

Some cultures are careful to keep personal information private, which may seem overly secretive to more open cultures.

explains how these various forms of disclosure and feedback operate in them. Knowing these processes can help us make wise disclosure decisions depending on the type and life cycle stage of our relationship.

7-2a Social Penetration

Not all self-disclosure is equally revealing. In other words, some messages reveal more about our thoughts and feelings than others. Irwin Altman and Dalmas Taylor (197) have conceptualized a model of self-disclosure based on the breadth and depth of information shared. *Breadth* has to do with the range of different subjects you discuss with your partner. *Depth* has to do with the quality of information shared, which can range from relatively impersonal and "safe" to very confidential and "risky." For example, when Whitney and Paige first met, the breadth of subjects they discussed focused on their families, hometowns, and things they were learning in class. As their relationship became more intimate they added subjects about career ambitions, feelings about people they were dating, and feelings about their own relationship. The depth of disclosure also deepened. For example, in addition to sharing impersonal information, such as how many siblings they each have, they also disclosed characteristics they liked and did not like about their brothers and sisters. Discussions about their hometowns became deeper as they shared personal stories about positive and negative experiences they had growing up. And discussions about class grew to include opinions each had about whether what they were learning would help them achieve their career goals. Paige and Whitney's social penetration model is illustrated in Figure 7.1.

7-2b The Johari Window

Whereas we once believed that more disclosure between partners naturally resulted in increased intimacy, today we realize that relational closeness depends on appropriate self-disclosure along with appropriate feedback and other-disclosure. One way to understand the nature of disclosure and feedback in interpersonal relationships

is through the Johari window. The Johari window, named after its two originators, Joe Luft and Harry Ingham (1970), consists of four panes that comprise all information about you. You and your partner each know some (but not all) of this information (see Figure 7.2).

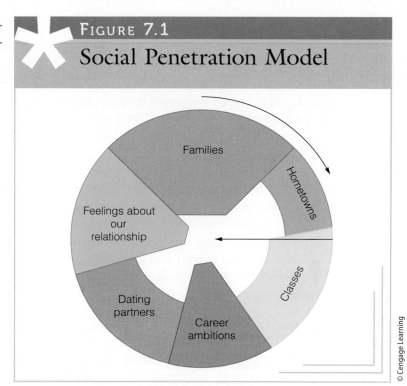

Figure 7.1

Social Penetration Model

© Cengage Learning

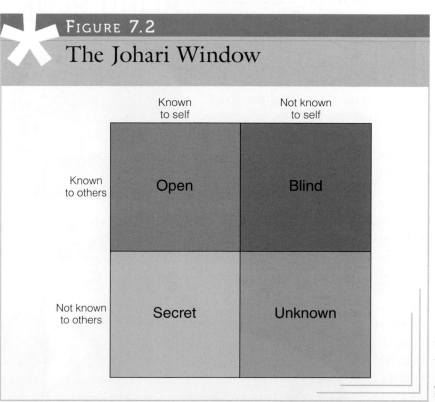

Figure 7.2

The Johari Window

© Cengage Learning

The Open Pane

The first quadrant in the Johari window is called the "open" pane because it represents the information about you that both you and your partner know. It includes information you have self-disclosed and observations about you that your partner has shared with you. It might include mundane information that you share with most people, such as your college major, but it also may include information that you disclose to relatively few people. Similarly, it could include simple observations that your partner has made, such as how you doodle when you're bored, or more serious ones such as how you behave when you're angry.

The Secret Pane

The second quadrant is called the "secret" pane. It contains all those things that you know about yourself but that your partner does not yet know about you. Secret information is made known through the process of self-disclosure. The information moves into the open pane of the window once you share it with your partner. For example, suppose you were once engaged to be married but your partner broke the engagement. You may not want to share this part of your history with casual acquaintances, so it will be in the secret pane of your window in many of your relationships. But when you disclose this fact to a friend, it moves into the open part of your Johari window with this person. As you disclose information, the secret pane becomes smaller and the open pane grows larger.

The Blind Pane

The third quadrant is called the "blind" pane. This is the place for information that the other person knows about you, but about which you are unaware. They may have discovered it by observing you or from other-disclosure shared by a mutual friend or acquaintance. Information moves from the blind area of the window to the open area through feedback. When someone gives you an insight about yourself and you accept the feedback, then the information moves into the open pane. Thus, the open pane of the Johari window becomes larger and the blind pane becomes smaller.

The Unknown Pane

The fourth quadrant is called the "unknown" pane. It contains information that neither you nor your partner knows about you. Obviously, you cannot develop a list of this information. So how do we know that it exists? Well, because periodically we discover it. If, for instance, you have never tried hang gliding, then nobody knows how you will react at the point of takeoff. You might chicken out or follow through, do it well or crash, love every minute of it or be paralyzed with fear. But until you try it, this information is unknown. Once you try it, you gain information about yourself that becomes part of the secret pane, which you can move to the open pane through disclosure. Also, once you have tried it, others who observe your flight will have information about your performance that you may not know unless they give you feedback.

As you and your partner disclose information with each other, the sizes of the various windowpanes change. And the panes of the Johari window you have with different friends will vary in size depending on the nature of that relationship. Thus, disclosure and feedback are the communication processes through which each relationship moves back and forth through phases in its life cycle.

THE BLIND PANE

© Yuri Arcurs/Shutterstock.com

7-3 Stages of Relationships

Regardless of whether your relationship is with an acquaintance, a friend, or an intimate partner, every relationship develops and changes with time. Researchers have identified ten stages within the three phases of coming together, relational maintenance, and coming apart (Dindia, 2003; Knapp & Vangelisti, 2009). Our relationships move among these stages based on the *information* we share with our partners and "by the *interpretation* of such things" by them (Duck, 2007, p. 80).

7-3a Coming Together: Beginning Relationships

The stages in the coming together phase focus on beginning

and developing relationships. Communication during the stages of coming together focuses on reducing uncertainty by increasing your knowledge of the other person. Your goal is to understand how he or she sees the world (Berger, 1987). Noted interpersonal communication scholar Steve Duck (1999) conceived the Relationship Filtering Model to explain the process that relationships go through in the beginning stages. According to the model, when you first meet someone you assume he or she is similar to you until what his/ her words or actions tell you otherwise. You begin by communicating very generally about noncontroversial topics and asking questions about surface information such as hometowns and hobbies. Based on what you learn, you make inferences about the person's general attitudes, values, and ways of thinking. If you decide you have enough common interests and attitudes, you will choose to develop the relationship by disclosing more about yourself.

Let's look again at Whitney and Paige, who have decided to become college roommates. At first they are nervous, wondering if they will be compatible. To reduce this uncertainty, they get to know each other better through disclosure and feedback. They may talk about what they did in high school, what major each is pursuing, what hobbies they like, and their favorite foods, movies, and music. As they learn more about each other, they find that although Whitney is majoring in fine arts and Paige is pre-med, both are passionate environmentalists and vegetarians. As they learn more, they begin to relax and find that although they have many differences, they like and respect each other. Over the semester, they each socialize with different friends, but they continue to have evening meals in the dining hall together. Life in the room they share begins to take on a predictable pattern. When Whitney is working on a class project, materials are strewn all over the room, so Paige accommodates her by studying in the library. When Paige is freaking out over her midterm exam in chemistry, Whitney gets her a Red Bull from the Quick Mart and then goes to the lounge to watch TV while Paige studies.

Relationships can begin in face-to-face or online environments. Increasingly, the beginning stage may occur online (Ward & Tracy, 2004). Online communication may present a potentially less difficult way to meet others than traditional face-to-face interactions. The initial interaction can occur in the comfort of your own home and at your own pace. You need not be concerned about your (or your partner's) physical appearance, and you can more precisely select what you are going to say (Ward & Tracy, 2004).

7-3b Coming Together: Developing Relationships

As the relationship develops, you continue coming together by disclosing more to one another, engaging in more physical contact, and feeling a deepening psychological closeness (Duck, 1999). Through disclosure and feedback, partners identify and capitalize on their similarities and tolerate or negotiate their differences.

Partners also tend to share greater physical contact during this developing relationship stage. Physical contact may involve sitting closer together, leaning toward each other, and engaging in more eye contact and touch. Such physical behaviors may or may not involve romantic feelings. Even platonic friends increase physical contact with each other as the relationship develops, for example, through hugs, high-fives, and fist bumps. Let's say the relationship between Whitney and Paige is working out well. They spend time together, get to know each other well, and consider themselves to be intimate friends. By second semester, they hug each other when they return from spring break, share clothes, and do each other's hair, makeup, and nail polish.

Of course, cultural norms also affect how people engage in physical contact in relationships. In some cultures, for instance, male friends who are not romantic partners may hold hands in public or kiss to greet one another. In contrast, for orthodox Jews and observant Muslim women, touching men is abhorred.

As a relationship develops, partners will feel psychologically closer as well (Duck, 1999). Partners who do not feel relaxed and comfortable will remain casual acquaintances and may even decide to avoid having any relationship with one another. If you share no common interests, attitudes, or ways of interpreting the world, you are not likely to choose to develop a deeper relationship. Think about the people you met during your first weeks on campus. Which ones did not become your friends and why? Most likely, during your initial encounters you gathered information that reduced uncertainty about them, but what you learned was that they did not share enough common interests or attitudes to warrant developing a relationship.

We know that relationships can develop via face-to-face or online interactions; it may come as a surprise that some people report that they achieve more closeness in online relationships than in equivalent face-to-face

relationships (Brooks, 2011). Indeed, rapid and exaggerated intimacy can be part of the fun of online relationships (Rabby & Walther, 2003).

Relational Maintenance

Once a relationship has developed into what others identify as a relationship, we employ communication strategies to maintain it. **Relational maintenance** consists of those communication strategies used to keep a relationship operating smoothly and satisfactorily (Dindia, 2003). Maintaining a relationship means that both people continue to invest emotionally in the relationship in ways that demonstrate an ongoing commitment to their partner. Researchers have catalogued many relational maintenance strategies (Rusbult, Olsen, Davis, & Hannon, 2004), such as engaging in prosocial behaviors (e.g., being friendly and polite), observing ceremonial occasions (e.g., birthdays, anniversaries, regular "date nights," and memorable shared experiences), and not becoming overly critical or taking the other for granted. For example, Paige and Whitney celebrate one another's birthdays by going bowling and then to dinner at a favorite restaurant. Paige also tries not to be overtly critical when Whitney strews papers around while working on a big project, knowing that Whitney will tidy things up when she is finished. Instead, Paige admires Whitney for having such a serious work ethic.

Other strategies include spending time together (both with one another and with mutual friends), communicating honestly and frequently about both deep and everyday topics, and offering words and actions that demonstrate affection and respect for one another. Whitney and Paige, for example, gave each other "best friend" status on their Facebook pages, decided to join some of the same clubs, and even visited each other's hometowns to meet each other's families and high school friends.

Partners also **sacrifice** by putting their needs or desires on hold to attend to the needs of their partner or the relationship. For example, when Whitney was ill, Paige sacrificed a date in order to stay home and take care of her sick roommate. Because all relationships involve give and take, being willing to do what is

Relational maintenance includes prosocial behaviors such as celebrating birthdays.

© Grafica/Shutterstock.com

best for the other person or for the relationship itself can help maintain it.

Finally, because conflict is inevitable in developed relationships, we may do or say things that hurt our partner. If not handled properly, such transgressions can harm the relationship and move it to a less intimate level. By forgiving minor transgressions, we can keep a relationship at the desired level of closeness. For example, Whitney and Paige each have little habits that annoy the other, but they choose not to let these annoyances get in the way of a good friendship.

7-3c Coming Apart: Declining and Dissolving Relationships

When one or both partners fail to engage actively in relational maintenance strategies, the relationship may begin to come apart and could eventually end altogether. Relationships between acquaintances, casual friends, coworkers, and neighbors are more likely to end than highly developed ones (Parks, 2007). The communication in declining relationships is marked by four stages: circumscribing, stagnating, avoiding, and terminating.

Circumscribing

The first sign that a relationship is coming apart is known as the **circumscribing stage**, which is where communication decreases in both quantity and quality. Rather than discuss a disagreement, for example, both parties ignore it outwardly even if it troubles them inside. Even though Whitney and Paige were close during their first two years of college, they drifted apart as they each met people with more aligned personal and professional interests. They found they had less and less to talk about when they were together, so they started spending less time with each other.

Stagnating

If circumscribing continues, it may eventually lead to the **stagnating stage**, when partners just go through the motions of interacting with each other routinely without enthusiasm or emotion. When employees reach this stage, we say they have "job burnout" as they go through the motions without joy or passion. Because Whitney and Paige share a dorm room, they continue to engage in the routines they had developed for studying, cleaning, and entertaining friends there. But they often

> Avoiding coworkers can signal dissatisfaction with your relationships.

do so in silence, neither of them wanting to make the effort to initiate a conversation about meaningless topics.

Avoiding

When remaining in a relationship that has stagnated becomes too painful, partners move into the **avoiding stage** by creating physical distance between themselves and by making excuses not to do things together. They communicate about "safe" topics if they even interact at all. The overriding tone is usually not marked by hostility but by indifference. When Whitney tells Paige she is moving into an apartment with other friends, Paige responds with "Whatever."

Terminating

Of course, not all relationships end. However, when partners decide the relationship is no longer satisfying and no longer worth trying to maintain, they have reached the **terminating stage**. Basically, a relationship has ended when the people involved no longer interact with each other. People give many reasons for terminating

circumscribing stage relationship stage during which communication decreases in both quantity and quality

stagnating stage relationship stage during which partners just go through the motions of interacting with each other routinely without enthusiasm or emotion

avoiding stage relationship stage during which partners create physical distance by making excuses not to do things with the other person in the relationship

terminating stage relationship stage in which partners no longer interact with each other

grave-dressing
attempts to explain why
a relationship failed

relationship transformation
the process of changing
a relationship from one
level of intimacy to
another

relationships, including poor communication, lack of fulfillment, differing lifestyles and interests, rejection, outside interference, absence of rewards, and boredom (Cupach and Metts, 1986). These attempts to explain why the relationship failed are called **grave-dressing** (Duck, 1982).

Unfortunately, partners sometimes look for reasons to blame each other rather than trying to find equitable ways of bringing the relationship to an acceptable conclusion. They do so by using strategies of manipulation, withdrawal, and avoidance (Baxter, 1982). Though misguided and inappropriate, manipulation involves being indirect and failing to take any responsibility for ending the relationship. Manipulators may purposely sabotage the relationship in hopes that the other person will break it off. Withdrawal and avoidance, also unsuitable strategies, are passive approaches that lead to the slow and often painful death of the relationship.

The most competent way to end a relationship is to be direct, open, and honest. Clearly state your wish to end the relationship while being respectful of the other person and sensitive to the resulting emotions. If two people have had a satisfying and close relationship, they owe it to themselves and to each other to be forthright and fair about communicating during the terminating stage of the relationship.

Even when partners agree that their relationship in its current form is over, they may continue to interact and influence each other through a different type of relationship. This is called **relationship transformation**. Romantic relationships may transform into friendships, best friends may become casual friends, and even marriages may continue on friendly terms or as a type of business relationship where child-rearing practices and expenses are coordinated (Parks, 2007). After Whitney and Paige graduate, their

friendship may be transformed into that of acquaintances who enjoy seeing each other at reunions.

7-3d Mediated Communication and Interpersonal Relationships

Almost all of us have met someone online, used the Internet to keep connected to a friend or loved one who lives far away, or used e-mail and text messaging to "converse" with friends and family. Internet technology and social media have changed how we build and maintain our relationships in several important ways:

- People can begin friendships and even meet their soul mates online. Sometimes these relationships stem from shared interests, such as online gaming or forums for specific hobbies like home-brewing beer or practicing martial arts.

- Our online partners usually respond to our verbal messages rather than our physical appearance or nonverbal cues. As a result, we are more likely to develop "pure relationships" based on mutual interests unconstrained by pressures to maintain the social order. This increases the likelihood that we will form relationships that cross boundaries of race, class, and sex (Baym & Ledbetter, 2009; Clark, 1998; Giddens, 1993; Mesch & Talmud, 2006; Rawlins, 1992).

- Social media makes it very easy to stay connected and maintain our existing relationships. When we are temporarily separated from our friends and loved ones, we can still be together in cyberspace. In addition, we can communicate with our partners whenever it is convenient for us, regardless of the time.

- Meeting people online can sometimes be riskier than meeting in person since we don't know whether the "cyber-self" being presented is an accurate reflection of who the person

© John Cowie/iStockphoto.com

really is. On the other hand, online relationships can also be less risky because we can get to know people at a distance before meeting face-to-face.

When people meet online, they don't experience what we traditionally call interpersonal communication. Rather, they experience **hyperpersonal communication**, which differs from face-to-face interaction in that senders have a greater capacity to strategically manage their self-presentation because nonverbal and relevant contextual cues are more limited (Walther, 1996). As you would expect, they "put their best foot forward." So, hyperpersonal communication receivers are left to fill in the blanks. They do this by assuming that their partner is similar to them and by using implicit personality theory. Thus, partners who begin their relationships online seem to like each other more than partners who first meet face-to-face (Walther, 1996).

Technology and the Relationship Cycle

Relationships that begin online show a predictable pattern of adding additional media as they develop, each bringing more nonverbal and contextual cues into play. Partners who meet in an online group, like a class blog, may begin to exchange private e-mails, exchange pictures, then make phone calls, conduct video chats, and finally arrange face-to-face meetings. In one study, over 50 percent of the people who met online had followed this progression through to a face-to-face meeting (McKenna, Green, & Gleason, 2002).

Relationships that begin in face-to-face settings may also use digital technology and social media as the relationship develops. Research suggests, in fact, that many of us find self-disclosure and feedback easier online (McKenna, et al., 2002). In addition, one study found that Americans reported being more honest with family members online than they are in face-to-face encounters (Rainie, Lenhart, Fox, Spooner, & Horrigan, 2000). As we interact online, we also develop new "rites of passage" that signal important relationship transitions. For example, giving your partner the passwords to your social networking pages and e-mail accounts might signal a deepening bond of trust (Gershon, 2010).

We also use digital technology to maintain relationships. Most of our ongoing relationships are characterized by **media multiplexity**, which simply means that we use more than one medium to maintain our relationships. Interestingly, research has found that closer relationships use more media (Haythornthwaite, 2005). Although you are likely to e-mail or call your coworkers, you are more likely to also text and video chat with close friends and family members. We also maintain our relationships using social networking sites (SNS) like Facebook (Gilbert, Karahalios, & Sandvig, 2008; Golder, Wilkinson, & Huberman, 2007).

Finally, not only do we begin, develop, and maintain our relationships online, but we also often use mediated technology to disengage from relationships. Just as we distance ourselves physically in face-to-face relationships, digitally connected partners signal a desire to disengage by exchanging fewer e-mails, texts, and phone calls. For example, Brian began letting phone calls from Ruth go to voice mail rather than picking up. He also began ignoring her e-mails and texts. Ruth, who was not ready to let go of the relationship, began checking Brian's Facebook page more frequently to figure out why he wasn't responding to her messages. Some research suggests that young adults today choose to "break up" using technology rather than by having a face-to-face conversation even though they believe such behavior is inappropriate (Gershon, 2010).

hyperpersonal communication
online interaction in which senders have a greater capacity to strategically manage their self-presentation because nonverbal and relevant contextual cues are more limited

media multiplexity
using more than one medium to maintain relationships

7-4 Dialectics in Interpersonal Relationships

Have you ever felt ambivalent about a relationship? On the one hand, you really wanted to become close to someone, but at the same time you wanted your "space." Or have you met someone who seemed a bit too nosy yet you really wanted to get to know the person? Have you

© Wojtek Kryczka/iStockphoto.com

ever enjoyed the stability of a long-term relationship, but at the same time longed for the same excitement as when you first met? If so, you were experiencing what scholars call a relational dialectic. A **dialectic** is a tension between conflicting forces. **Relational dialectics** are the competing psychological tensions that exist in any relationship. At any one time, one or both people may be aware of these tensions. Let's take a look at some specific relational dialectics and then discuss some ways to manage these inevitable tensions in our relationships.

7-4a **Relational Dialectics**

Three dialectics common to most relationships are the tugs between autonomy and connection, openness and closedness, and novelty and predictability (Baxter & Montgomery, 1996; Baxter & West, 2003). How these tensions are dealt with can alter the stage and life cycle of a relationship.

Autonomy/Connection

Autonomy is the desire to do things independent of your partner. **Connection** is the desire to link your actions and decisions with your partner. Joel and Shelly have been dating for about a year. At this point in their relationship, Shelly wants to spend most of her free time with Joel and enjoys talking with him before acting or making decisions. Joel, however, has begun to feel hemmed in. For example, he wants to be able to play basketball with the guys without having to clear it first with Shelly. At the same time, though, he doesn't want to hurt Shelly's feelings or ruin the closeness of their relationship. Shelly is happy with their relationship and may not recognize any tension between autonomy and connection. On the other hand, Joel is feeling the tension between wanting to be more autonomous without jeopardizing his connection to Shelly. If Joel begins to act autonomously, he may relieve his own tension but at the same time create tension in the relationship.

Openness/Closedness

Openness is the desire to share intimate ideas and feelings with your partner. **Closedness** is the desire to maintain privacy. Let's say that Joel discloses quite a bit to Shelly. He believes it is important to divulge his feelings to Shelly, and he expects her to do the same. In other words, the open quadrant of Joel's Johari window in his relationship with Shelly is quite large. Shelly, however, is a more private person. She does disclose to Joel, but not as much as he would like. The secret pane of her Johari window is larger than Joel would like it to be. The fact that Shelly and Joel differ in their preferred levels of self-disclosure is one source of tension in their relationship. But Joel does not want complete openness all the time. He realizes it is sometimes appropriate to refrain from self-disclosure. So he seeks both openness and closedness in this relationship. Likewise, Shelly, although wanting more closedness than Joel does, still wants some openness. So, like Joel, she wants both forces to occur simultaneously in this relationship.

Novelty/Predictability

Novelty is the desire for originality, freshness, and uniqueness in your own or your partner's behavior or in the relationship. **Predictability** is the desire for consistency, reliability, and dependability. People experience tension between their desires for novelty and predictability. Because Shelly and

dialectic
a tension between conflicting forces

relational dialectics
the competing psychological tensions in a relationship

autonomy
the desire to do things independent of one's partner

connection
the desire to do things and make decisions with one's partner

openness
the desire to share intimate ideas and feelings with one's partner

closedness
the desire to maintain one's privacy in a relationship

novelty
originality, freshness, and uniqueness in a relationship

predictability
consistency, reliability, and dependability in a relationship

Joel have been dating for a year, much of the uncertainty is gone from their relationship. But they do not want to eliminate uncertainty altogether. With no uncertainty at all, a relationship becomes so predictable and so routine that it is boring. Although Shelly and Joel know each other well, can predict much about each other, and have quite a few routines in their relationship, they also want to be surprised and have new experiences with each other. Shelly and Joel may differ in their needs for novelty and predictability. Shelly may yearn for Joel to surprise her with a mystery date, or she may shock Joel by spontaneously breaking into their favorite song in the middle of the mall. At this point in their relationship, Joel may be comfortable operating by the routines they have established and may be embarrassed and upset by Shelly's song. This is another tension between the two that must be managed in their relationship. But they must also cope with the fact that they each need some amount of both novelty and predictability in the relationship.

Although our example of Shelly and Joel is an intimate relationship, it is important to remember that dialectical tensions exist in all relationships—and they are always in flux. Sometimes these dialectical tensions are active and in the foreground; at other times they are in the background. Nevertheless, when we experience them, they influence the nature of our relationship (Wood, 2000).

7-4b Managing Dialectical Tensions

You may be wondering how you can cope with dialectical tensions in relationships. How do people satisfy opposite needs at the same time? Several researchers (Baxter & Montgomery, 1996; Wood, 2000) have studied how people manage dialectical tensions in relationships. Four strategies include temporal selection, topical segmentation, neutralization, and reframing.

Temporal selection is the strategy of choosing one desire and ignoring the other for the time being. Perhaps you and a friend realize that you have spent too much time apart lately (autonomy), so you make a conscious decision to pursue connection. That is, you agree that over the next few months you will make a point of spending more time together. You schedule lots of activities together so that you can be more connected. Over time, however, you may feel that you are spending too much time together, and so you may find yourself cancelling dates. Seesawing back and forth like this is one way to temporarily manage a relational dialectic.

Topical segmentation is the strategy of choosing certain topics with which to satisfy one desire and other topics for the opposite desire. You and your mom may practice openness by sharing your opinions and feelings about certain topics such as school, work, and politics but maintain your privacy concerning your sex lives. This segmentation satisfies both your needs for balance in the openness/closedness dialectic.

Neutralization is the strategy of compromising between the desires of one person and the desires of the other. Neutralization partially meets the needs of both people but does not fully meet the needs of either. A couple might pursue a moderate level of novelty and spontaneity in their lives, which satisfies both of them. The amount of novelty in the relationship may be less than what one person would ideally want and more than what the other would normally desire, but they have reached a middle point comfortable to both.

Reframing is the strategy of changing your perception about the level of tension. Reframing involves looking at your desires differently so that they no longer seem quite so contradictory. Maybe you are tense because you perceive that you are more open and your partner is more closed. So you think about how much you disclose to him and how little he discloses to you. You might even discuss this issue with your partner. Perhaps during the conversation, you begin to realize the times that you have held back (closedness), as well as the instances when he was open. After the conversation, you no longer see a strong contradiction. You see yourselves as more similar than different on this dialectic. You have reframed your perception of the tension.

In most cases when you are developing, maintaining, or trying to repair a deteriorating relationship, it helps to openly talk with your partner about the tensions you are feeling and come to an agreement about how you will manage the dialectic going forward. Through self-disclosure and feedback, you and your partner may be able to negotiate a new balance that satisfies both of you. At times, however, partners will be unable to resolve the tensions. When this happens, one or both of you will probably experience dissatisfaction and the relationship may deteriorate or end.

temporal selection
the strategy of choosing one desire and ignoring its opposite for a while

topical segmentation
the strategy of choosing certain topics with which to satisfy one dialectical tension and other topics for its opposite

neutralization
the strategy of compromising between the desires of the two partners

reframing
the strategy of changing one's perception about the level of tension

Quick Quiz

T F 1. Sometimes a relationship may deteriorate simply because the partners are not vigilant in doing what is necessary to maintain the relationship at its current level.

T F 2. Decreased communication is an initial sign of relationship decline.

T F 3. Autonomy is the desire to link your actions and decisions with your partner.

T F 4. Originality, freshness, and uniqueness in your own or your partner's behavior or in the relationship is referred to as novelty.

T F 5. Topical segmentation is the strategy of compromising between the desires of one person and the desires of the other.

6. A relationship with people whom you share a high degree of commitment, trust, interdependence, and disclosure is called
   a. platonic.
   b. intimate.
   c. romantic.
   d. impersonal.
   e. professional.

7. An intimate relationship in which the partners are not sexually attracted to each other or do not act on an attraction they feel is called
   a. platonic.
   b. intimate.
   c. romantic.
   d. impersonal.
   e. professional.

8. The Johari window is a tool for examining the
   a. relationship between disclosure and feedback in a relationship.
   b. level of trust in an intimate relationship.
   c. gender difference in communication styles.
   d. strength of a close friendship.
   e. life cycle of a relationship.

9. When romantic relationships turn into friendships, best friends become casual friends, and marriages continue on friendly or business-like terms because of shared values on child-rearing, this is an example of
   a. relationship maintenance.
   b. relationship connection.
   c. relational dialectics.
   d. relationship transformation.
   e. None of the above is correct.

10. Which of the following is a strategy in managing dialectical tensions in relationships?
   a. choosing one desire and ignoring the other for the time being
   b. compromising between the desires of one person and the desires of the other person
   c. changing your perception about the level of tension in the relationship
   d. choosing certain topics to satisfy one desire and other topics to satisfy the opposite desire
   e. All of the above are strategies in managing tensions in relationships.

Answers: 1. T, 2. T, 3. F, 4. T, 5. F, 6. B, 7. A, 8. A, 9. D, 10. E

USE THE TOOLS.

• Rip out the Review Cards in the back of your book to study.

Or Visit CourseMate to:

• Read, search, highlight, and take notes in the interactive eBook
• Review Flashcards (Print or Online) to master key terms
• Test yourself with Auto-Graded Quizzes
• Bring concepts to life with Games, Videos,
  and Animations!

Go to CourseMate for COMM to begin using these tools.
Access at **www.cengagebrain.com**

Complete the Speak Up
survey in CourseMate at
www.cengagebrain.com

f **Follow us at**
www.facebook.com/4ltrpress

© iStockphoto.com/A-Digit | © Cengage Learning

Interpersonal
Communication

Learning Outcomes

8-1 Discuss how to provide emotional support

8-2 Examine the tension between openness and privacy

8-3 Understand how to express desires and expectations

8-4 Discuss conflict management styles

In the last chapter, you learned about how we begin, maintain, and end relationships and the dialectical tensions that pull partners between competing desires. As you and your partner interact, you create the **communication climate**—the overall emotional tone of your relationship—through the messages you exchange (Cissna & Seiberg, 1995). A **positive communication climate** is one where partners feel valued and supported. We use **confirming communication messages** to convey that we care about our partner (Dailey, 2006). We can say "you're important to me" and "you matter to me" verbally through skillfully wording our messages. At the same time, we need to avoid **disconfirming communication messages**, which signal a lack of regard for our partner. In this chapter, we look at how to create confirming messages when we want to (1) respond to a partner who is experiencing emotional distress, (2) share or keep private some of our personal information, (3) express a personal desire or expectation, and (4) resolve a conflict.

What do you think?
Conflict can help people grow closer together.

1	2	3	4	5	6	7	8	9	10
STRONGLY DISAGREE									STRONGLY AGREE

communication climate
the overall emotional tone of your relationship

positive communication climate
communication climate in which partners feel valued and supported

confirming communication messages
messages that convey that we care about our partner

disconfirming communication messages
messages that signal a lack of regard for our partner

8-1 Providing Emotional Support

Can you recall a time when you were emotionally distraught? Perhaps someone close to you died unexpectedly, or the person you thought you would spend the rest of your life with dumped you, or someone you trusted betrayed you, or you were treated unjustly by someone with power over you. If so, you probably appreciated the emotional support you received from some friends and family members and might have been perplexed or even angered by inappropriate statements made by others. Most likely, you have also helped those close to you during times of distress. **Comforting** is helping others feel better about themselves, their behavior, or their situation by creating a safe space to express feelings and to work out a plan for the future. Comforting can also help those who provide emotional support by improving their self-esteem and their relationship with the person being comforted (Burleson, 2003). Comforting usually occurs over several turns in a conversation or over several conversations that may span weeks, months, or even years.

Many people believe that women expect, need, and provide more emotional support than men. However, a growing body of research suggests that both men and women value emotional support from their partners in a variety of relationships, including same-sex friendships, opposite-sex friendships, romantic relationships, and sibling relationships (Burleson, 2003). Providing emotional

support is also generally valued across cultural and co-cultural groups (Burleson, 2003).

8-1a Comforting Guidelines

The following guidelines can help you successfully provide emotional support.

1. Clarify supportive intentions. When people are experiencing emotional turmoil, they may have trouble trusting the motives of those who want to help. You can clarify your supportive intentions by openly stating that your goal is to help. Notice how David does this:

> **David** (noticing Paul sitting in his cubicle with his head in his lap and his hands over his head): Paul, is everything OK?
>
> **Paul** (sitting up and looking miserable and then defiant): Like you should care. Yeah, everything is fine.
>
> **David:** Paul, I do care. You've been working for me for five years. You're one of our best technicians. So if something is going on, I'd like to help, even if all I can do is listen. So what's up?

2. Buffer face threats with politeness. Face is the perception we want others to have of our worth (Ting-Toomey & Chung, 2005). **Positive face needs** are the desires we have to be appreciated, liked, and honored. **Negative face needs** are the desires we have to be free from imposition and intrusion. The very act of providing comfort can threaten your partner's face needs. For example, your partner might worry that you will respect, like, or value him or her less because of the situation. Or your partner might worry that you will think he or she cannot handle the situation independently. So effective comforting messages must be phrased in ways that address the other person's positive and negative face needs. **Buffering messages** cushion the effect by using both positive and negative politeness skills. When David says to Paul, "You're one of our best technicians," he attends to Paul's positive face need to be valued. When David says that all he can do is listen, he attends to Paul's negative face need for independence.

© Sheff/Shutterstock.com

3. Encourage understanding through other-centered messages. Other-centered messages encourage those feeling emotional distress to talk about what happened and how they feel about it. Other-centered messages can be questions that encourage others to elaborate or may simply be vocalized encouragement (e.g., um, uh-huh, wow, I see). Other-centered messages are the most highly valued type of comforting message among most cultural and co-cultural groups (Burleson, 2003).

4. Reframe the situation. When people are emotionally distressed, we might **reframe the situation** by offering ideas, observations, information, or explanations that help them understand the situation in a different light. For example, imagine that Travis returns from class and tells his roommate, Abe, "Well, I'm flunking calculus. It doesn't matter how much I study, I just can't get it. I might as well just drop out of school before I flunk out completely. I can ask for a full-time schedule at work and not torture myself with school anymore." To reframe the situation, Abe might remind Travis that he has been putting in many hours of overtime at work and ask Travis if he thinks the heavy work schedule might be cutting into his study time. Or he might suggest that Travis seek help at the tutoring center, a resource many of their mutual friends found helpful. In each case, Abe has provided new observations and information that can help Travis reframe the situation from the seemingly impossible to the manageable.

5. Give advice. We can also comfort by **giving advice**—presenting relevant suggestions for resolving a problem or situation. You should not give advice, however, until your supportive intentions have been understood, you have attended to your partner's face needs, and you have sustained an other-centered conversation for some time. Even then, always ask permission before offering advice and always acknowledge that your advice is only one suggestion. Present the potential risks or costs associated with your advice and affirm that it's OK if your partner chooses not to follow it.

8-2 Managing Privacy and Disclosure

As you recall from chapter 7, people in relationships experience dialectical tensions, one of which is the tension between openness and closedness. When we want more openness, we use disclosure skills to share information and feelings. When we want more closedness, we manage privacy to limit what others know about us.

Disclosure is revealing confidential or secret information about yourself (self-disclosure) and about others (other-disclosure) (Petronio, 2002). Suppose Juanita tells Kirsten that she wet the bed until she was 12 years old (self-disclosure) but had never told anyone because she had always been afraid of being teased. If Kirsten later tells a friend that Juanita was once a bed wetter, Kirsten is also disclosing, but she is disclosing Juanita's private information, not her own (other-disclosure).

Privacy management is maintaining confidential or secret information to enhance autonomy or minimize vulnerability (Margulis, 1977). The concept of privacy assumes that people own their personal information and have the right to control it by determining whether or not to communicate it (Petronio, 2002). Like Juanita, you can choose whether to reveal or conceal personal information to your partner. Then either of you can choose to reveal that sensitive information to others or maintain it within the privacy of your relationship.

If your partner has your permission to share some of your personal information, then disclosing it to others is unlikely to affect your relationship. However, if you have not given your partner permission to disclose certain information and you expect it to remain between the two of you, then disclosure is likely to damage your relationship. So when Juanita learns that Kirsten has told a mutual friend that Juanita is a former bed wetter, she may feel embarrassed, hurt, and betrayed if she believes Kirsten has breached her confidentiality. On the other hand, if Juanita doesn't care that others know, she may be unaffected.

Controlling who has access to your personal information is becoming more complicated with our ever-increasing use of technology. For example, search engines such as Google routinely track our searches. A bug in Apple software recently allowed people to access photos stored on others' personal cell phones (Bilton, 2012). And whenever we post

other-centered messages
comforting messages that encourage relational partners to talk about and elaborate on what happened and how they feel about it

reframing the situation
offering ideas, observations, information, or alternative explanations that might help a relational partner understand a situation in a different light

giving advice
presenting relevant suggestions that a person can use to resolve a situation

disclosure
revealing confidential or secret information about others as well as yourself

privacy management
maintaining confidential or secret information to enhance autonomy or minimize vulnerability

collaborating have not been successful. For example, if Heather and Zachary need to meet outside of class to complete a class project but both have busy schedules, they may compromise to meet at a time that isn't ideal for either of them but which they can both live with.

8-4e Collaborating (Win–Win)

Collaborating occurs when people work through the problem together to discover a mutually acceptable solution. It is assertive and cooperative and is typically characterized as a win–win approach. Collaborating may be appropriate when the issue is too important for a compromise, when the relationship is important, and when we want to come up with a creative solution to a problem. We collaborate by discussing the issues, describing feelings, and identifying the characteristics of a solution that will satisfy everyone. For example, Fadi really wants to vacation alone with Aliana, but Aliana wants to invite their friends, Greg and Shelly. Aliana may explain how she thinks that vacationing with friends

Collaboration
allows everyone to ...

... work together
to make
a whole.

would lower the cost of the trip. Fadi may describe his desire to have "alone time" with Aliana. As they discuss their vacation goals, they arrive at a plan that meets both of their needs. For example, they may decide to vacation alone, but camp rather than stay in hotels to lower their expenses. Or they may share a condo with their friends, but schedule alone time each day.

8-4f Collaboration Guidelines

When you decide that collaboration is the best strategy for resolving a conflict, several guidelines can help assist you:

- **Identify and own the problem.** "Hi, I'm trying to study and I need your help."

- **Describe the problem in terms of behavior, consequences, and feelings.** "When I hear your music, I listen to it instead of studying, and then I get frustrated and behind schedule."

- **Refrain from blaming or accusing.** "I know you aren't trying to ruin my study time and are just enjoying your music."

- **Find common ground.** "I would guess that you have had times when you became distracted from something you needed to do, so I'm hoping that you can help me out by lowering the volume a bit."

- **Mentally rehearse so that you can state your request briefly.**

It is more difficult to collaborate when you have to respond to a conflict that someone initiates in a confrontational manner. But you can shape the conversation toward collaboration by following these guidelines:

- **Disengage.** Mentally "put up your shield" and avoid a defensive response by emotionally disengaging. Remember, your partner has a problem and you want to help.

- **Respond with genuine concern.** Sometimes you need to allow your partner to vent before the partner will be ready to problem solve: "I can see that you're angry. Tell me about it."

- **Paraphrase and ask questions.** "Is it the volume of my music or the type of music that is making it difficult for you to study?"

- **Seek common ground.** "I can understand that you would be upset about losing precious study time."

- **Ask for alternative solutions.** "Can you give me a couple of ideas about how we could resolve this so your study is more effective?"

Quick Quiz

T F 1. Negative face needs are the desires to be free from imposition and intrusion.

T F 2. The use of technology to develop and maintain relationships is impacting people's decisions about what to disclose and what to keep private.

T F 3. In a crowded line, your friend accidentally bumps into a man's wife. The man proceeds to yell at your friend for being inconsiderate. The man has an assertive communication style.

T F 4. When sharing personal feelings, it is most appropriate to begin with the "trigger" and follow with a "feeling."

T F 5. Flattery is described as disclosing a specific positive behavior or accomplishment of another person and the effect that behavior has on others.

6. _____ means helping people feel better about themselves, their behavior, or their situation by creating a safe conversational space where they can express their feelings and work out a plan for the future.
   a. Encouraging
   b. Buffering
   c. Advising
   d. Welcoming
   e. Comforting

7. Which of the following is considered a direct communication strategy that you can use when being pressed to disclose something that you are not comfortable sharing?
   a. giving a vague answer
   b. changing the subject
   c. masking your feelings
   d. telling a white lie
   e. setting a boundary

8. A straight-faced poker player whose expression is impossible to decipher has become a master of
   a. self-disclosure.
   b. rapport-talk.
   c. report-talk.
   d. masking feelings.
   e. managing privacy.

9. A(n) _____ person has the skill to stand up for himself or herself in interpersonally effective ways.
   a. passive
   b. assertive
   c. aggressive
   d. accommodating
   e. passive-aggressive

10. When people submit to others' demands even when it is inconvenient, against their best interests, or violates their rights, it is considered
    a. passive behavior.
    b. passive-aggressive behavior.
    c. assertive behavior.
    d. aggressive behavior.
    e assertive-aggressive behavior.

Answers: 1. T, 2. T, 3. F, 4. T, 5. F, 6. E, 7. E, 8. D, 9. B, 10. A

Communicating in Groups

Learning Outcomes

9-1 Identify different types of groups

9-2 Analyze the characteristics of healthy groups

9-3 Understand how groups develop

9-4 Describe the nature of conflict in groups

You probably belong to many formal and informal groups. Each group has different purposes and expects different things of you. But one thing all groups have in common is that their effectiveness depends on communication. In fact, year after year, surveys conducted by the National Association of Colleges and Employers report "the ability to work well in groups" is one of the top ten skills sought in college graduates. Although students are often asked to do group projects, very few graduate from college with any formal training in how to communicate effectively in groups.

In this chapter and the one that follows, we discuss how groups function and how to communicate most effectively within them. We begin by defining the nature and types of different groups, as well as some of the communication challenges you are likely to face when interacting in each of them. Then we describe key characteristics of healthy groups and the stages of development groups often follow over the course of their existence. We end this chapter with a discussion about conflict in groups and provide guidelines for managing conflict effectively.

9-1 The Nature and Types of Groups

Take a moment to think about the groups of people you interact with consistently. Examples may range from student clubs to friendship groups to family groups to study groups to online networking groups. What makes each of these a group rather than a mere assembly of people? A **group** is

group
a collection of about three to 20 people who interact and attempt to influence each other to accomplish a common purpose

a collection of about three to 20 people who feel a sense of belonging and attempt to influence each other to accomplish a common purpose. **Group communication**, which consists of all the verbal and nonverbal messages shared among members, is what makes participating in groups a positive or negative experience. Let's look at some of the most common group types and the role communication plays in them.

9-1a Families

A **family** is "a group of intimates who through their communication generates a sense of home and group identity, complete with strong ties of loyalty and emotion, and experiences a history and a future" (Galvin, Byland, & Brommel, 2007). Families can be nuclear (consisting of two parents who live together with their biological or adopted children), single parent (consisting of one adult living with his or her children), extended (consisting of a parent or parents and children living with grandparents, cousins, aunts and uncles, or other relatives), blended (consisting of committed or married adults living with the children of their previous

marriages and relationships as well as the children of their union), as well as unrelated by either blood or marriage.

Research suggests that families typically function using one of four family communication patterns (Koerner & Fitzpatrick, 2002). In *protective families*, issues are not discussed and are decided solely by the family authority figure. In the movie *The Sound of Music,* prior to Maria's arrival, the Von Trapp family exemplified this family dynamic. In *consensual families*, all members engage in conversation about an issue but a family authority figure still makes the final decision. Many television sitcoms from the 1950s, 60s, and 70s, such as *Father Knows Best, Leave It to Beaver*, and *The Brady Bunch*, portray families with a benevolent and self-sacrificing father filling this role. In *pluralistic families*, all members engage in conversation about an issue and everyone participates in the decision making. These families may have formal family meetings to decide important family issues. The popular 1980s television sitcom *Full House,* in which three men raised children together, operated as a pluralistic family. Finally, in *laissez-faire families*, members may converse about an issue, but each member makes his or her own decision and is responsible for its consequences. The cartoon family portrayed on *The Simpsons* tends to function this way.

We initially learn how to communicate in groups based on how our family members communicated with each other while we were growing up. Healthy family communication builds self-concept and self-esteem through messages of (1) praise (e.g., "awesome job on that painting"), (2) acceptance (e.g., "whether you decide to go to college or get a full-time job, just know that we support you"), and (3) love (e.g., "I love you no matter what"). Unfortunately, however, not all families engage in healthy communication.

9-1b Social Friendship Groups

A **social friendship group** is composed of people who genuinely care about each other's welfare and enjoy spending time together. Their interactions are characterized by "interpersonal ties and positive,

©jannoon028/Shutterstock.com

amiable preexisting relationships among members" (Thompson, 2003, p. 239). Most of us belong to more than one social friendship group. You may have had a group of friends you were close to in high school, a group of buddies you were close to when you served in the military, or a group of friends you play golf or softball with regularly. Sometimes people who work together evolve into a social friendship group when they begin to get together for social activities outside of work. Popular TV programs such as *New Girl, How I Met Your Mother,* and *The League* provide examples of social friendship groups.

Because social friendship groups fill our needs to be accepted and to belong, communication in these groups should (1) encourage quieter members to participate in conversations ("Hey Jules, you haven't had a chance to catch us up on how your Dad is doing"); (2) protect members from playful harassment ("Hey Jenna, back off, you've been picking on Pam all evening"); and (3) provide opportunities for friends to disclose problems and receive support ("Hey, Zach, I heard that your sister was in a bad accident. How's she doing?").

9-1c Support Groups

A **support group** is composed of people who come together to provide encouragement, honest feedback, and a safe environment for expressing deeply personal feelings about a problem common to the members. Support groups include addiction recovery groups such as AA (Alcoholics Anonymous), grief counseling support groups, survivor or caregiver support groups, and abuse recovery groups such as the ASCA (Adult Survivors of Child Abuse). Support groups can meet face-to-face as well as online.

Support groups must create an environment in which members feel safe to disclose highly personal information. So members need to make sure that their messages follow guidelines for comforting (see chapter 8), which include clarifying supportive intentions, buffering face threats, using other-centered language, framing, and selectively offering advice.

9-1d Interest Groups

An **interest group** is composed of individuals who come together because they share a common interest, hobby, or activity. These groups may be formal with defined goals and tasks (such as a 4-H club or community theater troupe) or they may be informal (like a

Social Support Groups Thrive Online

Online outlets for co-cultural groups can be a good thing (Pascoe, 2008). One example is the vast online community of gay, lesbian, bisexual, and transgendered (GLBT) teenagers. These teens, who can have a difficult time finding friends or dates in their physical communities, can easily find other GLBT teenagers online on sites like the It Gets Better project (http://www.itgetsbetter.org). The site was originally created by syndicated columnist and author Dan Savage in response to a rash of bullying-related suicides among GLBT youth. It Gets Better provides a place where GLBT youth and adults, along with straight allies, can come together to share their stories without judgment and find support from other members, showing that the Internet can be a place where healthy groups can be created.

neighborhood book or gardening club). They may be part of a larger organization like La Raza, the Urban League, or the Houston Area Apple Users Group. Some interest groups are externally focused on a common political or social issue and adopt an agenda to achieve change. MADD (Mothers Against Drunk Driving) is an example. Other interest groups are internally focused on increasing members' skills or knowledge. Toastmasters, for instance, helps its members improve their public speaking skills. Some interest groups meet online. Meetup.com is an Internet site that helps people find others who share their interests.

Because interest group members share some passion, all members ought to have an opportunity to communicate their expertise by (1) encouraging members to share success stories ("I'm really glad that Brian was able to get Ace Hardware to donate all the bathroom fixtures for our project. Brian, can you tell us what you said and did?") and (2) allowing all members to highlight what they know without demeaning the knowledge or opinions of others ("I really liked hearing Brian's story and I'd like to know how other people approach getting donations.").

support group
a group consisting of people who come together to provide encouragement, honest feedback, and a safe environment for expressing deeply personal feelings about a problem common to the members

interest group
a group consisting of individuals who come together because they share a common concern, hobby, or activity

9-1e Service Groups

A **service group** is composed of individuals who come together to perform hands-on charitable works or to raise money to help organizations that perform such work. Service groups may be local affiliates of larger secular or religious organizations like Lions Club International, the Red Cross, the Salvation Army, and Habitat for Humanity. Other service groups are local and function independently. Examples include small soup kitchens and community beautification groups.

Because service groups are both voluntary and task-oriented, they need to be dedicated to the task as well as sensitive to the emotional needs of members. So communication should (1) be clear about individual tasks, roles, and responsibilities ("Jim, as I recall, you agreed to work on patching the roof"); (2) encourage and praise member accomplishments ("I was really impressed with how sensitive you were when you said no to her"); and (3) be polite ("Martina, it would be really helpful if you would stuff envelopes today. Thanks so much!").

9-1f Work Group Teams

A **work group team** is a collection of three or more people formed to work together to solve a problem or accomplish a specific task. Examples of work group teams include class project groups (established to create a joint presentation, paper, or other learning project) and workplace teams (established as needed to perform specific activities in the workplace). Effective work group teams have an appropriate number of members with diverse skills and viewpoints, clearly defined goals, and explicit roles and rules for members (Katzenbach & Smith, 2003).

What is the best size for a work group team? In general, research suggests that the ideal size for most work group teams is five to seven members (Bonito, 2000; Henley & Price, 2002). However, the best size is the smallest number of people capable of effectively achieving the goal (Sundstrom, DeMeuse, & Futrell, 1990). As the size of the group increases, discussion time also increases. Smaller groups can make decisions more quickly than larger ones. If the goals and issues are complex, however, a group with more members is more likely to have the breadth of information, knowledge, and skills needed to make high-quality decisions (Bonito, 2000; Henley & Price, 2002).

More important than the number of people is the right combination of people on the team. Effective work group teams consist of people who offer different but relevant knowledge and skills (Valacich, George, Nonamaker, & Vogel, 1994). A **heterogeneous group** is usually better than a **homogeneous group**. In homogeneous groups, members are likely to know the same things and come at the problem from the same perspective; consequently, they are likely to overlook some important information or take shortcuts in the problem-solving process. In contrast, heterogeneous groups are more likely to have diverse information, perspectives, and values; consequently, they tend to thoroughly discuss issues before reaching a decision. For example, a medical group composed of seven nurses who are all young white females would be considered a homogeneous group; a medical group composed of nurses, doctors, nutritionists, and physical therapists of different ages, races, and sexes would be considered a heterogeneous group. The heterogeneous medical group would probably make a more comprehensive decision about a patient's care than the homogeneous group of nurses.

© Christopher Futcher/iStockphoto.com

↘ CrossFit is an organization for people interested in developing broad, general, and inclusive fitness through high-intensity workouts. These groups meet in smaller gyms called "boxes" all over the world and compete in one large annual competition called the CrossFit Games.

service group
a group consisting of individuals who come together to perform hands-on charitable works or to raise money to help organizations that perform such work

work group team
a collection of three or more people formed to solve a problem

heterogeneous group
a group in which various demographics, levels of knowledge, attitudes, and interests are represented

homogeneous group
a group in which members have a great deal of similarity

Work Group Team Goals

What are the elements of an effective work group team goal? An effective **work group team goal** is a clearly stated objective desired by enough members to motivate the group to work toward achieving it (Johnson & Johnson, 2003). Effective work group team goals meet four important criteria (see box "Effective Work Group Team Goals").

Work group teams should develop explicit member roles and rules (Katz & Koenig, 2001). Because the goals of work group teams are typically quite challenging, all members must understand and perform their specific roles for the group to succeed (LaFasto & Larson, 2001). These roles and rules are always discussed and sometimes even written down in a formal or informal contract.

Most work group team communication focuses on task-related issues and should (1) update other members on the status of individual efforts ("I thought you all should know that I will be about two days late with that feasibility report because the person providing me with the cost data is on vacation"); (2) appropriately credit the contributions of other team members ("Today I am presenting the conclusions, but Len did the initial

© iofoto/iStockphoto.com

research and Mavis did the quantitative analysis that led to them"); (3) keep the discussion focused on the task ("Georgia, let's talk more about your party after the meeting, ok?"); and (4) seek collaboration to resolve conflicts ("Felicia, I'm stuck and I really need your help").

9-1g Virtual Groups

Until recently, group communication occurred almost exclusively in face-to-face settings. A **virtual group** is a group whose members "meet" via technological media from different physical locations. We can interact with our families, social friendship groups, support groups, interest groups, service groups, and work group teams from different physical locations through e-mail, teleconferences, and videoconferences; online social networks such as LinkedIn, Facebook, and Twitter; and other technologies (Timmerman & Scott, 2006). We can also use technology to form groups without ever meeting other members in person.

Because these technologies have changed the communication landscape, and are continuing to do so, research about how communication functions in them is still in its youth. We do know, however, that while effective **virtual group communication** follows the same fundamental principles as effective communication in face-to-face groups it is also unique in several ways. Technology makes virtual group communication possible (1) at the same time and location, (2) at the same time but from different locations, (3) at different times but from the same location, and (4) at different times and from different

Effective Work Group Team Goals

1. **Effective goals are specific.** For example, the crew at a local fast-food restaurant set the specific goal: "During the next quarter, the crew will increase profitability by reducing food costs by 1 percent. They will do so by throwing away less food due to precooking."

2. **Effective goals serve a common purpose.** Achieving one goal must not prevent achieving another. For the fast-food crew, all members must believe that reducing the amount of precooked food on hand will not hinder their current level of service.

3. **Effective goals are challenging.** Achieving them will require hard work and team effort.

4. **Effective goals are shared.** People tend to support things they help create. So group members who participate in setting the goals are likely to exert high effort to achieve them as well.

work group team goal
a future state of affairs desired by enough members to motivate the group to work toward its achievement

virtual group
a group whose members "meet" via technological media from different physical locations

virtual group communication
communication that occurs in virtual groups

locations (Becker-Beck, Wintermantel, & Borg, 2005). Teleconferences and videoconferences are examples of virtual group communication taking place in **real time**, which means at the same time. Communication in videoconferences most closely resembles group communication in face-to-face settings because participants can interact using both verbal and nonverbal messages. By contrast, virtual group communication that occurs on social networking sites, blogs, and Web sites takes place at the same location (on a particular Internet page) but not necessarily at the same time. Virtual group communication that occurs via e-mail typically occurs at different times; a group member can send a message and wait hours or days before getting a reply.

9-1h Mediated Communication and Virtual Groups

Have you ever participated in a threaded online discussion? Perhaps you have done so as part of a course requirement or as part of a work team. Or have you ever held a three-way telephone conversation with your friends to decide where to go on a Friday night? If so, you have been part of a virtual group. There are several types of virtual groups, as illustrated in Figure 9.1.

Virtual groups and virtual group meetings have become popular for a number of reasons. First, members need not be physically present to communicate. Before these technologies, group members had to meet face-to-face to exchange information or make a decision. But today, group members can interact while in different cities, states, and countries. Second, asynchronous virtual groups allow people to participate across time. Busy people often struggle to find a meeting time that works with everyone's schedule. So a group can "meet" and

FIGURE 9.1
Types of Virtual Groups

Type of Group	Description
Computer conferences (threaded discussions)	Asynchronous virtual forums in which comments related to an issue are organized by topic and available for all group members to read and comment upon
Online social networks	Internet sites that focus on building social relationships among people who share interests, activities, and backgrounds
Teleconferences	Multiperson telephone meetings using telephone conferencing technology
Video chats	Synchronous informal meetings using personal computer video capabilities
Videoconferences	Synchronous formal meetings using video conferencing technology provided at various sites

© Cengage Learning

communicate using a threaded discussion instead. Third, virtual meetings can save money. Before these technologies, meeting participants often had to travel to a meeting site, which can be expensive. Because virtual group meetings can be conducted over the phone or Internet, meeting costs can be reduced for both participants and hosts.

These benefits also come with potential costs. For example, research has found that communication problems can impact both task and relationship outcomes (Andres, 2002). Face-to-face groups are often more dedicated to task (Olsen & Teasley, 1996), and the rich communication environment leads to more effective interactions and results than virtual teams. Face-to-face groups are also better at maintenance functions. They are more cohesive (Huang, Wei, Watson, & Tan, 2003), have stronger social ties (Warkentin, Sayeed, & Hightower, 1997), and are more dedicated to other team members (Olsen & Teasley, 1996).

Because the use of virtual groups is becoming increasingly common in both education and industry, improving virtual group communication can increase work quality and member satisfaction. We offer several guidelines for doing so.

© Mash Audio Visuals Pvt. Ltd. Agency/iStockphoto.com

1. Train members to use the technology. First and foremost, all members must be skilled in appropriately using the technology. Provide training if needed. Also, don't assume that someone who has used a particular technology before understands all of its capabilities or how it can be used with the current situation. And just because someone has used a similar program (e.g., Skype) doesn't necessarily mean he or she will be able to comfortably use another (e.g., iChat) without training.

2. Create opportunities for members to become acquainted as the group is forming. Just as members of face-to-face groups take time to socialize to get to know each other when forming, so must members of virtual groups. For example, many successful virtual groups encourage members to develop and share personal Web pages with pictures, self-descriptions, and places to update what is happening in their lives. To be successful, you may even need to allow more time in virtual groups to form social bonds before turning to task considerations.

3. Use the richest form of technology available. While e-mails and threaded discussions allow people the freedom to do group work at their own convenience, these asynchronous technologies also convey the fewest social cues. So whenever possible, use scheduled synchronous audio or video meetings along with text-based technologies.

4. Develop group ground rules. Functional norms are crucial for effective group communication in both face-to-face and virtual settings. Set ground rules such as how quickly members should respond to messages, turn-taking, and **netiquette** (etiquette rules users follow when communicating over computer networks). These include being courteous and respectful, using emoticons, keeping messages short, refraining from the use of all capital letters, thinking before posting, being patient with new users, obeying copyright laws, and keeping personal information private (Shoemaker-Galloway, 2007).

5. Create opportunities to meet outside the virtual environment. Members of virtual groups can feel closer to one another if they can also have side conversations. One way to accomplish this is to set up an instant messaging system that allows members to contact each other for short "conversations," much like those that can occur when we are physically present in face-to-face settings.

6. Provide clear structure. Virtual groups perform better when there is a clear plan guiding their tasks. So the leader should develop a series of threaded discussions that clearly outline the expected outcomes and process.

7. Create regular opportunities to evaluate the technology and its use. Regularly scheduled surveys of virtual group members can identify emerging problems members are experiencing in order to correct them before they undermine the group's work.

Now that we have illustrated some of the different types of groups you are likely to belong to and the role communication plays in them, let's turn to a discussion of the similarities among healthy groups regardless of type.

netiquette
etiquette rules users follow when communicating over computer networks

healthy group
a group formed around a constructive purpose and characterized by ethical goals, interdependence, cohesiveness, productive norms, accountability, and synergy

interdependent group
a group in which members rely on each other's skills and knowledge to accomplish the group goals

9-2 Characteristics of Healthy Groups

Healthy groups are formed around a constructive purpose and are characterized by ethical goals, interdependence, cohesiveness, productive norms, accountability, and synergy.

9-2a Healthy Groups Have Ethical Goals

Sometimes the actual goal of a group is unethical; other times, fulfilling the goal would require some or all group members to behave in unethical ways. For example, criminal gangs can be highly effective but unethical groups. They may make lots of money, but at the expense of society at large and often by risking the welfare of members. By contrast, healthy groups have goals that benefit both members and the larger society. Fulfilling these goals may require sacrifice and hard work, but accomplishing them does not depend on illegal or unethical behavior.

9-2b Healthy Groups Are Interdependent

In **interdependent groups**, members rely on each other's skills and knowledge to accomplish the ultimate group goal(s). One concrete way to understand interdependence is to observe a musical group—a symphony orchestra, for instance. One reason the music we hear is so beautiful is not only because the various instruments sound different but because the parts in the musical score for each instrument are well-balanced with each other. If any of the musicians did not perform their part well, the beautiful sound would be compromised. Likewise, in any group, if one person tries to do all the work, or if anyone performs poorly, or if everyone does the same task while others are left unattended, then that group is not interdependent will consequently be ineffective.

9-2c Healthy Groups Are Cohesive

Cohesiveness is the force that brings group members closer together (Eisenberg, 2007). In a highly cohesive group, members genuinely respect each other and work cooperatively to reach the group's goals (Evans & Dion, 1991). Because cohesiveness is such an important characteristic of healthy groups, many newly formed groups often engage in **team-building activities** designed to build rapport and develop trust among members (Midura & Glover, 2005). Research suggests that five factors help foster cohesiveness in groups (Balgopal, Ephross, & Vassil, 1986; Widmer & Williams, 1991; Wilson, 2005). First, members are attracted to its purpose. Daniel, for example, joined the local Lions Club because he was attracted to its community service mission. Second, groups are generally more cohesive when membership is voluntary. If Daniel had joined the Lions Club because he felt obligated to do so, cohesiveness would have suffered. Third, members feel safe expressing themselves even when they disagree with others. Fourth, members support, encourage, and provide positive feedback to each other. Finally, members perceive the group to be achieving its goals and celebrate their accomplishments. For example, when the local chapter of the Lions Club surpassed its previous fundraising record for the

Trigger Warning: Tumblr and "Pro-Ana" Diarists

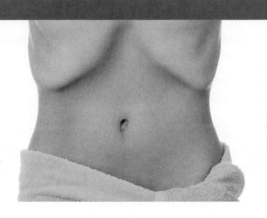
© Piotr Marcinski/iStockphoto.com

A thriving "pro-ana" (promoting anorexia nervosa) scene exists on some popular social media sites such as Tumblr, driven in large part by the diary format that allows users to track weight loss, post diet tips, and share images and quotes that provide "thinspiration" for themselves and others striving to achieve their "ultimate goal weight" (Gregoire, 2012). Although initially these sites may seem to provide a positive environment, posts often encourage people to develop and continue dangerous behaviors.

Many young women stumble on these sites while searching for "fitspo" or fit-inspiration images. What they see on "thinspo" pages may turn some away, but others flock to the so-called supportive community. They Skype, exchange texts, and e-mail to encourage each other not to binge. They've co-opted second-wave feminist terms to describe their "lifestyle choice." According to body image expert Jess Weiner, this desire for connectivity sustains thinspo blogs—but the danger comes from forming a community around hatred and shame of your body (Gregoire, 2012).

Some sites, like Facebook, are working to establish guidelines to report and flag encouragement of disordered-eating and unhealthy lifestyle choices. *Vogue Italia* pulled photos of popular model Karlie Kloss from its Web site when the images began to appear on pro-ana sites. But the television show *Skins* continues to feature the pro-ana poster girl, Cassie, whose character is described as a starry-eyed, anorexic, pill-popping teen (Gregoire, 2012).

While awareness of eating disorders is on the rise, and much media is paying attention to how women and men are portrayed, there is still an easily accessible "support" community for disorders that was not there before the Internet. It is a community founded on unhealthy group communication that can trigger bad habits and relapses in participants.

© Luke Daniek/iStockphoto.com

↘ Some companies build group cohesion through adventure team-building activities, such as high-ropes courses, hiking, or white-water rafting.

annual Journey for Sight 5K Community Run, the group celebrated the accomplishment with a picnic in the park.

9-2d Healthy Groups Develop and Abide by Productive Norms

Norms are expectations about the way group members are to behave. Healthy groups develop norms that help them achieve their goals (Shimanoff, 1992) and foster cohesiveness (Shaw, 1981). Norms can be developed through formal discussions or informal group processes (Johnson & Johnson, 2003). Some groups choose to formulate explicit **ground rules**, prescribed behaviors designed to help the group meet its goals and conduct its conversations. These may include sticking to the

agenda, refraining from interrupting others, making brief comments rather than lengthy monologues, expecting everyone to participate, focusing on issues rather than personalities, and sharing decision making.

In most groups, however, norms evolve informally. When we join a new group, we act in ways that were considered appropriate in the groups we participated in previously. When members of our new group respond positively to our actions, an informal norm is established. For example, suppose Daniel and two others show up late for a Lions Club meeting. If the latecomers are greeted with disapproving glares, then Daniel and the others will learn that this group has an on-time norm. A group may never actually discuss informal norms, but members understand what they are, follow them, and educate new members about them.

9-2e Healthy Groups Are Accountable

Accountability means all group members are held responsible for adhering to the group norms and working toward the group's goal. This means a group will penalize a member who violates a group norm. The severity of the penalty depends on the importance of the norm, the extent of the violation, and the status of the person who violated it. Violating a norm that is central to a group's performance or cohesiveness will generally receive a harsher penalty than violating a norm that is less central. In addition, violations by newcomers to the group are generally punished less severely than violations by veteran group members. As a new Lions Club member, for example, Daniel's "penalty" for arriving late was merely a stern look from the others. Group members who have achieved higher status in the group also tend to receive more lenient penalties—or even escape them altogether.

Being accountable can also mean changing counterproductive norms. For example, suppose a few folks spend more time socializing than seriously discussing community service issues at the Lions Club meetings. If the group does not effectively control this behavior, then it could become a counterproductive group norm. As a result, work toward the group's goals could be delayed, set aside, or perhaps even forgotten. If counterproductive behavior

norms
expectations for the way group members are to behave while in the group

ground rules
prescribed behaviors designed to help a group meet its goals and conduct its conversations

accountability
group members being held responsible for adhering to the group norms and working toward the group's goal

synergy
the multiplying force of a group working together that results in a combined effort greater than any of the parts

forming
the initial stage of group development characterized by orientation, testing, and dependence

storming
the stage of group development characterized by conflict and power plays as members seek to have their ideas accepted and to find their place within the group's power structure

continues for several meetings and becomes a norm, it will be very difficult (though not impossible) to change.

What can a group member do to try to change a norm? You can help your group change a counterproductive norm by (1) observing the norm and its outcome, (2) describing the results of the norm to the group, and (3) soliciting opinions of other group members (Renz & Greg, 2000). For instance, Daniel observed that every Lions Club meeting began 15–20 minutes late and that this was making it necessary to schedule additional meetings. When members express their frustration about holding extra meetings, he could bring up his observations and the consequences and ask the group for their reaction.

9-2f Healthy Groups Are Synergetic

The old saying "two heads are better than one" captures an important characteristic of healthy groups. **Synergy** is the multiplying force of a group of individuals working together that results in a combined effort greater than any of the parts (Henman, 2003). For instance, the sports record books are filled with "no-name teams" that have won major championships over opponents with more talented players. A healthy group can develop a collective intelligence and a dynamic energy that translate into an outcome that exceeds what even a highly talented individual could produce. When a group has ethical goals and is interdependent, cohesive, and held accountable to productive norms, the group is well on its way toward achieving synergy.

9-3 Stages of Group Development

Just as interpersonal relationships go through identifiable life cycles, so too do groups move through overlapping stages of development. Although numerous models have been proposed to describe these stages, psychologist, Bruce Tuckman's (1965) model has been widely accepted because it identifies central issues facing a group at each stage. In this section, we describe each of these stages and the nature of communication during each one.

9-3a Forming

Forming is the initial stage of group development characterized by orientation, testing, and dependence. Members try to understand precisely what the goal is, what role they will play in reaching the goal, and what the other group members are like. As the goal becomes clearer, members assess how their skills, talents, and abilities might be used in accomplishing it. Group interactions are typically polite and tentative as members become acquainted with each other and find their place in the group. Any real disagreements between people often remain unacknowledged during this stage because members want to be perceived as flexible and likable. During the forming stage, you should communicate a positive attitude; refrain from making abrasive or disagreeable comments; self-disclose appropriately benign information and feelings; and demonstrate open-minded and genuine interest in others (Anderson, 1988).

© Ljupco Smokovski/Shutterstock.com

9-3b Storming

As members figure out the goal and become comfortable with each other, they begin to express their honest opinions and vie for power and position. This signals the beginning of the second stage. The **storming** stage is characterized by conflict and power plays as members seek to have their ideas accepted and to find their place within the group's power structure. Constructive disagreements help the group clarify its goal and the resolution of power plays clarifies the group structure. During the storming stage, the politeness exhibited during forming may be replaced by pointedly aggressive

New members may experience leniency as they learn norms.

© Helder Almeida/Shutterstock.com

groupthink
a deterioration of mental efficiency, reality testing, and moral judgment that results from in-group pressure to conform

norming
the stage of group development during which the group solidifies its rules for behavior, resulting in greater trust and motivation to achieve the group goal

performing
the stage of group development when the skills, knowledge, and abilities of all members are combined to overcome obstacles and meet goals successfully

adjourning
the stage of group development in which members assign meaning to what they have done and determine how to end or maintain interpersonal relations they have developed

transforming
the stage of group development that occurs when a group continues to exist with a new goal

exchanges between some members. While storming, members may also take sides and form coalitions. Although storming occurs in all groups, some groups manage it better than others. When storming is severe, it can threaten the group's survival. However, if a group does not storm, it may experience **groupthink**, a deterioration of mental efficiency, reality testing, and moral judgment that results from in-group pressure to conform (Janis, 1982). To avoid groupthink, members need to communicate in ways that encourage constructive disagreement, avoid name-calling and inflammatory language, and use active listening skills with an emphasis on paraphrasing and honest questioning (Anderson, 1988).

9-3c Norming

Norming is characterized by increased cohesion, collaboration, emerging trust among members, and motivation to achieve the group goal. Having expressed honest opinions, resolved major differences, and sorted out specific roles, members become loyal to each other and to the group goal. During this stage, members come to appreciate their differences, strengthen their relationships, and freely express their ideas and opinions. Members accept the norms established by the group and provide positive and constructive feedback to each other.

9-3d Performing

Performing is characterized by harmony, productivity, problem solving, and shared leadership. During this stage, the group capitalizes on the skills, knowledge, and abilities of all members to work toward achieving its goal; conversations are focused on sharing task-related information and problem solving. Groups cannot achieve their full potential in this stage unless they have successfully resolved storming conflicts and developed productive norms.

9-3e Adjourning and Transforming

Adjourning is characterized by celebrating goal accomplishment and disengagement. The group usually engages in some type of formal or informal celebration during which they recognize their accomplishment and the role each member played. They may rehash parts of their work and try to capture what they learned about group process or their own behavior. Finally, group members will begin to disengage from their relationships with each other. Sometimes the group will formally disband but a few members will continue to interact interpersonally with one another. Other times, rather than adjourn and disband, the group will engage in **transforming** and continue to exist with a new goal. The new goal will inevitably cause the members to revisit the earlier stages of group development, but the cohesion, trust, and norms developed earlier are likely to help the group move quickly and more smoothly through them.

9-4 Conflict in Groups

Just as conflict is inevitable in interpersonal relationships, so is it to be expected in group interactions (Kraus, 1997). As we discussed earlier, groups that experience no conflict are likely to engage in groupthink. Groups that experience conflict but fail to manage it effectively are likely to stall out and never achieve their goal (Nussbaum, Singer, Rosas, Castillo, Flies, Lara, & Sommers, 1999). The key is to manage conflict effectively. Conflict can be directed toward other members (interpersonal conflict) or ideas (issues) or both (Li & Hambrick, 2005; Wilmot & Hocker, 2007). Let's look at three types of conflict that will inevitably occur during group interactions and reveal some communication strategies you can employ to manage the disagreements effectively.

9-4a Pseudo-Conflict

Pseudo-conflict occurs when group members who actually agree about something believe they disagree due to poor communication. Since *pseudo* means *fake,* the perceived conflict is essentially a misperception. To manage or resolve pseudo-conflict, employ the effective listening, perception-checking, and paraphrasing skills we discussed in chapters 6, 7, and 8. This will reveal misinterpretations and result in a moment of revelation that you are actually on the same page after all.

9-4b Issue-Related Group Conflict

Issue-related group conflict occurs when two or more group members' goals, ideas, or opinions about the topic are incompatible. One major

advantage of collaboration is the synergy that occurs as a result of expressing diverse points of view. So issue-related conflict is actually a good thing when handled appropriately. To manage issue-related conflict effectively, begin by clarifying your position and the position of the other group member using perception-checking and paraphrasing skills. Then, as we discussed in chapter 8, express your position using assertive communication supported with facts rather than opinions or feelings. Finally, make the conflict a group discussion by asking others for input; if possible, postpone making a final decision until later. This will provide time to conduct additional research to make an informed decision as well as for tensions among members to subside.

9-4c Personality-Related Group Conflict

Personality-related group conflict occurs when two or more group members become defensive because they feel like they are being attacked. Typically, personality-related conflicts are rooted in a power struggle (Sell, Lovaglia, Mannix, Samuelson, & Wilson, 2004).

Personality-related conflicts sometimes emerge from poorly managed issue-related conflict. For example, Jack thought the group should do something fun to celebrate the end of finals. Jill thought they should do a service project to give something back to the community before everyone headed home for the summer. What began as an issue-related conflict turned sour as Jill exclaimed, "Jack, all you ever think about is yourself. You are so cold-blooded and self-centered!" and Jack retorted with, "You are such a square, Jill. You don't even know HOW to have fun. That's why you end up sitting alone in your room so much!" Factions emerged and, ultimately, some group members sided with Jill and others with Jack. The group ended up doing nothing to mark the successful completion of the semester. Had the group handled the issue-related conflict effectively, they could probably have done something both fun *and* useful. Instead, they did neither and departed feeling frustrated and dissatisfied.

To manage personality-related conflict effectively, try to turn the conflict

Penalties for breaking norms keep the group functioning well.

© Ljupco Smokovski/Shutterstock.com

into an issue-related problem to be solved rather than a conflict someone must win. Develop rules that allow for differences of opinion. Be descriptive rather than evaluative. Use "I" language and perception-checking. Finally, if the conflict isn't central to the group's goal, agree to disagree and move on.

9-4d Culture and Conflict

As we discussed in chapter 3, as well as throughout this book, people who belong to different cultural and co-cultural groups tend to abide by unique communication norms. When managing conflict in groups, keep in mind that cultural differences may exist. For instance, people who identify with individualistic cultural norms tend to use direct verbal methods to manage conflict, whereas those who identify with collectivist norms tend to use indirect nonverbal methods (Ting-Toomey & Oetzel, 2003). Knowing that cultural differences may exist can help you select communication strategies both for managing group conflict effectively and for interpreting the messages of others accurately.

9-4e Virtual Groups and Conflict

Managing conflict effectively in virtual groups poses an additional set of challenges because it can be more difficult to catch the subtle meanings of group members' messages. This is due, in part, to the fact that most technology channels reduce our ability to send and receive nonverbal messages, particularly emotional and relational cues. Although most of us use emoticons and acronyms to represent missing nonverbal cues, a smiley face can be offered sincerely or sarcastically and it can be difficult for the receiver to perceive the difference. Unfortunately, conflict goes unresolved more often in virtual groups than in face-to-face groups because in most virtual settings we cannot see the nonverbal reactions of frustration that are visible when interacting in person (Bordia, DiFonzo, & Chang, 1999). However, when communication is effective, the bonds among virtual group members can be even stronger than those in face-to-face groups (Jiang, Bazarova, & Hancock, 2011; Wang, Walther, & Hancock, 2009).

To manage potential conflict effectively in virtual groups, then, work to overcome the limitations of virtual communication by making a conscious effort to communicate both what you *think* and how you *feel* about a topic. You can do so most clearly in your verbal messages, although emoticons and acronyms can also help when used deliberately to aid communication.

© Rommel Canlas/Shutterstock.com

Quick Quiz

T F 1. In the norming stage, group members may take sides and form coalitions.

T F 2. The use of paraphrasing and honest questioning helps a group avoid groupthink.

T F 3. A nuclear family consists of two parents who live together with their biological or adoptive children.

T F 4. Studies show that group meetings must be face-to-face to be effective.

T F 5. Habitat for Humanity is an example of an interest group.

6. A _____ group is one in which various demographics, levels of knowledge, attitudes, and interests are represented.

a. homogeneous
b. heterogeneous
c. cohesive
d. problem-solving
e. synergistic

7. All of the following are factors leading to cohesiveness in groups except

a. attractiveness of the group's purpose.
b. commitment to specific ground rules.
c. voluntary membership.
d. feeling free to share opinions.
e. celebration of accomplishments.

8. The stage of group development during which the group clarifies its goals and determines the roles each member will have in the group power structure is called

a. forming.
b. storming.
c. norming.
d. performing.
e. adjourning.

9. Which is the correct sequence in the stages of group development model?

a. forming, norming, storming, performing, adjourning, transforming
b. storming, transforming, forming, norming, performing, adjourning
c. forming, performing, transforming, norming, storming, adjourning
d. norming, transforming, forming, storming, performing, adjourning
e. None of these is correct.

10. In _____ families, members may converse about an issue, but each member makes his or her own decision and is responsible for its consequences.

a. laissez-faire
b. consensual
c. protective
d. pluralistic
e. progressive

Answers: 1. F, 2. T, 3. T, 4. F, 5. F, 6. B, 7. B, 8. B, 9. E, 10. A

Group Leadership and Problem Solving

Learning Outcomes

10-1 Understand how leadership functions in teams

10-2 Describe how to run effective meetings

10-3 List the six steps of systematic problem solving

10-4 Know the various methods for communicating group solutions

10-5 Evaluate group effectiveness using provided guidelines

> ### *What do you think?*
> When I work in a group, I like to be a follower, not a leader.
>
> **1 2 3 4 5 6 7 8 9 10**
> STRONGLY DISAGREE   STRONGLY AGREE

When group meetings are ineffective, it is easy to point the finger at the leader. But the responsibility for any "waste of time" lies not with one person; instead, it is part of the complex nature of making decisions in groups. Although working in groups can have its disadvantages, it is the preferred approach in business and industry today (Katzenbach & Smith, 2003; O'Hair, O'Rourke, & O'Hair, 2001; Snyder, 2004; Teams that succeed, 2004). Business leaders realize that when groups work effectively to solve problems, they generate greater breadth and depth of ideas, promote positive group morale, and increase productivity. You can expect to work in groups many times throughout your professional life (Tullar & Kaiser, 2000). You will also work to make decisions and solve problems in community groups, in service groups, and even in your family. This chapter focuses on effective leadership and problem solving in groups. We begin by discussing what effective group leadership means and the responsibilities of every group member in achieving it. Then we illustrate how shared leadership and effective communication plays out before, during, and after group meetings. From there we turn our attention specifically to problem solving and take you through a systematic problem-solving process. Finally, we propose methods for communicating your results with others and evaluating group effectiveness.

10-1 Effective Leadership

Leadership is a process "whereby an individual influences a group of individuals to achieve a common goal" (Northouse, 2007, p. 3). Traditionally, leadership leads

> **leadership**
> a process whereby an individual influences a group of individuals to achieve a common goal

formal leader
a person designated or elected to facilitate the group process

informal emergent leaders
members who help lead the group to achieve different leadership functions

shared leadership functions
the sets of roles that group members perform to facilitate the work of the group and help maintain harmonious relationships between members

role
a specific communication behavior that group members perform

task leadership roles
sets of behaviors that help a group acquire, process, or apply information that contributes directly to completing a task or goal

maintenance leadership roles
sets of behaviors that help a group develop and maintain cohesion, commitment, and positive working relationships

us to think of a person who is in charge (Gardner, 2011). However, in the modern usage, leadership is a set of communication functions performed by any group member at various times based on each one's unique strengths and expertise (Fairhurst, 2001; Frey & Sunwulf, 2005). So, although a group may have a **formal leader**, a person designated or elected to oversee the group process, a series of **informal emergent leaders**, members who help lead the group to achieve different leadership functions, make for effective leadership in groups.

Shared leadership functions are the sets of roles you and other members perform to facilitate the work of the group and help maintain harmonious relationships among members. A **role** is a specific communication behavior that group members perform to address the needs of the group at a given point in time. When these roles are performed effectively, the group functions smoothly. The three sets of shared leadership functions can be categorized as task, maintenance, and procedural roles.

10-1a Task Roles

Task leadership roles help the group acquire, process, or apply information that contributes directly to completing a task or goal.

- **Givers:** Information or opinion givers provide content for the discussion. People who perform this role are well informed on the content of the task and share what they know with the group. Your ability to assume this role depends on your command of high-quality information that the group needs to complete its task. "Well, the articles I read seem to agree that . . ." and "Based on how my sorority raised money for the Ronald McDonald House, we could . . ." are statements typical of information and opinion givers.

- **Seekers:** Information or opinion seekers probe others for their ideas and opinions during group meetings. Typical comments by information and opinion seekers include "Before going further, what information do we have about how raising fees is likely to affect membership?" or "How do other members of the group feel about this idea?"

- **Analyzers:** Information or opinion analyzers help the group scrutinize the content and the reasoning of discussions. They may question what is being said and help members understand the hidden assumptions in their statements. Information or opinion analyzers make statements such as "Enrique, you seem to be generalizing from only one instance. Can you give us some others?"

10-1b Maintenance Roles

Maintenance leadership roles are the sets of behaviors that help the group develop and maintain cohesion, commitment, and positive working relationships.

- **Supporters:** Supporters encourage others to give opinions through positive body language or encouraging words. When someone contributes an idea or opinion, supporters may smile, nod, or vigorously shake their heads. They might also say things like "Good point, Ming," "I really like that idea, Paolo," or "It's obvious you've really done your homework, Janelle."

- **Interpreters:** Interpreters use their knowledge about the different social, cultural, and gender orientations of group members to help group members understand each other (Jensen & Chilberg, 1991). For example, an interpreter might say, "Paul, Lin Chou is Chinese, so when she says that she will think about your plan she might mean that she does not support your ideas, but she doesn't want to embarrass you in front of the others."

- **Harmonizers:** Harmonizers intervene when conflict is threatening to harm group cohesiveness or a relationship between specific group members by speaking to the group with positive and calming words. Harmonizers are likely to make statements such as "Tom, Jack, hold it a second. I know you're on opposite sides of this, but let's see where you might have some agreement" or "Cool it, everybody, we're coming up with some good stuff; let's not lose our momentum by name-calling."

- **Mediators:** Mediators are impartial arbiters who guide the discussion to help find a mutually acceptable resolution. Mediators do this by maintaining their own neutrality, keeping the discussion focused on issues and not personalities, helping to identify areas of common ground, and using paraphrasing and perception checking.

- **Tension relievers:** Tension relievers recognize when group members are stressed or tired and intervene to relieve the stress and reenergize the group, usually through humor. We know that humor "facilitates communication, builds relationships, reduces stress, provides perspective, and promotes attending and energizes" (Martin, Kuiper, Olinger, & Dance, 1993, p. 89). Fortune 500 companies such as General Electric, AT&T, Lockheed, and IBM all emphasize the value of workplace humor in their training programs. People who are effective in this leadership role might tell a joke, kid around, or tell a lighthearted story. A single well-placed one-liner can get a laugh, break the tension, and jolt the group out of its lethargy. Although the tension reliever momentarily distracts the group from its task, this action helps the group remain cohesive.

10-1c Procedural Roles

Procedural leadership roles are sets of communication behaviors that provide logistical support, keep the group focused on the task, and record the group's accomplishments and decisions.

- **Logistics coordinators:** Logistics coordinators arrange for appropriate spaces for group meetings, procure the supplies and equipment needed, and manage other details to meet the group's physical needs. The logistics coordinator's leadership role is usually carried out behind the scenes, but it is crucial to a group's success.

- **Expediters:** Expediters keep track of the group's objectives and help move the group through the agenda. When the group strays, expediters make statements like "I'm enjoying this, but I can't quite see what it has to do with resolving the issue" or "Let's see, aren't we still trying to find out whether these are the only criteria that we should be considering?"

- **Gatekeepers:** Gatekeepers manage the flow of conversation so that all members have an opportunity to participate. If one or two members begin to dominate the conversation, the gatekeeper acknowledges

> **procedural leadership roles** sets of behaviors that provide logistical support, keep the group focused on the task, and record the group's accomplishments and decisions

Gatekeepers manage the flow of conversation.

this and invites other group members to participate. Gatekeepers also notice nonverbal signals that indicate that a member wishes to speak. The gatekeeper is the one who sees that Juanita is on the edge of her chair, eager to comment, and says, "We haven't heard from Juanita, and she seems to have something she wants to say."

- *Recorders:* Recorders take careful notes of group decisions and the evidence upon which they are based, sometimes called *minutes*. Recorders usually distribute edited copies of their notes to group members prior to the next meeting.

10-1d **Shared Leadership Responsibilities**

For shared leadership to work, all members must do their part. We propose five key shared leadership responsibilities (see Figure 10.1) that all members must abide by for the group to function effectively.

1. Be committed to the group goal. Being committed to the group goal means finding a way to align your expertise with the agreed-upon goal of the group. In addition to demonstrating responsibility, being committed to the group goal conveys both integrity and respect.

2. Keep discussions on track. It is every member's responsibility to keep the discussion on track by offering only comments that are relevant and by gently reminding others to stay focused if the discussion starts to get off track. It is unproductive to talk about personal issues during the team's work time. Moreover, it is unethical to try to get the discussion off track because you disagree with what is being said.

3. Complete individual assignments on time. One potential advantage of group work is that tasks can be divided among members. However, each member is responsible for completing his or her tasks thoroughly and on time.

4. Encourage input from all members. All too often, quiet members are overshadowed by extroverts. If you are an extrovert, you have a special responsibility to refrain from dominating the discussion and to ask others for their opinions. If you tend to be an introvert, make a conscious effort to express yourself.

5. Manage conflict among members. As you learned in chapter 9, all small groups experience some *conflict*—disagreements or clashes among ideas, principles, or people. If managed appropriately, conflict can actually be beneficial to the group goal by stimulating thinking, fostering open communication, encouraging diverse opinions, and enlarging members' understanding of the issues (Rahim, 2001). So do your part to manage pseudo-conflict, issue-related conflict, and personality-related conflict effectively when it arises.

Now that we have a clear understanding of effective leadership in groups, let's turn our attention to one of the most common group communication workplace events—meetings.

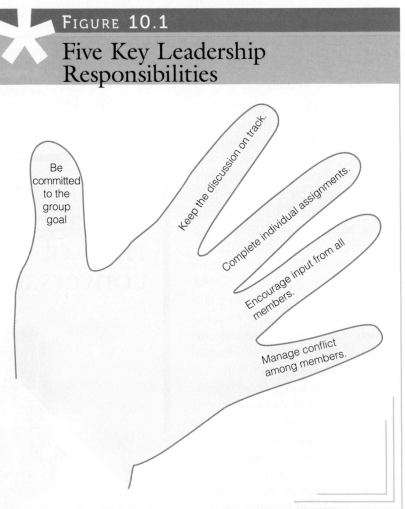

FIGURE 10.1

Five Key Leadership Responsibilities

Be committed to the group goal

Keep the discussion on track.

Complete individual assignments.

Encourage input from all members.

Manage conflict among members.

© Cengage Learning

10-2 Effective Meetings

In a survey of managers, business consultant Mike Drummond (2004) discovered that over 50 percent of managers spend at least six hours per week in meetings and these same managers feel 50 percent of their meeting time is wasted! To ensure that your meetings are not a waste of time, let's look at several guidelines for both leaders and participants.

10-2a Guidelines for Meeting Leaders

Most of us will be responsible for convening a group meeting at some point in our lives. Whether you are the designated formal leader for a class project or a task force at work or simply substituting for your manager at the monthly department meeting, you need to know how to effectively plan for, facilitate, and follow up after meetings.

© Natalia Siverina/Shutterstock.com

Before the Meeting

Meeting leaders should follow these guidelines before the meeting begins.

1. Prepare and distribute an agenda. An **agenda** is an organized outline of the information and decision items to be covered during a meeting. It is a road map that lets the members know the purpose of the meeting and what they are expected to accomplish as a result of attending. Agenda items should move the group toward its goals. You can identify the items for your agenda by

- reviewing your notes and the formal minutes of the previous meeting;

- clarifying what the group decided to accomplish between meetings; and

- identifying what decisions the group expected to make in this next session.

Then you can structure the agenda into information items and decision items. In other words, you can have members report on their assignments (information items), then make decisions and determine next steps.

It is critical to distribute the agenda at least 24 hours before the meeting so that members have time to prepare. You can e-mail the agenda, post it to the group's Web page, or hand-deliver it. None of us likes to come to a meeting and be embarrassed because we forgot to complete an assignment or be called on to make decisions about something we have not had time to think about. As the meeting leader, you are responsible for providing the information members need to come prepared. Figure 10.2 shows an agenda for a group meeting to decide which one of three courses to offer over the Internet next semester.

> **agenda**
> an organized outline of the information and decision items that will be covered during a meeting

2. Decide who should attend the meeting. In most cases, all group members will attend meetings. Occasionally, one or more members may not need to attend a particular meeting but may merely be informed of the outcomes later.

3. Manage meeting logistics. You may choose to carry out this role or ask another group member to do so. But even if you delegate, it remains your responsibility to confirm that the meeting arrangements are made and appropriate. As a general rule, meetings should be shorter than 90 minutes, or have breaks scheduled every 90 minutes to reduce fatigue.

Face-to-face meetings need:

- an appropriately sized room based on the number of people attending,

- any equipment to be available and operational,

- and a table set up to encourage interaction (usually with chairs around it).

Remote meetings need:

- technology for remote interface that is available and operational.

4. Speak with each participant prior to the meeting. As the leader, you need to understand members' positions and personal goals. Time spent discussing issues in advance allows you to anticipate conflicts that might emerge during the meeting and plan how to manage them effectively if they do.

During the Meeting

Meeting leaders should follow these guidelines as the meeting proceeds.

1. Review and modify the agenda. Begin the meeting by reviewing the agenda and modifying it based on members' suggestions. Reviewing the agenda ensures that the group will be working on items that are still relevant and gives members a chance to provide input into what will be discussed.

2. Monitor member interaction. If other group members are assuming the task-related, maintenance, and procedural leadership functions, you need do nothing. But when there is a need for a particular role and no one is assuming it, you should do so. For example, if you notice that some people are talking more than their fair share and no one is trying to draw out quieter members, you should assume the gatekeeper role and invite reluctant members to comment. Similarly, if a discussion becomes too heated, you may need to take on the role of harmonizer or tension reliever.

3. Monitor the time. Although another group member may serve as expediter, it is ultimately your responsibility to make sure the group stays on schedule.

4. Praise in public and reprimand in private. Meetings provide an excellent opportunity to praise individuals or the entire group for jobs well done. Being recognized among one's peers often boosts self-esteem and group morale. Conversely, criticizing individuals or the entire group during a meeting has the opposite effect. The humiliation of public criticism can deflate self-esteem, group morale, and motivation.

5. Check periodically to see if the group is ready to make a decision. You should listen carefully for agreement among members and move the group into its formal decision-making process when the discussion is no longer adding insight.

6. Implement the group's decision rules. You are responsible for executing the decision-making rule the group has agreed to use. If the group is deciding by consensus, for example, you must make sure all members feel they can support the chosen alternative. If the group is deciding by majority rule, you call for the vote and tally the results.

7. Summarize decisions and assignments. You should summarize what has been and is left to accomplish, as well as assignments tasked to various members.

8. Set the next meeting. Clarify when future meetings will take place if necessary.

FIGURE 10.2

Agenda for Internet Course Committee

March 1, 2013

To: Campus computer discussion group

From: Janelle Smith

Re: Agenda for discussion group meeting

Meeting Date: March 8, 2013

Place: Student Union, Conference Room A

Time: 3:00 p.m. to 4:30 p.m.

Meeting objectives

☐ We will familiarize ourselves with each of three courses that have been proposed for Internet-based delivery next semester.

☐ We will evaluate each course against the criteria we developed last month.

☐ We will use a consensus decision process to determine which of the three courses to offer.

Agenda for group discussion

☐ Review and discussion of Philosophy 141 (Report by Justin)

☐ Review and discussion of Art History 336 (Report by Marique)

☐ Review and discussion of Communication 235 (Report by Kathryn)

Consensus-building discussion and decision

☐ Which proposals fit the criteria?

☐ Are there non-criteria-related factors to consider?

☐ Which proposal is more acceptable to all members?

Discussion of next steps and task assignments

Set date of next meeting

Following Up

Meeting leaders should follow these guidelines after the meeting is over.

1. Review the meeting outcomes and process. A good leader learns how to be more effective by reflecting on how well the meeting went. Did the meeting accomplish its goals? Was group cohesion improved or damaged in the process? What will you do differently next time to improve the experience?

2. Prepare and distribute a meeting summary. Although some groups have a designated recorder, many groups rely on their leader to take notes of the discussion. If your group has a designated recorder, be sure to review the minutes and compare them to your notes before they are distributed. Summaries are most useful when they are distributed within two or three days of the meeting when everyone's memories are still fresh.

3. Repair damaged relationships. If any heated debate occurred during the meeting, some members may have left angry or hurt. You should help repair relationships by seeking out these participants and talking with them. Through empathic listening, you can soothe hurt feelings and spark a recommitment to the group.

4. Conduct informal progress reports. When participants have been assigned specific task responsibilities, you should periodically check to see if they have encountered any problems in completing those tasks and how you might help them.

10-2b Guidelines for Meeting Participants

Just as there are guidelines for effective meeting leaders to follow before, during, and after meetings, there are also guidelines for meeting participants.

Before the Meeting

Too often people think of group meetings as a "happening" that requires attendance but no preparation. Countless times we have observed people arriving at a meeting unprepared even though they come carrying packets of material they received in advance. Here are some important preparation guidelines for meeting participants.

1. Study the agenda. Consider the meeting's purpose and determine what you need to do to be prepared. If you had an assignment, make sure you are ready to report on it.

© sturti/iStockphoto.com

INFORMAL PROGRESS REPORTS CAN HELP ENSURE THAT RESPONSIBILITIES ARE FULFILLED AND THAT PROBLEMS ARE SOLVED QUICKLY.

2. Study the minutes. If this is one in a series of meetings, read the minutes and your own notes from the previous meeting. This should prepare you for the next meeting.

3. Do your homework. Read the material distributed prior to the meeting and inform yourself about each agenda item. Bring any materials to the meeting that may help the group accomplish its objectives.

4. List questions. Make a list of questions related to any agenda items that you would like to have answered during the meeting.

5. Plan to play a leadership role. Consider which leadership functions and roles you are best at and decide what you will do to enact them during the meeting.

During the Meeting

Go into the meeting planning to be a full participant.

1. Listen attentively. Concentrate on what others say so you can complement, supplement, or counter what is presented.

2. Stay focused. It is easy to get off track during meetings. Keep your comments focused on the specific agenda item under discussion. If others get off the subject, do what you can to get the discussion back on track.

3. Ask questions. Honest questions help stimulate discussion and build ideas.

4. Take notes. Even if someone else is responsible for providing the official minutes, you'll need notes to remember what occurred and any tasks you agreed to take on after the meeting.

5. Play devil's advocate. When you think an idea has not been fully discussed or tested, be willing to voice disagreement or encourage further discussion.

6. Monitor your contributions. Well-prepared group members tend to dominate discussion. Make sure that you are neither dominating the discussion nor abdicating your responsibility to share insights and opinions.

Following Up

When meetings end, too often people leave and forget about what took place until they arrive at the next meeting. Instead:

1. Review and summarize your notes.
Do this soon after the meeting while the discussion is still fresh in your mind. Make sure your notes include what you need to do before the next meeting.

2. Evaluate your effectiveness. How effective were you in helping the group move toward achieving its goals? Where were you strong? Where were you weak? What should you do next time to improve, and how? For example, if you didn't speak up as much as you would have liked to, perhaps you'll decide to write down questions or topics when you think of them to use as notes to encourage you to speak up next time.

3. Review decisions. Make notes about what your role was in making decisions. Did you do all that you could have done? If not, what will you do differently next time, why, and how?

4. Communicate progress. Inform others who need to know about information conveyed and decisions made in the meeting.

5. Complete your tasks. Make sure you complete all assignments you agreed to take on in the meeting.

6. Review minutes. Compare the official meeting minutes to your own notes and report any discrepancies to the member who prepared them.

Sometimes the goal of a workplace meeting is to regroup and refocus as we perform the regular duties assigned to us. Other times, however, we will meet as part of a work group team charged with a specific problem-solving challenge. In these situations, we will be most successful if we work through the problem using a systematic problem-solving process.

10-3 Systematic Problem Solving

When a work group team is charged with tackling a problem together, members may use an orderly series of steps or a less-structured spiral pattern in which they refine, accept, reject, modify, and combine ideas, then circle back to the previous discussion as they go along.

Whether the deliberations are linear or spiral, groups that arrive at high-quality decisions accomplish the six tasks that make up what is known as the Systematic Problem-Solving Process. This process, first described by John Dewey in 1933 and since revised by others, remains a tried and true approach to individual or group problem solving (Duch, Groh, & Allen, 2001; Edens, 2000; Levin, 2001; Weiten, Dunn, & Hammer, 2011).

10-3a Step One: Identify and Define the Problem

The first step is to identify the problem and define it in a way that all group members understand and agree with. Even when a group is commissioned by an outside agency that provides a description of the problem, the group still needs to understand precisely what is at issue and needs to be resolved. Many times, what appears to be a problem is only a symptom of a problem; if the group focuses on solutions that eliminate only a symptom, the underlying problem will remain. For example, let's say that a group's budget crisis stems from a recession-related membership drop. How does the group know that the inability to fund the budget is the problem and not just a symptom of the problem? What if their membership drop has some other cause? If that is the case, then cutting the budget may be a temporary fix but will not solve the problem. One way to see if you have uncovered the root cause or real problem is to ask, "If we solve this problem, are we confident that the consequences of the problem will not recur?" If we cut the budget, are we confident that we won't need to make additional cuts later? If not, then we probably need to look further for the root problem. We will need to look more closely at causes for the drop in membership and other ways besides dues for funding the budget. The real problem may be how to fund the budget.

Once your group agrees about the nature of the root problem, you will want to draft a **problem definition**, which is a formal written statement describing the problem. An effective problem definition is stated as a question of fact, value, or policy; it contains only one central idea; and it uses specific, precise, and concrete language. **Questions of fact** ask the group to determine what is true or to what extent something is true. "What percentage of our projected expenses can be covered with our existing revenue?" is a question of fact. **Questions of value** ask the group to determine or judge whether something is right, moral, good, or just. Questions of value often contain words such as *good, reliable, effective,* or *worthy*—for instance, "What is the most effective way to recruit new members?" **Questions of policy** concern what course of action should be taken or what rules should be adopted to solve a problem—for example, "Should we sponsor an annual fund-raising event with the local Public Relations Society of America chapter to help fund our budget?" After some discussion, the student chapter decided that the problem they needed to solve was a policy question that could be best stated: "How can we increase our revenues to meet our budget in the current economic conditions?"

10-3b Step Two: Analyze the Problem

Problem analysis involves finding out as much as possible about the problem. Most groups begin this process with each member sharing information he or she already knows about the problem. Then members determine which additional questions they need to answer and search for additional information to answer them. Some members may be assigned to conduct library or online research about the problem, others may interview experts, and still others may conduct surveys to gather information from particular target groups. The information gathered by group members should help the group answer key questions about the nature of the problem such as those listed in Figure 10.3.

During the information gathering and analysis step, group members should be encouraged to share information that is new or contradicts the sentiments or preferences expressed in the group. A group that is willing to consider new and unexpected information will more deeply analyze the problem and, therefore, will likely come to a more effective solution.

problem definition
a formal written statement describing a problem

question of fact
a question asked to determine what is true or to what extent something is true

question of value
a question asked to determine or judge whether something is right, moral, good, or just

question of policy
a question asked to determine what course of action should be taken or what rules should be adopted to solve a problem

© Vadim Georgiev/Shutterstock.com

10-3c Step Three: Determine Criteria for Judging Solutions

Criteria are standards used for judging the merits of proposed solutions. They provide a blueprint for how the group will evaluate the virtues of each alternative solution. Research suggests that when groups develop criteria before they think about specific solutions, they are more likely to come to a decision that all members can accept (Young, Wood, Phillips, & Pedersen, 2007). Without clear criteria, group members may argue for their preferred solution without regard to whether it will adequately address the problem and whether it is feasible. Figure 10.4 provides a list of questions that can help a group think about the types of criteria that a solution might need to meet.

Once you've agreed on the list of solution criteria, the group needs to prioritize the list. Although rank ordering the list from most to least important may be unwieldy and counterproductive, it is probably useful to agree which criteria are major (must meet) and which are minor (would like to meet).

10-3d Step Four: Identify Alternative Solutions

Ending up with a good solution depends on having a wide variety of possible solutions to choose from. Therefore, one of the most important activities of problem solving is coming up with solution ideas. Many groups fail to generate solution ideas because they criticize the first ideas expressed; this discourages members from taking the risk to put their ideas out for the group to consider. One way to encourage everyone's ideas is to use the technique of brainstorming. **Brainstorming** is an uncritical, non-evaluative process of generating possible solutions by being creative, suspending judgment, and combining or adapting ideas.

During a brainstorming session, members offer ideas without censoring themselves. Other members may build on ideas that have been presented, combine two or more ideas, or even offer off-the-wall thoughts. What members may *not* do is criticize, poke fun at, or in any other way evaluate the ideas. While the group is brainstorming, one member should record the ideas for all to see (e.g., on a whiteboard, smartboard, or projector).

FIGURE 10.3

Questions to Guide Problem Analysis

- ☐ What are the symptoms of this problem?
- ☐ What are the causes of this problem?
- ☐ What have others who have faced this problem done?
- ☐ How successful have they been with the solutions they attempted?
- ☐ How is our situation similar to and different from theirs?
- ☐ Does this problem consist of several smaller problems? If so, what are their symptoms, causes, previously tried solutions, and so forth?
- ☐ What would be the consequences of doing nothing?
- ☐ What would be the consequences of trying something and having it fail?

© Cengage Learning

FIGURE 10.4

Questions to Guide Discussion of Solution Criteria

- ☐ What are the quantitative and qualitative measures of success that a solution must be able to demonstrate?
- ☐ Are there resource constraints that a good solution must meet (costs, time, personnel)?
- ☐ Is solution simplicity a factor?
- ☐ What risks are unacceptable?
- ☐ Is ease of implementation a consideration?
- ☐ Is it important that no constituency be unfairly harmed or advantaged by a solution?

© Cengage Learning

10-3e Step Five: Evaluate Solutions and Decide

After generating potential solutions, the group must find the one or ones that will best solve the problem. To do this, the group must compare each alternative to the decision criteria established earlier. If many solutions were generated during brainstorming, the group will probably want to quickly review the list and eliminate those that obviously do not meet the criteria. Then it can concentrate on evaluating the remaining solutions, discussing how well each meets specific criteria and comparing the positive features of each. This discussion may result in only one solution that meets all the criteria, but often there will be more than one viable solution.

Decision making is the process of choosing among alternatives. Sometimes your group will not be responsible for choosing among the remaining alternatives. Instead, you will present the results of your work to others who will make the final decision. At other times, though, your group will make the decision. Five methods are commonly used to reach a group decision.

1. The expert opinion method. Once the group has eliminated those alternatives that do not meet the criteria, the group asks the member who has the most expertise to make the final choice. Obviously, this method is quick and useful if one member is much more knowledgeable about the issues or has a greater stake in the implementation of the decision.

2. The average group opinion method. In this approach, each group member ranks each of the alternatives that meet all the criteria. Their rankings are then averaged, and the alternative receiving the highest average becomes the choice. This method is useful for routine decisions or when a decision needs to be made quickly. It can also be used as an intermediate straw poll so the group can eliminate low-scoring alternatives before moving to a different process for making the final decision.

decision making
the process of choosing among alternatives

3. The majority rule method. In this method, the group votes on each alternative, and the one that receives a majority of votes is selected. Although this method is considered democratic, it can create problems. If the majority voting for an alternative is slight, then nearly as many members oppose the choice as support it. If these minority members strongly object to the choice, they may sabotage implementation of the solution either actively or passively.

4. The unanimous decision method. In this method, the group must continue deliberation until every member of the group believes that the same solution is the best. As you would expect, it is very difficult and time-consuming to arrive at a truly unanimous decision. When a group reaches unanimity, however, each member is likely to be committed to selling the decision to others and helping to implement it.

5. The consensus method. This method is an alternative to the unanimous decision method. In consensus, the group continues deliberation until all members of the group find an acceptable solution, one they can support and are committed to helping implement. Some group members may believe there is a better solution than the one chosen, but all can live with the chosen solution. Arriving at consensus, although easier than reaching unanimity, is still difficult. Although the majority rule method is widely used, the consensus method is a wise investment if the group needs everyone's support to implement the decision successfully.

Sometimes a group will choose only one solution. But frequently a group will decide on a multi-pronged approach that combines two or three of the acceptable solutions.

10-3f Step Six: Implement the Agreed-Upon Solution and Assess It

Finally, the group may be responsible for implementing the agreed-upon solution or, if the group is presenting the solution to others for implementation, making recommendations for how the solution should be implemented. The group has already considered implementation in terms of selecting a solution but now must fill in the details. What tasks are required by the solution(s)? Who will carry out these tasks? What is a reasonable time frame for implementation generally and for each of the tasks specifically? Because the agreed-upon solution may or may not prove effective, the group should determine a point at which they will revisit and assess its success. Doing so builds in an opportunity to revise or replace the solution if warranted.

10-4 Communicating Group Solutions

Once a group has completed its deliberations, it is usually expected to communicate its results. **Deliverables** are tangible or intangible products of your work that must be provided to someone else. Although some deliverables are objects, typically the deliverables from problem-solving groups are communications of the information gathered, analyses, decisions, and recommendations. These kinds of intangible deliverables can be communicated in written formats, oral formats, or virtual formats.

10-4a Written Formats

1. Written brief. A **written brief** is a very short document that describes the problem, background, process, decision, and

deliverables
tangible or intangible products of work that must be provided to someone else

written brief
a very short document that describes a problem, background, process, decision, and rationale so that a reader can quickly understand and evaluate a group's product

comprehensive report
a written document that provides a detailed review of the problem-solving process used to arrive at a recommendation

WoW Problem Solving

For some, mention of games like *World of Warcraft* might conjure up a stereotypical image of a teenage boy typing away at his computer alone. But role-playing games are actually social interactions that encourage successful group problem solving

World of Warcraft (WoW) is a popular MMORPG (massively multiplayer online role-playing game). *World of Warcraft* is played online and players communicate with one another using text or voice chat programs. To advance in the game, players must work with others to defeat monsters, find treasure, and gain experience (Newman, 2007).

In a *BusinessWeek* Online article, researcher John Seely Brown and business consultant John Hagel (2009) argue that many aspects of *WoW* encourage group problem solving and can even be applied as innovative workplace strategies. They claim that *WoW* creates opportunities for teams to self-organize around challenging performance targets; provides opportunities to develop tacit knowledge without neglecting the exchange of broader knowledge; and encourages frequent and rigorous performance feedback.

Based on these benefits, some MMORPGs are actually being developed for a range of "real-life" applications. For example, the Bill and Melinda Gates Foundation recently awarded a $3 million grant to the MIT Education Arcade to develop games that help high school students learn math and biology. The games enable self-directed and collaborative learning experiences, where the players take on the roles of scientists, engineers, and mathematicians.

rationale so that the reader can quickly understand and evaluate the group's product. Most briefs are one or two pages long. When preparing a brief, begin by describing your group's task. What problem were you attempting to solve and why? Then briefly provide the background information the reader will need to evaluate whether the group has adequately studied the problem. Present solution steps and timelines for implementation as bullet points so the reader can quickly understand what is being proposed. Close with a sentence or very short paragraph that describes how the recommendation will solve the problem, as well as any potential side effects.

2. Comprehensive report. A **comprehensive report** is a written document that provides a detailed review of the problem-solving process used to arrive at the recommendation. A comprehensive report is usually organized into sections that parallel the problem-solving process.

Because comprehensive reports can be very long, they usually include an executive summary. An **executive summary** is a one-page synopsis of the report. This summary contains enough information to acquaint readers with the highlights of the full document without reading it. Usually, it contains a statement of the problem, some background information, a description of any alternatives, and the major conclusions.

10-4b Oral Formats

1. Oral brief. An **oral brief** is essentially a summary of a written brief delivered to an audience by a group member. An oral brief can typically be delivered in less than 10 minutes.

2. Oral report. An **oral report** is similar to a comprehensive report. It provides a more detailed review of a group's problem-solving process. Oral reports can range from 30 to 60 minutes.

3. Symposium. A **symposium** is a set of prepared oral reports delivered sequentially by group members before a gathering of people who are interested in the group's work. A symposium may be organized so that each person's speech focuses on one step of the problem-solving process, or it may be organized so that each speaker covers all of the steps in the problem-solving process as they relate to one of several issues or recommendations that the group worked on or made. In a symposium, the speakers usually sit together at the front of the room. One member acts as moderator, offering the introductory and concluding remarks and providing transitions between speakers. When introduced by the moderator, each speaker may stand and walk to a central spot, usually a lectern. Speakers who use a computerized slideshow should coordinate their slides so that there

are seamless transitions between speakers. Symposiums often conclude with a question-and-answer session facilitated by the moderator, who directs one or more of the members to answer based on their expertise. Questions can be directed to individuals or to the group as a whole.

4. Panel discussion. A **panel discussion** is a structured problem-solving discussion held by a group in front of an audience. One member serves as moderator, introducing the topic and providing structure by asking a series of planned questions that panelists answer. Their answers and the interaction among them provide the supporting evidence. A well-planned panel discussion seems spontaneous and interactive but

executive summary
a one-page synopsis of a comprehensive report

oral brief
a summary of a written brief delivered to an audience by a group member

oral report
a detailed review of a group's problem-solving process delivered to an audience by one or more group members

symposium
a set of prepared oral reports delivered sequentially by group members before a gathering of people who are interested in the group's work

A set-up like this may be for larger meetings or symposiums, where one person speaks at a time either giving a report or part of a report.

© Pressmaster/Shutterstock.com

requires careful planning and rehearsal to ensure that all relevant information is presented and that all speakers are afforded equal speaking time. After the formal discussion, the audience is often encouraged to question the participants. Perhaps you've seen or heard a panel of experts discuss a topic on a radio or television talk show like *SportsCenter* or *The Doctors*.

10-4c Virtual Formats

1. Remote access reports. A **remote access report (RAR)** is a computer-mediated audiovisual presentation of the group's process and outcome that others can receive electronically. One or more group members prepare the RAR with slideshow software to provide a visual overview of the group's process, decisions, and recommendations. Effective RARs typically consist of no more than 15 to 20 slides. Slides are titled and content is presented in outline format or with bullet-point phrases or key words (rather than complete sentences or paragraphs), as well as through visual representations of important information. RARs may be self-running so that the slides automatically forward after a certain number of seconds, but it is better to let the viewer choose the pace and control when the next slide appears. RARs can be silent or narrated. When narrated, a voice-over accompanies each slide, providing additional or explanatory information.

2. Streaming videos. A **streaming video** is a recording that is sent in compressed form over the Internet. You are probably familiar with streaming video from popular Web sites such as YouTube. Streaming videos are a great way to distribute oral briefs, but they also can be used to distribute recordings of oral reports, symposiums, or panel presentations. Streaming videos are useful when everyone who needs to know the results of the group's work cannot meet at one time or in one place.

10-5 Evaluating Group Effectiveness

As with any communication skill, group communication can improve over time based on practice, reflective assessment, and revision. In this section, we offer some guidelines for evaluating the group communication process and a group presentation.

10-5a Group Dynamics

Group dynamics is the way a group interacts to achieve its goal. Effective groups periodically stop to evaluate how their interactions affect what they are accomplishing and how members perceive themselves and others. At times you may be asked to provide a formal evaluation of the group dynamics of a class project group or other work team. One way you might evaluate members is to describe how each member performed his or her specific tasks and how well his or her communication contributed to the cohesiveness, problem solving, and conflict resolution processes in the group. Figure 10.5 is one example you can use for evaluating class project group member participation. Alternatively, in a class project group, members could prepare a "reflective thinking process paper," which details in paragraph form what each member did well and could improve upon as well as a self-analysis of their own contributions and what they could do to improve.

Like the performance evaluations business managers make of employees, these evaluations document the efforts of group members. They can be submitted to the instructor, just as they would be submitted to a supervisor. In business, these documents provide a basis for determining promotion, merit pay, and salary adjustments. In the classroom, they can provide a basis for determining one portion of each member's grade.

10-5b Group Presentations

Effective group presentations depend on quality individual presentations as well as overall group performance. So evaluations of group presentations should consist of both an individual and a group component (see Figure 10.6). And, if you are serious about improving your individual presentation skills, you will also evaluate yourself to discover areas where you can improve (see Figure 10.7).

FIGURE 10.5

Group Dynamics Evaluation Form

Meeting Date: _____

Your name: _____

Directions

After each requried group meeting, provide ethical critiques for both your group members and yourself. Rate each individual on his or her performance in the group. Justify the rating with specific examples. As you rate each member, consider the following:

- ☐ committed to the group goal
- ☐ fulfills individual assignments
- ☐ manages interpersonal conflicts
- ☐ encourages group participation
- ☐ helps keep the discussion on track

Yourself _____

Circle overall individual rating

0	1	2	3	4	5	6	7
(poor)			(met requirements)			(excellent)	

Tasks accomplished:

Tasks assigned:

Ethical critique:

Group member _____

Circle overall individual rating

0	1	2	3	4	5	6	7
(poor)			(met requirements)			(excellent)	

Tasks accomplished:

Tasks assigned:

Ethical critique:

Group member _____

Circle overall individual rating

0	1	2	3	4	5	6	7
(poor)			(met requirements)			(excellent)	

Tasks accomplished:

Tasks assigned:

Ethical critique:

Group member _____

Circle overall individual rating

0	1	2	3	4	5	6	7
(poor)			(met requirements)			(excellent)	

Tasks accomplished:

Tasks assigned:

Ethical critique:

Group member _____

Circle overall individual rating

0	1	2	3	4	5	6	7
(poor)			(met requirements)			(excellent)	

Tasks accomplished:

Tasks assigned:

Ethical critique:

FIGURE 10.6

Sample Evaluation Form for Group Presentations

Group Member Name: _____ **Critic (your name):** _____

Directions: Evaluate the effectiveness of each group member according to each of the following criteria for effective presentations individually and as a group.

Rating Scale:
Circle overall individual rating

0	1	2	3	4	5	6	7

(poor)   (met requirements)   (excellent)

_____

Individual Performance Critique

_____ **Content** (Breadth and depth and listener relevance)

(rating) **Critique** (Provide a rationale for the rating you gave):

_____ **Structure** (Macrostructure and microstructure/language)

(rating) **Critique** (Provide a rationale for the rating you gave):

_____ **Delivery** (Use of voice and use of body)

(rating) **Critique** (Provide a rationale for the rating you gave):

Group Performance Critique

_____ **Content** (Thematic? Focused? Thorough? Construction of presentational aids?)

(rating) **Critique** (Provide a rationale for the rating you gave):

_____ **Structure** (Balanced? Transitions/Flow? Attention Getter/Clincher?)

(rating) **Critique** (Provide a rationale for the rating you gave):

_____ **Delivery** (Teamwork? Cooperation? Fluency? Use of aids?)

(rating) **Critique** (Provide a rationale for the rating you gave):

Overall Comments:

© Cengage Learning

FIGURE 10.7

Sample Self-Critique Form for Group Presentations

Directions: Complete the items below with regard to your presentation in the group symposium.

1. If I could do my portion of the oral presentation over again, I would do the following things differently:
   a.
   b.

2. In terms of content, I did the following things well in my oral presentation:
   a.
   b.

3. In terms of structure, I did the following things well in my oral presentation:
   a.
   b.

4. In terms of delivery, I did the following things well in my oral presentation:
   a.
   b.
   c.

5. In terms of my role as a group member, I am most proud of how I:

6. In terms of my role as a group member, I am least proud of how I:

7. Overall, I would give myself a grade of _____ for the group speech because:

© Cengage Learning

Quick Quiz

T F 1. Criteria are standards or measures that provide the blueprint for how a group will evaluate the virtues of each alternative solution.

T F 2. Leadership is the set of roles performed to facilitate group work and to maintain relationships among members.

T F 3. A tension reliever's main role is to momentarily distract the group from its task, which helps break monotony or tension within the group.

T F 4. An oral brief is similar to a comprehensive report, whereas an oral report is a summary of a written brief delivered to an audience by a group member.

T F 5. Panel discussions require careful planning and rehearsal to ensure that all relevant information is presented and that each speaker is afforded equal speaking time.

6. According to the problem-solving method, a process of identifying an alternative solution can be reached through

a. analyzing.
b. defining.
c. developing criteria.
d. evaluation.
e. brainstorming.

7. In which decision-making method does a group continue deliberations until every member of the group believes that the same solution is best?

a. the average group opinion method
b. the unanimous decision method
c. the majority rule method
d. the expert opinion method
e. None of these is correct.

8. _____ are neutral and impartial arbiters who guide discussions, whereas _____ intervene in the group's discussion when conflict is threatening group cohesiveness.

a. Tension relievers; interpreters
b. Interpreters; mediators
c. Mediators; harmonizers
d. Harmonizers; mediators
e. Supporters; mediators

9. Which procedural role do you play when you ensure that everyone has an opportunity to speak and be heard?

a. gatekeeper
b. encourager
c. harmonizer
d. peacekeeper
e. initiator

10. When running a meeting, be sure to complete each of the following tasks except

a. modifying the agenda based on members' suggestions.
b. monitoring the roles that members assume.
c. encouraging conflict and arguments among group members to elicit everyone's true feelings.
d. implementing the group's decision rules.
e. periodically checking to see if the group is ready to make a decision.

Answers: 1. T, 2. F, 3. T, 4. F, 5. T, 6. E, 7. B, 8. C, 9. A, 10. C

Topic Selection
and Development

What do you think?
It makes me nervous
to speak in public.

1 2 **3** 4 5 6 7 **8** 9 10
STRONGLY DISAGREE   STRONGLY AGREE

Learning Outcomes

11-1 Understand how the various factors that create the rhetorical situation impact topic selection

11-2 Identify and select appropriate topics for your speech

11-3 Identify the general and specific goals of your speech

11-4 List the three different types of sources you can draw from to develop your speech and explain how to evaluate them

11-5 Know how to identify and cite sources

Developing effective public speaking skills is empowering. Effective speakers can influence the thinking of others. Effective public speaking skills are essential to advancing your career. Whether giving a "job talk" speech during an interview, presenting oral reports and proposals, responding to questions, or training other workers, you will spend a good portion of your work life in activities that require effective public speaking skills. This chapter focuses on the first steps in effective speechmaking: (1) selecting a specific speech goal that is adapted to the rhetorical situation and (2) gathering and evaluating information to develop your speech.

rhetorical situation
a state in which you, the audience, and the occasion overlap

11-1 The Rhetorical Situation

As Figure 11.1 illustrates, the **rhetorical situation** is a state in which you (and your knowledge and intentions), the audience (and their knowledge and expectations), and the occasion (and the constraints of it) overlap. Effective speakers address all three of these components throughout the speech

ACTION STEPS

Action Step 1
Select a Specific Speech Goal That Is Adapted to the Rhetorical Situation

Action Step 2
Gather and Evaluate Information to Develop Your Speech

exigence
the reason the speech needs to be given

audience analysis
the study of the intended audience for your speech

audience adaptation
the process of tailoring your speech to the needs, interests, and expectations of your audience

uncertainty reduction theory
explains the processes we go through to get to know strangers

subject
a broad area of knowledge

topic
some specific aspect of a subject

demographics
the statistical characteristics of a specific group of people

preparation and presentation process. Lloyd Bitzer (1968), an esteemed professor and rhetorician, coined the term *exigence* to capture the notion that speeches address a real or perceived need. In other words, **exigence** is *the reason the speech needs to be given*. And because the audience is a critical component of the rhetorical situation, your specific speech goal must be based on **audience analysis**, the study of the intended audience for your speech, and **audience adaptation**, the process of tailoring your speech to their needs, interests, and expectations. Audience analysis and adaptation is rooted in what communication scholars refer to as **uncertainty reduction theory**, which explains the processes we go through to get to know strangers (Berger & Calabrese, 1975). Although effective speakers adapt their speech to the audience throughout the speech preparation and presentation process, audience adaptation and analysis begins when they select a topic and speech goal.

To determine a specific speech goal that is adapted to the rhetorical situation, begin by identifying several subjects and topics that interest you. A **subject** is a broad area of knowledge, such as contemporary cinema, renewable energy, computer technology, or Middle Eastern politics. A **topic** is a narrow, specific aspect of a subject. Then, based on your analysis of both the audience and the occasion, narrow your list of topics appropriately. Ultimately, a good speech is one that interests you, is adapted to address the needs, interests, and expectations of the audience, and is appropriate for the occasion.

ACTION STEP 1

Select a Specific Speech Goal That Is Adapted to the Rhetorical Situation

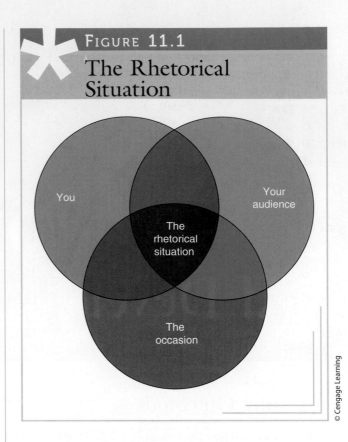

FIGURE 11.1
The Rhetorical Situation

You

Your audience

The rhetorical situation

The occasion

© Cengage Learning

11-1a Analyze the Audience

Addressing the specific needs and expectations of your intended audience is integral to the rhetorical situation. To select an appropriate topic, therefore, you need to analyze the audience's demographic characteristics and subject-specific knowledge. You will use the information you learn from audience analysis during topic selection as well as throughout the speechmaking process.

Demographic Data
Demographics are the statistical characteristics of a specific group of people. Helpful demographic information includes each audience member's approximate age, education, sex, income, occupation, race, ethnicity, religion, geographic uniqueness, and language, among other characteristics. Figure 11.2 presents a list of questions that will help you uncover important demographic information about your audience.

Subject-Related Data
You also want to collect subject-related audience data, including how knowledgeable audience members are about the subject and potential topics you are considering, as well as their initial level of interest in and attitude toward the topics. Once you determine what your audience already knows about the subject, you can use a process of elimination to choose a topic that will offer new

information and insight. Similarly, when you understand their initial level of interest regarding your subject, you can choose a topic that builds on that interest or adapt your material to capture their interest. Understanding your audience's attitude toward your subject is especially important when you want to influence their beliefs or move them to action. Knowing your audience members' attitudes toward your subject will help you choose a topic and tailor it in ways that influences them without alienating them.

Suppose, for example, you want to give a speech on blogging. If you're not sure your audience understands what blogging is, you may infer what they know by examining demographic data. Are most of the audience members young, educated, and from a middle-class background? If so, you can infer that they will have heard about blogging and know some of the basics. So you might adapt your speech topic to offer insights about blogging of which they may be unaware, such as the dangers or "dark side" of blogging. But if your audience is from different demographic groups, then you might need to collect subject-related data to learn what they know about blogging and then pick an appropriately focused topic within the general subject area of blogging. If you discover that most of your audience members have never written or even read a blog, then you may need to adapt your topic to introduce them more generally to what blogging is.

Data-Gathering Methods

You can use several different methods to gather data about your audience.

1. Conduct a survey. Although it is not always possible, the most direct way to collect audience data is to survey them. A **survey** is an examination of people to gather information about their ideas and opinions. Some surveys are done as interviews, others as written questionnaires. The four most common types of questions used in a survey are two-sided, multiple-response, scaled, and open-ended. *Two-sided questions* force respondents to choose between two answers (e.g., yes/no, for/against). *Multiple-response questions* give respondents several alternatives from which to choose. *Scaled questions*

survey
an examination of people to gather information about their ideas and opinions

---

FIGURE 11.2

Audience Analysis Questions

Age: What is the average age range of the people in your audience?

Educational Level: What percentage of your audience has a high school, college, or postgraduate education?

Sex: What percentage of your audience is male? Female?

Occupation: Is a majority of your audience from a single occupational group, industry, or major? Or do they come from a variety of occupations, industries, or majors?

Socioeconomic Status: What percentage of your audience comes from high-, middle-, or low-income families?

Race: Are most members of your audience of the same race, or is there a mixture of races represented?

Ethnicity: What cultural and co-cultural groups do your audience members identify with?

Religion: What religious traditions are represented?

Geographic Uniqueness: Are audience members from the same state, city, or neighborhood?

Language: What language (if any) is spoken by all audience members? What are the most common primary languages?

© Cengage Learning

marginalizing
ignoring the values, needs, interests, and subject-specific knowledge of some audience members

stereotyping
assuming all members of a group have similar knowledge levels, behaviors, or beliefs simply because they belong to that group

measure the direction of intensity of respondents' feelings or attitudes toward something (e.g., on a scale from 1 to 5, with 5 being "very likely," . . .). *Open-ended questions* encourage respondents to elaborate on their opinions without forcing them to answer in a predetermined way. Figure 11.3 gives examples of each type.

2. Observe informally. If you are familiar with the members of your audience (as you are with members of your class audience), you can learn a lot through informal observation. For instance, after being in class for even a couple of sessions, you should be able to estimate the approximate age or age range of the class as well as the ratio of men to women. As you listen to your classmates talk, you will learn more about their interest in, knowledge of, and attitudes about many issues.

3. Question a representative. When you are invited to speak to a group you are unfamiliar with, ask your contact person for demographic and subject-related audience data. You should specifically ask for data that are somewhat important for you as you choose a topic or work to adapt your material. For the blogging speech, for example, you would want to know if the audience members have a basic understanding of what a blog is.

4. Make educated guesses. If you can't get information in any other way, you can make educated guesses based on indirect data such as the general makeup of the people who live in a certain community, belong to a certain organization, or who are likely to attend a speech of this nature.

11-1b Ethical Use of Audience Data

Once you have collected audience data, you can use it to tailor your speech to your audience's interests, needs,

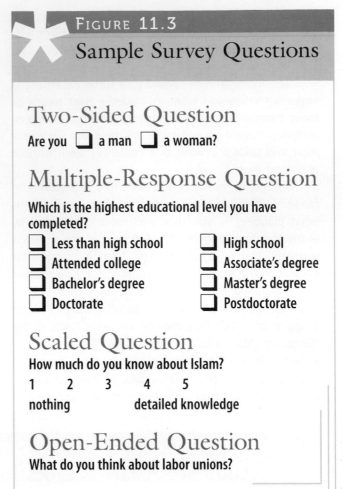

FIGURE 11.3
Sample Survey Questions

Two-Sided Question
Are you ☐ a man ☐ a woman?

Multiple-Response Question
Which is the highest educational level you have completed?
☐ Less than high school ☐ High school
☐ Attended college ☐ Associate's degree
☐ Bachelor's degree ☐ Master's degree
☐ Doctorate ☐ Postdoctorate

Scaled Question
How much do you know about Islam?
1   2   3   4   5
nothing   detailed knowledge

Open-Ended Question
What do you think about labor unions?

© Cengage Learning

and expectations. But adapting to your audience also means creating a speech that all audience members can relate to. So you will want to avoid two potential pitfalls: marginalizing and stereotyping.

Marginalizing is the practice of ignoring the values, needs, interests, and subject-specific knowledge of some audience members, leaving them to feel excluded. For example, if you find out that most of your audience members have blogged, you want to avoid marginalizing the few members who have never blogged. So you might provide a quick definition of blogging and show an example as a visual aid before going into your speech about the dangers of blogging.

Stereotyping is assuming all members of a group have similar knowledge, behaviors, or beliefs simply because they belong to that group. If, for instance, you find out that the average age of your audience is 65, you might stereotype and assume that most of them know nothing about blogging when, in fact, many of them not only know about blogs but have created them. To avoid stereotyping based on demographic data, you also need to collect subject-related data from your audience.

© Pixsooz/Shutterstock.com

You also can reduce your chances of marginalizing or stereotyping by identifying and acknowledging the diversity represented in your audience. **Audience diversity** is the range of demographic characteristics and subject-specific differences represented in an audience. So while the average age of your audience may be 65, there may also be some in the audience who are much younger.

11-1c Examine the Occasion

The **occasion** is the expected purpose for the speech and the setting where it will be given. Answers to several questions about the occasion should guide you when selecting your topic and throughout the speech-making process.

1. What is the intended purpose of the speech? In other words, why does the audience think this speech is being given? At a Sunday church service, the congregation expects the minister's sermon to have a religious theme. At a national sales meeting, the field representatives expect to hear about new products. For your classroom speeches, a major expectation is that your speech will meet the assignment criteria.

2. What is the expected length? Time limits for classroom speeches are usually quite short, so you will want to choose a topic that is narrow enough to be covered in the brief time allotted. For example, "Three Major Causes of the Declining Honeybee Population" could probably be covered in a five-minute speech; however, "A History of Human Impact on the Environment" could not. Speakers who speak for more or less than the allotted time can seriously interfere with event programming and lose the respect of both their hosts and their audience.

3. Where will the speech be given? Rooms vary in size, shape, lighting, and seating arrangements. Some are a single level, some have stages or platforms, and some have tiered seating. The space affects the speech. For example, in a long, narrow room, you may have to speak loudly to be heard in the back row. If you are speaking in an auditorium to a large group of people, you will need to speak loudly and perhaps use a microphone. You will also need to use large gestures and presentational aids that can be seen and heard easily in all parts of the room. The brightness of the room and the availability of shades may affect the kinds of visual aids you can use. So you will want to know and consider the layout of the room as you plan your speech. At times, you might request that the room be changed or rearranged so that the space is better suited to your needs.

4. When will the speech be given? A speech given early in the morning requires a different approach from one given right after lunch or in the evening. If a speech is scheduled after a meal, for example, the audience may be lethargic, mellow, or even on the verge of sleep. So you

> **audience diversity**
> the range of demographic characteristics and subject-specific differences represented in an audience
>
> **occasion**
> the expected purpose and setting for the speech

ACTION STEP 1a

Analyze Your Audience

1. **Decide on the audience characteristics (demographic and subject-related data) you want to research to adapt your topic and speech effectively.**

2. **Choose a method for gathering audience information.**

3. **Collect the data.**

Large auditorium?   OR   Small conference room?

may want to plan more material that gains and regains their interest throughout the speech. Similarly, where you are placed on the schedule of events should influence your speech planning. For example, if you are first, you may need to "warm up" the audience and be prepared to deal with the distraction of latecomers entering the room while you are speaking. If you speak later in the program, you will need to integrate attention-catching material to keep the interest of a weary audience.

5. What equipment is necessary and available? Would you like to use a microphone, lectern, flip chart, smartboard, computer and LCD projector, or Internet during your speech? If so, you need to check with your host to make sure that the equipment can be made available to you. In some cases, the unavailability of equipment may limit your topic choice. Regardless of the arrangements that have been made, however, experienced speakers expect that something may go wrong and always prepare a backup plan. For example, although computer slide shows can be very effective, technological glitches can sometimes interfere with their use. So it's a good idea to bring handouts as a backup.

The history of Tex-Mex is a topic in the larger subject of U.S. food history.

11-2 Identifying and Selecting Speech Topics

Choosing a good speech topic can be tough, and it can make a real difference in the outcome of your speech. Good speech topics come from subject areas that you have some knowledge about and interest in. (Recall that a subject is a broad area of knowledge, whereas a topic is a narrow, specific aspect of a subject.) To some extent, your analysis of the audience and your topic selection will occur simultaneously. It helps to have some idea of your subject as you develop your audience profile.

11-2a Subjects

You can identify subjects by listing those that (1) you think are important and (2) you know something about. Subjects may be related to careers that interest you, your major area of study, special skills or competencies you have or admire, your hobbies, or even your social, economic, or political interests. So if your major is marketing, favorite hobbies are skateboarding and snowboarding, and special concerns are substance abuse and childhood obesity, then these are *subjects* from which you can identify potential speech topics.

At this point, you might be thinking, "What if my audience isn't interested in the subjects that interest me?" In reality, topics in any subject area can be of interest when they are adapted to address the needs and expectations of the audience. Figure 11.4 contains a list of subjects that Holly,

---

ACTION STEP 1b

Analyze the Occasion

Hold a conversation with the person who arranged for you to speak and get answers to the following questions:

1. **What is the intended purpose of the speech?**
   _____

2. **What is the expected length for the speech?**
   _____

3. **Where will the speech be given and to how many people?**
   _____

4. **When will the speech be given?**
   _____

5. **What equipment is necessary to give the speech?**
   _____

Write a short paragraph discussing which aspects of the occasion are most important to consider for your speech and why.

_____

_____

_____

_____

a beginning communication student, identified as she began thinking about her upcoming speech. She chose to organize her subject areas under three headings: (1) career interests, (2) hobbies, and (3) issues of concern.

11-2b Brainstorm and Concept Map

Because a topic is a specific aspect of a subject, you can identify many topics related to one subject. Two methods for identifying topics are brainstorming and concept mapping.

As you recall from chapter 10, *brainstorming* is an uncritical, nonevaluative process of generating associated ideas. When you brainstorm, you list as many ideas as you can think of without evaluating them. Holly, for example, decided she wanted to give a speech on the subject of social networking. By brainstorming, she came up with a list of potential topics that included the history of social networking, future trends in social networking, comparisons of popular social networking sites, the downside of social networking, and the social impacts of online social networks.

Concept mapping is a visual means of exploring connections between a subject and related ideas (Callison, 2001). To generate connections, you might ask yourself questions about your subject, focusing on who, what, where, when, and how. In Figure 11.5, you can see Holly's concept map on the subject of endangered birds.

concept mapping
a visual means of exploring connections between a subject and related ideas

---

FIGURE 11.4
Holly's Subject Lists

Career Interests	Hobbies	Issues of Concern
• Teacher	• Social Networking	• Endangered Birds
• Web Site Designer	• Rowing	• Child Pornography Online
• Information Systems Specialist	• Big Brothers/Big Sisters Organizations	• Personal Privacy and the Internet
• Technology Trainer	• Birding	• Water Pollution
• Public Relations	• Photography	• Global Warming/Climate Change

© Cengage Learning

FIGURE 11.5
Holly's Endangered Birds Concept Map

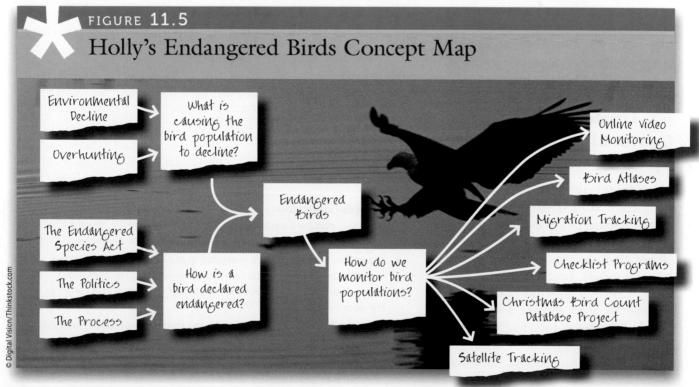

© Digital Vision/Thinkstock.com

general goal
the overall intent
of the speech

11-2c Select a Topic

As you review your topic list, compare each to your audience profile. Are any topics too simple or too difficult for this audience's knowledge base? If so, eliminate those topics. Are some topics likely to bore the audience and you can't think of any way to pique their interest? Eliminate those as well. How might the audience's age range, ethnicity, and other demographic characteristics mesh with each topic? By asking these and similar questions, you will be able to identify topics that are appropriate for the audience. Also consider the occasion. Are some topics inappropriate for the intended purpose? Are some too broad to cover adequately in the time allotted? Would any require equipment that cannot be made available where you will be speaking? Answers to these kinds of questions will help you identify topics appropriate to the occasion. Finally, the topics that remain should be appropriate for the rhetorical situation. Choose one that you would enjoy preparing and sharing with the audience.

ACTION STEP 1c

Brainstorm and Concept Map for Topics

1. **Develop a subject list.**
   a. **Divide a sheet of paper into three columns. Label column 1 "career interests," column 2 "hobbies," and column 3 "issues of concern."**
   b. **Working on one column at a time, identify subjects that interest you. Try to identify at least three subjects in each column.**
   c. **Place a check mark next to one subject in each column you might enjoy speaking about.**
   d. **Keep these lists for future use in choosing a topic for an assigned speech.**
2. **For each subject you checked, brainstorm a list of potential speech topics related to it.**
3. **Then, for each subject you checked, develop a concept map to identify potential speech topics.**

11-3 Write a Speech Goal Statement

Once you have chosen your topic, you are ready to identify the general goal of your speech and then to write your specific goal statement tailored to the audience and occasion.

11-3a Understanding General and Specific Speech Goals

The **general goal** is the overall intent of the speech. Most speeches intend to entertain, inform, or persuade, even though each type can include elements of the others. Consider the following examples. Jimmy Kimmel's opening monologue on *Jimmy Kimmel Live* is generally intended to entertain, even though it may include persuasive material. Presidential campaign speeches are intended to persuade, even though they also include informative

ACTION STEP 1d

Select a Topic

Use your responses to Action Steps 1a, 1b, and 1c to complete this step.

1. **Write each of the topics that you checked in Action Step 1c on the lines below:**

   _____

   _____

   _____

   _____

   _____

   _____

2. **Using the information you compiled in Action Step 1a (audience analysis), compare each topic to your audience profile. Draw a line through topics that seem less appropriate for your audience.**
3. **Using the information you compiled in Action Step 1b (analysis of the occasion), compare the remaining topics to the expectations of the occasion. Draw a line through topics that seem less suited to the occasion.**
4. **From the remaining topics, choose one that you would find enjoyable preparing and sharing in your speech.**

material. The general goal is usually dictated by the occasion. (In this course, your instructor is likely to specify it.)

Whereas the general goal is typically determined by the occasion, the **specific goal** (or specific purpose) is a single statement that identifies the desired response a speaker wants from the audience. For a speech about vanishing honeybees, for instance, you might state a specific goal as, "I want my audience to understand the four reasons honeybees are vanishing" if your general goal is to inform. If your general goal is to persuade, you might state as your specific goal, "I want my audience to donate money to *Honeybee Advocacy International,* a group trying to solve the problem and stop the crisis." Figure 11.6 offers additional examples of informative and persuasive speech goals.

11-3b Phrasing a Specific Goal Statement

A specific speech goal statement must be carefully crafted because it lays the foundation for organizing your speech. The following guidelines can help you create a specific goal statement.

1. Write a first draft of your specific speech goal statement. Julia, who has been concerned with and is knowledgeable about the subject of illiteracy, drafts the following: "I want my audience to understand the effects of illiteracy." Julia's draft is a complete sentence, and it specifies the response she wants from the audience: *to understand* the effects of illiteracy. Thus, she is planning to give an informative speech.

specific goal
a single statement of the exact response the speaker wants from the audience

2. Make sure the goal statement contains only one central idea. Suppose Julia had written: "I want the audience to understand the nature of illiteracy and innumeracy." This would need to be revised because it includes two distinct ideas: illiteracy and innumeracy. It would be difficult to adequately address both within one speech. If your goal statement includes the word *and*, you probably have more than one idea and need to narrow your focus.

3. Revise the statement until it clearly articulates the desired audience response. The draft "I want my audience to understand illiteracy" is a good start, but it is fairly broad. Julia narrows the statement to: "I want my audience to understand three effects of illiteracy." This version is more specific but still does not clearly capture her intention, so she revises it again to: "I would like the audience to understand three effects of illiteracy in the workplace." Now the goal is limited by Julia's focus not only on the specific number of effects but also on a specific situation.

FIGURE 11.6

Informative and Persuasive Speech Goals

Informative Goals

Increasing Understanding: I want my audience to understand the three basic forms of a mystery story.

Increasing Knowledge: I want my audience to learn how to light a fire without a match.

Increasing Appreciation: I want my audience to appreciate the intricacies of spiderweb designs.

Persuasive Goals

Reinforce Belief : I want my audience to maintain its belief in drug-free sports.

Change Belief: I want my audience to believe that SUVs are environmentally destructive.

Motivation to Act: I want my audience to join Amnesty International.

© Cengage Learning

ACTION STEP 1e

Write a Specific Speech Goal Statement

General speech goal

_____

1. **Write a draft of your specific speech goal, using a complete sentence that specifies the type of response you want from the audience:** *to learn about, to understand,* **or** *to appreciate* **the topic.**
2. **Review the specific goal statement. If it contains more than one idea, select one and redraft your specific goal statement.**

Write your revised specific speech goal statement:

_____

_____

_____

11-4 Evaluating and Selecting Information Sources

How can you quickly find the best information related to your specific speech goal? You can start by assessing your own knowledge and experience. Then you can move to **secondary research**, which is the process of locating information discovered by other people. This includes doing Internet and library searches for relevant books, articles, general references, and Web sites. If the information you find from secondary sources doesn't answer all your questions, you may need to conduct **primary research**, which is the process of collecting data about your topic directly from the real world.

11-4a Personal Knowledge and Experience

Because you will be speaking on a topic you know something about, you can include examples from your personal experiences. For instance, a saxophone player knows how to select and care for a reed. Likewise, entrepreneurs know the key features of a business plan, and dieticians have a wealth of information about healthy diets. So Diane, a skilled long-distance runner, can draw from her own knowledge and experience to develop her speech on "How to Train for a Marathon." If you have personal knowledge and experience about the topic, however, you should also share your **credentials**—your experiences or education that qualifies you to speak with authority on a subject. For Diane, establishing her credentials means briefly mentioning her training and expertise as a long-distance runner before she launches into her speech about training for a marathon.

11-4b Secondary Research

Even if you are an expert on your topic, you may need to do secondary research as you adapt the information for your intended audience. To conduct secondary research, you'll need to know how to locate sources, what types of sources you can draw from, and how to skim and evaluate sources.

© René Mansi/iStockphoto.com

Locating Sources

Begin by locating potential sources. Today we usually start searching for potential sources online. Because there is so much material available on the Internet, we can quickly access many sources from which to collect general facts about a topic, as well as quickly identify some of the outlets that tend to publish material on it. We can also locate relevant material found on personal and commercial Web sites, blogs, and discussion boards, as well as original content created by people on sites such as YouTube.

You can also do online library searches to locate secondary sources about your topic. Some of these materials will be available digitally. Others may require you to visit a library to pick up hard copies. When you locate a source that is not available digitally or in your local library, you may be able to get it through interlibrary loan.

Visiting the library can prove helpful when you get stuck trying to locate information for your speech. Although you can ask librarians for help online via an "ask the librarian" link, visiting with them face-to-face affords you their undivided attention until you are satisfied with the sources they've helped you locate. Librarians are free resources, experts who can demystify thorny research problems. Helping you is their job, so you're not imposing on them when you seek their advice.

Types of Sources

You'll want to draw from a variety of source types. You can find pertinent information in encyclopedias, books, articles in academic journals and magazines, newspapers, statistical sources, biographies, quotation books and Web sites, and government documents.

1. Encyclopedias Encyclopedia entries can serve as a good starting point by providing an overview acquainting you with the basic terminology associated with a topic. But because encyclopedias provide only overviews, they should never be the only source you rely on. General encyclopedias contain short articles about a wide variety of subjects. In addition, specialized encyclopedias focus on areas such as art, history, religion, philosophy, and science.

2. Books If your topic has been around for awhile, books have probably been written about it. Although books are excellent sources of in-depth material about a topic, keep in mind that most of the information in a book is likely to be at least two years old by the time it is published. So books are not a good resource if you're looking for the latest information on a topic.

3. Articles Articles may contain more current or highly specialized information on your topic than a book. They are published in **periodicals**—magazines and journals that appear at regular intervals. The information in periodical articles is often more current than that published in books because many periodicals are published weekly, biweekly, or monthly. So a periodical article is likely to be a better source if a topic is one that's "in the news." Four frequently available periodical databases are InfoTrac College Edition, InfoTrac University Library, Periodical Abstract, and EBSCO.

periodicals
magazines and journals that appear at regular intervals

4. Newspapers Newspaper articles are excellent sources of facts about and interpretations of both contemporary and historical issues and provide information about local issues and perspectives. Keep in mind, however, that most authors of newspaper articles are journalists who are not experts themselves on the topics they write about. Therefore, it is best not to rely solely on newspaper articles for your speech. Today, most newspapers are available online, which makes them very accessible.

5. Statistical Sources Statistical sources present numerical information on a wide variety of subjects. When you need facts about demography, continents, heads of

To Wikipedia or Not to Wikipedia?

Wikipedia is one of the top ten Web sites used worldwide, offering over 18 million articles in 279 different languages; the English language section alone features 3.77 million articles (Cohen, 2011; Kirkpatrick, 2011) Nonetheless, hoaxes and other incidents have spurred a "credibility" backlash against the site. U.S. courts have begun ruling that Wikipedia cannot be used as legal evidence, and in October 2011, Wikipedia member Sven Manguard reported the community was facing a huge backlog of editorial work with over 250,000 articles lacking even a single citation to support them (Manguard, 2011). Though Wikipedia and its community plan to take steps to address the problem and ensure more quality content in the future, these sorts of issues have led many educators to discourage their students from using Wikipedia as a research tool. Some schools have even banned access to it completely. Even Wikipedia founder Jimmy Wales cautions against relying on the site as a primary source (Helm, 2005).

But some educators argue that to simply dismiss Wikipedia as a "bad" source misses the opportunity for students to think critically about how to do authoritative research. Many university librarians suggest that instead of simply banning Wikipedia's use, today's college students need to be taught to develop information literacy skills that will help them navigate an increasingly complex information environment. For example, instead of uncritically accepting a Wikipedia entry as "fact," students should, at the very least, verify the information by clicking on the sources in the "Notes" section at the end of an entry to see if it comes from a primary and trusted source.

© Sergej Khakimullin/Shutterstock.com

© Kozirsky/Shutterstock.com

skimming
rapidly viewing a work to determine what is covered and how

abstract
a short paragraph summarizing the research findings

valid sources
sources that report factual information that can be counted on to be true

accurate sources
sources that present unbiased information that includes a balanced discussion of controversial ideas

reliable sources
sources with a history of presenting accurate information

state, weather, or similar subjects, access one of the many single-volume sources that report such data.

6. Biographies When you need an account of a person's life, from thumbnail sketches to reasonably complete essays, you can use a biographical reference source. Although you can access some biographical information online, you will find information of more depth and breadth by reading full-length biographies and by consulting biographical references such as *Who's Who in America* and *International Who's Who*.

7. Quotation Books and Web Sites A good quotation can be especially provocative as well as informative, and there are times you want to use a quotation from a respected person. *Bartlett's Familiar Quotations* is a popular source of quotes from historical as well as contemporary figures. But many other collections of quotations are also available.

8. Government Documents If your topic is related to public policy, government documents may provide useful information. The *Federal Register* publishes daily regulations and legal notices issued by the executive branch of the United States and all federal agencies. The *Monthly Catalog of United States Government Publications* covers publications of all branches of the federal government.

Skim Sources

Because your search of secondary sources is likely to uncover far more information than you can use, you

will want to skim sources to determine whether or not to read them in full. **Skimming** is a method of rapidly viewing a work to determine what is covered and how.

As you skim an article, think about whether it really presents information on the area of the topic you are exploring and whether it contains any documented statistics, examples, meaningful visuals, or quotable opinions. Many journal articles are printed with an **abstract**—a short paragraph summarizing the research findings—which may make it easier for you to determine if you can use the information in your speech. As you skim a book, read the table of contents carefully, look at the index, and review the headings and visuals in pertinent chapters, asking the same questions as you would for a magazine article. A few minutes spent skimming will save you hours of time.

Evaluate Sources

The validity, accuracy, and reliability of secondary sources vary widely. **Valid sources** report factual information that can be counted on to be true. Tabloid magazines and tabloid newspapers are generally considered less valid sources for information on celebrities than mainline news organizations that use "fact-checkers" before publishing an article. **Accurate sources** present unbiased information that often includes a balanced discussion of controversial ideas. For example, the *Congressional Record* provides an accurate account of what each member of U.S. Congress has said on the House or Senate floor. A newspaper account of a member's speech, however, may only report part of what was said and may distort the remark by taking it out of context. **Reliable sources** are those with a history of presenting accurate information. For example, the *Bureau of Labor Statistics* is an accurate source for information about U.S. employment. A union newsletter, on the other hand, may sometimes report accurate information about employment trends and at other times may report only information that supports its case. Four criteria can help you assess the validity, accuracy, and reliability of sources.

Authority. The first test of a source is the expertise of its author and/or the reputation of the publishing or sponsoring organization. When an author is listed, you can check the author's credentials through biographical references or by seeing if the author has a home page listing professional qualifications. Use the electronic periodical indexes or check the Library of Congress to see what else the author has published in the field.

On the Internet, you will sometimes find information that is anonymous or credited to someone whose background is not clear. In these cases, your ability to trust the information depends on evaluating the qualifications of the sponsoring organization. URLs ending in .gov (governmental), .edu (educational), and .org are noncommercial sites with institutional publishers. The domain name .com indicates that the Web site sponsor is a for-profit organization. If you do not know whether you can trust the sources, do not use the information.

Objectivity. Although all authors have a viewpoint, be wary of information that seems excessively slanted. Documents that have been published by business, government, or public interest groups should be carefully scrutinized for obvious biases or good public relations fronts. To evaluate the potential biases in articles and books, read the preface or identify the thesis statement. These often reveal the author's point of view. When evaluating a Web site with which you are unfamiliar, look for its purpose. Most home pages contain a purpose or mission statement (sometimes in a link called "About"). Armed with this information, you are in a better position to recognize potential biases in the information.

Currency. In general, newer information is more accurate than older information (unless, for example, you are documenting a historical event). So when evaluating your sources, unless your speech covers a historical event, be sure to consult the latest information you can find. One of the reasons for using Web-based sources is that they can provide more up-to-date information than printed sources. But just because a source is found online

does not mean that the information is timely. To determine how current the information is, you will need to find out when the book was published, the article was written, the study was conducted, or the article was placed on the Web or revised. Web page dates are usually listed at the end of the article. If there are no dates listed, you have no way of judging how current the information is.

> **fieldwork observations**
> a research method focused on careful observations of people or groups of people while immersed in their community

Relevance. During your research, you will likely come across a great deal of interesting information. Whether that information is appropriate for your speech is another matter. Relevant information is directly related to your topic and supports your main points, making your speech easier to follow and understand. Irrelevant information will only confuse listeners, so you should avoid using it no matter how interesting it is.

11-4c Primary Research

When there is little secondary research available on your topic or on a main idea you want to develop in your speech, or when you wonder whether what you are reading about is true in a particular setting, consider doing primary research. Recall that *primary research* is conducting your own study in the real world. But keep in mind that primary research is much more labor intensive and time consuming than secondary research—and, in the professional world, much more costly. You can conduct fieldwork observations, surveys, interviews, original artifact or document examinations, or experiments.

Fieldwork Observations

You might choose to learn about a group of people and their practices by conducting **fieldwork observations**, which is a method focused on careful observation of people or groups of people while immersed in their community. You can conduct fieldwork as a *participant observer* by engaging in interactions and activities with the people you are studying, or as a *non-participant observer* by observing but not engaging with them. If, for instance, you are planning to talk about how social service agencies help the homeless find shelter and job training, or the process involved in adopting a pet, you can learn more by visiting or even volunteering for a period of time at a homeless shelter or humane society. By focusing on specific behaviors and taking notes on your observations, you will have a record of specifics that you can use in your speech.

© Mihai Simonia/Shutterstock.com

↘ Evaluate all Web sources carefully for trustworthy information. Citing bad sources decreases your credentials.

expert
a person who has mastered a specific subject, usually through long-term study

anecdotes
brief, often amusing stories

narratives
accounts, personal experiences, tales, or lengthier stories

comparisons
illuminate a point by showing similarities

contrasts
illuminate a point by highlighting differences

plagiarism
the unethical act of representing a published author's work as your own

annotated bibliography
a preliminary record of the relevant sources you find as you conduct your research

necessary are opinions. Whether they are expert opinions depends on who made the statements. An **expert** is a person who has mastered a specific subject, usually through long-term study, and who is recognized by other people in the field as being a knowledgeable and trustworthy authority. When you use expert opinions in your speech, remember to cite their credentials.

11-5c Elaborations

Both factual information and expert opinions can be elaborated upon through anecdotes and narratives, comparisons and contrasts, or quotable explanations and opinions.

Anecdotes and Narratives

Anecdotes are brief, often amusing stories; **narratives** are accounts, personal experiences, tales, or lengthier stories. Because holding audience interest is important and because audience attention is likely to be captured by a story, anecdotes and narratives are worth looking for or creating. The key to using them is to be sure the point of the story directly addresses the point you are making in your speech. Good anecdotes and narratives may be humorous, sentimental, suspenseful, or dramatic.

Comparisons and Contrasts

One of the best ways to give meaning to new ideas or facts is through comparison and contrast. **Comparisons** illuminate a point by showing similarities, whereas **contrasts** highlight differences. Although comparisons and contrasts may be literal, like comparing and contrasting the murder rates in different countries or during different eras, they may also be figurative.

- *Figurative comparison*: "In short, living without health insurance is as much of a risk as having uncontrolled diabetes or driving without a safety belt" (Nelson, 2006, p. 24).

- *Figurative contrast:* "If this morning you had bacon and eggs for breakfast, I think it illustrates the difference. The eggs represented 'participation' on the part

of the chicken. The bacon represented 'total commitment' on the part of the pig!" (Durst, 1989, p. 325).

Quotations

At times, information you find will be so well stated that you want to quote it directly in your speech. Because the audience is interested in listening to your ideas and arguments, you should avoid using quotations that are too long or too numerous. But when you find that an author or expert has worded an idea especially well, quote it directly and then verbally acknowledge the person who said or wrote it. Using quotations or close paraphrases without acknowledging their source is **plagiarism**, the unethical act of representing another person's work as your own.

11-5d Seek Information from Multiple Cultural Perspectives

With many topics, the way we perceive facts as well as the opinions we hold are influenced by our cultural background. Therefore, it is important to seek information from a variety of cultural perspectives by drawing from sources with different cultural orientations and by interviewing experts with diverse cultural backgrounds. For example, when Carrie was preparing her speech on proficiency testing in grade schools, she purposefully searched for articles written by noted Hispanic, Asian-American, African-American, and European-American authors. In addition, she interviewed two local school superintendents—one from an urban district and another from a suburban district. Doing so boosted Carrie's confidence that her speech would accurately reflect multiple sides of the debate on proficiency testing.

11-5e Record Information

As you find information to use in your speech, you need to record it accurately and keep a careful account of your sources so you can cite them appropriately during your speech. How should you keep track of the information you plan to use? One way is to compile an annotated bibliography of the sources you believe are relevant and create a research card for each individual item of information you plan to cite in the speech.

Annotated Bibliography

An **annotated bibliography** is a preliminary record of the relevant sources you find as you conduct your research. Each entry in an annotated bibliography includes a short summary of information in that source. You can compile an annotated bibliography on your computer as you work. When you identify the exact information you want to use in the speech, you can edit your bibliography to create your speech reference list. A good annotated bibliography for speech planning includes:

- A complete bibliographic citation for each source based on the type of source (such as book, article, or Web site) and the style guide (such as APA or MLA) you are using;

- Two or three sentences summarizing the information in the source;

- Two or three sentences explaining how the source is related to your speech topic; and

- Any direct quotations you might want to include verbatim in your speech.

research cards
individual cards or facsimiles that record one piece of relevant information for your speech

oral footnotes
references to an original source, made at the point in the speech where information from that source is presented

FIGURE 11.7
Sample Research Card

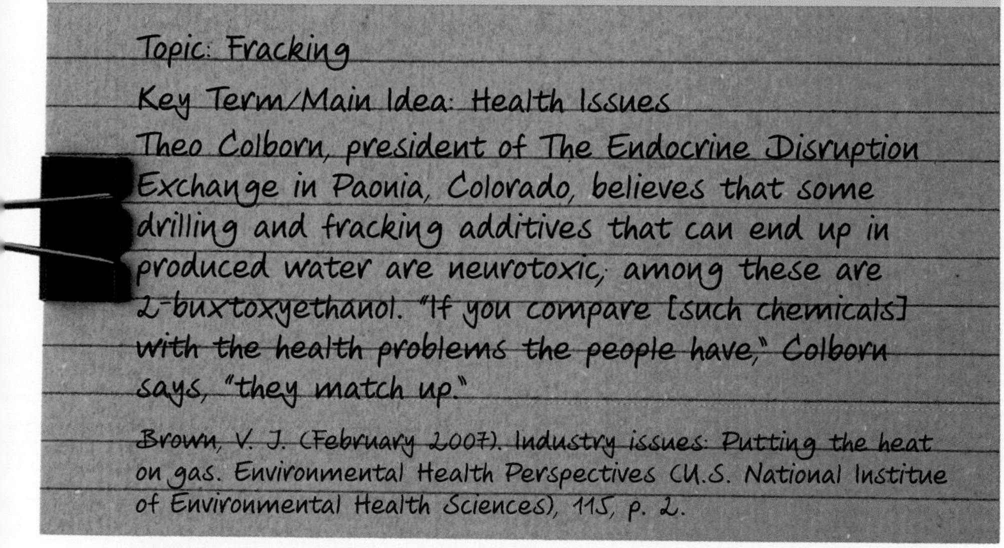

Topic: Fracking

Key Term/Main Idea: Health Issues

Theo Colborn, president of The Endocrine Disruption Exchange in Paonia, Colorado, believes that some drilling and fracking additives that can end up in produced water are neurotoxic; among these are 2-buxtoxyethanol. "If you compare [such chemicals] with the health problems the people have," Colborn says, "they match up."

Brown, V. J. (February 2007). Industry issues: Putting the heat on gas. Environmental Health Perspectives (U.S. National Institue of Environmental Health Sciences), 115, p. 2.

ACTION STEP 2b

Prepare Research Cards: Record Facts, Opinions, and Elaborations

The goal of this step is to review the source material you identified in Action Step 2a and to record specific items of information that you might wish to use in your speech.

1. Carefully read all print and electronic sources (including Web site material) you have identified and evaluated as appropriate sources for your speech. Review your notes and any tapes from interviews and observations.

2. As you read an item (fact, opinion, example, illustration, statistic, anecdote, narrative, comparison/contrast, quotation, definition, or description) that you think might be useful in your speech, record it on a research card or on the appropriate electronic note card form available on the *COMM3* CourseMate site. If you are using an article from a periodical that you read online, use the periodical research card form.

Research Cards

Research cards are individual three-by-five-inch or four-by-six-inch index cards or electronic facsimiles that record one piece of information relevant to your speech along with a key word or main idea and the bibliographic information identifying where you found it. Recording each piece of information using a key word or main idea identifier on a unique research card allows you to easily find, arrange, and rearrange individual pieces of information as you prepare your speech.

As your stack of research cards grows, you can sort the material and place each item under the heading to which it is related. Figure 11.7 shows a sample research card.

11-5f Cite Sources

As with any communication in which you use information that is not your own, you need to acknowledge the sources of the information you use in your speeches. Specifically mentioning your sources not only helps the audience evaluate them but also enhances their perception of you as knowledgeable. Frankly, failure to cite sources constitutes plagiarism. Just as you would provide internal citations or footnotes in a written document, you must provide oral footnotes during your speech. **Oral footnotes** are references to an original source, made at the point in the speech where information from that source is presented. The key to preparing oral footnotes is to include enough information for listeners to access the sources themselves and to offer enough credentials to enhance the credibility of the information you are citing. Figure 11.8 has some examples.

ACTION STEP 2c

Cite Sources

On the back of each research card, write a short phrase that you can use in your speech as an oral footnote.

FIGURE 11.8

Oral Footnotes

"Thomas Friedman, noted columnist for *The New York Times*, stated in his book *The World Is Flat* . . ."

"In an interview with *New Republic* magazine, Governor Chris Christie stated . . ."

"According to an article in last week's *Time* magazine, the average college graduate . . ."

"In the latest Gallup poll cited in the February 10 issue of *The New York Times* online . . ."

"But to get the complete picture, we have to look at the statistics. According to the *2012 Statistical Abstracts*, the level of production for the European Economic Community fell from . . ."

"During the Indo-U.S. Strategic Dialogue in Afghanistan in 2012, Secretary of State John Kerry stated . . ."

© Cengage Learning

Quick Quiz

T F 1. A well-worded specific goal statement should always contain three central ideas.

T F 2. Experience and education that qualify you to speak with authority on a subject are called credentials.

T F 3. Encyclopedias are excellent sources of facts about and interpretations of both contemporary and historical issues.

T F 4. Primary research is much more labor intensive and costly than secondary research.

T F 5. Footnotes can be written or oral.

6. A _____ is a broad area of expertise about something such as movies, cognitive psychology, or computer technology.

   a. subject
   b. talking point
   c. topic
   d. main idea
   e. bullet point

7. Demographic information of an audience member includes

   a. occupation, income, and education.
   b. gender and age.
   c. race and language.
   d. ethnicity and religion.
   e. All of these are correct.

8. Each of the following questions should be asked about the speech occasion to help with speech planning beforehand except

   a. What are the special expectations for the speech?
   b. Will a meal be served before the speech?
   c. What is the appropriate length for the speech?
   d. How large will the audience be?
   e. Where will the speech be given?

9. Although _____ are excellent sources of in-depth material about a topic, most of the information is likely to be at least two years old at the time of publishing.

   a. statistical sources
   b. encyclopedias
   c. periodicals
   d. books
   e. government documents

10. When presenting information in a speech that you've learned from a secondary source, it is crucial to _____ or you could be accused of _____.

   a. tell the truth; ethical behavior
   b. cite sources; plagiarism
   c. fabricate statistics; lying
   d. read your full bibliography during the speech; being sloppy
   e. show confidence; concept mapping

Answers: 1. F, 2. T, 3. F, 4. T, 5. T, 6. A, 7. E, 8. B, 9. D, 10. B

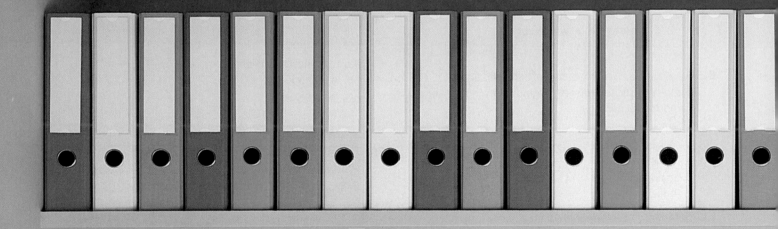

Organizing
Your Speech

What do you think?
Speeches that are funny
are the most memorable.

1	2	3	4	5	6	7	8	9	10
STRONGLY DISAGREE									STRONGLY AGREE

Learning Outcomes

12-1 Describe methods for developing the body of your speech

12-2 Explain how to create an introduction

12-3 Explain how to prepare a conclusion

12-4 Examine guidelines for listing sources

12-5 Develop a method for reviewing the outline

We often hear speeches that are packed with interesting information and delivered in ways that hold our attention, but when we reflect on what was said we find it difficult to recall the speaker's main ideas, or even the overall goal of the speech. Although every speech should have an introduction, a body, and a conclusion, not all speeches that have these components are well organized. So we may listen to a speech and find that, even though we have been entertained, the speaker's words have no lasting impact on us.

Well-constructed speeches have impact. When a speech is over, we must remember not only the opening joke or a random story, but we must also remember the main ideas that the speaker presented. In this chapter, we describe the third of the five speech plan action steps. When you have completed this step, you can be confident that your speech not only will maintain your audience's interest but will help your audience understand and remember what you have said.

Organizing, the process of structuring the material you will present in your speech, is guided by what you learned when you conducted your audience analysis. When the audience's expectations are violated or when they can't understand your goal or follow your main

organizing
the process of structuring the material to be presented in the speech

ACTION STEPS

Action Step 3
Organize Ideas into a Well-Structured Outline

points, they may get frustrated, "tune out," or even become hostile. To turn your ideas into a well-organized outline, begin by developing the body, then the introduction, and finally the conclusion.

12-1 Developing the Body

Once you have completed the first two action steps (identified your general and specific speech goal and assembled a body of information on your topic), you are ready to plan the body of your speech by (a) choosing the main points, (b) crafting them into a well-phrased thesis statement, (c) outlining the body of the speech, and (d) creating transitions.

12-1a Choose Main Points

Begin to organize the body of your speech by identifying the main ideas you want to share. The **main points** are complete sentence statements of the two to four central ideas your audience needs to understand if you are to achieve your speech goal. You will then develop each main idea with supporting material. Usually, the difference between a five-minute speech and a 25-minute speech with the same speech goal is not the number of main points but the extent to which each one is developed with supporting material.

For some goals, determining the main points is easy. For example, if your goal is to teach your audience how to create a Web site, your main points will likely be the steps involved in developing a very basic one. Most times, however, it is more difficult to identify main points that achieve your speech goal. How can you identify the main ideas when they aren't obvious? First, begin by listing the ideas you believe relate to your specific goal. You will probably find it easy to list as many as nine or more. Second, eliminate ideas that your analysis suggests your audience already understands. Third, eliminate any ideas that might be too complicated or too broad for your audience to comprehend in the time allotted for your speech. Fourth, check to see if some of the ideas can be grouped together under a broader concept. Finally, from

Raise a Glass: Giving a Toast

While a celebratory toast may not seem like the place for a prepared and structured speech, most experts suggest it's best to prepare your remarks ahead of time. This will give you a chance to gather your thoughts and help you manage your nerves when you actually give the toast. Practicing aloud in advance will also help you to sound more natural and conversational because you are less likely to simply read it.

When considering how to structure your toast, begin by writing down your thoughts about the subject of the toast. From this brainstorming list, you can begin to structure your speech by pairing your research with your personal experience and your personal knowledge. A toast should focus on the personal. At a wedding, for example, humorous or heartfelt anecdotes about the couple can be a great way to personalize the speech and keep your audience interested. In fact, including a joke or a poignant memory about the bride or groom can be an effective way to start your toast and set the tone for the entire speech. Most experts recommend keeping such personal anecdotes positive rather than embarrassing. Be mindful of your audience, as it's unlikely that Grandma wants to hear a raunchy story about the bride's single days. Choosing an appropriate anecdote can help you structure the entire speech, as the emotions brought out in the anecdote can set up the well-wishes you use to end your toast. You can end with your own words or turn to popular quotations that exemplify the positive emotions you've expressed during your toast.

© Nyul/iStockphoto.com

the ideas that remain, choose two to four that are most central to your specific speech goal.

Let's look at how Katie used these steps to identify the main points for a speech whose goal was to "inform my classmates of the growing problem of Adderall abuse among college students." To begin, Katie listed ideas she had discovered while doing her research.

- What is a prescription drug?
- What is Adderall?
- What are the ingredients in Adderall?
- How is Adderall made?
- What is the history of Adderall?
- Who uses Adderall?
- Why is it prescribed?
- What are its benefits?
- What are its risks?
- How many college students use Adderall without a prescription?
- What are the demographics of college students who use Adderall without a prescription?
- Why do college students who don't have a prescription use it (perceived benefits)?
- What are the benefit myths?
- What are actual results or consequences of this behavior?

Second, Katie eliminated the idea "what is a prescription drug" because she knew her audience already understood this. Third, Katie noticed that several of the ideas seemed to be related. What is Adderall, why is it prescribed, and who uses it—as well as its risks and benefits—seemed to go together. How many people use Adderall, user demographics, and perceived benefits of college students who use Adderall without a prescription also seemed to be related. Benefit myths and actual results/consequences could be grouped together as well. Fourth, Katie decided that she could not discuss the ingredients, history, and manufacture of Adderall in the time allotted for the speech; she further determined that these topics were not directly related to her goal.

Based on this examination, Katie decided her main points would be: (1) Adderall is a prescription drug developed for a specific purpose; (2) Adderall's ability to increase memory retention has made it a popular drug among college students looking for an edge; and

(3) Using Adderall as a study aid can cause serious problems. These main points became the framework for the body of Katie's speech. When she finished her analysis and synthesis, Katie's list looked like Figure 12.1.

12-1b Write the Thesis Statement

A **thesis statement** is a one- or two-sentence summary of your speech that incorporates your general and specific goals and previews the main points. Katie crafted the following thesis statement for her speech on Adderall: "I want to inform my audience about the growing problem of college students taking Adderall without a prescription by explaining the nature and purpose of Adderall as a prescription drug, its growing popularity as a study aid among college students, and problems associated with using Adderall without a prescription."

thesis statement
a one- or two-sentence summary of your speech that states your general and specific goals and previews the main points

ACTION STEP **3a**

Choose Main Points

The goal of this activity is to help you determine two to four main ideas or main points that you can use as the framework for your speech.

1. List all the ideas you have found that relate to the specific goal of your speech.

_____

_____

_____

_____

2. If you have trouble limiting the number, do the following:
   a. Draw a line through each idea that you believe the audience already understands, that you have no supporting information for, or that just seems too complicated.
   b. Combine ideas that can be grouped together under a single heading.
3. From the ideas that remain, choose the two to four you will use as main points in your speech.

12-1c Outline the Speech Body

Once you have chosen your main points and written a thesis statement, you can begin to organize the information you want to present under each main point. The most effective way to do this is to outline your speech. **Speech outlines** are full-sentence written frameworks of the sequential and hierarchical relationships among the ideas presented in a speech. In most speeches, three levels of hierarchy are all you will need: main points (numbered with Roman numerals), subpoints that support a main point (ordered under each main point with capital letters), and sometimes sub-subpoints (numbered under the relevant subpoint with Arabic numbers). Figure 12.2 shows the general form of most speech outlines. Notice that this outline proposes between two and four main points and offers at least two subpoints under each main point.

Writing your main points and subpoints in complete sentences will help you clarify the relationships between main points and subpoints. Once you have worded each main point and determined its relevant subpoints, you are ready to choose an organizational pattern that fits your thesis. Let's look at how Katie developed her outline in the following sections.

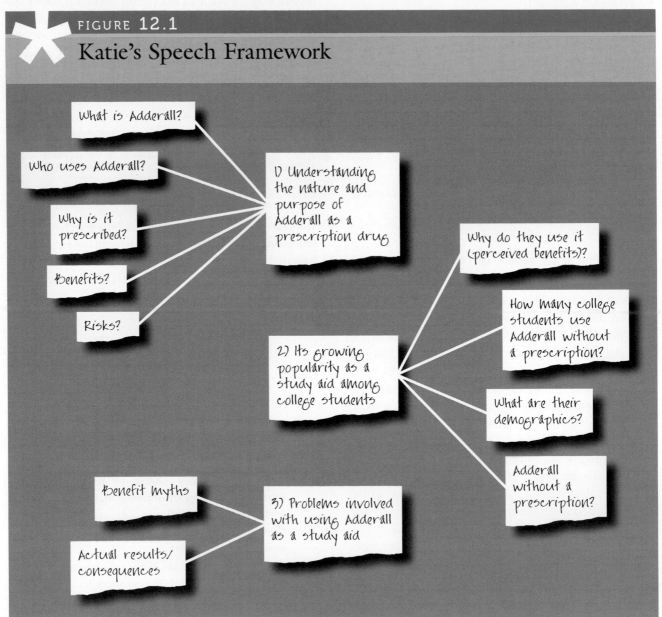

FIGURE **12.1**

Katie's Speech Framework

What is Adderall?

Who uses Adderall?

Why is it prescribed?

Benefits?

Risks?

1) Understanding the nature and purpose of Adderall as a prescription drug

Why do they use it (perceived benefits)?

How many college students use Adderall without a prescription?

2) Its growing popularity as a study aid among college students

What are their demographics?

Adderall without a prescription?

Benefit Myths

3) Problems involved with using Adderall as a study aid

Actual results/ consequences

© Cengage Learning

Word Main Points

Recall Katie's main points: understanding the nature and purpose of Adderall as a prescription drug, Adderall's growing popularity as a study aid among college students, and the risks involved in using Adderall without a prescription. Her thesis statement was: "Today I want to alert you to the uses and abuses of Adderall among college students. We'll do so by, first, discussing its nature and legal uses as a prescription drug, then its growing popularity as a study aid among college students, and, finally, the problems associated with abusing Adderall." Suppose she wrote her first draft of main points as follows:

I. What exactly is Adderall, and why is it prescribed?

II. College student use

III. Risks

From this wording, Katie would have drafted some ideas of the main points she was going to talk about and then create complete sentences for each. So she might clarify her main points like this:

I. What exactly is Adderall?

II. An increasing number of American college students are using Adderall.

III. Abusing Adderall is risky.

Study these statements. Do they seem a bit vague? Notice that we have emphasized that this is a first draft. Sometimes, the first draft of a main point is well expressed and doesn't need additional work. More often, however, we find that our first attempt doesn't quite capture what we want to say. So we need to rework our points to make

them clearer. Let's consider Katie's draft statements more carefully. Katie has made a pretty good start. Her three main points are complete sentences. Now let's see how Katie might use two test questions to assure herself that she has achieved the best wording for her points.

1. Is the relationship between each main point and the goal statement clearly specified? Katie's first main point statement doesn't indicate what purposes Adderall serves as a prescription medicine. So she could improve this statement by saying:

What exactly is Adderall, and what is it prescribed for?

Similarly, she can improve the second main point statement by saying:

Adderall abuse is becoming increasingly common among American college students.

The third point might be redrafted to state:

Abusing Adderall as a study aid is dangerous.

2. Are the main points worded with parallel structure? Main points are *parallel* to one another when their wording follows the same structural pattern.

FIGURE 12.2
General Form for a Speech Outline

I. **Main point one**
  A. Subpoint A for main point one
    1. Sub-subpoint one (optional)
    2. Sub-subpoint two (optional)
  B. Subpoint B for main point one
II. **Main point two**
  A. Subpoint A for main point two
    1. Sub-subpoint one (optional)
    2. Sub-subpoint two (optional)
  B. Subpoint B of main point two
III. **Main point three**
  A. Subpoint A for main point three
    1. Sub-subpoint one (optional)
    2. Sub-subpoint two (optional)
  B. Subpoint B of main point three
  . . . and so on.

© Cengage Learning

ACTION STEP 3b

Write a Thesis Statement

The goal of this activity is to use your specific goals and the main points you have identified to develop a well-worded thesis statement for your speech.

1. Write the general and specific goals you developed in chapter 11 with Action Step 1e.

2. List the main points you determined in Action Step 3a.

3. Now write a complete sentence that combines your specific goal with your main point ideas.

Parallel structure is not a requirement, but it can help the audience recognize main points when you deliver your speech. Katie notices that she could make her main points parallel with a small adjustment:

I. First, what exactly is Adderall, and why is it prescribed?

II. Second, a growing number of American college students are using Adderall.

III. Third, abusing Adderall as a study aid is dangerous.

Parallelism can be achieved in many ways. Katie used numbering: "first . . . second . . . third." Another way is to start each sentence with an active verb. Suppose Adam wants his audience to understand the steps involved in writing an effective job application cover letter. He might write the following first draft of his main points:

I. Format the heading elements correctly.

II. The body of the letter should be three paragraphs long.

III. When concluding, use "sincerely" or "regards."

IV. Then you need to proofread the letter carefully.

After further consideration, Adam might revise his main points to make them parallel in structure by using active verbs (italicized):

I. *Format* the heading elements correctly.

II. *Organize* the body into three paragraphs.

III. *Conclude* the letter with "sincerely" or "regards."

IV. *Proofread* the letter carefully.

Notice how the similarity of structure clarifies the message. The audience can immediately identify the key steps in the process and the parallel structure makes the main points easier to remember.

Select an Organizational Pattern

A speech can be organized in many different ways. An **organizational pattern** is a logical way to structure information that makes it easy for an audience to follow what is being said. Although speeches may use many different organizational patterns, four fundamental patterns are time (a.k.a. sequential or chronological) order, narrative order, topical order, and logical reasons order.

1. Time order, sometimes called **sequential order** or **chronological order**, arranges main points in sequence or by steps in a process. When you are explaining how to do something, how to make something, how something works, or how something happened, you will use time order. Adam's speech on the steps in writing a job application and cover letter followed a time order pattern. Let's look at another example of time order.

Thesis statement: The four steps involved in developing a personal network are to analyze your current networking potential, to position yourself in places for opportunity, to advertise yourself, and to follow up on contacts.

I. First, analyze your current networking potential.

II. Second, position yourself in places for opportunity.

III. Third, advertise yourself.

IV. Fourth, follow up on contacts.

2. Narrative order structures your ideas through a story or series of stories. Narrative order is rooted in narrative theory, which suggests that one important way people communicate is through storytelling. We use stories to teach and learn, to entertain, and to make sense of the world around us (Fisher, 1987). While a narrative may be presented in chronological order, it may also use a series of flashbacks or flash forwards to increase the dramatic effect. The main points in a narrative may be the events in a single story that highlights the thesis, or the main points may be individual stories, each of which dramatizes the thesis. Lonna shared her story about having anorexia to help listeners understand the impact of the condition on someone's life.

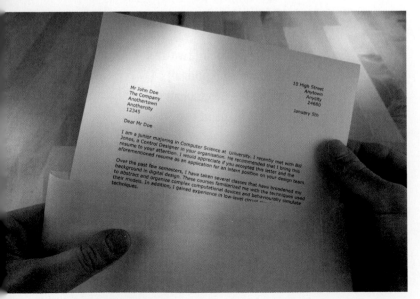

© peepo/iStockphoto.com

Thesis statement: Today, I want to share my story as a person living with anorexia. I'll start by describing what a typical day is like for me as a recovering anorexic, then how I became anorexic, and finally, who saved my life.

I. Let me begin by telling you a story about what a typical day is like for me today as a recovering anorexic.

II. Becoming anorexic was a gradual process that began when I was a high school gymnast.

III. When I nearly died as a college sophomore, I got the help I needed thanks to two people I consider to be angels on earth.

3. Topical order structures the main points using some logical relationship among them. Main points may be organized to progress from general to specific, least to most important, most to least familiar, and so forth. In the following example, the most important point is presented last and the second most important point is presented first, which is the order that the speaker believes is most suitable for the audience and speech goal.

Thesis statement: To maintain good health, let's discuss three proven methods for ridding our bodies of harmful toxins: staying hydrated, reducing animal foods, and eating natural whole foods.

I. One proven method for ridding our bodies of harmful toxins is reducing our intake of animal products.

II. A second proven method for ridding our bodies of harmful toxins is eating more natural whole foods.

III. A third proven method for ridding our bodies of harmful toxins is keeping well hydrated.

4. Logical reasons order structures the main points as reasons for accepting the thesis as desirable or true. Logical reasons order is usually used when your goal is to persuade.

Thesis statement: Donating to the United Way is appropriate because your one donation can be divided among many charities, you can stipulate which specific charities you wish to support, and a high percentage of your donation goes to charities.

I. When you donate to the United Way, your one donation can be divided among many charities.

© Monkey Business Images/Shutterstock.com

THE LAST POINT, STAYING HYDRATED, IS HIGHLIGHTED IN THE TOPICAL ORGANIZATION STRUCTURE.

II. When you donate to the United Way, you can stipulate which charities you wish to support.

III. When you donate to the United Way, you know that a high percentage of your donation will go directly to the charities you've selected.

These four organizational patterns are the most basic ones. In chapters 16 and 17, you will be introduced to several additional patterns for structuring the main points of informative and persuasive speeches.

Identify Subpoints

Subpoints are statements that elaborate on a main point. A main point may have two, three, or even more subpoints depending on the complexity of it. Subpoints use **supporting material**—developmental material you gathered through secondary and primary research.

topical order
an organizational pattern that structures the main points using some logical relationship among them

logical reasons order
an organizational pattern that structures the main points as reasons for accepting the thesis as desirable or true

subpoints
statements that elaborate on a main point

supporting material
developmental material you gathered through secondary and primary research

Subpoints and/or sub-subpoints may be elaborated with definitions, examples, statistics, personal experiences, stories, quotations, and other items.

As a first step, you can sort the research cards you prepared earlier into piles that correspond to each of your main points. Or color-code your annotated bibliography to indicate which sources relate to which main points. After categorizing each piece of information by main points, make a list of the subpoints that belong to each main point. Then look for relationships between and among ideas. As you analyze, you can draw lines connecting items of information that fit together logically, cross out information that seems less important or doesn't really fit, and combine similar ideas using different language. One subpoint in each main point should be a **listener relevance link**, a piece of information that alerts listeners to why the main point is related to them or why they should care about this point.

Outline Subpoints

Subpoints should also be represented on the outline in full sentences. It helps to include internal references for items of information you found in secondary sources. Doing so will remind you to cite them during the speech, which will enhance listeners' perception of you as an authority on the subject and help you avoid unintentional plagiarism. As with main points, subpoints should be revised until they are clearly stated. Katie developed her first main point this way:

I. Adderall is a psychostimulant prescribed to treat three conditions.

   A. Adderall, the brand name for amphetamine-dextroamphetamine is a psychostimulant, one of a class of drugs intended to promote concentration, suppress hyperactivity, and promote healthy social experiences for patients.

      1. Adderall stimulates the central nervous system by increasing the amount of dopamine and norepinephrine in the brain. These chemicals are neurotransmitters that help the brain send signals between nerve cells.

      2. Mentally, Adderall brings about a temporary improvement in alertness, wakefulness, endurance, and motivation.

      3. Physically, it can increase heart rate and blood pressure and decrease perceived need for food or sleep.

ACTION STEP 3c

Outline the Main Points

The goal of this activity is to help you phrase and order your main points.

1. **Write your thesis statement (Action Step 3b).**

2. **Using the thesis statement you wrote in Action Step 3b, underline the two to four main points for your speech.**

3. **Review the main points as a group.**

   a. **Is the relationship of each main point statement to the goal statement clearly specified? If not, revise.**

   b. **Are the main points parallel in structure? If not, revise.**

4. **Choose an organizational pattern for your main points.**

5. **Write your main points down in this order. Place a "I." before the main point you will make first, a "II." before your second point, and so on.**

B. Adderall is prescribed for the medical treatment of attention deficit/hyperactivity disorder (ADHD) in children and adults as well as for narcolepsy and clinical depression.

   1. ADHD is a neurobehavioral developmental disorder characterized by problems of attention coupled with hyperactivity.

      a. Since the mid-1990s, there has been a documented increase in the number of American children diagnosed and treated for ADHD.

      b. According to the *Diagnostic and Statistical Manual of Mental Disorders (2000)*, symptoms must be present for at least six months for diagnosis, and symptoms must be excessive for medicinal treatment.

      c. The drugs Ritalin and Dexedrine are also used to treat ADHD. Adderall, however, remains the most widely prescribed of these drugs.

      d. According to the Centers for Disease Control and Prevention, approximately 4.4 million American children have been diagnosed with ADHD, and more than 2.5 million of those patients have been prescribed medicine to treat the condition.

Identify and Outline Subpoints

The goal of this activity is to help you develop and outline your subpoints. Complete the following steps for each of your main points.

1. **List the main point.**
2. **Using your research cards or annotated bibliography, list the key information related to that main point.**
3. **Analyze that information and cross out items that seem less relevant or don't fit.**
4. **Look for items that seem related and can be grouped under a broader heading.**
5. **Try to group information until you have between two and four supporting points for the main point.**
6. **Write those supporting subpoints in full sentences.**
7. **Repeat this process for all main points.**
8. **Write an outline using Roman numerals for main points, capital letters for supporting points, and Arabic numbers for material related to supporting points.**

2. Adderall is also prescribed to treat narcolepsy, which occurs when the brain can't normally regulate cycles of sleep and waking, so sufferers experience excessive daytime sleepiness that results in episodes of suddenly falling asleep.

3. Adderall can also be used to treat clinical depression, a disorder that is characterized by low mood, a loss of interest in normal activities, and low self-esteem.

12-1d **Create Transitions**

Transitions are words, phrases, or sentences that allow you to move smoothly from one point to another by showing the relationship between the two ideas. Good transitions are important in writing, but they are even more important in speaking. If listeners get lost or think they have missed something, they cannot go back and check as they can when reading. Transitions can come in the form of section transitions or signposts.

Section Transitions

Section transitions are complete sentences that show the relationship between or bridge major parts

of the speech. They typically summarize what has just been said in one main point and preview the next main idea. Essentially, section transitions are the "glue" that links the main points of your speech together.

For example, suppose Adam just finished his introduction on creating a cover letter and is now ready to launch into his main points. Before stating his first main point, he might say, "Creating a good cover letter is a process that has four steps. Now, let's consider the first one." When his listeners hear this transition, they are signaled to listen to and remember the first main point. When he finishes his first main point, he will use another section transition to signal that he is finished speaking about the first main point and is moving on to the second main point: "Now that we understand what is involved in creating the heading elements, let's move on to discuss what to include in the body of the letter."

You might be thinking that this sounds repetitive or patronizing, but section transitions are important for two reasons. First, they help the audience follow the organization of ideas in the speech. Second, they help audience members remember information. To help remember and use section transitions, write them in complete sentences between the appropriate main points on your speech outline.

Signposts

Signposts are words or phrases that connect pieces of supporting material to the main point or subpoint they address. Sometimes signposts number ideas: *first, second, third,* and *fourth*. Sometimes they help the audience focus on a key idea: *foremost, most important,* or *above all*. Signposts can also be used to introduce an explanation: *to illustrate, for example, in other words, essentially,* or *to clarify*. Signposts can even signal that a lengthy anecdote, or even the speech itself, is coming to an end: *in short, finally, in conclusion,* or *to summarize*. Just as section transitions serve as the glue that holds

transitions
words, phrases, or sentences that show the relationship between or bridge ideas

section transition
a complete sentence that shows the relationship between or bridges major parts of a speech

signposts
short word or phrase transitions that connect pieces of supporting material to the main point or subpoint they address

Prepare Section Transitions

The goal of this exercise is to help you prepare section transitions. Section transitions appear as parenthetical statements before or after each main point. Using complete sentences:

1. **Write a transition from your first main point to your second.**
2. **Write a transition from each remaining main point to the one after it.**
3. **Add these transitional statements to your outline.**

your big-picture main points together, signposts connect your subpoints and supporting material together within each main point.

12-2 Developing the Introduction

Once you have developed the body of the speech, you can decide how to introduce it. Because the introduction is so important to your speech's success, you will want to develop two or three different introductions and then select the one that seems best for your specific goal and the audience you will be addressing. An introduction is generally about 10 percent of the length of the entire speech, so for a five-minute speech (approximately 750 words), an introduction of about 30 seconds (approximately 60–85 words) is appropriate.

An effective introduction achieves four primary goals: (1) it gets the audience's attention, (2) it identifies the relevance of the topic to the audience, (3) it begins to establish speaker credibility, and (4) it states the thesis (speech goal and main point preview).

startling statement
a shocking expression or example used to arouse an audience's interest

questions
requests for information that encourage an audience to think about something related to your topic

rhetorical question
a question that doesn't require an overt response from an audience

direct question
a question that demands an overt response from an audience

12-2a Get Attention

An audience's physical presence does not guarantee people will actually listen to your speech. Your first goal, then, is to create an opening that will win your listeners' attention by arousing their curiosity and motivating them to want to know more about your topic. Let's look at several strategies for getting attention: startling statements, questions, stories, jokes, personal references, quotations, action, and suspense.

Startling Statements

A **startling statement** is a shocking expression or example. Chris used this startling statement to get his listeners' attention for his speech about how automobile emissions contribute to global warming:

Look around. Each one of you is sitting next to a killer. That's right. You are sitting next to a cold-blooded killer. Before you think about jumping up and running out of this room, let me explain. Everyone who drives an automobile is a killer of the environment. Every time you turn the key to your ignition, you are helping to destroy our precious surroundings.

Questions

Questions are requests for information that encourage the audience to think about something related to your topic. Questions can be *rhetorical* or *direct*. A **rhetorical question** is one that doesn't require an overt response. Notice how a student began her speech on counterfeiting with three short, rhetorical questions:

What would you do with this $20 bill if I gave it to you? Would you take your friend to a movie? Or would you treat yourself to pizza and drinks? Well, if you did either of these things, you could get in big trouble—this bill is counterfeit!

Notice that the speaker didn't ask the question to find out what her audience members would actually do with the money, but to set up the speech on counterfeiting.

Unlike a rhetorical question, a **direct question** demands an overt response from the audience. It might be a "yea" or "nay" or a show of hands. For example, here's how author and motivational speaker Harvey MacKay started his

© dra_schwartz/iStockphoto.com

commencement address at the University of Southern California in 2009:

Let me start by asking all of you in the audience this question: How many people talk to themselves? Please raise your hands. I count approximately 50 percent. To the other 50 percent who didn't raise your hands, I can just hear you now, saying to yourself: "Who me? I don't talk to myself!"

Well I think all of you will be talking to yourself about the day's events on your way home this evening. This is an unforgettable moment among many fine hours you will have in your career and life. (Mackay, 2009)

Direct questions get audience attention because they require a physical response. However, getting listeners to actually comply with your request can also pose a challenge.

Stories

A **story** is an account of something that has happened (actual) or could happen (hypothetical). Most people enjoy a well-told story, so it makes a good attention getter. One drawback is that stories can sometimes take more time to tell than is appropriate for the length of your speech. Use a story only if it is short or if you can abbreviate it so that it is just right for your speech length.

Jokes

A **joke** is an anecdote or a piece of wordplay designed to make people laugh. A joke can be used to get attention when it meets the *three R's test:* It must be realistic, relevant, and repeatable (Humes, 1988). In other words, the joke can't be too far-fetched, unrelated to the speech purpose, or potentially offensive to some listeners. In his speech about being a person of integrity, for example, Joel Osteen offered this joke to get attention:

A kindergarten teacher asked one of her students what she was drawing a picture of. The little girl said, "I'm drawing a picture of God." The teacher replied, "Oh honey, nobody knows what God looks like." Without missing a beat, the little girl replied, "They will in a minute . . ." (Osteen, 2012)

Personal References

A **personal reference** is a brief account of something that happened to you or a hypothetical situation that listeners can imagine themselves in. In addition to getting attention, a personal reference can engage listeners as active participants. A personal reference like the one that follows is suitable for a speech of any length:

Were you panting when you got to the top of those four flights of stairs this morning? I'll bet there were a few of you who vowed you're never going to take a class on the top floor of this building again. But did you ever stop to think that maybe the problem isn't that this class is on the top floor? It just might be that you are not getting enough exercise.

Quotations

A **quotation** is a comment made by and attributed to someone other than the speaker. A particularly vivid or thought-provoking quotation can make an excellent introduction as long as it relates to your topic.

Action

An **action** is an attention-getting act designed to highlight and arouse interest in your topic. You can perform an action yourself, just as Juan did when he split a stack of boards with his hand to get attention for his speech on karate, or you can ask volunteers from the audience to perform the action. For example, Cindria used three audience members to participate in breaking a piñata to create interest in her speech on the history of the piñata. If you choose to use audience members, consider soliciting participants ahead of time to avoid the possibility of having no volunteers when you ask for them during your speech. Finally, you can ask your entire audience to perform some action related to your speech topic. If you'd like to ask your whole audience to perform an action, realistically assess whether what you are asking is something your audience is likely to comply with.

Suspense

To create **suspense**, word your attention-getter so that what is described generates uncertainty or mystery and excites the audience. When your audience wonders, "What is she leading up to?" you have created suspense.

story
an account of something that has happened or could happen

joke
an anecdote or a piece of wordplay designed to be funny and make people laugh

personal reference
a brief account of something that happened to you or a hypothetical situation that listeners can imagine themselves in

quotation
a comment made by and attributed to someone other than the speaker

action
an act designed to highlight and arouse interest in a topic

suspense
wording your attention-getter so that it generates uncertainty and excites the audience

© Mike Flippo/Shutterstock.com

A suspenseful opening is especially valuable when your audience is not particularly interested in hearing about your topic. Consider this suspenseful introduction from Midori's speech:

It costs the United States more than $116 billion per year. It has cost the loss of more jobs than a recession. It accounts for nearly 100,000 deaths a year. I'm not talking about drug abuse—the problem is alcoholism. Today I want to show you how we can avoid this inhumane killer by abstaining from alcohol.

By putting the problem, alcoholism, near the end of her suspenseful comments, Midori encourages the audience to try to anticipate her topic. And because the audience may well be thinking the problem is drugs, the revelation that the answer is alcoholism is likely to be that much more effective.

12-2b Establish Relevance

Even if you successfully get your listeners' attention, to *keep* their attention you will need to motivate them to listen to your speech. You can do this by offering a clear listener relevance link in the introduction. Recall that a listener relevance link is a statement of how and why your speech relates to or might affect your audience. Sometimes your attention-getting statement will serve this function, but if it doesn't, you will need to provide a personal connection between your topic and your audience. Notice how Tiffany created a listener relevance link for her speech about being a vegetarian by asking her audience to consider the topic in relation to their own lives:

Although a diet rich in eggs and meat was once the norm in this country, more and more of us are choosing a vegetarian lifestyle to help lower blood pressure, reduce cholesterol, and even help prevent the onset of some diseases.

When creating a listener relevance link, answer these questions: Why should my listeners care about what I'm saying? In what way(s) might they benefit from hearing about it? How might my speech address my listeners' needs or desires for such things as health, wealth, well-being, self-esteem, success, and so forth?

12-2c Establish Credibility

If someone hasn't formally introduced you, audience members are going to wonder who you are and why they should pay attention to what you say. So another goal of the introduction is to begin to build your credibility. **Credibility** is the perception your audience has about your competence and character. You want to provide some indication that you are an authority on the subject of your speech and that you care about the audience and the occasion. Remember, though, that your goal is to highlight that you are a credible speaker on this topic, one who respects the audience and occasion, not that you are *the* or even *a* final authority on the subject.

12-2d State the Thesis

Because audiences want to know what the speech is going to be about, it's important to state your thesis. After Miguel gained the audience's attention and established relevance and credibility, he introduced his thesis, "In the next five minutes, I'd like to explain to you that romantic love consists of three elements: passion, intimacy, and commitment."

Stating main points in the introduction is necessary unless you have some special reason for not revealing the details of the thesis. For instance, after getting the attention of his audience, Miguel might say, "In the next five minutes, I'd like to explain the three aspects of romantic love," a statement that specifies the number of main points but leaves specifics for transition statements immediately preceding the main points. In a commencement address at Stanford University, Steve Jobs stated the main points in his introduction in this way: "Today I want to tell you three stories from my life. That's it. No big deal. Just three stories" (Jobs, 2005).

ACTION STEP 3f

Write Speech Introductions

The goal of this activity is to create choices for how you will begin your speech.

1. For the speech body you outlined earlier, write three different introductions that you believe meet the goals of effective introductions and that you believe would set an appropriate tone for your speech goal and audience.

2. Of the three you drafted, which do you believe is the best? Why?

3. Write that introduction in outline form.

12-3 Developing the Conclusion

Shakespeare once said, "All's well that ends well." Effective conclusions heighten the impact of a good speech by summarizing the main ideas and leaving the audience with a vivid impression. Even though the conclusion is a relatively short part of the speech—seldom more than 5 percent (35 to 40 words for a five-minute speech)—your conclusion should be carefully planned. As with your speech introduction, you should prepare two or three conclusions and then choose the one you believe will be the most effective with your audience.

12-3a Summarize Main Points

An effective speech conclusion includes an abbreviated restatement of your thesis. An appropriate summary for an informative speech on how to improve your grades might be "So I hope you now understand [informative goal] that three techniques to help you improve your grades are to attend classes regularly, to develop a positive attitude toward the course, and to study systematically [main points]." A short ending for a persuasive speech on why you should exercise might be "So you should exercise for at least 30 minutes each day [persuasive goal] to improve your appearance as well as your physical and mental health [main points]."

12-3b Clinch

Although a good summary helps the audience remember your main points, a good clincher leaves the audience with a vivid impression. A **clincher** is a short memorable statement that provides a sense of closure by driving home the importance of your speech goal in a memorable way. If you can, try to devise a clincher that refers back to the introductory comments in some way. Two effective strategies for clinching are using vivid imagery and appealing to action.

Vivid Imagery

To develop vivid imagery, you can use any of the devices we discussed for getting attention (startling statement, question, story, joke, personal reference, quotation, action, or suspense). For example, in Tiffany's speech about being a vegetarian, she referred back to the personal reference she had made in her introduction about a vegetarian Thanksgiving meal:

So now you know why I made the choice to become a vegetarian and how this choice affects my life today. As a vegetarian, I've discovered a world of food I never knew existed. Believe me, I am salivating just thinking about the meal I have planned for this Thanksgiving: fennel and blood orange salad; followed by baked polenta layered with tomato, Fontina, and Gorgonzola cheeses; an acorn squash tart; marinated tofu; and with what else but pumpkin pie for dessert!

Sounds good, doesn't it? Clinchers with vivid imagery are effective because they leave listeners with a picture imprinted in their minds.

Appeal to Action

The appeal to action is a common clincher for persuasive speeches. The **appeal to action** describes the behavior that you want your listeners to follow after they have heard your arguments.

Notice how Matthew Cossolotto, president and founder of Study Abroad Alumni International, concludes his speech on global awareness and responsibility with a strong appeal to action:

So, yes, you should have this re-entry program. Yes, you should network and explore international career opportunities. That's all good.

But I also encourage you to Globalize Your Locality. I urge you to Think Global. . . . Act Global. . . . Be Global.

This is an urgent call to action . . . for you and other study abroad alumni . . . to help us reduce the global awareness deficit.

You can do so by becoming involved with SAAI . . . and other organizations such as the National Council for International Visitors, Sister Cities, or Rotary International.

You can speak to local schools and community organizations about your study abroad experience and the need for more global awareness.

When you studied abroad, I'm sure you were told many times that you would be serving as unofficial ambassadors of the United States . . . your campus . . . and even your community back home.

Now that you're home again, I hope you'll become ambassadors for the value of the study abroad experience and for the need for greater international awareness.

In wrapping up . . . I'd like to leave you with this image . . . just picture in your mind's eye

clincher
a one- or two-sentence statement that provides a sense of closure by driving home the importance of your speech in a memorable way

appeal to action
describes the behavior you want your listeners to follow after they have heard your arguments

that iconic photograph of planet earth. I'm sure you've seen it. Taken over four decades ago . . . in December 1968 . . . on the Apollo 8 mission to the moon.

The photograph—dubbed Earthrise—shows our small, blue planet rising above a desolate lunar landscape. This photo was a true watershed in human history . . . marking the first time earthlings . . . fellow global citizens had traveled outside earth's orbit and looked back on our lonely planet.

The widespread publication of Earthrise had a lot to do with launching the worldwide environmental movement. It's no accident that the first Earth Day—on April 22, 1970—took place so soon after the publication of this remarkable photograph.

We're all privileged to inhabit this same planet—truly an island in space. And voices to the contrary notwithstanding . . . whether we want to admit it or not . . . we are all, undeniably and by definition, citizens of the world.

The only question is: will we accept the responsibilities of global citizenship?

Your future . . . and perhaps the survival of the planet . . . just may depend on how many of us answer yes to that question. (Cossolotto, 2009)

12-4 Compiling the Reference List

Regardless of the type or length of your speech, you'll want to prepare a list of the sources you use in it. This list will enable you to direct audience members to the specific source of any information you used and allow you

to quickly find the information at a later date. The two standard methods of organizing source lists are (1) alphabetically by author's last name or (2) by content category, with items listed alphabetically by author within each category. For speeches with a short list, the first method is efficient. But for long speeches with a lengthy source list, it is helpful to group sources by content categories.

Many formal bibliographic style formats can be used (e.g., MLA, APA, Chicago, CBE). The "correct" form differs by professional or academic discipline. Check to see if your instructor has a preference about which style you use for this class. Figure 12.3 gives examples of Modern Language Association (MLA) and American Psychological Association (APA) citations for the most commonly used sources.

12-5 Reviewing the Outline

Now that you have created all of the parts of the outline, it is time to put them together in complete outline form and edit them to make sure the outline is well organized and well worded. Use this checklist to complete the final review of your outline.

1. Have I used a standard set of symbols to indicate structure? Main points are indicated by Roman numerals, major subpoints by capital letters, sub-subpoints by Arabic numerals, and further subdivisions by lowercase letters.

2. Have I written main points and major subpoints as complete sentences? Complete

FIGURE 12.3

Examples of MLA and APA Citation Forms for Speech Sources

	MLA Style	APA Style
Book	Jones, Phillip March. *Points of Departure: Roadside Memorial Polaroids*. Lexington, KY: The Jargon Society, 2011.	Jones, P. M. (2011). *Points of departure: Roadside memorial polaroids*. Lexington, KY: The Jargon Society.
Academic Journal	Von Burg, Ron. "Decades Away or *The Day After Tomorrow?*: Rhetoric, Film, and the Global Warming Debate." *Critical Studies in Media Communication*, 29.1(2012):7–26.	Von Burg, R. (2012). Decades away or *The Day After Tomorrow?*:Rhetoric, film, and the global warming debate. *Critical Studies in Media Communication, 29*(1) 7–26.
Magazine	Abrahamson, Rachel Paula. "Destroyed by Plastic Surgery." *US Weekly*, 19 March, 2012: 54–55.	Abrahamson, R. P. (2012, March 19). Destroyed by plastic surgery. *US Weekly, 892*, 54–55.
Web Site	"Supplier Responsibility at Apple." Apple.com. n.d. Web. 01 June 2012.	Apple. (n.d.). Supplier responsibility at Apple. Retrieved from http://www.apple.com /supplierresponsibility/
Blog Post	Ramsey, G. "UK Hoops Dominates SEC Awards." Cat Scratches: The Official Blog of UK Athletics. ukathletics.com. 29 February 2012. Web. 01 June 2012.	Ramsey, G. (2012, February 29). UK hoops dominates SEC awards [Web blog post]. Retrieved from http://www.ukathletics.com/blog/2012/02/uk-hoops -dominates-sec-awards.html
Movie	*The Iron Lady*. Dir. Phyllida Lloyd. Prod. Damien Jones. Pathe, 2011. DVD.	Jones, D. (Producer), & Lloyd, P. (Director). (2011). *The iron lady* [Motion picture]. United Kingdom: Pathe.
Online Video	"Barry Schwartz: The Paradox of Choice." TEDtalks. *YouTube*. 2007. Web. 01 June 2012.	TEDtalksDirector. (2007, January 16). *Barry Schwartz: The paradox of choice* [Video file]. Retrieved from http://www.youtube.com/watch?v=VO6XEQIsCoM

© Cengage Learning

sentences help you to see (1) whether each main point actually develops your speech goal and (2) whether the wording makes your intended point.

3. Do main points and major subpoints each contain a single idea? This guideline ensures that the development of each part of the speech will be relevant to the point. Thus, rather than:

Organically produced food is good for the environment and good for animals and good for you.

Divide the sentence so that each part is stated separately:

I. *Organically produced food is good for the environment.*

II. *Organically produced food is good for animals.*

III. *Organically produced food is good for you.*

4. Does each major subpoint relate to or support its major point? This principle, called subordination, ensures that you don't wander off point and confuse your audience. For example:

I. *Proper equipment is necessary for successful play.*

A. *Good gym shoes are needed for maneuverability.*

B. *Padded gloves will help protect your hands.*

C. *A lively ball provides sufficient bounce.*

D. *A good attitude doesn't hurt either.*

Notice that the main point deals with equipment. Subpoints A, B, and C (shoes, gloves, and ball) all relate to the main point. But D, attitude, is not equipment and should appear under some other main point, if at all.

5. Are potential subpoint elaborations indicated? Recall that subpoint elaborations help build the speech. Because you don't know how long it might take you to discuss these elaborations, you should include more than you are likely to use. During rehearsals, you may discuss each a different way.

Now that we have considered the various parts of an outline, let us put them together for a final look. The complete outline for Katie's speech on Adderall illustrates the principles in practice.

Speech Outline

Using and Abusing Adderall: What's the Big Deal?

by Katie Anthony
University of Kentucky

© Marioci/Shutterstock.com

General goal:

I want to inform my audience.

Specific goal:

I would like the audience to understand the uses and abuses of Adderall by college students.

Thesis statement:

I want to inform you about the growing problem of off-label Adderall usage by college students, explaining the nature and legal uses of Adderall, its growing popularity as a study aid for college students, and the problems associated with abusing Adderall.

Introduction

I. Attention getter: Raise your hand if anyone you know has taken the drug Adderall. Keep your hand raised if the person you know to be taking Adderall is doing so without a prescription for the drug.

   ▶ *Attention getter*

II. Listener relevance: The illegal use of stimulants like Adderall among college students has increased dramatically over the past decade. The latest National Study on Drug Use and Health found that nearly 7 percent of full-time college students reported using Adderall without a prescription. So if you know ten people who are in college, it is likely that you know someone who is abusing Adderall.

   ▶ *Listener relevance*

III. Speaker credibility: I became interested in this topic my freshman year when my roommate received a call from her mother telling her that her best friend, who was a sophomore at a different college, had died suddenly from an Adderall-induced heart attack. Because I had several friends who were also using Adderall without a prescription but who thought it was safe to do so, I began to read all I could about the drug, its use, and its risks. Not only have I become versed in the written information on Adderall, but I have also interviewed several faculty here who are studying the problem, and I have become an undergraduate research assistant helping one faculty member to collect data on this problem. Today, I want to share with you some of what I have learned.

   ▶ *Speaker credibility*

IV. Thesis statement: Specifically, I want to inform you about the growing problem of off-label Adderall usage by college students, explaining the nature and legal uses of Adderall, its growing popularity as a study aid for college students, and the problems associated with abusing Adderall.

   ▶ *Thesis statement*

Body

I. Adderall is a psychostimulant prescribed to treat three conditions.

Listener relevance link: Understanding the intended medical uses of the drug Adderall may help you understand why the drug is so widely abused by collegians.

⊙ *Listener relevance link*

A. Adderall, the brand name for amphetamine-dextroamphetamine, is a psychostimulant, one of a class of drugs intended to promote concentration, suppress hyperactivity, and promote healthy social experiences for patients (Willis, 2001).

   1. Adderall stimulates the central nervous system by increasing the amount of dopamine and norepinephrine in the brain. These chemicals are neurotransmitters that help the brain send signals between nerve cells (Daley, 2004, April 20).

   2. Mentally, Adderall brings about a temporary improvement in alertness, wakefulness, endurance, and motivation.

   3. Physically, it can increase heart rate and blood pressure and decrease perceived need for food or sleep.

B. Adderall is prescribed for the medical treatment of attention deficit/hyperactivity disorder (ADHD) in children and adults as well as for narcolepsy and clinical depression.

   1. ADHD is a neurobehavioral developmental disorder characterized by problems of attention coupled with hyperactivity.

      a. Since the mid-1990s, there has been a documented increase in the number of American children diagnosed and treated for ADHD (McCabe, Teter, & Boyd, 2004).

      b. According to the *Diagnostic and Statistical Manual of Mental Disorders* (2000), symptoms must be present for at least six months for diagnosis and symptoms must be excessive for medicinal treatment.

      c. The drugs Ritalin and Dexedrine are also used to treat ADHD. Adderall, however, remains the most widely prescribed of these drugs (Willis, 2001).

      d. According to the Centers for Disease Control, approximately 4.4 million American children have been diagnosed with ADHD, and over 2.5 million of those patients have been prescribed medicine to treat the condition (2005).

   2. Adderall is also prescribed to treat narcolepsy, which occurs when the brain can't normally regulate cycles of sleep and waking.

      a. Sufferers of narcolepsy experience excessive daytime sleepiness that results in episodes of suddenly falling asleep.

      b. A chronic sleep disorder, narcolepsy affects between 50,000 and 2.4 million Americans. (National Heart, Lung, and Blood Institute, 2008).

3. Adderall can also be used to treat clinical depression.

    a. Clinical depression is a disorder characterized by low mood, a loss of interest in normal activities, and low self-esteem.

    b. According to the National Institute of Mental Health, 9.5% of the adult population—that is nearly 1.8 million American adults suffer from clinical depression.

Now that we understand the basic properties and medical uses of the drug Adderall, let's assess the increasing level of abuse of the drug by college students.   ▶ *Transition*

II. Unfortunately, Adderall has become popular among college students, who use it as a study aid and for recreational purposes.

Listener relevance link: As college students, we need to be aware of what students believe about Adderall and why they are abusing it.   ▶ *Listener relevance link*

A. College students who don't suffer ADHD, narcolepsy, or depression will take it with no prescription because they believe that it will improve their focus and concentration, allowing them to perform better on academic tasks (Teter, McCabe, Crandford, Boyd, & Gunthrie, 2005).

    1. Adderall abuse among college students occurs especially at stressful times of the semester when students get little sleep.

        a. DeSantis, Webb, and Noar (2008) found that 72 percent of the students they surveyed reported using the drug to stay awake so that they could study longer when they had many assignments due.

        b. Katherine Stump, a Georgetown University student, reported in the school newspaper: "During finals week here at Georgetown, campus turns into an Adderall drug den. Everyone from a cappella singers to newspaper writers become addicts, while anyone with a prescription and an understanding of the free market becomes an instant pusherman" (Jaffe, 2006, January 1).

        c. Collegians report using the drug frequently during stressful times of the semester. One student said, "I use it every time I have a major paper due" (Daley, 2004, April 20).

B. Students also use Adderall for purposes other than academic ones.

    1. A survey of undergraduate and graduate students revealed that students engage in Adderall abuse for partying at a frequency just slightly less than taking the drug for academic purposes (Prudhomme White, Becker-Blease, & Grace-Bishop, 2006).

    2. DeSantis, Webb, and Noar (2007) report that students take the drug for its energizing effects. Other students report taking the drug to make them more social and outgoing at parties.

    3. Some college students, especially women, report using the drug for its use as an appetite suppressant for dieting purposes (Daley, 2004, April 20).

Now that we understand that Adderall abuse is prevalent on university campuses among students, it is important to understand the detrimental effects that can accompany the illegal use of Adderall.

▶ *Transition*

III. Whether students acknowledge the dangers or not, there are great risks involved in illegally using Adderall.

Listener relevance link: As we have now discussed the pervasiveness of Adderall abuse, statistically, it is likely that several of you have used this substance without a prescription to either enhance your academic performance or your social outings. Thus, it is important that we all recognize the adverse effects that result from taking Adderall without a prescription.

▶ *Listener relevance link*

A. Adderall abuse can cause negative health effects for individuals not diagnosed with ADHD (Daley, 2004, April 20).

1. Adderall is reported to cause a heightened risk for heart problems when used inappropriately. Problems include sudden heart attack or stroke, sudden death in individuals with heart conditions, and increased blood pressure and heart rate (FDA, 2010).

2. Adderall abuse also can result in a myriad of mental problems, including manifestation of bipolar disorder, an increase of aggressive thoughts, and a heightened risk for psychosis similar to schizophrenia (FDA, 2010).

B. Adderall is highly addictive.

1. Adderall is an amphetamine, and while amphetamines were once used to treat a variety of ailments including obesity in the 1950s and 1960s, the drugs began to be much more closely regulated once their addictive nature was realized (Daley, 2004, April 20).

2. Adderall has similar properties to cocaine, and, as a result, abuse of the drug can lead to substance dependence (FDA, 2010).

C. Though clear risks are associated with the illegal use of Adderall, unlike other drugs, collegians do not view the inappropriate use of Adderall as harmful or illegal.

1. College students typically view stimulant abuse as morally acceptable and physically harmless. In a 2010 study, DeSantis and Hane found that students were quick to justify their stimulant abuse by claiming its use was fine in moderation.

2. The *Kentucky Kernel*, the student newspaper at the University of Kentucky, published an editorial of a student who flippantly described the use of Adderall among college students. He states, "If you want to abuse ice cream, amphetamines or alcohol, then there are going to be serious problems; however, let's not pretend a person using Adderall twice a semester to help them study is in any way likely to die a horrible death or suffer terrible side effects" (Riley, 2010, May 3).

3. In a study assessing the attitudes of college students toward the inappropriate use of stimulants, the authors found that "the majority of students who reported misuse or abuse were not concerned about the misuse and abuse of prescription stimulants, and a number of students thought that they should be more readily available (Prudhomme White, Becker-Blease, & Grace-Bishop, 2006, p. 265).

Conclusion

I. Restatement of thesis: Adderall is a prescription stimulant that is increasingly being abused by college students primarily as a study aid.

II. Main point review: We have examined today what the drug Adderall is, its growing popularity among college students especially as a study aid, and the risks associated with using the drug illegally.

III. Clincher: The next time you or a friend considers taking Adderall as a study aid, think again. The potential harm that the drug could cause to your body is not worth even a perfect grade point average.

▶ *Restatement of thesis*

▶ *Main point review*

▶ *Clincher*

References

American Psychiatric Association. (2000). *Diagnostic and statistical manual of mental disorders*. Arlington, VA: Author.

Centers for Disease Control and Prevention. (2005, September 2). *Morbidity and Mortality Weekly Report (MMWR)*. Retrieved from http://www.cdc.gov

Daley, B. (2004, April 20). Perspective: Miracle drug? Adderall is prescribed for individuals with ADD and ADHD; for nonprescribed users there can be some serious risks. *Daily Pennsylvanian*. Retrieved from http://www.vpul.upenn.edu

DeSantis, A. D., & Hane, A. C. (2010). "Adderall is definitely not a drug": Justifications for the illegal use of ADHD stimulants. *Substance Use & Misuse, 45*, 31–46.

DeSantis, A. D., Webb, E. M., & Noar, S. M. (2008). Illicit use of prescription ADHD medications on a college campus: A multimethodological approach. *Journal of American College Health, 57*, 315–324.

Food and Drug Administration. (2010). *Drugs @ FDS: FDA approved drug products*. Retrieved from http://www.accessdata.fda.gov

National Heart, Blood, and Lung Institute (2008). "What is narcolepsy?" *National Heart, Blood, and Lung Institute Diseases and Conditions Index*. Retrieved from http://www.nhlbi.nih.gov/health/dci/Diseases/nar/nar_what.html

Jaffe, H. (2006, January 1). ADD and abusing Adderall. *The Washingtonian*. Retrieved from http://www.washingtonian.com

McCabe, S. E., Teter, C. J., & Boyd, C. J. (2004). The use, misuse and diversion of prescription stimulants among middle and high school students. *Substance Use and Misuse, 39*, 1095–1116.

Prudhomme White, B., Becker-Blease, K. A., & Grace-Bishop, K. (2006). Stimulant medication use, misuse, and abuse in an undergraduate and graduate student sample. *Journal of American College Health, 54*, 261–268.

Riley, T. (2010, May 3). Prescription drug abuse is a personal choice. *Kentucky Kernel*. Retrieved from http://kykernel.com

Substance Abuse and Mental Health Services Administration, Office of Applied Studies. (2009, April 7). *The NSDUH report: Nonmedical use of Adderall among full-time college students*. Rockville, MD.

Teter, J. C., McCabe, S. E., Crandford, J. A., Boyd, C. J., & Gunthrie, S. K. (2005). Prevalence and motives for illicit use of prescription stimulants in an undergraduate student sample. *Journal of American College Health, 53*, 253–262.

Willis, F. (2001). Attention deficit disorder. *Modern Drug Discovery, 4*, 84–86.

Quick Quiz

T F 1. A speech should always be organized according to sequential order.

T F 2. A direct question seeks a mental response from the audience, whereas a rhetorical question demands an overt response from the audience.

T F 3. A clincher is a restatement of your speech's goal and summary of the main points.

T F 4. If your speech is particularly short, it would be appropriate to list your sources alphabetically, by authors' last name.

T F 5. Startling statements, rhetorical questions, quotations, and personal references can all be used to state the thesis.

6. A plot, characters, and settings to dramatize the thesis are used in which organizational pattern?

a. topic order
b. logical reasons order
c. story order
d. narrative order
e. time order

7. Which of the following is NOT a technique used to get your audience's attention?

a. personal references
b. startling statements
c. stories
d. suspense
e. signposts

8. _____ is used in a speech when the main points are the rationale or proof that support the thesis.

a. A thesis statement
b. Logical reasons order
c. Time order
d. Topic order
e. Persuasive order

9. In the conclusion of a speech, you should

a. summarize the main points.
b. read the sources compiled from the bibliographic information recorded on research note cards for the audience.
c. get the audience's attention.
d. introduce the thesis.
e. establish credibility.

10. In the final review of the outline before you move into adaptation and rehearsal, you should ask yourself all of these questions EXCEPT

a. Have I used a standard set of symbols to indicate structure?
b. Have I written main points and major subdivisions as complete sentences?
c. Do main points and major subdivisions each contain multiple ideas to hold the audience's attention?
d. Does the outline include no more than one-third the total number of words anticipated in the speech?
e. Are potential subdivision elaborations indicated?

Answers: 1. F, 2. F, 3. F, 4. T, 5. F, 6. D, 7. E, 8. B, 9. A, 10. C

Presentational Aids

Learning Outcomes

13-1 Understand why you should incorporate presentational aids into your speech

13-2 Describe the different types of presentational aids you can choose from

13-3 Choose the appropriate visual aid for your presentation and prepare it correctly

13-4 Learn about various media you can use to display your presentational aids

We live in an era when the written, oral, visual, and digital modes of communicating are merging. Whether it is a TV news program, your professor's lecture, or a motivational speech, audiences have come to expect messages to be enhanced with presentational aids. This means that as you prepare your speech, you will need to decide which presentational aids will enhance your verbal message and motivate your audience to both pay attention and remember it. In fact, presentational aids have become so important to public speeches that they are essentially a form of supporting material you should be looking for when conducting your research. You might use them to get attention in the introduction, to support a main point in the body, or to clinch the conclusion.

A **presentational aid** is any visual, audio, audiovisual, or other sensory material used to enhance a verbal message. **Visual aids** enhance a speech by allowing audience members to see what you are describing or explaining. Examples of visual aids include actual objects, models, photographs, drawings and diagrams, maps,

What do you think?
There are few ways to make a speech more engaging for the audience: they're either interested or not.

1 2 3 4 5 6 7 8 9 10
STRONGLY DISAGREE   STRONGLY AGREE

presentational aid
any visual, audio, audiovisual, or other sensory material used to enhance a verbal message

visual aids
presentational aids that enhance a speech by allowing audience members to see what you are describing or explaining

ACTION STEPS

Action Step 4
Identify, Prepare, and Use Appropriate Presentational Aids

charts, and graphs. **Audio aids** enhance a speaker's verbal message through sound. Some examples include musical clips from CDs and iTunes, recorded clips from conversations, interviews, famous speeches, and recordings of nature sounds like bird calls and whale songs. **Audiovisual aids** enhance a speech using a combination of sight and sound. Examples of audiovisual aids include clips from movies and television, YouTube videos, and podcasts, as well as other events or observations captured on video. Other sensory aids include materials that enhance your ideas by appealing to smell, touch, or taste. For example, a speaker can enhance the verbal description of the fragrance of a particular perfume by allowing audience members to smell it, and the flavor of a particular entrée by allowing audience members to taste it.

13-1 Benefits of Presentational Aids

Research documents several benefits for using presentational aids. First, they clarify and dramatize your verbal message. Second, they help audiences remember information (Tversky, 1997). Third, they allow you to address the diverse learning style preferences of your audience (Kolb, 1984). Fourth, they increase persuasive appeal. In fact, some research suggests that speakers who use presentational aids are almost two times more likely to convince listeners than those who do not (Hanke, 1998). Finally, using presentational aids may help you feel more competent and confident (Ayers, 1991).

Today, presentational aids are usually developed into computerized slide shows using presentation software such as PowerPoint, MediaPro, Adobe Acrobat, or Photodex and projected onto a large screen via a computer and LCD projector. These programs allow you to

Ignite: The Power(Point) of eXtreme Audience Adaptation

Ignite is a global event, organized by volunteers, where participants are given five minutes to speak about their ideas and personal or professional passions, accompanied by 20 slides. Ignite asks speakers, "If you had five minutes on stage, what would you say? What if you only had 20 slides and they rotated automatically after 15 seconds?" ("What Is Ignite?" n.d.). Ignite challenges speakers to engage in what could be called extreme audience adaptation, sharing information in a timely and relevant manner so that audiences can easily comprehend it.

Speeches at Ignite events range from "Fighting Dirty in Scrabble" and "Causal Inference Is Hard" to "How I Learned to Appreciate Dance: Being Married to a Ballerina," "Geek Generation," and "How to Buy a Car Without Getting Screwed" ("Ignite Seattle 7," 2009; Guzman, 2009). The emphasis on extreme brevity as a way to share ideas is reflected in Ignite Seattle's tagline: "Enlighten us, but make it quick," and reveals the importance of well-designed visual aids to successful public speaking (*Ignite Seattle*, n.d.). Since Ignite presenters are given just 20 slides, each slide must be carefully crafted to concisely and creatively express an idea in only a few seconds. Part of Ignite's success has been its ability to adapt to the interests of its various

© Blend_Images/iStockphoto.com

audiences. For example, cocreator Brady Forrest attempts to balance the gender of the speakers and to keep topics only moderately tech-oriented so that more audience members can relate to them (Guzman, 2009). Ignite presentations are even finding their way into college classrooms. Tailoring assignments to Ignite's short presentation style helps students develop as speakers by honing their ability to analyze and distill research into its most important points as well becoming comfortable with creating and delivering presentations using digital media.

embed audio and audiovisual links from local files and the Internet, which makes it fairly simple to create effective multimedia presentations. Whether you are creating multimedia presentations or developing simpler presentational aids, the purpose is the same: to enhance your message without overpowering it. Speakers who violate this purpose end up with "death by PowerPoint," a situation where the audience is overwhelmed by the aids and the message gets lost. In this chapter, we describe various types of presentational aids, criteria to consider when choosing and preparing them, and methods for displaying them during your speech.

13-2 Types of Presentational Aids

Presentational aids range from those that are readily available from existing sources to those that are custom produced for a specific speech.

13-2a Visual Aids

Visual aids enhance your verbal message by allowing listeners to see what you are describing or explaining. They include actual objects and models, photographs, drawings and diagrams, maps, charts, and graphs.

Actual Objects

Actual objects are inanimate or animate physical samples of the idea you are communicating. Inanimate objects make good visual aids if they are (1) large enough to be seen by all audience members, (2) small enough to transport to the speech site, (3) simple enough to understand visually, and (4) safe. A volleyball or a Muslim prayer rug would be appropriate in size for most classroom audiences. An iPhone or Blackberry might be OK if the goal is to show what a smartphone looks like, but it might be too small if you want to demonstrate how to use any of the phone's specialized functions.

On occasion, *you* can be an effective visual aid. For instance, you can use descriptive gestures to show the height of a tennis net; you can use posture and movement to show the

© WilleeCole/Shutterstock.com

motions involved in a golf swing; or you can use your clothing to illustrate the traditional attire of a particular country. Sometimes it can be appropriate to use another person as a visual aid, such as when Jenny used a friend to demonstrate the Heimlich maneuver. Animals can also be effective visual aids. For example, Josh used his AKC Obedience Champion dog to demonstrate the basics of dog training. But keep in mind that some animals placed in unfamiliar settings can become difficult to control and can distract from your message.

Models

When an actual object is too large or too small for the room where you'll be speaking, too complex to understand visually, or potentially unsafe or uncontrollable, a model of it can be an effective visual aid. A **model** is a three-dimensional scaled-down or scaled-up version of an actual object that may also be simplified to aid understanding. In a speech on the physics of bridge construction, a scale model of a suspension bridge would be an effective visual aid. Likewise, in a speech on genetic engineering, a scaled-up model of the DNA double helix might help the audience understand what happens during these microscopic procedures.

Photographs

If an exact reproduction of material is needed, enlarged photographs can be excellent visual aids. In a speech on smart weapons, enlarged before-and-after photos of target sites would be effective in helping the audience understand the pinpoint accuracy of these weapons. When choosing photographs, be sure that the image is large enough for the audience to see, that the object of interest in the photo is clearly identified, and, ideally, that the object is in the foreground. For example, if you are giving a speech about your grandmother and show a photo of her with her college graduating class, you might circle her image so that she can easily be seen.

Simple Drawings and Diagrams

Simple drawings and **diagrams** (a type of drawing that shows how

actual objects
inanimate or animate physical samples of the idea being communicated

model
a three-dimensional scaled-down or scaled-up version of an actual object

diagram
a type of drawing that shows how the whole relates to its parts

Language

Learning Outcomes

14-1 Describe the ways that oral style differs from written style

14-2 Use language strategies that allow you to speak appropriately and connect with the audience

14-3 Choose clear and specific language that helps the audience understand and remember your ideas

14-4 Choose language that helps the audience see and experience your ideas

Recall from chapter 11 that audience adaptation is the process of tailoring your speech to your specific audience. In this chapter, we turn our focus to tailoring your language and oral style to the audience.

We begin by clarifying how oral style differs from written style, as well as how the formal oral style we use in public speeches differs from the informal oral style we use in conversations with friends and family. Then we review several aspects of semantic, pragmatic, and sociolinguistic word meanings we introduced in chapter 4 as they relate specifically to public speaking.

> ### What do you think?
> Word choice does not have much to do with how an audience understands a speech.
>
> 1 2 3 4 5 6 7 8 9 10
> STRONGLY DISAGREE   STRONGLY AGREE

14-1 Oral Style

Oral style refers to how we convey messages through the spoken word. An effective oral style differs quite a bit from written style, though when giving a speech your oral style is still more formal than everyday talk. Your goal is to adapt your language to your purpose, the audience, and the occasion. For example, when you are speaking to a small audience of colleagues at a business meeting, your language will be more formal than when

> **oral style**
> the manner in which one conveys messages through the spoken word

ACTION STEPS

Action Step 5
Practice Oral Language and Delivery Style

slang
informal, nonstandard vocabulary and definitions assigned to words by a social group or subculture

vocalized pauses
unnecessary words interjected to fill moments of silence

vivid language
words that are full of life

sensory language
words that appeal to seeing, hearing, tasting, smelling, and feeling

words her friend understands. In short, limit your use of jargon in speeches to general audiences and always define jargon in simple terms the first time you use it.

Slang refers to informal, nonstandard vocabulary and nonstandard definitions assigned to words by a social group or subculture. For example, today the word *wicked,* which has a standard definition denoting something wrong or immoral, can mean quite the opposite in some social groups and co-cultures (Rader, 2007). You should generally avoid slang in your public speeches not only because you risk being misunderstood but also because the use of slang doesn't sound professional and can hurt your credibility.

Overusing and misusing abbreviations and acronyms can also hinder clarity. Even if you think the abbreviation or acronym is common, always define it the first time you use it in the speech to ensure intelligibility. For example, in his speech about stock car racing, Jared initially refers to the sport's sanctioning organization by its full name and then provides the acronym: "National Association for Stock Car Auto Racing, or NASCAR." Providing the full and abbreviated forms of the name will ensure clarity for all listeners. If you are assuming right now that everyone knows what NASCAR is, it might benefit you to know one of your authors had to look it up to include it in this book!

14-3c Details and Examples

Sometimes the word we use may not have a precise synonym. In these situations, clarity can be achieved by adding details or examples. Saying "He lives in a really big house," for instance, can be clarified by adding, "He lives in a fourteen-room Tudor mansion on a six-acre estate."

14-3d Vocalized Pauses

Vocalized pauses are unnecessary words interjected into sentences to fill moments of silence. Words commonly used for this purpose are "like," "you know," "really," and "basically," as well as "um" and "uh." We sometimes refer to vocalized pauses as "verbal garbage" because they do not serve a meaningful purpose and actually distract audience members from the message. Although a few vocalized pauses typically don't hinder clarity, practicing your speech aloud will help you eliminate them.

14-4 Speaking Vividly

Because listeners cannot "reread" what you have said, you must speak in ways that help them remember your speech. Speaking vividly is one effective way to maintain your audience's interest and help them remember what you say. **Vivid language** is full of life—vigorous, bright, and intense. For example, a mediocre football announcer might say, "Jackson made a great catch," but a better commentator's vivid account might be, "Jackson stretched for the ball and grasped it in both hands, struggling to keep both feet in bounds, and successfully made the touchdown as he crashed into the reporters." The words *stretched, grasped, struggling,* and *crashed* paint an intense verbal picture of the action. You can make your ideas come to life by using sensory language and by using rhetorical figures and structures of speech.

14-4a Sensory Language

Sensory language is language that appeals to the senses of seeing, hearing, tasting, smelling, and feeling. Vivid sensory language begins with vivid thought. You are much more likely to express yourself vividly if you can physically or psychologically sense the meanings you are trying to convey. If you feel the "bite of the wind" or "the sting of freezing rain," or if you hear and smell "the thick, juicy sirloin steaks sizzling on the grill," you will be able to describe these sensations. Does the cake "taste good"? Or do your taste buds "quiver with the sweet double-chocolate icing and velvety feel of the rich, moist cake"?

To develop vivid sensory language, begin by considering how you can re-create what something, someone, or some place *looks like.* Consider, too, how you can help listeners imagine how something *sounds*. How can you use language to convey the way something *feels* (textures, shapes, temperatures)? How can language re-create a sense of how something *tastes* or *smells*? To achieve this in your speech, use colorful descriptors. They make your ideas more concrete and can arouse emotions. They invite listeners to imagine details. Here's an example about downhill skiing:

> Sight: *As you climb the hill, the bright winter sunshine glistening on the snow is blinding.*
>
> Touch and feel: *Just before you take off, you gently slip your goggles over your eyes. They are bitterly cold and sting your nose for a moment.*
>
> Taste: *You start the descent and, as you gradually pick up speed, the taste of air and ice and snow in your mouth invigorates you.*
>
> Sound: *An odd silence fills the air. You hear nothing but the swish of your skis against the snow beneath your feet. At last, you arrive at the bottom of the slope. Reality hits as you hear the hustle and bustle of other skiers and instructors directing them to their next session.*
>
> Smell and feel: *You enter the warming house. As your fingers thaw in the warm air, the aroma from the wood stove in the corner comforts you as you ready yourself to drift off into sleep.*

By using colorful descriptors that appeal to the senses, you arouse and maintain listener interest and make your ideas more memorable.

14-4b Rhetorical Figures and Structures of Speech

Rhetorical figures of speech make striking comparisons between things that are not obviously alike to help listeners visualize or internalize what you are saying. **Rhetorical structures of speech** combine ideas in a particular way. Either of these devices can make your speech more memorable—as long as they aren't overused. Let's look at some examples.

A **simile** is a direct comparison of dissimilar things using the words *like* or *as*. Clichés such as "He walks like a duck" and "She's as busy as a bee" are similes. If you've seen the movie *Forrest Gump,* you might recall Forrest's use of the simile: "Life is like a box of chocolates. You never know what you're going to get." Similes

© Paul Pegler/iStockphoto.com

can be effective because they make ideas more vivid in listeners' minds. But they should be used sparingly or they lose their appeal. Clichés should be avoided because their predictability reduces their effectiveness.

A **metaphor** is an implied comparison between two unlike things, expressed without using *like* or *as*. Instead of saying that one thing is *like* another, a metaphor says that one thing *is* another. Thus, problem cars are "lemons," and the leaky roof is a "sieve." Metaphors can be effective because they make an abstract concept more concrete, strengthen an important point, or heighten emotions. Notice how one speaker used a metaphor effectively to conclude a speech: "It is imperative that we weave our fabric of the future with durable thread" (Schertz, 1977).

An **analogy** is an extended metaphor. Sometimes, you can develop a story from a metaphor that makes a concept more vivid. If you were to describe a family member as the "black sheep in the barnyard," that's a metaphor. If you went on to talk about the other members of the family as different animals on the farm and the roles ascribed to them, you would be extending the metaphor into an analogy. Analogies can be effective for holding your speech together in a creative and vivid way. Analogies are particularly useful to highlight the similarities between a complex and unfamiliar concept with one that is familiar.

Alliteration is the repetition of consonant sounds at the beginning of words that are near one another. Tongue twisters such as "She sells seashells by the seashore" use alliteration. In her speech about the history of jelly beans, Sharla used alliteration when she said, "And today there are more than fifty fabulous fruity flavors from which to choose." Used sparingly, alliteration can catch listeners' attention and make the speech memorable. But overuse can hurt the message because listeners might focus on the technique rather than the content of your message.

rhetorical figures of speech
language that makes striking comparisons between things that are not obviously alike

rhetorical structures of speech
language that combines ideas in a particular way

simile
a direct comparison of dissimilar things using the words *like* or *as*

metaphor
an implied comparison between two unlike things, expressed without using *like* or *as*

analogy
an extended metaphor

alliteration
the repetition of consonant sounds at the beginning of words that are near one another

assonance
the repetition of vowel sounds in a phrase or phrases

onomatopoeia
the use of words that sound like the things they stand for

personification
attributing human qualities to a concept or an inanimate object

repetition
restating words, phrases, or sentences for emphasis

antithesis
combining contrasting ideas in the same sentence

Assonance is the repetition of vowel sounds in a phrase or phrases. "How now brown cow" is a common example. Sometimes the words rhyme, but they don't have to. As with alliteration, assonance can make your speech more memorable as long as it's not overused.

Onomatopoeia is the use of words that sound like the things they stand for, such as "buzz," "hiss," "crack," and "plop." In the speech about skiing, the "swish" of the skis is an example of onomatopoeia.

Personification attributes human qualities to a concept or an inanimate object. When Madison talked about her truck, "Big Red," as her trusted friend and companion, she used personification. Likewise, when Rick talked about flowers dancing on the front lawn, he used personification.

Repetition is restating words, phrases, or sentences for emphasis. Martin Luther King Jr.'s "I Have a Dream" speech is a classic example:

I say to you today, my friends, so even though we face the difficulties of today and tomorrow, I still have a dream. It is a dream deeply rooted in the American dream.

I have a dream that one day this nation will rise up and live out the true meaning of its creed: "We hold these truths to be self-evident: that all men are created equal."

I have a dream that one day on the red hills of Georgia the sons of former slaves and the sons of former slave owners will be able to sit down together at the table of brotherhood.

I have a dream that one day even the state of Mississippi, a state sweltering with the heat of injustice, sweltering with the heat of oppression, will be transformed into the oasis of freedom and justice.

I have a dream that my four little children will one day live in a nation where they will not be judged by the color of their skin but by the content of their character. I have a dream today.

Reprinted by arrangement with the Estate of Martin Luther King, Jr. c/o Writers House as agent for the proprietor New York, NY. Copyright 1963 Dr. Martin Luther King, Jr., copyright renewed 1991 Coretta Scott King.

Antithesis is combining contrasting ideas in the same sentence, as when John F. Kennedy said, "My fellow Americans, ask not what your country can do for you; ask what you can do for your country." Likewise, astronaut Neil Armstrong used antithesis when he first stepped on the moon: "That's one small step for [a] man, one giant leap for mankind." Speeches that offer antithesis in the concluding remarks are often very memorable.

ACTION STEP 5a

Adapt Oral Language and Style

The goal of this activity is to help you plan how you will adapt your language and style to the specific audience. Write your thesis statement:

_____

_____

_____

Review the audience analysis that you completed in Action Steps 1 through 4. Now verbally adapt to your audience by answering the following questions:

1. How can I adapt my language to foster verbal immediacy with this audience?

2. How can I adapt my language choices to demonstrate respect for this audience?

3. Where can I adapt my language to be most intelligible for this audience?

4. How can I use sensory language and rhetorical figures of speech to make my ideas more vivid for this audience?

Quick Quiz

T F 1. The skill of audience adaptation involves both verbally and visually preparing presentational aids that facilitate audience understanding.

T F 2. In order to be timely, you must adapt the information in your speech so that audience members view it as important to them.

T F 3. Saying that Bryony is an excellent female architect is an example of marking.

T F 4. Palani notes in a speech that human traffickers often use containers to run their illegal trade. This is specific language.

T F 5. When you are speaking in a second language, audience members are less likely to tolerate your mistakes.

6. When you are choosing the supporting material for your speech, it's important to select materials that
   a. are relevant to the audience.
   b. are not offensive to the audience.
   c. establish common ground between you and the audience.
   d. maintain or develop credibility.
   e. accomplish all of these things.

7. A speech that includes information about the audience's neighborhood or town is establishing
   a. relevance.
   b. timeliness.
   c. proximity.
   d. personal impact.
   e. credibility.

8. Which is NOT one of the five guidelines that can aid in adapting the information of your speech so that the audience can more easily understand it?
   a. avoiding jargon
   b. using precise words
   c. limiting words like "um" and "like"
   d. using rhetorical structures of speech
   e. using technical language where necessary

9. Millie begins her speech by saying, "I've decided to talk today about volcanoes and their impact on Hawaiians. I'll tell you about native Hawaiian culture and how volcanoes have influenced that culture." Millie needs to
   a. use personal pronouns.
   b. ask rhetorical questions.
   c. speak Hawaiian .
   d. increase her verbal immediacy.
   e. use a visual aid.

10. A fashion design professor giving a lecture describes coated denim as having a strong conviction and strength of character. She is using
   a. a simile.
   b. a metaphor.
   c. alliteration.
   d. personification.
   e. onomatopoeia.

Answers: 1. F, 2. F, 3. T, 4. F, 5. F, 6. E, 7. C, 8. E, 9. A, 10. D

Delivery

What do you think?

The best-delivered speeches are the ones that are spontaneous.

1	2	3	4	5	6	7	8	9	10
STRONGLY DISAGREE									STRONGLY AGREE

Learning Outcomes

15-1 Describe symptoms and causes of public speaking apprehension and some methods for managing it

15-2 Identify the characteristics of an effective delivery style

15-3 Discuss the characteristics of the effective use of voice

15-4 Discuss the characteristics of the effective use of the body

15-5 Identify the characteristics of different delivery methods

15-6 Analyze what makes a rehearsal effective

15-7 Identify criteria for evaluating speeches

The difference between a good speech and a great speech is often how well it is delivered. In fact, research suggests that listeners are often influenced more by speech delivery than content (Decker, 1992; Gardner, 2003; Towler, 2003). Although some people seem to be naturally fluent and comfortable speaking to a group, most of us are actually a bit nervous and maybe even downright frightened. What you'll learn in this chapter will help you manage your nervousness as you deliver effective speeches.

In the last chapter, we focused on one aspect of the fifth action step: oral language style. In this chapter, we turn our attention to the other aspect: delivery style. We begin by discussing stage fright and ways to manage it effectively. Then we explain how to use your voice and body effectively, as well as three common methods for delivering a speech. We then introduce a process designed to make your practice sessions productive and some delivery guidelines to consider while giving the actual speech. Finally, we offer several criteria you can use to evaluate your speeches and apply that criteria to a sample student speech.

ACTION STEPS

Action Step 5
Practice Oral Language and Delivery Style

15-1 Public Speaking Apprehension

Most of us feel some fear about public speaking. In fact, as many as 76 percent of experienced public speakers feel some fear before presenting a speech (Hahner, Sokoloff, & Salisch, 2001). Did you know, for example, that award-winning actors Meryl Streep and Kim Basinger, entertainers Barbra Streisand and Donny Osmond, professional football player Ricky Williams, and evangelist Billy Graham all experience a fear of public speaking? In spite of their fear, they are all effective public speakers.

Public speaking apprehension is the level of fear we experience when anticipating or actually speaking to an audience. Fortunately, we can benefit from the results of a good deal of research about managing public speaking apprehension effectively. We say *manage* because having some fear actually makes us better speakers. Just as an adrenaline boost helps athletes, musicians, and actors perform better, it can also help us deliver better public speeches (Kelly, Duran, & Stewart, 1990; Motley, 1997; Phillips, 1977).

15-1a Symptoms and Causes

The symptoms of public speaking apprehension vary from individual to individual and range from mild to debilitating. Symptoms can be cognitive, physical, or emotional. Cognitive symptoms stem from negative self-talk (e.g., "I'm going to blow it" or "I just know I'll make a fool of myself"), which is also the most common cause of speech apprehension (Richmond & McCroskey, 2000). Physical symptoms may be stomach upset (or butterflies),

flushed skin, sweating, shaking, light-headedness, rapid or pounding heartbeats, stuttering, and vocalized pauses ("like," "you know," "ah," "um," and so on). Emotional symptoms include feeling anxious, worried, or upset.

In addition to negative self-talk, previous experience, modeling, and negative reinforcement can also cause public speaking apprehension. Previous experience has to do with being socialized to fear public speaking as a result of modeling and negative reinforcement (Richmond & McCroskey, 2000). Modeling has to do with observing how your friends and family members react to speaking in public. If they tend to be quiet and reserved and avoid public speaking, your fears may stem from modeling. Negative reinforcement concerns how others have responded to your public speaking endeavors. If you experienced negative reactions, you might be more apprehensive about speaking in public than if you had been praised for your efforts (Motley, 1997).

Luckily, our apprehension gradually decreases for most of us as we speak. Researchers have identified three phases we proceed through: anticipation, confrontation, and adaptation (Behnke & Carlile, 1971). Figure 15.1 illustrates these phases. The **anticipation phase** is the anxiety we experience before giving the speech, both while preparing it and waiting to speak. The **confrontation phase** is the surge of anxiety we feel as we begin delivering the speech. The **adaptation phase** is the period during which our anxiety level gradually decreases. It typically begins about one minute into the presentation and tends to level off after about five minutes (Beatty & Behnke, 1991).

What if they laugh?

15-1b Management Techniques

We propose five techniques you can use to help manage your apprehension effectively: communication orientation, visualization, systematic desensitization, cognitive restructuring, and public speaking skills training.

Communication Orientation Motivation

Communication orientation motivation (COM) techniques reduce anxiety by helping us adopt a *communication* rather than *performance* orientation toward speeches (Motley, 1997). When we have

---

public speaking apprehension
the level of fear you experience when anticipating or actually speaking to an audience

anticipation phase
anxiety we experience before giving a speech

confrontation phase
the surge of anxiety we experience when beginning to deliver a speech

adaptation phase
the period during a speech when our anxiety gradually decreases

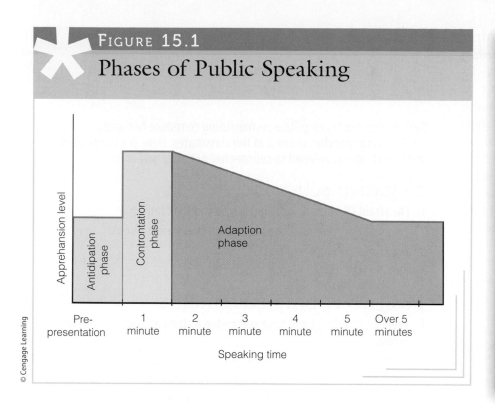

FIGURE 15.1
Phases of Public Speaking

Apprehension level

Antidipation phase

Controntation phase

Adaption phase

| Pre-presentation | 1 minute | 2 minute | 3 minute | 4 minute | 5 minute | Over 5 minutes |

Speaking time

© Cengage Learning

a **performance orientation**, we believe we must *impress* a hypercritical audience with our knowledge and delivery. On the other hand, when we have a **communication orientation**, we focus on talking with our audience about an important topic and *getting a message across to them*—not about how they might be judging our performance.

Visualization
Visualization helps us reduce anxiety by developing a mental picture of ourselves giving a masterful speech. If we visualize ourselves going through an entire speech-making process successfully, we are more likely to be successful when we actually deliver the speech (Ayres & Hopf, 1990; Ayres, Hopf, & Ayres, 1994).

Systematic Desensitization
Systematic desensitization can help reduce anxiety by gradually visualizing and engaging in increasingly more frightening speaking events while remaining in a relaxed state. The process starts with consciously tensing and then relaxing muscle groups to learn how to recognize the difference between the two states. Then, while in a relaxed state, you first imagine yourself and then engage in successively more stressful situations—for example, researching a speech topic in the library, practicing the speech out loud to a roommate, and finally giving a speech. The ultimate goal of systematic desensitization is to transfer the calm feelings we attain while visualizing to the actual speaking event. Calmness on command—it works.

Cognitive Restructuring
Cognitive restructuring helps reduce anxiety by changing negative thoughts about public speaking. In other words, we replace anxiety-arousing negative self-talk with anxiety-reducing positive self-talk through a four-step process.

1. Identify your fears. Write down all the fears that come to mind when you know you must give a speech.

2. Determine whether or not these fears are rational. Most of your fears about public speaking are irrational because public speaking is not life threatening.

3. Develop positive coping statements to replace each negative self-talk statement. There is no list of coping statements that will work for everyone. Psychologist Richard Heimberg of the State University of New York at Albany reminds his clients that most listeners don't notice or even care if the clients do what they're afraid of doing when giving a speech. Ultimately, he asks them, "Can you cope with the one or two people who [notice or criticize or] get upset?"

4. Incorporate positive coping statements into your life so they become second nature. You can do this by writing your statements down and reading them aloud to yourself each day, as well as before you give a speech. The more you repeat your coping statements, the more natural they will become (see Figure 15.2).

Public Speaking Skills Training

Public speaking skills training is systematically practicing the skills involved in preparing and delivering an effective public speech. Skills training is based on the assumption that some public speaking anxiety is caused by not knowing how to be successful. So if we learn the skills associated with effective speech making (e.g., audience analysis, topic selection and development, organization, oral language, and delivery style), then we will be less anxious (Kelly, Phillips, & Keaten, 1995).

15-2 Effective Delivery Style

Think about the best speaker you have ever heard. What made this person stand out in your mind? In all likelihood, how the speaker delivered the speech had a lot to do with it. **Delivery** is how a message is communicated orally and visually through the use of voice and body. So we achieve effective delivery by adapting the types of nonverbal communication introduced in chapter 5 to a public speaking situation. An effective public speaking delivery style is both conversational and animated.

15-2a Conversational

You have probably heard ineffective speakers whose delivery was overly dramatic and affected or stiff and mechanical. In contrast, effective delivery is **conversational.** The audience perceives you as *talking with* them and not performing *in front of* or *reading to* them. The hallmark of a conversational style is spontaneity. **Spontaneity** is the ability to sound natural—as though you are really thinking about the ideas and getting them across to your audience—no matter how many times you've practiced.

15-2b Animated

Have you ever been bored by a professor reading a well-structured lecture while looking at the lecture notes rather than the students and making few gestures other than turning the pages? Even a well-written speech given by an expert can bore an audience unless its delivery is **animated**, that is, lively and dynamic.

How can you sound conversational and animated at the same time? The secret is to focus on conveying the passion you feel about the topic through your voice and body. When we are passionate about sharing something with someone, almost all of us become more animated in our delivery. Your goal is to duplicate this level of liveliness when you deliver your speeches. The next two sections focus more closely on how you can use your voice and your body to achieve effective conversational and animated delivery.

FIGURE 15.2
Cognitive Restructuring

Beth decided to try cognitive restructuring to reduce her anxiety about giving speeches in front of her classmates. Here are the positive statements she developed to counter her negative self-talk:

Negative self-talk
1. I'm afraid I'll stumble over my words and look foolish.
2. I'm afraid everyone will be able to tell that I am nervous.
3. I'm afraid my voice will crack.
4. I'm afraid I'll sound boring.

Positive coping statements
1. Even if I stumble, I will have succeeded as long as I get my message across.
2. They probably won't be able to tell I'm nervous, but as long as I focus on getting my message across, that's what matters.
3. Even if my voice cracks, as long as I keep going and focus on getting my message across, I'll succeed at what matters most.
4. I won't sound bored if I focus on how important this message is to me and to my audience. I don't have to do somersaults to keep their attention, because my topic is relevant to them.

---

public speaking skills training
the systematic teaching of the skills associated with preparing and delivering an effective public speech, with the intention of improving speaking competence and thereby reducing public speaking apprehension

delivery
how a message is communicated orally and visually through the use of voice and body

conversational style
presenting a speech so that your audience feels you are talking with them

spontaneity
a naturalness that seems unrehearsed and unmemorized

animated
lively and dynamic

15-3 Use of Voice

Recall from chapter 5 that your *voice* is the sound you produce using your vocal organs. How your voice sounds depends on its pitch, volume, rate, and quality. As a public speaker, you can achieve a conversational and animated delivery style by varying your pitch, volume, rate, and quality in ways that make you more intelligible and expressive.

15-3a Intelligibility

To be **intelligible** means to be understandable. All of us have experienced situations in which we couldn't understand what was being said because the speaker was talking too softly or too quickly. If you practice your speech using appropriate pitch, volume, rate, and vocal quality, you can improve the likelihood that you will be intelligible to your audience.

Most of us speak at a pitch that is appropriate for us and intelligible to listeners. However, some people naturally have voices that are higher or lower in register or become accustomed to talking in tones that are either above or below their natural pitch. Speaking at an appropriate pitch is particularly important if your audience includes people who have hearing loss because they may find it difficult to hear a pitch that is too high or too low.

Appropriate volume is key to intelligibility. You must speak loudly enough, with or without a microphone, to be heard easily by the audience members in the back of the room but not so loudly as to cause discomfort to listeners seated in the front. You can also vary your

↘ If you don't speak intelligibly, you may sound like you are talking with your mouth full!

volume to emphasize important information. For example, you may speak louder when you introduce each main point or when imploring listeners to take action.

The rate at which you speak can also influence intelligibility. Speaking too slowly gives your listeners time to let their minds wander after they've processed an idea. If you speak too quickly, especially when sharing complex ideas and arguments, listeners may not have enough time to process the information completely. Because nervousness may cause you to speak more quickly than normal, monitor your rate and adjust if you are speaking more quickly than normal.

In addition to vocal characteristics, articulation and accent can affect intelligibility. **Articulation** is using the tongue, palate, teeth, jaws, and lips to shape vocalized sounds that combine to produce a word. Many of us suffer from minor articulation and **pronunciation** problems such as adding an extra sound ("athalete" for *athlete*), leaving out a sound ("libary" for *library*), transposing sounds ("revalent" for *relevant*), and distorting sounds ("troof" for *truth*).

Accent is the inflection, tone, and speech habits typical of native speakers of a language. When you misarticulate or speak with a heavy accent during a conversation, your

intelligible
understandable

articulation
using the tongue, palate, teeth, jaw movement, and lips to shape vocalized sounds that combine to produce a word

pronunciation
the form and accent of various syllables of a word

accent
the articulation, inflection, tone, and speech habits typical of the native speakers of a language

listeners can ask you to repeat yourself until they understand you. But in a speech setting, audience members are unlikely to interrupt to ask you to repeat what you have just said. If your accent is "thick" or very different from that of most of your audience, practice pronouncing key words so that you are easily understood, speak slowly to allow your audience members more time to process your message, and consider using visual aids to reinforce key terms, concepts, and important points.

15-3b Vocal Expression

Vocal expression is achieved by changing your pitch, volume, and rate; stressing certain words; and using pauses. Doing so clarifies the emotional intent of your message and helps animate your delivery. Generally, speeding up your rate, raising your pitch, or increasing your volume reinforces emotions such as joy, enthusiasm, excitement, anticipation, and a sense of urgency or fear. Slowing down your rate, lowering your pitch, or decreasing your volume can communicate resolution, peacefulness, remorse, disgust, or sadness.

A total lack of vocal expression produces a **monotone**—a voice in which the pitch, volume, and rate remain constant, with no word, idea, or sentence differing significantly in sound from any other. Although few people speak in a true monotone, many severely limit themselves by using only two or three pitch levels and relatively unchanging volume and rate when giving public speeches. An actual or near monotone not only lulls an audience to sleep but, more importantly, diminishes the chances of audience understanding. For instance, if the sentence "Congress should pass laws limiting the sale of pornography" is presented in a monotone, listeners will be uncertain whether the speaker is concerned with *who* should be taking action, what Congress should *do*, or *what* the laws should be.

Pauses, moments of silence strategically used to enhance meaning, can also mark important ideas. If you use one or more sentences in your speech to express an important idea, pause before each sentence to signal that something important is coming or pause afterward to allow the idea to sink in. Pausing one or more times within a sentence can also add impact. Nick included several short pauses within and a long pause after his sentence "Our government has no compassion (*pause*), no empathy (*pause*), and no regard for human feeling" (*longer pause*).

15-4 Use of Body

Because your audience can see as well as hear you, how you use your body also contributes to how conversational and animated your audience perceives you to be. Body

If you expect your audience to dress like this . . .

© Andresr/Shutterstock.com

language elements that affect speech delivery include appearance, posture, poise, eye contact, facial expressions, gestures, and movement.

15-4a Appearance

Some speakers think that what they wear doesn't or shouldn't affect the success of their speech. But studies show that a neatly groomed and professional appearance sends important messages about a public speaker's commitment to the topic and occasion, as well as about the speaker's credibility (ethos) (Bates, 1992; Hammer, 2000; Sellnow & Treinen, 2004). Your appearance should complement your message, not detract from it. Three guidelines can help you decide how to dress for your speech.

1. Consider the audience and occasion. Dress a bit more formally than you expect members of your audience to dress. If you dress too formally, your audience is likely to perceive you to be untrustworthy and insincere; if you dress too casually, your audience may view you as uncommitted to your topic or disrespectful of them or the occasion (Morris, Gorham, Cohen, & Huffman, 1996).

2. Consider your topic and purpose. In general, the more serious your topic, the more formally you should dress. For example, if your topic is AIDS and you are trying to convince your audience to be tested for HIV, you will want to look like someone who is an authority by dressing the part. But if your topic is yoga and you are trying to convince your audience to take a yoga class at the new campus recreation center, you might dress more casually, or even in sportswear.

3. Avoid extremes. Your attire shouldn't detract from your speech. Avoid gaudy jewelry, over- or undersized clothing, and sexually suggestive attire. Remember: You want your audience to focus on your message, so your appearance should be neutral, not distracting.

15-4b Posture

Recall from chapter 5 that *posture is* how you hold your body. When giving a public speech, an upright stance and squared shoulders communicate a sense of confidence. Speakers who slouch may be perceived as lacking self-confidence and

© Warren Goldswain/Shutterstock.com

Dress like this.

not caring about the topic, audience, and occasion. As you practice, be aware of your posture and adjust it so that you do not slouch; keep your weight equally distributed on both feet.

15-4c Poise

Poise is a graceful and controlled use of the body that gives the impression that you are self-assured, calm, and dignified. Mannerisms that convey nervousness, such as swaying from side to side, drumming fingers on the lectern, taking off or putting on glasses, jiggling pocket change, smacking the tongue, licking the lips, or scratching the nose, hand, or arm should be noted during practice sessions and avoided during the speech.

15-4d Eye Contact

When giving a public speech, effective *eye contact* involves looking at people in all parts of an audience throughout the speech. As long as you are looking at someone (those in front of you, in the left rear of the room, in the right center of the room, and so on) and not at your notes or the ceiling, floor, or window, everyone in the audience will perceive you as having good eye contact with them. Generally, you should look at your audience at least 90 percent of the time, glancing at your notes only when you need a quick reference point. Maintaining eye contact is important for several reasons.

1. Maintaining eye contact helps audiences concentrate on the speech. If you do not look at audience members while you talk, audience members are unlikely to maintain eye contact with you. This break in mutual eye contact often decreases concentration on the message.

2. Maintaining eye contact bolsters ethos. Just as you are likely to be skeptical of people who do not look you in the eye as they converse, so too audiences will be skeptical of speakers who do not look at them. In the United States, eye contact is perceived as a sign of sincerity. Speakers who fail to maintain eye contact with audiences are almost always perceived as ill at ease and often as insincere or dishonest (Burgoon, Coker, & Coker, 1986; Levine, Asada, & Park, 2006).

3. Maintaining eye contact helps you gauge the audience's reaction to your ideas. Because communication is two-way, audience members communicate with you while you are speaking to them. In conversation, the audience's response is likely to be both verbal and nonverbal. In public speaking, the audience's response is likely to occur only through nonverbal cues. Bored audience members might yawn, look out the window, slouch in their chairs, and even sleep. Confused audience members might look puzzled by furrowing their brows or shaking their head. Audience members who understand or agree with something you say might nod their heads. By monitoring your audience's behavior, you can adjust by becoming more animated, offering additional examples, or moving more quickly through a point.

When speaking to large audiences of 100 or more people, you must create a *sense* of looking listeners in the eye even though you actually cannot. This process is called **audience contact**. You can create audience contact by mentally dividing your audience into small groups. Then, tracing the letter Z with your gaze, talk for four to six seconds with each group as you move through your speech.

15-4e Facial Expressions

Recall from chapter 5 that *facial expression* is the arrangement of facial muscles to express emotions. For public speakers, effective facial expressions can convey **nonverbal immediacy** by communicating that you are personable and likable. They can also help animate your speech. Speakers who do not vary their facial expressions during their speech but instead wear a deadpan expression, perpetual grin, or permanent scowl tend to be perceived as boring, insincere, or stern. To assess whether you are using effective facial expressions during your speech, practice delivering it to yourself in a mirror or record your rehearsal and evaluate your facial expressions as you watch it.

15-4f Gestures

As we discussed in chapter 5, *gestures* are the movements of your hands, arms, and fingers. You can use gestures when delivering speeches to describe or emphasize what you are saying, refer to presentational aids, or clarify structure. For example, as Aaron began to speak about the advantages of smart phone apps, he said, "on one hand" and lifted his right hand face up. When he got to the disadvantages, he lifted his left hand face up as he said, "on the other hand." Recall from chapter 5, however, that certain gestures mean different things in different cultures.

Some people who are nervous when giving a speech clasp their hands behind their backs, bury them in their pockets, or grip the lectern. Unable to pry their hands free gracefully, they wiggle their elbows or appear stiff, which can distract listeners from the message.

As with facial expressions, effective gestures must appear spontaneous and natural even though they are carefully planned and practiced. When you practice and then deliver your speech, leave your hands free so that you will be available to gesture as you normally do.

15-4g Movement

Recall that *movement* refers to changing your body position. During your speech, it is important to engage only in **motivated movement**, movement with a specific purpose such as emphasizing an important idea, referencing a presentational aid, or clarifying structure. To emphasize a particular point, you might move closer to the audience. To create a feeling of intimacy before telling a personal story, you might walk out from behind a lectern and sit down on a chair placed at the edge of the stage. Each time you begin a new main point, you might take a few steps to one side of the stage or the other. To use motivated movement effectively, you need to practice when and how you will move so you can do so in a way that appears spontaneous and natural while remaining "open" to the audience (not turning your back to them).

© Steve Devenport/iStockphoto.com

Avoid such unmotivated movement as bobbing, weaving, shifting from foot to foot, or pacing from one side of the room to the other; unplanned movements distract the audience from your message. Because many unplanned movements result from nervousness, you can minimize them by paying mindful attention to your body as you speak. At the beginning of your speech, stand up straight on both feet. If you find yourself fidgeting, readjust and position your body with your weight equally distributed on both feet.

15-5 Delivery Methods

Speeches vary in the amount of content preparation and practice you do ahead of time. The three most common delivery methods are impromptu, scripted, and extemporaneous.

15-5a Impromptu Speeches

An **impromptu speech** is one that is delivered with only seconds or minutes of advance notice for preparation and is usually presented without referring to notes of any kind. Because impromptu speakers must quickly gather their thoughts just before and while they speak, carefully organizing and developing ideas can be challenging. As a result, they may leave out important information or confuse audience members. Delivery can suffer as speakers often use "ahs," "ums," "like," and "you know" to buy time as they scramble to collect their thoughts. That's why the more opportunities you have to organize and deliver your thoughts using an impromptu method, the better you'll become at doing so.

Common situations that will require you to use the impromptu method include employment and performance review interviews, business meetings, classes, social ceremonies, and speaking to the media. In each situation, having practiced organizing ideas quickly and conveying them intelligibly and expressively will bolster your ethos and help you succeed in business and in life.

© Blaj Gabriel/Shutterstock.com

You can improve your impromptu performances by practicing mock impromptu speeches. For example, if you are taking a class in which the professor calls on students at random to answer questions, you can prepare by anticipating the questions that might be asked on the readings for the day and practice giving your answers aloud. Over time, you will become more adept at organizing your ideas and thinking on your feet.

15-5b Scripted Speeches

At the other extreme, a **scripted speech** is one that is prepared by creating a complete written manuscript and then delivered by reading from or memorizing a written copy. Obviously, effective scripted speeches take a great deal of time to prepare because both an outline and a word-for-word transcript must be prepared, practiced, and delivered in a way that sounds both conversational and animated. When you memorize a scripted speech, you face the increased anxiety of forgetting your lines. When you read a scripted speech, you must become adept at looking at the script with your peripheral vision so that you don't appear to be reading and sound conversational and animated.

Because of the time and skill required to effectively prepare and deliver a scripted speech, they are usually reserved for important occasions that have important consequences. Political speeches, keynote addresses at conventions, commencement addresses, and CEO remarks at annual stockholder meetings are examples of occasions when a scripted speech might be appropriate and worth the extra effort.

impromptu speech
a speech that is delivered with only seconds or minutes of advance notice for preparation

scripted speech
a speech that is prepared by creating a complete written manuscript and delivered by rote memory or by reading a written copy

15-5c Extemporaneous Speeches

Most speeches, whether in the workplace, in the community, or in class, are delivered extemporaneously. An **extemporaneous speech** is researched and planned ahead of time, but the exact wording is not scripted and will vary somewhat from presentation to presentation. When speaking extemporaneously, you may refer to speaking notes reminding you of key ideas, structure, and delivery cues as you speak. Some speakers today use their computerized slideshows as speaking notes. If you choose to do so, however, be careful not to include too many words on any given slide, which will ultimately distract listeners from focusing on you as you speak.

Extemporaneous speeches are the easiest to give effectively. Unlike with impromptu speeches, when you speak extemporaneously you can prepare your thoughts ahead of time and have notes to prompt you. Unlike scripted speeches, extemporaneous speeches do not require as lengthy a preparation process to be effective.

15-5d Delivering Speeches through Mediated Technology

When great orators like Plato, Aristotle, and Cicero engaged in public speaking to conduct business, debate public issues, and gain and maintain power, the communication event occurred in real time with both the speaker and audience physically present. Thanks to technology, however, public speeches today may be delivered in both face-to-face and virtual environments. Technology also makes it possible to record public speeches and watch them again and again. A professor can record and upload a speech to the class Web site. Later, students can watch, critique, and prepare assignments critiquing themselves or each other.

Technology also makes it possible to speak publicly to multiple audiences across the country and around the world. For example, a speech posted to YouTube could reach an audience far beyond the classroom. Although public speaking certainly still occurs in traditional face-to-face settings, it is no longer limited by place and time—far from it!

President Franklin Delano Roosevelt (FDR) is credited as one of the first public figures to capitalize on the benefits of technology to break through the *place* limitation

© Fliegenwulf/Shutterstock.com

Politics, Politicians, and Public Speech Delivery

In political speeches, it is not always *what* you say that resonates with audiences, but *how* you say it. Politicians are often criticized for exhibiting an overly rehearsed speaking style that leaves audiences believing that the speaker is simply saying what he or she thinks we want to hear.

On the other hand, New Jersey governor Chris Christie is often celebrated for using a blunt and straightforward speaking style that contrasts with the scripted style exhibited by many politicians. He is well known for routinely using words like "stupid," "crap," and "insane" in news briefings, town hall meetings, and even more formal political speeches (Barron, 2011). Christie supporters champion his spirited style as evidence of his real commitment to his goals of political reform and his rejection of political pandering. In an era when Americans are increasingly frustrated with Washington political bickering, Christie's straightforward style seems like a welcome alternative.

However, not everyone is a fan of Christie's frank and confrontational style. Some critics suggest that his combative delivery style makes him come off as a bully; others worry that Christie's tendency to allow his emotions get the better of him during his public speeches does not fit with the need for rational and measured debate within the political realm. But his supporters say it is exactly this heartfelt and authentic expression of his ideas that makes Christie appealing as a politician.

to reach a wider audience. Throughout his presidency in the 1930s and 1940s, FDR delivered *fireside chats*, weekly radio addresses about important issues facing the country (Mankowski & Jose, 2012). These speeches could be heard by anyone who chose to tune in. U.S. presidents have been offering weekly addresses ever since! In fact, today President Obama even posts weekly addresses on YouTube and the White House Web site (Obama, *Your Weekly Address*).

Perhaps one of the most significant examples of technology overcoming the limitation of *time* comes from Martin Luther King, Jr. Over 200,000 people were at the political rally in Washington, D.C., on August 28, 1963, to hear his famous "I Have a Dream" speech live and in person. More than 50 years later, we can join the 200,000 who made up that first audience to hear him deliver this powerful oration by clicking on any number of Web sites where it is archived. In fact, a quick *Google* search of "I Have a Dream speech" yields more than 37,400,000 *hits*.

The benefits of overcoming *place* and *time* barriers also come with some new challenges, particularly regarding *audience analysis and adaptation*. While many fundamentals of effective public speaking remain true, today speakers must also adapt to multiple audiences and to some unique demands of a mediated platform.

To reach multiple audiences successfully, we must consider not just those who are informed about the topic and issue, but also those who may not be informed, may be apathetic, and perhaps may even be hostile toward it. Those who have analyzed Dr. King's speech, for instance, claim he did so by using the rhetorical devices common to the black preacher style, and at the same time, transcending the typical Civil Rights–era speeches that were aimed at supportive audiences. In the first half of the speech, King addressed his remarks to the assembled throng, but he then moved from addressing the grievances of black Americans to focus on the bedrock of American values. Linking civil rights to the American Dream appealed not only to the audience present on the Washington Mall, but also to the millions of noncommitted Americans who watched the speech on TV. Today, more than 50 years later, it continues to resonate as representing American values and the American dream.

Technology today brings with it a challenge to address mediated audiences that we intentionally target, as was the case with King. However, because speeches today may be easily uploaded to websites like YouTube with or without our permission and then quickly go viral, we also must always be cognizant of possible audiences we never intended to target. Not doing so can result in devastating consequences. For example, in 2011 Texas

governor and then–GOP presidential hopeful Rick Perry discovered this when a speech he delivered to a group of supporters in New Hampshire went viral. Blog posts and newspaper editorials blamed his giggling and rambling remarks on being "drunk" or "drugged" (Camia, 2011).

Guidelines for Public Speaking in a Virtual World

The benefits of mediated public speaking to overcome *place* and *time* barriers can be traced to FDR's fireside chats in the 1930s. However, the unique challenges it poses are only beginning to surface. So, the following list of guidelines provides a starting point that will inevitably grow as we learn more about the role technology and digital media play in effective public speaking.

1. Adapt your speech to address multiple audiences. Assume that any speech you give may be recorded and made available to those who are not in your immediate target audience. Always consider how you might adapt your content, structure, and delivery to accurately and respectfully address uninformed, apathetic, and oppositional audiences who may view your speech virtually.

2. Adapt your speech to account for unintended audiences. Don't say anything to one specific audience that you would not want broadcast to a wider audience. With just a few clicks of an iPhone or BlackBerry, an audience member can record a video and post it online. So make sure your content, language, and humorous anecdotes are accurate and respectful.

3. Choose presentational aids carefully. Make sure the visuals and audiovisuals you use can be easily viewed and heard in an online format. Also, be sure to explain them so that those who only have audio access or who view them on a small smartphone

rehearsing
practicing the
presentation of your
speech aloud

speaking notes
word or phrase
outlines of your
speech

screen can understand the information on them.

4. Become proficient with technology. Consult with communication technology experts at your university, college, place of business, or professional organization to learn how to use the technologies effectively. Consider taking a course or seminar devoted to developing these competencies.

5. Employ the fundamentals of effective public speaking. Although this might seem to go without saying, be sure to adhere to the strategies of effective public speaking even when delivering your speech online to mediated audiences. In other words, use an attention getter to pique curiosity, thesis statement with preview to frame what is to come, and transitions to help your audience follow along. Use accurate, clear, and vivid language, and employ verbal and nonverbal techniques that are intelligible, conversational, and animated.

15-6 Rehearsals

Rehearsing is the process of repeatedly practicing your speech aloud. A speech that is not practiced out loud is likely to be far less effective than it would have been had you given yourself sufficient time to revise, evaluate, and mull over all aspects of the speech (Menzel & Carrell, 1994). Figure 15.3 provides a useful timetable for preparing a classroom speech.

In this section, we describe how to rehearse effectively by preparing speaking notes, handling presentational aids, and recording, analyzing, and refining delivery.

15-6a Preparing Speaking Notes

Prior to your first rehearsal session, prepare a draft of your speaking notes. **Speaking notes** are a keyword outline of your speech including hard-to-remember information or quotations and delivery cues. The best notes contain the fewest words possible written in lettering large enough to be seen instantly at a distance.

To develop your notes, begin by reducing your speech outline to an abbreviated outline of key phrases and words. Then, if there are details you must cite exactly accurately—such as a specific example, a quotation, or a set of statistics—add these in the appropriate spots. You might also put these on a separate card as

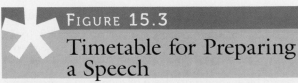

FIGURE 15.3
Timetable for Preparing a Speech

8 days before	Select topic; begin research
7 days before	Continue research
6 days before	Outline body of speech
5 days before	Work on introduction and conclusion
4 days before	Finish outline; find additional material if needed; have all presentational aids completed
3 days before	First rehearsal session
2 days before	Second rehearsal session
1 day before	Third rehearsal section
Due Date	Deliver speech

a "Quotation Card" to refer to when delivering direct quotations during the speech, which is what Alyssa did (see Figure 15.4). Next, indicate exactly where you plan to share presentational aids. Finally, incorporate delivery cues indicating where you want to use your voice and body to enhance intelligibility or expressiveness. For example, indicate where you want to pause, gesture, or make a motivated movement. Capitalize or underline words you want to stress. Use slash marks (//) to remind yourself to pause. Use an upward-pointing arrow to remind yourself to increase rate or volume.

For a 3- to 5-minute speech, you should need no more than three 3 × 5-inch note cards to record your speaking notes. For longer speeches, you might need one card for the introduction, one for each main point, and one for the conclusion. If your speech contains a particularly important and long quotation or a complicated set of statistics, you can record this information in detail on a separate card. Speakers who use computerized slideshows often use the "notes" feature on the program for their speaking notes.

Use your notes during practice sessions as you will when you actually give the speech. If you will use a lectern, set the notes on the speaker's stand or, alternatively, hold them in one hand and refer to them only when needed. How important is it to construct good speaking notes? Speakers often find that the act of making the notes is so effective in helping cement ideas in the mind that during practice, or later during the speech itself, they rarely refer to them at all.

FIGURE 15.4

Alyssa's Speaking Notes

NOTE CARD 1: Introduction
PLANT FEET . . . DIRECT EYE CONTACT . . . POISE/ETHOS!
I. Famous Indian peace activist Mahatma Gandhi: "We must become the change we seek in the world." Tall order . . . We can make a difference right here in Lexington, KY
II. Think for a moment . . . child/homework, neighbor/leaves, stranger/groceries . . . It's easy for college students like us to get involved.
III. I volunteer at LRM and reaped benefits (Slide 1)
IV. Benefits volunteering . . .
   a. get acquainted
   b. responsibility & privilege
   c. résumé-building skills
BLANK SLIDE, WALK RIGHT, EYE C. Let's begin by explaining the ways volunteering can help us connect to our local community.

NOTE CARD 2: Body
I. GREAT WAY to become acquainted ☺ ☺
   LR: Comforts of home . . . unfamiliar city . . . volunteering . . . easy and quick way . . .
   Natalie Cunningham–May 2nd (Q. CARD #1) Social issues and conditions
   Acc. to a 1991 article published in the J. of Prevention and Intervention in the Community by Cohen, Mowbray, Gillette, and Thompson raise awareness . . .
   My experience at LRM (SLIDES 2 & 3)
   BLANK SLIDE, WALK LEFT, EYE C. Not only is volunteering important . . . familiar and social issues . . . FRANKLY . . . dem society . . .
II. Civic responsibility AND privilege . . . LR: We benefit college . . . give back
   I agree with Wilson and Musick who said in their 1997 article in Social Forces active participation or deprived. (SLIDES 4 & 5)
   Also a privilege . . . make a difference . . . feel good . . . self-actualization (SLIDE #6)

NOTE CARD 3: Body & Conclusion
BLANK SLIDE, WALK RIGHT, EYE C: privilege & responsibility . . . résumé-building . . .
III. Life skills
   Article "Employability Credentials: A Key to Successful Youth Transition to Work" by I. Charner–1988 issue of the Journal of Career Development . . . (Q. CARD #2)
   Laura Hatfield . . . leadership, teamwork, and listening skills Andrea Stockelman, volunteer (SLIDE #7) (Q. CARD #3) MY RESUME (SLIDE #8)
   BLANK SLIDE, WALK TO CENTER, EYE C: Today, we've discussed . . . get acquainted, responsibility & privilege, résumé-building life skills help after grad.
   CL: So, I'm hoping the next time you recall . . . not distant past. Instead, I hope you'll be thinking about how you ARE being the change you seek in the world by volunteering right here ///in Lexington///right now!
PAUSE, EYE CONTACT, POISE, NOD ☺

Quotation Card
#1: "My first group of students needed rides to all the various volunteer sites b/c they had no idea where things were in the city. It was really easy for the students who lived on campus to remain ignorant of their city, but while volunteering they become acquainted with Lexington and the important issues going on here."
#2: "Employers rely on credentials to certify that a young person will become a valuable employee. Credentials that document the experiences and employability skills, knowledge, and attitude."
#3: "I learned that there was a lot more that went into preparing food for the homeless than I ever thought possible. It was neat to be a part of that process."

15-6b Handling Presentational Aids

Many speakers think that once they have prepared good presentational aids, they will have no trouble using them in the speech. However, many speeches with good aids have become a shambles because the aids were not well handled. You can avoid problems by following these guidelines:

1. Carefully plan when to use presentational aids. Indicate in your speaking notes exactly when you will reveal and conceal each aid. Practice introducing and using your aids until you can use them comfortably and smoothly.

2. Consider audience needs carefully. As you practice, eliminate any presentational aid that does not contribute directly to the audience's attention to, understanding of, or retention of the key ideas in the speech.

3. Position presentational aids and equipment before beginning your speech. Make sure your aids and equipment are where you want them and that everything is ready and in working order. Test electronic equipment to make sure everything works and that excerpts are cued correctly.

4. Reveal a presentational aid only when talking about it. Because presentational aids will draw audience attention, practice sharing them only when you are talking about them, then conceal them when they are no longer the focus of attention.

Because a single presentational aid may contain several bits of information, practice revealing only the portion you are currently discussing. On computerized slideshows, you can do so by using the "custom animation" feature to allow only one item to appear at a time. You can also strike the "B" key for a black screen when you aren't directly referencing the aid and insert blank slides where ideas in your speech are not being supplemented with something on the slideshow.

5. Display presentational aids so that everyone in the audience can see and hear them. The

© Rreza Estakhrian/Stone/Getty Images

inability to see or hear an aid is frustrating. If possible, practice in the space where you will give your speech so you can adjust equipment accordingly. If you cannot practice in the space ahead of time, then arrive early enough on the day of the presentation to practice quickly with the equipment you will use.

6. Reference the presentational aid during the speech. Because you already know what you want your audience to see in a visual aid, tell your audience what to look for, explain the various elements in it, and interpret figures, symbols, and percentages. For an audio or audiovisual aid, point out what you want your audience to listen for before you play the excerpt. When showing a visual or audiovisual aid, use the "turn-touch-talk" technique.

- When you display the visual, walk to the screen—that's where everyone will look anyway. Slightly turn to the visual and touch it—that is, point to it with an arm gesture or a pointer if necessary. Then, with your back to the screen and your body still facing the audience at a slight forty-five-degree angle, talk to your audience about it.

- When you finish making your comments, return to the lectern or your speaking position and conceal the aid.

7. Talk to your audience, not to the presentational aid. Although you will want to acknowledge the presentational aid by looking at it occasionally, it is important to maintain eye contact with your audience as much as possible. As you practice, resist the urge to stare at your presentational aid.

8. Resist the temptation to pass objects through the audience. People look at, read, handle, and think about whatever they hold in their hands. While they are so occupied, they are not likely to be listening to you. If you have handouts or objects to distribute, do so after the speech rather than during it.

15-6c Rehearsing and Refining Delivery

As with any other activity, effective speech delivery requires practice, and the more you practice, the better your speech will be. During practice sessions, you have three major goals. First, practice wording your ideas so that they are appropriate, accurate, clear, and vivid. Second, practice your speech aloud until your voice and body convey your ideas conversationally, intelligibly, and expressively. Third, practice using presentational aids. As part of each practice, analyze how well it went and set goals for the next practice session.

Let's look at how you can proceed through several practice rounds.

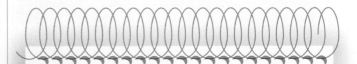

First Practice

Your initial rehearsal should include the following steps:

1. Record (audio and video) your practice session. You may also want to have a friend sit in on it.

2. Read through your complete sentence outline once or twice to refresh your memory. Then put the outline out of sight and practice the speech using only your speaking notes.

3. Make the practice as similar to the speech situation as possible, including using the presentational aids you've prepared. Stand up and face your imaginary audience. Pretend that the chairs, lamps, books, and other objects in your practice room are people.

4. Write down the time that you begin.

5. Begin speaking. Regardless of what happens, keep going until you have presented your entire speech. If you goof, make a repair as you would have to do if you were actually delivering the speech to an audience.

6. Write down the time you finish. Compute the length of the speech for this first rehearsal.

Analysis

Watch and listen to the recorded performance while reviewing your complete outline. How did it go? Did you leave out any key ideas? Did you talk too long on any one point and not long enough on another? Did you clarify each of your points? Did you adapt to your anticipated audience? (If you had a friend or relative watch and listen to your practice, have him or her help with your analysis.) Were your speaking notes effective? How well did you do with your presentational aids? Make any necessary changes before your second rehearsal.

Second Practice

Repeat the six steps outlined for the first rehearsal. By practicing a second time right after your analysis, you are more likely to make the kind of adjustments that begin to improve the speech.

Additional Practices

After you have completed one full rehearsal session consisting of two practices and the analysis in between them, put the speech away until that night or the next day. Although you should rehearse the speech at least a couple more times, you will not benefit if you cram all the practices into one long rehearsal time. You may find that a final practice right before you go to bed will be very helpful; while you are sleeping, your subconscious will continue to work on the speech. As a result, you are likely to find significant improvement in your mastery of the speech when you practice again the next day.

15-6d Adapting while Delivering the Speech

Even when you've practiced your speech to the point that you know it inside and out, you must be prepared to adapt to your audience and possibly change course a bit as you give your speech. Remember that your primary goal as a public speaker is to generate shared understanding with your listeners, so pay attention to the audience's feedback as you speak and adjust accordingly. Here are six tips for adapting to your audience.

1. Be aware of and respond to audience feedback. As you make eye contact with members of your audience, notice how they react to what you say. For instance, if you see quizzical looks on the faces of several listeners, you may need to explain a particular point in a different way, perhaps by providing an additional example to clarify the point. On the other hand, if you see listeners nodding impatiently, recognize that you don't need to belabor your point and move on. If you notice that many audience members look bored, adjust your voice and try to rekindle their interest by showing your enthusiasm for what you are saying.

2. Be prepared to use alternative developmental material. Your ability to adjust to your audience's needs depends on how much additional alternative information you have to share. If you have prepared only one example, you wouldn't be ready if your audience is confused and needs another. If you have prepared only one definition for a term, you may be unable to rephrase an additional definition if needed. As you prepare, try to anticipate where your audience may be confused or already knowledgeable and practice adding or dropping examples and other details.

3. Correct yourself when you misspeak. Every speaker makes mistakes. They stumble over words, mispronounce terms, forget information, and mishandle presentational aids. It's normal. What's important is what you do when you make that mistake. If you stumble over a phrase or mispronounce a word, correct yourself and move on. Don't make a big deal of it by laughing, rolling your eyes, or in other ways drawing unnecessary attention to it. If you suddenly remember that you forgot to provide some information, consider how important it is for your audience to have that information. If what you forgot to say will make it difficult for your audience to understand a point that comes later, figure out how and when to provide the information later in your speech. Usually, however, information we forgot to share is not critical to the audience's understanding and it's better to leave it out and move on.

4. Adapt to unexpected events. Maintain your composure if something unexpected happens, such as a cell phone ringing or someone entering the room while you're speaking. Simply pause until the disruption ceases and then move on. If the disruption causes you to lose your train of thought or has distracted the audience, take a deep breath, look at your speaking notes, and continue your speech at a point slightly before the interruption occurred. This will allow both you and your audience to refocus on your speech. You might acknowledge that you are backtracking by saying something like, "Let's back up a bit and remember where we were . . ."

5. Adapt to unexpected audience reactions. Sometimes, you'll encounter listeners who disagree strongly with your message. They might show their disagreement by being inattentive, heckling you belligerently, or rolling their eyes when you try to make eye contact with them. If these behaviors are limited to one or only a few members of your audience, ignore them and focus on the rest of your listeners. If, however, you find that your audience analysis was inaccurate and that the majority of your audience is hostile to what you are saying, try to anticipate and address their concerns. You might begin by acknowledging their feedback and then try to convince your audience to suspend their judgment while they listen. For example, you could say something like, "I can see that most of you don't agree with my first point. But let me ask you to put aside your initial reaction and think along with me on this next point. Even if we end up disagreeing, at least you will understand my position."

6. Handle questions respectfully. It is rare for audience members to interrupt speakers with questions during a speech. But if you are interrupted, be prepared to deal respectfully with the question. If the question is directly related to understanding the point you are making, answer it immediately. If it is not, acknowledge the question, indicate that you will answer it later, and then do so.

In most professional settings, you will be expected to answer questions when you've finished your speech.

Some people will ask you to clarify information. Some will ask you for an opinion or to draw conclusions beyond what you have said. Whenever you answer a question, be honest about what you know and don't know. If an audience member asks a question you don't know the answer to, admit it by saying something like, "That's an excellent question. I'm not sure of the answer, but I would be happy to follow up on it later if you're interested." Then move on to the next question. If someone asks you to state an opinion about a matter you haven't thought much about, it's okay to say, "You know, I don't think I have given that enough thought to have a valid opinion."

Be sure to monitor how much time you have to answer questions. When the time is nearly up, mention that you'll entertain one more question to warn listeners that the question-and-answer period is almost over. You might also suggest that you'll be happy to talk more with individuals one on one later—this provides your more reserved listeners an opportunity to follow up with you.

15-7 Evaluating Speeches

In addition to learning to prepare and present speeches, you are learning to evaluate (critically analyze) the speeches you hear. From an educational standpoint, critical analysis of speeches provides the speaker with an analysis of where the speech went right and where it went wrong; it also gives you, the critic, insight into the methods that you can incorporate or avoid in your own speeches. In this section, we look at some general criteria for evaluating public speeches.

The critical assumption is that if a speech has good content that is adapted to the audience, is clearly organized, and is delivered well, it is likely to achieve its goal. Thus, you can evaluate any speech by answering questions that relate to the basics of content, structure, and delivery. Figure 15.5 is a speech critique checklist. You can use this checklist to analyze your first speech during your rehearsal period and to critique sample student speeches at the end of this chapter as well as speeches delivered by your classmates.

FIGURE 15.5
Speech Critique Checklist

Check all items that were accomplished effectively.

Content

☐ 1. Was the goal of the speech clear?

☐ 2. Did the speaker offer breadth and depth to support each main point?

☐ 3. Did the speaker use high-quality information and sources?

☐ 4. Did the speaker provide appropriate listener relevance links?

☐ 5. Were presentational aids appropriate?

Structure

☐ 6. Did the introduction gain attention, establish relevance and listener relevance, and lead into the speech using a thesis with main point preview?

☐ 7. Were the main points clear, parallel, and in meaningful complete sentences?

☐ 8. Did section transitions lead smoothly from one point to another?

☐ 9. Was the language appropriate, accurate, clear, and vivid?

☐ 10. Did the conclusion tie the speech together by summarizing the goal and main points and providing a clincher?

Delivery

☐ 11. Did the speaker appear and sound conversational?

☐ 12. Did the speaker appear and sound animated?

☐ 13. Was the speaker intelligible?

☐ 14. Was the speaker vocally expressive?

☐ 15. Was the speaker's appearance appropriate?

☐ 16. Did the speaker have good posture and poise?

☐ 17. Did the speaker look directly at and throughout the audience at least 90% of the time?

☐ 18. Did the speaker have good facial expressions?

☐ 19. Were the speaker's gestures and movement appropriate?

☐ 20. Did the speaker handle the presentational aids effectively?

Based on these criteria, evaluate the speech as (check one):

☐ excellent ☐ good ☐ satisfactory

☐ fair ☐ poor

ACTION STEP 5a

Rehearse Your Speech

The goal of this activity is to rehearse your speech, analyze it, and rehearse it again. One complete rehearsal includes a practice, an analysis, and a second practice.

1. Find a place where you can be alone to practice your speech. Follow the six points for the first practice explained earlier.

2. Review your outline as you watch and listen to the recording and then answer the following questions.

Are you satisfied with how well . . .

the introduction got attention and led into the speech? _____

main points were clearly stated? _____

main points were developed? _____

material was adapted to the audience? _____

section transitions were used? _____

the conclusion summarized the main points? _____

Did you . . .

leave the speech on a high note? _____

use presentational aids? _____

express ideas vividly? _____ and clearly? _____

sound conversational throughout? _____

sound animated? _____ sound intelligible? _____

use natural gestures and movement? _____

use effective eye contact? _____

monitor your facial expression? _____ monitor your posture? _____ and consider your appearance? _____

List the three most important changes you will make in your next practice session:

One: _____

Two: _____

Three: _____

3. Go through the six steps outlined for the first practice again.

Then assess: Did you achieve the goals you set for the second practice?

_____

Reevaluate the speech using the checklist and continue to practice until you are satisfied with all parts of your presentation.

Sample Informative Speech

Read the speech adaptation plan developed by Alyssa Grace Millner in preparing her speech on volunteering and civic engagement. Then read the transcript of Alyssa's speech, using the speech critique checklist from Figure 15.5 to help you evaluate her speech. You can access a video clip of Alyssa's speech on Coursemate.

Adaptation Plan

1. **Key aspects of audience.** The majority of listeners know what volunteering is in a general sense, but they probably don't know the ways it can benefit them as college students.

2. **Establishing and maintaining common ground.** I'll use personal pronouns throughout the speech, as well as specific examples about volunteering from volunteers right here in Lexington.

3. **Building and maintaining interest.** I'll insert listener-relevance links in the introduction and for each main point that point out how volunteering is directly related to improving the lives of college students in some way.

4. **Building credibility.** I will point out right away that I volunteer and that I've done a good deal of research on it. I'll insert examples of my own experiences throughout the speech, as well as cite credible research to support my claims.

5. **Audience attitudes.** Some may be indifferent, but according to the research I've found, most will probably be open to the idea of volunteering. They might not know how easy it can be to get started though.

6. **Adapting to audiences from different cultures and language communities.** Although most of my classmates are U.S. citizens, there are a couple of international students in the class. So, when I talk about volunteering being a civic responsibility, I'll make sure to talk about how all of us are reaping the benefits of a U.S. education; that's why we are all responsible for giving back in some way. I'll talk about it as an ethical responsibility.

7. **Use presentational aids.** I will show photographs of people engaged in volunteer work throughout the speech. I think this will make my ideas very concrete for the audience and will enhance pathos (emotional appeal). I'll also show some graphs about homelessness in Lexington and the percentage of college students who believe in volunteering. I think these will bolster my ethos as the audience will see I've done research. Finally, I'll show my résumé with elements highlighted that I've been able to include because I've volunteered. I think this will drive home my point about the future benefits for college students who volunteer while still in school.

Speech Outline

College Student Volunteering and Civic Engagement

by Alyssa Grace Milner

General goal:

I want to inform my audience.

Specific goal:

I want my audience to realize the benefits of volunteering in Lexington while we are still students at the University of Kentucky.

Introduction

I. The famous Indian peace activist and spiritual leader Mahatma Gandhi is known for saying "We must become the change we seek in the world." That sounds at first like an awfully tall order, but today I'd like to show you how each of us can do just that and make a difference right here in Lexington, Kentucky.

Attention getter

II. Think for a moment of a time in your life when you did something kind for someone else. Maybe you helped a child do homework, or a neighbor rake leaves, or even a stranger get groceries from the store to the car. Do you remember how that made you feel? Well, that feeling can be a normal part of your week when you choose to be a volunteer. And for college students like us, it's easy to get involved as volunteers in our local community.

Listener relevance link

III. Personally, I volunteer at the Lexington Rescue Mission and have reaped many benefits by doing so. *(Show slide 1: picture of me volunteering at the Mission)* I've also done extensive research on volunteering and civic engagement.

Speaker credibility

IV. So, let's spend the next few minutes discussing the benefits volunteering can have for us as college students by focusing on how volunteering helps us get acquainted with the local community, why civic engagement is the responsibility of every one of us, and what volunteering can do to teach us new skills and build our résumés.

Thesis statement with main point preview

Let's begin by explaining the ways volunteering can connect each of us to our local community.

Transition

Body

I. Volunteering is a great way to become acquainted with a community beyond the university campus.

Most college students move away from the comforts of home to a new and unfamiliar city. Not knowing what there is to do or even how to get around can be overwhelming and isolating. Volunteering is an easy way to quickly become familiar with and begin to feel a part of this new city in addition to the campus community.

Listener relevance link

A. Volunteering allows you to learn your way around town.

1. In an interview I had with Natalie Cunningham, the volunteer coordinator of the Lexington Rescue Mission, she said, "My first group of

students needed rides to all the various volunteer sites because they had no idea where things were in the city. It was really easy for the students who lived on campus to remain ignorant of their city, but while volunteering they become acquainted with Lexington and the important issues going on here" (personal communication, May 2, 2010).

    2. It seems like a silly thing, but knowing your way around town starts to make any city feel like home. Volunteering gets you out into the local area and helps you begin to get acquainted with new people and places.

B. Volunteering can also open your eyes to local social issues and conditions.

    1. Many nonprofit organizations strive to raise awareness of important social issues, things like hunger and homelessness (Cohen, Mowbray, Gillette, & Thompson, 1991).

    2. The second time I showed up to volunteer at the Lexington Rescue Mission, I served food to the homeless. *(Show slide 2: group of volunteers in the kitchen)*

        a. I served soup and hung out with other volunteers and local homeless people. One of the "veteran" volunteers explained to me that Lexington has approximately 3,000 homeless people. *(Show slide 3: homelessness statistics in Lexington)*

        b. I was shocked to learn that we had such a large number of men, women, and children without a regular place to sleep. I wouldn't have known about this problem or the organizations working to end homelessness if I hadn't been a volunteer.

Not only is volunteering important because it helps us become familiar with a town and its social issues; frankly, as members of a democratic society, volunteering is our civic responsibility. ▶ Transition

II. Giving back to the community through volunteer work is our civic responsibility and a privilege.

Each of us in this room—whether as U.S. citizens or international students—are reaping the benefits of earning college degrees in this democratic society. With that benefit comes the responsibility and privilege of giving back. ▶ Listener relevance link

A. Volunteering is our civic responsibility.

    1. Wilson and Musick (1997) explain that, without active participation in the local community, civil society becomes deprived.

    2. I agree. Giving back by volunteering helps the community in so many ways. *(Show slides 4 and 5: volunteers sorting clothes at the mission and then volunteers playing cards with people served at the shelter)*

B. Volunteering is also a privilege. Making a difference by volunteering ends up making us feel better about ourselves and our role in the world we live in.

    1. In fact, college students aged 16 to 24 represent the largest growth in percentages of volunteers across the country (Corporation for National and Community Service, 2006). *(Show slide 6: bar graph of growth)*

2. A study of first-year college students done by the Higher Education Research Institute published in January 2009 revealed that 69.7 percent of students believe it is *essential or very important* to volunteer in order to help people in need (Pryor et al., 2009).

Certainly, the privilege of giving back as volunteers is our civic responsibility and helps our local community, but we can also reap valuable résumé-building life skills by volunteering.

▶ Transition

III. Volunteering helps teach us new skills.

These new skills and talents can actually make us more marketable for better jobs once we graduate.

▶ Listener relevance link

A. Being a consistent volunteer at a nonprofit organization while attending college can strengthen your résumé.

1. "Employers rely on credentials to certify that a young person will become a valuable employee. Credentials that document the experiences and employability skills, knowledge, and attitude" (Charner, 1988, p. 30).

2. Laura Hatfield, director of the Center for Community Outreach at the University of Kentucky, points out that volunteers can include leadership, teamwork, and listening skills on their résumés because they can document the experiences where they had to use them effectively in the real world.

3. Andrea Stockelman, another volunteer at the Lexington Rescue Mission, explained some of the new skills she picked up with volunteering. She said, "I learned that there was a lot more that went into preparing food for the homeless than I ever thought possible. It was neat to be a part of that process" (personal communication, April 28, 2010). *(Show slide 7: photo of Andrea preparing food)*

B. Volunteering at the Lexington Rescue Mission taught me new skills that bolstered my résumé. *(Show slide 8: résumé with skills highlighted)*

1. I learned to coordinate the schedules of other volunteers.

2. I also practiced important people skills such as teamwork, empathy, conflict management, and listening.

Conclusion

I. Today we've discussed why volunteering is beneficial to college students by focusing on how volunteering can connect us quickly and easily to our local community, why it's both our responsibility and a privilege to do so, and how volunteering will benefit us after we graduate.

▶ Thesis restatement with main point summary

II. So, I'm hoping the next time you recall a time you really enjoyed making a difference by helping someone, that memory won't come from the distant past. Instead, I hope you'll be thinking about how you are being the change you seek in the world by volunteering right here in Lexington right now.

▶ Clincher

References

Charner, I. (1988). Employability credentials: A key to successful youth transition to work. *Journal of Career Development, 15*(1), 30–40.

Cohen, E., Mowbray, C. T., Gillette, V., & Thompson, E. (1991). Religious organizations and housing development. *Journal of Prevention and Intervention in the Community, 10*(1), 169–185.

Corporation for National and Community Service. (2006). *College students helping America.* Washington, DC: Author.

Pryor, J. H., Hurtado, S., DeAngelo, L., Sharkness, J., Romero, L., Korn, W. S., & Tran, S. (2009). *The American freshman: National norms for fall 2008.* Los Angeles, CA: Higher Education Research Institute.

Wilson, J., & Musick, M. A. (1997). Work and volunteering: The long arm of the job. *Social Forces, 76*(1), 251–272.

Speech and Analysis

The famous Indian peace activist and spiritual leader Mahatma Gandhi is known for saying "We must become the change we seek in the world." That sounds at first like an awfully tall order, but today I'd like to show you how each of us can do just that and make a difference right here in Lexington, Kentucky. Think for a moment of a time in your life when you did something kind for someone else. Maybe you helped a child do homework, or a neighbor rake leaves, or even a stranger get groceries from the store to the car. Do you remember how that made you feel? Well, that feeling can be a normal part of your week when you choose to be a volunteer. And for college students like us, it's easy to get involved as volunteers in our local community. Personally, I volunteer at the Lexington Rescue Mission and have reaped many benefits by doing so. *(Show slide 1: picture of me volunteering at the Mission)* I've also done extensive research on volunteering and civic engagement. So, let's spend the next few minutes discussing the benefits volunteering can have for us as college students by focusing on how volunteering helps us get acquainted with the local community, why civic engagement is the responsibility of every citizen, and what volunteering can do to teach us new skills and build our résumés. Let's begin by explaining the ways volunteering can connect each of us to our local community.

Volunteering is a great way to become acquainted with a community beyond the university campus. Most college students move away from the comforts of home to a new and unfamiliar city. Not knowing what there is to do or even how to get around can be overwhelming and isolating. Volunteering is an easy way to quickly become familiar with and begin to feel a part of this new city in addition to the campus community.

Volunteering allows you to learn your way around town. In an interview I had with Natalie Cunningham, the volunteer coordinator of the Lexington Rescue Mission, she said, "My first group of students needed rides to all the various volunteer sites because they had no idea where things were in the city. It was really easy for the students who lived on campus to remain ignorant of their city, but while volunteering they become acquainted with Lexington and the important issues going on here." It seems like a silly thing, but knowing

Analysis

▶ Notice how Alyssa uses a famous quotation to get the attention of her audience in a way that also piques interest about the topic.

▶ Here, Alyssa establishes listener relevance by pointing out that helping others makes us feel good and that volunteering can be easy.

▶ Alyssa mentions that she volunteers, which bolsters ethos and establishes her credibility to speak on the topic.

▶ Notice how Alyssa's thesis with main point preview gives us a sense of the organizational framework for her ideas.

▶ Again, as Alyssa introduces the first main point, she encourages us to tune in because we all know how overwhelming and isolating it can feel when we move to a new place.

▶ Quoting the volunteer coordinator is a great piece of developmental material that encourages us to trust Alyssa's message. (Note that interviews are not included in the reference section but are cited in the text of the outline.)

your way around town starts to make any city feel like home. Volunteering gets you out into the local area and helps you begin to get acquainted with new people and places.

Volunteering can also open your eyes to local social issues and conditions. According to Cohen, Mowbray, Gillette, and Thompson, many nonprofit organizations strive to raise awareness of important social issues, things like hunger and homelessness. The second time I showed up to volunteer at the Lexington Rescue Mission, I served food to the homeless. *(Show slide 2: group of volunteers in the kitchen)* I served soup and hung out with other volunteers and local homeless people. One of the "veteran" volunteers explained to me that Lexington has approximately 3,000 homeless people. *(Show slide 3: homelessness statistics in Lexington)* I was shocked to learn that we had such a large number of men, women, and children without a regular place to sleep. I wouldn't have known about this problem or the organizations working to end homelessness if I hadn't been a volunteer. Not only is volunteering important because it helps us become familiar with a town and its social issues; frankly, as members of a democratic society, volunteering is our civic responsibility.

Giving back to the community through volunteer work is our civic responsibility and a privilege. Each of us in this room—whether as U.S. citizens or international students—are reaping the benefits of earning college degrees in this democratic society. With that benefit comes the responsibility and privilege of giving back. Volunteering is our civic responsibility. Wilson and Musick explain that, without active participation in the local community, civil society becomes deprived. I agree. Giving back by volunteering helps the community in so many ways. *(Show slides 4 and 5: volunteers sorting clothes at the mission and then volunteers playing cards with people served at the shelter)*

Volunteering is also a privilege. Making a difference by volunteering ends up making us feel better about ourselves and our role in the world around us. In fact, research conducted by the Corporation for National and Community Service from 2002 to 2005 shows that college students age sixteen to twenty-four represent the fastest growing demographic of volunteers in this country. *(Show slide 6: bar graph showing growth)* Not only that, a study done by the Higher Education Research Institute published in January of 2009 shows that a whopping 69.7 percent of first-year college students believe it is essential or very important to volunteer to help people in need. Certainly, the privilege of giving back as volunteers is our civic responsibility and helps our local community, but we can also reap valuable résumé-building life skills by volunteering.

Volunteering helps teach us new skills. These new skills and talents can actually make us more marketable for better jobs once we graduate. Being a consistent volunteer at a nonprofit organization while attending college can strengthen your résumé. According to Charmer, in the *Journal of Career Development*, "Employers rely on credentials to certify that a young person will become a valuable employee. Credentials that document the experiences and employability skills, knowledge, and attitude." Laura Hatfield, director of the Center for Community Outreach at the University of Kentucky, points out that volunteers can include leadership, teamwork, and listening skills on their résumés because they can document the experiences where they had to use them effectively in the real world. Andrea Stockelman, another volunteer at the Lexington Rescue Mission, explained some of the new skills she picked up

▶ *Alyssa intersperses actual photos of herself and others volunteering throughout the speech. Doing so enhances her verbal message but doesn't replace it. The photos also provide pathos, making her ideas more emotionally compelling.*

▶ *Here and throughout the speech, notice how Alyssa uses effective section transitions to tie the point she is concluding into the next point to come. This makes her speech flow smoothly so listeners can follow her train of thought. It also bolsters her ethos because she sounds prepared.*

▶ *Alyssa's careful audience analysis reveals itself here as she reminds her audience that even those who are not American citizens are benefiting as students in our educational system, and thus have a responsibility to give back in some way.*

▶ *Alyssa's choice to include national statistics of college student volunteers boosts her credibility and provides listener relevance by reinforcing that college students are doing this kind of work, want to do this kind of work, and feel good about doing this kind of work.*

▶ *Students want to know how to market themselves to get good jobs. This main point will help maintain listener interest at a point when minds might tend to wander.*

with volunteering. She said, "I learned that there was a lot more that went into preparing food for the homeless than I ever thought possible. It was neat to be a part of that process." *(Show slide 7: photo of Andrea preparing food)*

Volunteering at the Lexington Rescue Mission taught me new skills that bolstered my résumé. *(Show slide 8: résumé with skills highlighted)* I learned to coordinate the schedules of other volunteers. I also practiced important people skills such as teamwork, empathy, conflict management, and listening.

Today we've discussed why volunteering is beneficial to college students by focusing on how volunteering can connect us quickly and easily to our local community, why it's both our responsibility and privilege to do so, and how volunteering will benefit us after we graduate. So, I'm hoping the next time you recall a time you really enjoyed making a difference by helping someone, that memory won't come from the distant past. Instead, I hope you'll be thinking about how you are being the change you seek in the world by volunteering right here in Lexington right now.

▶ By preparing a quotation from another volunteer, Alyssa insinuates that we don't have to take her word alone.

▶ This very clear thesis restatement with main point summary signals a sense of closure.

▶ Notice how Alyssa incorporates her opening quotation into her clincher, providing a sense of closure without saying "thank you." This lets listeners know that the speech is complete in a unique and memorable way.

Quick Quiz

T F 1. The symptoms of public speaking apprehension can be physical, emotional, or cognitive.

T F 2. Research has shown that being nervous or in a state of tension can help you do your best.

T F 3. Cognitive restructuring is transferring the calm feelings we attain while visualizing to the actual speaking event.

T F 4. A pause is the total lack of vocal expressiveness.

T F 5. You should show a visual aid only when talking about it.

6. How your voice sounds depends on its
   a. tone, pitch, quality, and rate.
   b. pitch, volume, rate, and quality.
   c. quality, volume, clarity, and tone.
   d. clarity, pitch, rate, and quality.
   e. volume, quality, clarity, and tone.

7. The position or bearing of your body while giving a speech is called
   a. articulation.
   b. gestures.
   c. posture.
   d. movement.
   e. poise.

8. The hallmark of a conversational style is
   a. poise.
   b. vocal expressiveness.
   c. spontaneity.
   d. fluency.
   e. eye contact.

9. Speeches that are researched and planned ahead of time, although the exact wording is not scripted and will vary from presentation to presentation, are called
   a. impromptu.
   b. scripted.
   c. extemporaneous.
   d. practiced.
   e. spontaneous.

10. When handling your presentational aids, what is the most important thing to consider?
    a. that you share the aid only when you are talking about it
    b. that you indicate on your outline exactly when you plan on revealing and concealing the presentational aid
    c. that you direct your attention to the audience, not the aid
    d. that you practice repeatedly the handling of your aid
    e. that you display your aid so everyone can see or hear it

Answers: 1. T, 2. T, 3. F, 4. F, 5. T, 6. B, 7. C, 8. C, 9. C, 10. D

Informative
Speaking

What do you think?
I can learn a lot from
listening to a speech.

1	2	3	4	5	6	7	8	9	10
STRONGLY DISAGREE									STRONGLY AGREE

Learning Outcomes

16-1 Identify the characteristics of effective informative speaking

16-2 Describe methods for conveying information

16-3 Discuss common patterns for informative speeches

An **informative speech** is one whose goal is to explain or describe facts, truths, and principles in a way that stimulates interest, facilitates understanding, and increases the likelihood of remembering. In short, informative speeches are designed to educate audiences. Informative speeches answer questions about a topic. For example, your informative speech might describe who popular singer-songwriter Adele is, define Scientology, compare and contrast the similarities and differences between Twitter and Facebook, tell the story of golf professional Rory McIlroy's rise to fame, or demonstrate how to create and post a video on a Web site like YouTube. Informative speaking differs from other speech forms (such as speaking to persuade, to entertain, or to celebrate) in that your goal is simply to achieve mutual understanding about an object, person, place, process, event, idea, concept, or issue.

In this chapter, we discuss five distinguishing characteristics of informative speeches and five methods of informing. Then, we discuss two common types of informative speeches (process and expository speeches) and provide an example of an informative speech.

16-1 Characteristics of Effective Informative Speaking

Effective informative speeches are intellectually stimulating, relevant, creative, memorable, and address diverse learning styles.

**informative
speech**
a speech whose
goal is to explain or
describe facts, truths,
and principles in a
way that increases
understanding

16-1a Intellectually Stimulating

Your audience will perceive information to be **intellectually stimulating** when it is new to them and when it is explained in a way that piques their curiosity and interest. By *new*, we mean information that most of your audience is unfamiliar with or fresh insights into a topic with which they are already familiar.

If your audience is unfamiliar with your topic, you should consider how you might tap their natural curiosity. Imagine you are an anthropology major who is interested in prehistoric humans, which is not an interest shared by most members of your audience. You know that in 1991, the 5,300-year-old remains of a man, now called Ötzi, were found surprisingly well preserved in an ice field in the mountains between Austria and Italy. Even though the discovery was big news at the time, your audience today probably doesn't know much about it. You can draw on their natural curiosity, however, as you present "Unraveling the Mystery of the Iceman," describing scientists' efforts to understand who Ötzi was and what happened to him ("Ötzi, the Ice Man," n.d.).

If your audience is familiar with your topic, you will need to identify fresh insight about it. Begin by asking yourself, "What things about my topic do listeners probably not know?" Then consider depth and breadth as you answer the question. *Depth* involves going into more detail than people's general knowledge of the topic. If you watch programs on the Food Network, that's what you'll find. Most people know basic recipes, but these programs show new ways to cook the same foods. *Breadth* involves looking at how your topic relates to associated

topics. Trace considered breadth when he informed his audience about Type 1 diabetes. He discussed not only the physical and emotional effects of the disease on a diabetic person, but also the emotional and relational effects on family and friends, as well as the financial effects on society.

16-1b Relevant

As you prepare an informative speech, do not assume that your listeners will recognize how the information is relevant to them. Remember to incorporate *listener relevance links* throughout the speech. As you prepare each main point, ask and answer the question: How would knowing this information make my listeners happier, healthier, wealthier, wiser, and so forth?

16-1c Creative

Your audience will perceive your information to be **creative** when it yields innovative ideas. You may not ordinarily consider yourself to be creative, but that may be because you have never recognized or fully developed your own innovative ideas. Contrary to what you may think, creativity is not a gift that some have and some don't; rather, it is the result of hard work. Creativity comes from doing good research, taking time, and practicing productive thinking.

Creative informative speeches begin with *good research*. The more you learn about a topic, the more you will have to work with to develop it creatively. Speakers who present information creatively have given themselves lots of supporting material to work with.

Rarely do creative ideas come when we are in a time crunch. Instead, they are likely to come when we least expect it—when we're driving our car, preparing for bed, or daydreaming. The creative process depends on having time to mull over ideas. If you complete a draft of your outline several days before you speak, you'll have time to consider how to present your ideas creatively.

For the creative process to work, you also have to *think productively*. **Productive thinking** occurs when we contemplate

The more you **know about** a topic, the more **creative** you can be with it.

something from a variety of perspectives. Then, with numerous ideas to choose from, we can select the ones that are best suited to our particular audience. In the article "A Theory about Genius," Michael Michalko (1998) describes several tactics you can use to become better at productive thinking. They include:

1. Rethink a problem, issue, or topic from many perspectives. As you brainstorm, try to think about a possible topic as it might be perceived by many different groups and co-cultural groups. Then as you conduct research, try to find sources that represent a variety of viewpoints and perspectives, as well.

2. Make your thoughts visible by sketching drawings, diagrams, and graphs. Concept mapping when generating possible topics is one example of this tactic.

3. Produce. Set regular goals to produce *something*. Don't let writer's block keep you from drafting an initial outline. You need to start somewhere. Getting ideas out of your head and onto the paper or computer screen gives you something to work with and revise. After all, you can't edit air.

4. Combine and recombine ideas, images, and thoughts in different ways. The Austrian monk, Gregor Mendel, combined mathematics and biology to come up with the laws of heredity, which still ground the modern science of genetics today. Jennifer's list of possible speech topics included gardening, something she loved to do, and the issue of rising college tuition costs. She put the two ideas together and came up with the idea of doing an informative speech about how to use gardening (services, produce, and products) to raise money to help pay for college.

Let's look at how productive thinking can help to identify different approaches to a topic. Suppose you want to give a speech on volunteering in the United States, and in your research, you ran across the data shown in Figure 16.1. With productive thinking, you can use this data in several ways to develop your speech. For instance, notice that roughly two-thirds of Utah's college students (ages 16 to 24) volunteer as much as or more than the general adult population. You could investigate why this is so and do a speech about it. Looking at the data from another perspective, you might notice that the percentage of both the general adult and college student populations that volunteer in three states (Minnesota, Nebraska, and Utah) is 40 percent or more. You might examine what types of volunteer work people do in

those states and why. Looking at these data yet another way reveals that Utah ranks first for the percentage of the general adult population that volunteers and Nevada ranks last. You could do a speech comparing volunteerism in those two states. Or you might notice that a majority low-ranking states are in the east, while many of the states that rank highest are in the Midwest and mountain west. Again, you could do a speech comparing volunteerism in these regions.

Productive thinking can also help us find alternative ways to make the same point. Using the information in Figure 16.1, we can quickly create two ways to support the point "On average, about 30 percent of the U.S. general adult population volunteers."

> ***Alternative A:*** *Eighteen of the fifty states plus the District of Columbia had volunteering rates between 25 and 30 percent. Twelve of them had volunteering rates between 30 and 35 percent. In other words, thirty of the fifty states plus D.C. (or 60 percent) report volunteering rates between 25 and 35 percent.*

> ***Alternative B:*** *If we exclude Nevada with its very low volunteering rate of 18.8 percent and Utah, Nebraska, and Minnesota with very high rates of 48 percent, 42.8 percent, and 40.7 percent, respectively, then we see that most states (forty-seven) reported volunteering rates between 20 and 40 percent.*

16-1d Memorable

If your speech is really informative, your audience will hear a lot of new information but will need help remembering what is most important. Emphasizing your specific goal, main points, and key facts are good starting points. Figure 16.2 summarizes ways to use presentational aids, repetition, transitions, humor, and mnemonics and acronyms to help your audience remember information you believe to be most important.

16-1e Address Diverse Learning Styles

Because audience members differ in how they prefer to learn, you will be most successful when you address diverse learning styles. You can appeal to people who prefer to learn through the feeling dimension by providing concrete, vivid images, examples, stories, and testimonials. Address the watching dimension by using visual aids. Address the thinking dimension by including definitions,

FIGURE 16.1

Volunteering Rates across the United States

State	General Adult Population		College Students, Ages 16–24	
	Volunteering Rate (in %)	State Rank	Volunteering Rate (in %)	State Rank
Alabama	28.9	32	34.8	16
Alaska	38.9	5	40.1	7
Arizona	24.9	45	30.8	32
Arkansas	25.6	43	31.7	22
California	26.1	40	28.5	38
Colorado	32.8	17	38.3	10
Connecticut	30.8	21	31.5	23
Delaware	26.7	37	26.4	42
District of Columbia	30.8	22	31.0	30
Florida	24.1	48	25.9	43
Georgia	25.9	41	21.4	51
Hawaii	25.4	44	29.6	35
Idaho	35.5	14	44.4	2
Illinois	29.7	28	31.2	27
Indiana	29.5	29	37.3	13
Iowa	39.2	4	31.1	29
Kansas	38.6	8	31.5	24
Kentucky	29.8	27	30.4	33
Louisiana	22.7	49	27.8	40
Maine	33.2	16	31.4	25
Maryland	30.3	25	30.2	34
Massachusetts	27.0	36	24.0	47
Michigan	32.1	18	37.4	12
Minnesota	40.7	3	39.9	8
Mississippi	26.4	39	33.1	20
Missouri	31.9	20	38.9	9
Montana	37.9	10	34.6	17
Nebraska	42.8	2	41.5	5
Nevada	18.8	51	23.6	49
New Hampshire	32.0	19	32.0	21
New Jersey	26.5	38	25.0	45
New Mexico	28.5	33	31.3	26
New York	21.3	50	23.4	50
North Carolina	29.1	30	28.8	37
North Dakota	36.5	13	33.7	19
Ohio	30.7	24	34.4	18
Oklahoma	30.0	26	43.0	3
Oregon	33.6	15	31.1	28
Pennsylvania	30.8	23	35.1	15
Rhode Island	24.9	46	25.8	44
South Carolina	28.0	35	28.3	39
South Dakota	38.8	6	31.0	31
Tennessee	25.9	42	24.0	48
Texas	28.3	34	29.2	36
Utah	48.0	1	62.9	1
Vermont	38.1	9	41.5	4
Virginia	29.0	31	24.6	46
Washington	36.8	12	37.6	11
West Virginia	24.6	47	27.4	41
Wisconsin	37.0	11	36.2	14
Wyoming	38.8	7	40.3	6

Source: Dote, Cramer, Dietz, and Grimm (2006). College students helping America. Washington, D. C.: Corporation for National and Community Service.

explanations, and statistics. Address the doing dimension by encouraging your listeners to do something during the speech or afterward. Rounding the learning cycle in this way ensures that you address the diverse learning style preferences of your audience and make the speech understandable, meaningful, and memorable for all.

16-2 Methods of Informing

We can inform through description, definition, comparison and contrast, narration, and demonstration. Let's look at each of these methods more closely.

16-2a Description

Description is an informative method used to create an accurate, vivid, verbal picture of an object, geographic feature, setting, event, person, or image. This method usually answers an overarching *who*, *what*, or *where* question. If the thing to be described is simple and familiar (like a lightbulb or a river), the description may not need to be detailed. But if the thing to be described is complex and unfamiliar (like a sextant or holograph), the description will need to be more comprehensive. Descriptions are, of course, easier

> **description**
> method of informing used to create an accurate, vivid, verbal picture of an object, geographic feature, setting, person, event, or image

---

FIGURE 16.2

Techniques for Making Informative Speeches Memorable

Technique	Use	Example
Presentational aids	To provide audience members with a visual, audio, or audiovisual conceptualization of important information	A diagram of the process of making ethanol
Repetition	To give the audience a second or third chance to retain important information by repeating or paraphrasing it	"The first dimension of romantic love is passion; that is, it can't really be romantic love if there is no sexual attraction."
Transitions	To help the audience understand the relationship between the ideas, including primary and supporting information	"So the three characteristics of romantic love are passion, intimacy, and commitment. Now let's consider five ways to keep love alive."
Humor and other emotional anecdotes	To create an emotional memory link to important ideas	"True love is like a pair of socks, you have to have two, and they've got to match. So you and your partner need to be mutually committed and compatible."
Mnemonics and acronyms	To provide an easily remembered memory prompt for a series or a list	"You can remember the four criteria for evaluating a diamond as the four Cs: carat, clarity, cut, and color." "As you can see, useful goals are SMART: S for specific, M for measurable, A for action-oriented, R for reasonable, and T for time-bound. That's SMART."

if you have a presentational aid, but vivid verbal descriptions can also create informative mental pictures. To describe something effectively, you can explain its size, shape, weight, color, composition, age, condition, and spatial organization. You can describe size subjectively as large or small and objectively by noting specific numerical measures. For example, you can describe New York City subjectively as the largest in the United States or more objectively as home to more than 8 million people with more than 26,000 people per square mile.

You can describe shape by reference to common geometric forms like round, triangular, oblong, spherical, conical, cylindrical, or rectangular, or by reference to common objects such as a book or a milk carton. For example, the Lower Peninsula of Michigan is often described as being shaped like a left-hand mitten. Shape is made more vivid by using adjectives, such as *smooth* or *jagged*.

You can describe weight subjectively as heavy or light and objectively by pounds and ounces or kilograms, grams, and milligrams. As with size, you can clarify weight with comparisons. For example, you can describe a Humvee (Hummer) as weighing about 7,600 pounds, or about as much as three Honda Civics.

You can describe color by coupling a basic color (such as black, white, red, or yellow) with a common object. For instance, instead of describing something as puce or ochre, you might describe the object as "eggplant purple" or "clay-pot orange."

You can describe the composition of something by indicating what it is made of, such as by saying the building was made of brick, concrete, or wood. Sometimes you might be clearer by describing what it looks like rather than what it is. For example, you might say something looks metallic, even if it is made of plastic rather than metal.

You can describe something by its age and by its condition. For example, describing a city as old and well

kept gives different mental pictures than describing a city as old and war torn.

Finally, you can describe by spatial organization going from top to bottom, left to right, outer to inner, and so on. A description of the Sistine Chapel, for example, might go from the floor to the ceiling, while a description of a NASCAR automobile might go from the body to the engine to the interior.

16-2b Definition

Definition is an informative method that explains the meaning of something. There are four ways to define something.

First, you can define a word or idea by classifying it and differentiating it from similar words or ideas. For example, in a speech on veganism, you might use information from the Vegan Society's Web site (www.vegansociety.com) to develop a definition of a vegan: "A vegan is a vegetarian who is seeking a lifestyle free from animal products for the benefit of people, animals, and the environment. Vegans eat a plant-based diet free from all animal products including milk, eggs, and honey. Vegans also don't wear leather, wool, or silk and avoid other animal-based products."

Second, you can define a word by explaining its derivation or history. For instance, the word *vegan* is made from the beginning and end of the word *vegetarian* and was coined in the United Kingdom in 1944, when the Vegan Society was founded. Offering this etymology will help your audience to remember the meaning of *vegan*.

Third, you can define a word by explaining its use or function. For example, in vegan recipes, you can use tofu or tempeh to replace meat and almond or soy milk to replace cow's milk.

The fourth, and perhaps the quickest way you can define something, is by using a familiar synonym or antonym. A **synonym** is a word that has the same or a similar meaning; an **antonym** is a word that has the opposite meaning. So you could define *vegan* by comparing it to the word *vegetarian*, which is a synonym with a similar although not identical meaning, or to the word *carnivore*, which is an antonym.

Eggplant purple is more descriptive than just purple.

© Valentyn Volkov/iStockphoto.com

16-2c Comparison and Contrast

Comparison and **contrast** is an informative method that focuses on how something is similar to and different from other things. For example, in a speech on veganism, you might tell your audience how vegans are similar to and different from other types of vegetarians. You can point out that like vegetarians, vegans don't eat meat. In contrast, semi-vegetarians eat fish or poultry. Like lacto vegetarians, vegans don't eat eggs, but unlike this group and lacto-ovo vegetarians, vegans don't use dairy products. So of all vegetarians, vegans have the most restrictive diet. Because comparisons and contrasts can be figurative or literal, you can use metaphors and analogies as well as making direct comparisons.

16-2d Narration

Narration is an informative method that recounts an autobiographical or biographical event, a myth, a story, or some other account. Narrations usually have four parts. First, the narration orients the listener by describing when and where the event took place and by introducing the important people or characters. Second, the narration explains the sequence of events that led to a complication or problem, including details that enhance the development. Third, the narration discusses how the complication or problem affected the key people in the narrative. Finally, the narration recounts how the complication or problem was solved. The characteristics of a good narration include a strong story line; use of descriptive language and detail that enhance the plot, people, setting, and events; effective use of dialogue; pacing that builds suspense; and a strong voice (Baerwald, n.d.).

Narrations can be presented in a first-, second-, or third-person voice. When you use first person, you report what you have personally experienced or observed, using the pronouns *I*, *me*, and *my* as you recount the events. "Let me tell you about the first time I tried to water-ski" might be the opening for a narrative story told in first person. When you use second person, you place your audience at the scene by using the pronouns *you* and *your*. You might say, for example, "Imagine that you have just gotten off the plane in Hong Kong. You look at the signs but can't read a thing. Which way is the terminal?" When you use third person, you describe to your audience what has happened, is happening, or will happen to other people by using pronouns like *he*, *she*, *his*, *her*, and *they*. "When the students arrived in Venice for their study-abroad experience, the first thing they saw was . . ."

© Blaj Gabriel/Shutterstock.com

16-2e Demonstration

Demonstration is an informative method that shows how something is done, displays the stages of a process, or depicts how something works. Demonstrations range from very simple with a few easy-to-follow steps (such as how to iron a shirt) to very complex (such as explaining how a nuclear reactor works). Regardless of whether the topic is simple or complex, effective demonstrations require expertise, developing a hierarchy of steps, and using vivid language and presentational aids.

In a demonstration, your experience with what you are demonstrating is critical. Expertise gives you the necessary background to supplement bare-bones instructions with personally lived experiences. Why are TV cooking shows so popular? Because the chef doesn't just read the recipe and do what it says. Rather, while performing each step, the chef shares tips that aren't mentioned in any cookbook. It is the chef's experience that allows him or her to say that one egg will work as well as two, or how to tell if the cake is really done.

In a demonstration, you organize the steps from first to last so that your audience will be able to remember the sequence of actions accurately. Suppose you want to demonstrate the steps in using a touch-screen voting machine. If you present 14 separate points, your audience is unlikely to remember them. However, if you group them under a few headings (I. Get ready to vote;

comparison and contrast
a method of informing that explains something by focusing on how it is similar and different from other things

narration
a method of informing that explains something by recounting events or stories

demonstration
a method of informing that explains something by showing how it is done, by displaying the stages of a process, or by depicting how something works

II. Vote; III. Review your choices; and IV. Cast your ballot), chances are much higher that your audience will be able to remember most of the items.

Although you could explain a process with only words, most demonstrations show the audience the process or parts of the process. That's one reason why TV shows like *What Not to Wear* and *Flip This House* are so popular. If what you are explaining is relatively simple, you can demonstrate the entire process from start to finish. However, if the process is lengthy or complex, you may choose to pre-prepare the material for some of the steps. Although you will show all stages in the process, you will not need to take the time for every single step as the audience watches. For example, many of the ingredients used by TV chefs are already cut up, measured, and separated into little bowls.

Effective demonstrations require practice. Remember that under the pressure of speaking to an audience, even the simplest task can become difficult. (Have you ever tried to thread a needle with 25 people watching you?) As you practice, you will want to consider the size of your audience and the configuration of the room. Be sure that all of the audience will be able see what you are doing.

16-3 Common Informative Patterns

Two of the most common patterns for organizing informative speech ideas are process patterns and expository patterns.

16-3a Process Speeches

The goal of a **process speech** is to demonstrate how something is done, is made, or works. Effective process speeches require you to carefully delineate the steps and the order in which they occur. These steps typically become the main points and explanations of each step become the subpoints. Process speeches rely heavily on the demonstration method of informing.

Although some process speeches require you to demonstrate, others are not suited to demonstrations. For these, you can use visual or audiovisual aids to help the audience see the steps in the process. In a speech

process speech
an informative speech that demonstrates how something is done, is made, or works.

expository speech
an informative presentation that provides carefully researched, in-depth knowledge about a complex topic

on remodeling a kitchen, for example, it would not be practical to demonstrate the process; however, you could greatly enhance the verbal description by showing pictures before, during, and after the remodeling.

16-3b Expository Speeches

The goal of an **expository speech** is to provide carefully researched, in-depth knowledge about a complex topic. For example, "understanding the health care debate," "the origins and classification of nursery rhymes," "the sociobiological theory of child abuse," and "viewing rap as poetry" are all topics on which you could give an interesting expository speech. Lengthy expository speeches are known as *lectures*.

All expository speeches require speakers to draw from an extensive research base, choose an organizational pattern best suited to the material and specific speech goal, and use a variety of informative methods (e.g., descriptions, definitions, comparisons and contrasts, narration, and short demonstrations) to sustain the audience's attention and help them understand the material presented.

Expository speeches include speeches that explain a political, economic, social, religious, or ethical issue; forces of history; a theory, principle, or law; and a creative work.

Exposition of Political, Economic, Social, Religious, or Ethical Issues

In an expository speech, you have the opportunity to help the audience understand the background or context of an issue, including the forces that gave rise to and continue to affect it. You may also present the various positions held about the issue and the reasoning behind these positions. Finally, you may discuss various ways that have been presented for resolving the issue.

The general goal of your speech is to inform, not to persuade. So you will want to present all sides of controversial issues, without advocating which side is better. You will also want to make sure that the sources you draw from are respected experts and are objective in what they report. Finally, you will want to present complex issues in a straightforward manner that helps your audience understand them, while refraining from oversimplifying knotty issues. Figure 16.3 provides examples of topic ideas for an expository speech about a political, economic, social, religious, or ethical issue.

For example, while researching a speech on fracking—the controversial method for extracting natural gas deposits—you need to be careful to consult articles and experts on all sides of this issue and fairly represent

FIGURE 16.3

Topic Ideas for Expository Speeches about Political, Economic, Social, Religious, or Ethical Issues

job search strategies	cyber bullying	fracking
global warming	digital remixing	capital punishment
teacher accountability	right to bear arms	Occupy Wall Street
patterns of immigration	media bias	cleaning up oil spills
Sikhism	celebrity culture	consequences of
stem cell research	European debt crisis	Arab Spring

© iStockphoto/Thinkstock.com

FIGURE 16.4

Topic Ideas for Expository Speeches about Historical Events and Forces

genocide	the colonization of Africa	Irish immigration
women's suffrage	Ghandi and his movement	the War on Terror
the Olympics	the Spanish Flu epidemic	the Ming Dynasty
the New Madrid earthquake	the Industrial Revolution	the Balfour Declaration
the papacy		

© iStockphoto/Thinkstock.com

and incorporate their views in your outline. You should discuss not only the technology that is used but also the controversies that surround its use. If time is limited, you might discuss just one or two of these issues, but you should at least inform the audience of others.

Exposition of Historical Events and Forces

It has been said that those who don't understand history may be destined to repeat it. So an expositional speech about historical events and forces can be fascinating for its own sake, but it can also be relevant for what is happening today. Unfortunately, some people think history is boring. So you have an obligation to seek out stories and narratives that can enliven your speech. And you will want to analyze the events you describe and their impact at the time they occurred, as well as the meaning they have today. Figure 16.4 proposes examples of topic ideas for an expository speech about historical events and forces.

Coloring the News: Is the Information Provided by the Media Biased?

The Pew Research Center for the People and the Press (2011) found that 77 percent of Americans across political affiliations think news organizations "tend to favor one side" and 66 percent believe news organizations are politically biased in their reporting. Though many Americans agree that media bias is a problem, there is little consensus about how to determine the nature of such bias or which side it even favors. For example, National Public Radio (NPR) has long been accused of having a liberal bias in its reporting, and some conservative critics have called for an end to federal funding of the organization. Some, like respected journalist Bill Moyers, have defended NPR as an independent news source that practices journalistic objectivity and balanced reporting because they don't take explicit stands on controversial issues like abortion and gay marriage (Moyers & Winship, 2011). Conservative critics, such as Bernard Goldberg (2011), counter that the partiality of NPR and other news organizations is rooted in ideological biases that shape what stories they choose to cover and how they are reported, such as the choice of sources and amount of time given to sources on each side of an issue. At times, bias may be as subtle as the language used to describe people on different sides of controversial issues. For example, consider how the pragmatics of messages change depending on whether a reporter chooses to label opponents as pro-choice vs. pro-life, pro-choice vs. antiabortion; anti-life vs. anti-abortion, or anti-life vs. pro-life. By choosing nonparallel labels to opposing sides, the reporter subtly colors the perceptions of unsophisticated audience members.

© REDAV/Shutterstock.com

Exposition of a Theory, Principle, or Law

The way we live is affected by natural and human laws and principles and is explained by various theories. Yet there are many theories, principles, and laws that we do not completely understand—or, at least, we don't understand how they affect us. The main challenge is to find material that explains the theory, law, or principle in language that is understandable to the audience. You will want to search for or create examples and illustrations that demystify complicated concepts and terminology. Using effective examples and comparing unfamiliar ideas with those that the audience already knows are techniques that can help you with this kind of speech. In a speech on the psychological principles of operant conditioning, for example, a speaker can help the audience understand the difference between continuous reinforcement and intermittent reinforcement by providing the following explanation:

> When a behavior is reinforced continuously, each time the person performs the behavior, a reward is given, but when the behavior is reinforced intermittently, the reward is not always given when the behavior is displayed. Behavior that is learned by continuous reinforcement disappears quickly when the reward no longer is provided, but behavior that is learned by intermittent reinforcement continues for long periods of time, even when not reinforced. Every day you can see the effects of how a behavior was conditioned. For example, take the behavior of putting a coin in a machine. If the machine is a vending machine, you expect to be rewarded every time you "play." And if the machine doesn't dispense the item, you might wonder if the machine is out of order and "play" just one more coin, or you might bang on the machine. In any case, you are unlikely to put in more than one more coin. But suppose the machine is a slot machine or a machine that dispenses instant-winner lottery tickets. How many coins will you "play" before you stop and conclude that the machine isn't going to give you what you want? Why the difference? Because you were conditioned to a vending machine on a continuous schedule, but a slot machine or automatic lottery ticket dispenser "rewards" you on an intermittent schedule.

FIGURE 16.5

Topic Ideas for Expository Speeches about Theories, Principles, or Laws

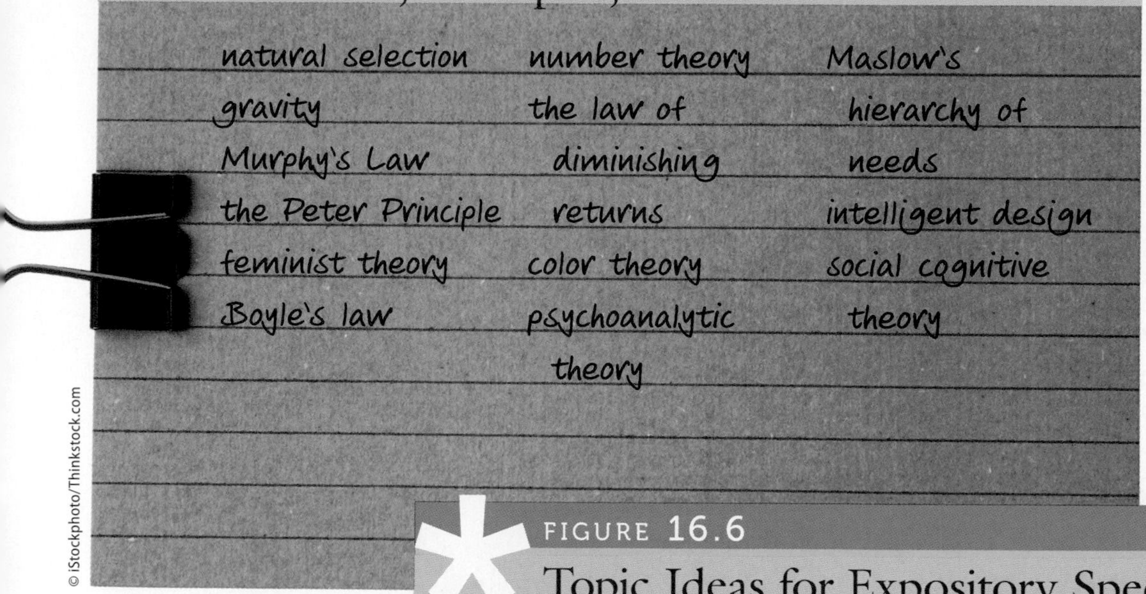
natural selection
gravity
Murphy's Law
the Peter Principle
feminist theory
Boyle's law
number theory
the law of diminishing returns
color theory
psychoanalytic theory
Maslow's hierarchy of needs
intelligent design
social cognitive theory

© iStockphoto/Thinkstock.com

FIGURE 16.6

Topic Ideas for Expository Speeches about Creative Works

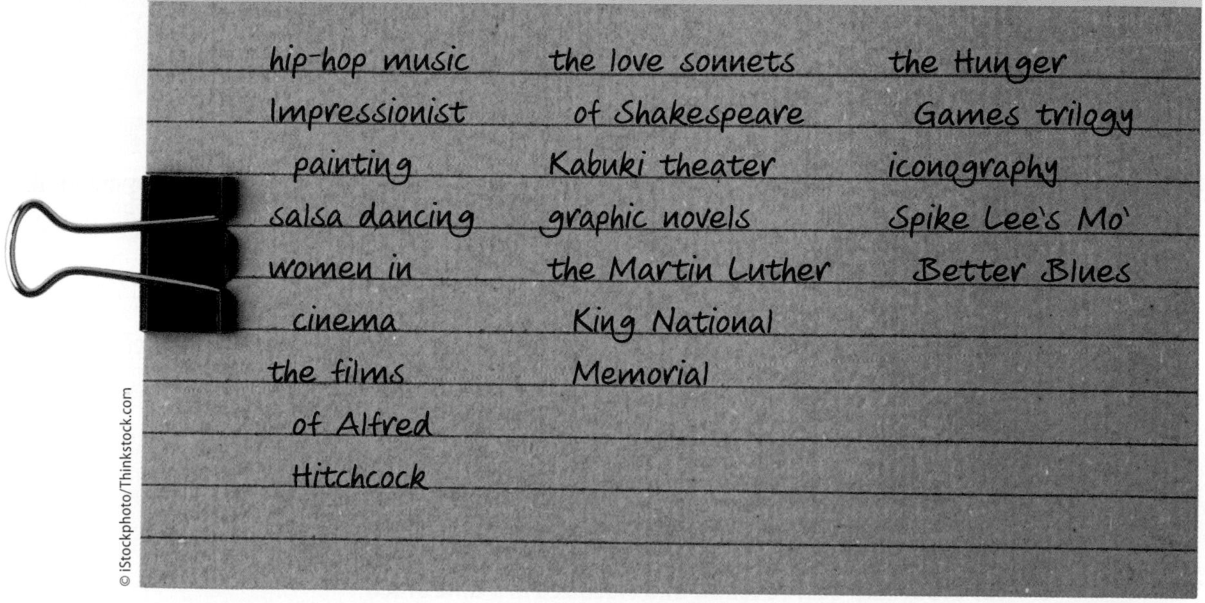
hip-hop music
Impressionist painting
salsa dancing
women in cinema
the films of Alfred Hitchcock
the love sonnets of Shakespeare
Kabuki theater
graphic novels
the Martin Luther King National Memorial
the Hunger Games trilogy
iconography
Spike Lee's Mo' Better Blues

© iStockphoto/Thinkstock.com

Figure 16.5 provides some examples of topic ideas for an expository speech about a theory, principle, or law.

Exposition of a Creative Work

Courses in art, theatre, music, literature, and film appreciation give students tools by which to recognize the style, historical period, and quality of a particular piece or group of pieces. Yet most of us know very little about how to understand a creative work, so presentations designed to explain creative works like poems, novels, songs, or even famous speeches can be very instructive for audience members.

When developing a speech that explains a creative work, you will want to find information on the work and the artist who created it. You will also want to find sources that educate you about the period in which this work was created and inform you about the criteria that critics use to evaluate works of this type. For example, if you wanted to give an expository speech on Freedrick Douglass's Fourth of July Oration given in Rochester, New York in 1852, you might need to orient your audience by first reminding them of who Douglass was. Then you would want to explain the traditional expectations for Fourth of July speakers in the mid-1800s. After this, you might want to summarize the speech and perhaps share a few memorable quotes. Finally, you would want to discuss how speech critics view the speech and why the speech is considered great.

Figure 16.6 presents examples of topics for expository speeches about creative works. Figure 16.7 is a checklist you can use to analyze any informative speech you rehearse or to critique the speeches of others.

FIGURE 16.7

Informative Speech Evaluation Checklist

Process Speech:
☐ **How something is done**
☐ **How something is made**
☐ **How something works**

Expository Speech:
☐ **Exposition of political, economic, social, religious, or ethical issue**
☐ **Exposition of historical events or forces**
☐ **Exposition of a theory, principle, or law**
☐ **Exposition of creative work**

General Criteria
_____ 1. **Was the specific goal clear?**
_____ 2. **Were the main points developed with breadth and depth of appropriate supporting material?**
_____ 3. **Was the introduction effective in creating interest and introducing the main points?**
_____ 4. **Was the speech organized and easy to follow?**
_____ 5. **Was the language appropriate, clear, and vivid?**
_____ 6. **Was the conclusion effective in summarizing the main points and providing closure?**
_____ 7. **Was the vocal delivery intelligible, conversational, and expressive?**
_____ 8. **Did the body actions appear poised, natural, spontaneous, and appropriate?**

Specific Criteria for Process Speeches
_____ 1. **Was the introduction clear in previewing the process to be explained?**
_____ 2. **Was the speech easy to follow and organized in a time order?**
_____ 3. **Were presentational aids used effectively to clarify the process?**
_____ 4. **Did the process use a demonstration method effectively?**

Specific Criteria for Expository Speeches
_____ 1. **Was the specific goal of the speech to provide well-researched information on a complex topic?**
_____ 2. **Did the speaker effectively use a variety of methods to convey the information?**
_____ 3. **Did the speaker emphasize the main ideas and important supporting material?**
_____ 4. **Did the speaker present in-depth, high-quality, appropriately cited information?**

© Cengage Learning

Sample Informative Speech

This section presents a sample informative speech given by a student, including an adaptation plan, an outline, and a transcript.

Read the speech adaptation plan developed by Louisa Greene in preparing her speech on making ethanol. Then read the transcript of Louisa's speech, using the speech critique checklist from Figure 16.7 to help you evaluate her speech. You can access a video clip of Louisa's speech on CourseMate.

Adaptation Plan

1. **Key aspects of audience.** Most people in my audience have probably heard of ethanol as an alternative to fossil fuels but don't know exactly what it is or how it's produced.

2. **Establishing and maintaining common ground.** I will begin my speech by asking the audience a question. Throughout the speech, I will refer to the audience's previous knowledge and experience.

3. **Building and maintaining interest.** Because my audience is initially unlikely to be interested in how to produce ethanol, I will have to work hard to interest them and to keep their interest through the speech. I will try to gain interest in the introduction by relating the production of ethanol, the fuel, to the production of "white lightning," the illegal alcohol, which might be of more interest to the average college student. Throughout the speech, I will use common analogies and metaphors to explain the complex chemical processes. Finally, I will use a well-designed PowerPoint presentation to capture attention.

4. **Audience knowledge and sophistication.** Because most of the class is not familiar with ethanol, I will introduce them to the four-part process of making ethanol. I believe that by relating the process to that of making alcohol that people can drink, my audience will be more likely to be interested in and retain the information.

5. **Building credibility.** Early in the speech, I will tell the audience about how I got interested in ethanol when I built a still as a science fair project in high school. I will also tell them that I am now a chemical engineering major and am hoping to make a career in the alternative fuel industry.

6. **Audience attitudes.** My audience is likely to be indifferent to my topic, so I need to capture their attention by using interesting examples. I then need to keep them interested by relating the topic to things they're familiar with.

7. **Adapting to audiences from different cultures and language communities.** I will use visual and audiovisual aids in my PowerPoint presentation to help those listeners from different cultures understand what I'm talking about even if English is not their native language.

8. **Using presentational aids to enhance understanding and memory.** Throughout the speech, I will use color-coded PowerPoint slides with headers to reinforce the steps being discussed.

Speech Outline
Making Ethanol
by Louisa Greene

General goal:
To inform

Specific goal:
I want my audience to understand the process for making ethanol from corn.

Introduction

I. Did you know that the first Model T cars were originally designed to run on ethanol or that Henry Ford said that ethanol was the fuel of the future? Did you know that in World War II about 75 percent of the German and American military vehicles were powered by ethanol since oil for gasoline was difficult to attain? ▶ *Attention getter*

II. The process for making ethanol is actually very similar to the process used to make moonshine, which may be why—during the first Arab oil embargo in 1978—when Robert Warren built a still to produce ethanol, he called the product "liquid sunshine" (Warren, 2006). Ethanol is an easy-to-make, inexpensive, and nearly pollution-free renewable alternative to gasoline. ▶ *Listener relevance link*

III. I became interested in ethanol in high school when I built a miniature ethanol still as a science fair project. I'm now a chemical engineering major and hope to make a career in the alternative fuel industry. ▶ *Speaker credibility*

IV. Today, I'm going to explain the commercial process that turns corn into ethanol. The four steps include, first, preparing the corn by making a mash; second, fermenting the mash by adding yeast to make beer; third, distilling the ethanol from the beer; and fourth, processing the remaining whole stillage to produce co-products such as animal feed (Ethanol Business, 2004). *(Slide 1. Shows the four-step flow process.)* ▶ *Thesis statement with main point preview*

Body

I. The first step in the commercial process of making ethanol, preparing the mash, has two parts: milling the corn and breaking the starch down into simple sugars (DENCO, n.d.). *(Slide 2. Title: Preparation. Shows corn flowing from a silo into a hammer mill and then into a holding tank where yeast is added.)*

In your saliva, you have enzymes that begin to break the bread and other starches you eat into sugar. In your stomach, you have other enzymes that finish this job of turning starch to simple sugar so your body can use the energy in the food you eat. In the commercial process of making ethanol, a similar transformation takes place. ▶ *Listener relevance link*

   A. The corn is emptied into a bin and passes into a hammer mill, where it is ground into coarse flour.

   B. After milling, the corn flour, a starch, must be broken down so that it becomes simple sugar by mixing in water and enzymes to form a thick liquid called slurry.

1. First the water and corn flour are dosed with the enzyme alpha-amylase and heated.

2. Then the starchy slurry is heated to help the enzyme do its work.

3. Later gluco-amylase is added to finish the process of turning the starch to simple sugar.

Once this mixture of sugar, water, and residual corn solids is turned into slurry or mash, it is ready to be fermented.   ▶ Transition

II. The second step of the commercial process for making ethanol is fermenting the slurry or mash by adding yeast (DENCO, n.d.). *(Slide 3. Title: Fermentation. Shows yeast added to the mash in a fermenter and carbon dioxide being released to form beer.)*

This step works in much the same way yeast is used to make bread dough rise. But in bread the carbon dioxide is trapped in the dough and causes it to rise, and the alcohol is burned off when the bread is baked. In making ethanol, carbon dioxide bubbles out of the mash and is released into the air.   ▶ Listener relevance link

A. The mash remains in the fermenters for about fifty hours.

B. As the mash ferments, the sugar is turned into alcohol and carbon dioxide.

C. The carbon dioxide bubbles out into the air.

D. What remains after the carbon dioxide is released is called "beer."

Once the yeast has done its job and the fermentation process is complete, we move on to distillation.   ▶ Transition

III. The third step of the commercial process for making ethanol is distilling the fermented mash, now called "beer," by passing it through a series of columns where the alcohol is removed from the mash (Tham, 1997–2006). *(Slide 4. Title: Distillation of Ethanol. Animated slide showing beer flowing into distillation tank, heat being applied to the beer, and ethanol vapors being released and captured in a condenser.)*

If you've ever seen moonshine cookers in real life or in the movies, that's basically the same process as what I'm explaining here (DENCO, n.d.).   ▶ Listener relevance link

A. Distillation is the process of boiling a liquid and then condensing the resulting vapor in order to separate out one component of the liquid.

B. In most ethanol production, distillation occurs through the use of cooling columns.

C. Once the ethanol has reached the desired purity or proof, it is denatured to be made undrinkable by adding gasoline to it.

D. The ethanol is ready to be transported from the plant.

Once this step is complete, you've successfully produced ethanol, but we aren't done until we complete step 4.   ▶ Transition

IV. The fourth step in commercial production is converting the remaining whole stillage into co-products (DENCO, n.d.). *(Slide 5. Title: Co-product. Shows a tank with remaining whole solids flowing into a condenser with output flowing into a bin of animal feed.)*

Not only is ethanol a renewable resource, but even its byproducts get put to good use!   ▶ Listener relevance link

Conclusion

I. As you can see, producing ethanol is a simple four-step process: preparing the corn into a slurry or mash, fermenting the slurry into beer, distilling the beer to release the ethanol, and processing the remaining water and corn solids into co-products. *(Slide 6: Same as slide 1.)*

II. In 1980, when Robert Warren was operating his still, only 175 million gallons of ethanol were being commercially produced in the United States. Twenty-five years later, 4.85 billion gallons were produced (Renewable Fuels Association, 2007). That's a whopping 2,674 percent increase! And it is a trend that is continuing. With today's skyrocketing gasoline prices and our increasing concerns about preserving our environment, you can see why this simple process of making liquid sunshine is getting more and more popular. I don't know about you, but I'm glad it is!

References

DENCO, LLC. (n.d.) Tour the plant. Retrieved July 2, 2007, from http://www.dencollc.com/DENCO%20WebSite_files/Tour.htm

Ethanol Business and Industry Center. (2004, May). Module 2: Ethanol science and technology. Retrieved July 3, 2007, from http://www.nwicc.com/pages/continuing/business/ethanol/Module2.htm

Renewable Fuels Association. (2007). Industry statistics: The ethanol industry. Retrieved July 9, 2007, from http://www.ethanolrfa.org/industry/statistics/

Tham, M. T. (1997–2006). Distillation: An introduction. Retrieved July 5, 2007, from http://lorien.ncl.ac.uk/ming/distil/distil0.htm

Warren, R. (2006, August). Make your own fuel. Retrieved July 3, 2007, from http://running_on_alcohol.tripod.com/index.html

Speech and Analysis

Did you know that the first Model T's were designed to run on ethanol and that Henry Ford said that ethanol was the fuel of the future? Or that in World War II about 75 percent of the German and American military vehicles were powered by ethanol since oil for gasoline was difficult to obtain? In 1978, during the first Arab oil embargo, when gas soared from 62 cents a gallon to $1.64, Californian Robert Warren and others built stills to produce what he called—no, not "white lightning"—but "liquid sunshine," which we call ethanol.

I became interested in ethanol in high school when I built a miniature ethanol still as a science fair project. I'm now a chemical engineering major and hope to make a career in the alternative fuel industry. So, today, I'm going to explain to you the simple process that takes corn and turns it into liquid sunshine. Specifically, I want you to understand the process that is used to make ethanol from corn.

According to the Ethanol Business and Industry Center at Northwest Iowa Community College, the four steps in the commercial process of making ethanol are, first, preparing the corn by making a mash; second, fermenting the mash by adding yeast to make beer; third, distilling the ethanol from the beer; and fourth, processing the remaining whole stillage to produce co-products like animal feed. *(Slide 1)*

Analysis

Thesis restatement with main points summary

Clincher

Louisa begins this speech with rhetorical questions designed to pique the audience's interest. At the time she prepared the speech, gasoline prices were again soaring, so these questions—coupled with the example of Warren's solution—provide a provocative introduction to her topic.

At this point, Louisa personalizes the topic with a self-disclosure that also establishes her credibility.

One thing Louisa could do better throughout the speech is to offer listener relevance links that more directly remind the audience of the speech's relevance to them whenever possible.

As this slide taken from the DENCO, LCC, "Tour the Plant" Web site depicts, the first step in the commercial process of making ethanol, preparing the mash, has two parts: milling the corn and breaking the starch down into simple sugars. *(Slide 2)*

The corn, which has been tested for quality and stored in a silo, is emptied into a bin and passes into a hammer mill, where it is ground into coarse flour. This is done to expose more of the corn's starchy material so that these starches can be more easily broken down into sugar.

In your saliva, you have enzymes that begin to break the bread and other starches you eat into sugar. In your stomach, you have other enzymes that finish this job of turning starch to simple sugar so your body can use the energy in the food you eat. In the commercial production of ethanol, a similar transformation takes place.

To break the milled corn flour starch into sugar, the milled flour is mixed with water and alpha-amylase, the same enzyme that you have in your saliva, and is heated. The alpha-amylase acts as Pacman and takes bites out of the long sugar chains that are bound together in the starch. What results are broken bits of starch that need further processing to become glucose. So later, gluco-amylase, which is like the enzyme in your stomach, is added, and these new Pacmen bite the starchy bits into simple glucose sugar molecules. Now this mixture of sugar, water, and residual corn solids, called slurry or mash, is ready to be fermented.

The second step in the commercial production of ethanol is to ferment the mash by adding yeast in an environment that has no oxygen and allowing the mixture to "rest" while the yeast "works." *(Slide 3)* This is accomplished by piping the slurry into an oxygen-free tank called a fermenter, adding the yeast, and allowing the mixture to sit for about fifty hours. Without oxygen, the yeast feeds on the sugar and gives off ethanol and carbon dioxide as waste products. Eventually, deprived of oxygen, the yeast dies.

This is similar to what happens when we add yeast to bread dough. But in bread the carbon dioxide is trapped in the dough and causes it to rise, while the alcohol is burned off when the bread is baked.

In ethanol production, the carbon dioxide is not trapped in the watery slurry. Because it is a gas, it bubbles out of the mixture and is captured and released into the outside air. The ethanol, however, remains in the mixture, which is now called "beer," with the water and the nonfermentable corn solids. At the end of the fermentation process, it is the ethanol in the mixture that retains much of the energy of the original sugar. At this point, we are now ready to separate or distill the ethanol from the other parts of the beer.

The third step in the commercial production of ethanol is distillation, which, according to M. T. Tham's book *Distillation: An Introduction*, is the process of purifying a liquid by heating it and then condensing its vapor. So, for example, if you boiled your tap water and condensed the steam that was produced, you would have purified water with no minerals or other impurities. But distilling ethanol is a bit more complicated since both the ethanol and the water in the beer are liquids and can be vaporized into steam by adding heat.

Luckily, different liquids boil at different temperatures, and since ethanol boils at 173°F while water boils at 212°F, we can use this boiling point difference to separate the two. So to simplify what is really a more complex process, *(Slide 4)* in the commercial distillation of ethanol, a column or series of columns

---

▶ Notice how Louisa has nested two steps, milling and breaking starch into sugars, under the more general heading of "Preparation." This grouping keeps the main points at a manageable number and will help her audience remember the steps. Her second slide is simple but effective because it reinforces the two substeps.

▶ Louisa helps the audience understand the unfamiliar starch-to-sugar conversion by comparing it to the familiar process of digestion.

▶ The Pacman analogy also helps the audience visualize what occurs during the starch-to-sugar conversion.

▶ The last sentence, mentioning slurry, is an excellent transition between the two main points.

▶ Louisa helps the audience stay with her by using the signpost "second step." Her third slide, a visual of the "fermentation equation," nicely simplifies the complex chemistry that underlies fermentation.

▶ Here she uses an effective transition statement to signal to her audience that she will be moving to the third step.

▶ Her fourth slide is much more elaborate than the others. The animation in the slide helps the audience visualize how distillation works. It would have been more effective had she been able to control the motion so that each stage was animated as she talked about it.

are used to boil off the ethanol and the water and then to separate these vapors so that the ethanol vapors are captured and condensed back into pure liquid ethanol. The liquid ethanol is then tested to make sure that it meets the specifications for purity and proof. At this point, ethanol is drinkable alcohol and would be subject to a $20 per gallon federal excise tax. To avoid this, it is "denatured"—made undrinkable by adding gasoline to it. After this, the ethanol is ready to be transported from the plant.

The fourth step in the commercial production process is converting the whole stillage into co-products. (Slide 5) One of the greatest things about producing ethanol is that the water and nonfermentable corn solids that are left after the ethanol is distilled aren't just thrown out as waste. Instead, the remaining water and nonfermentable corn solids can also be processed to make co-products that are primarily used as animal feed.

So as you have seen, the process of making ethanol is really quite simple. (Slide 6) One, prepare the corn by milling and breaking its starch into sugar. Two, ferment the mash using yeast. Three, distill off the ethanol from the beer, and four, process the co-products.

In 1980, when Robert Warren was operating his still, only 175 million gallons of ethanol were being commercially produced in the United States. Twenty-five years later, according to the Renewable Fuels Association, 4.85 billion gallons were produced. That's a whopping 2,674 percent increase! And it is a trend that is continuing. With today's skyrocketing gasoline prices and our increasing concerns about preserving our environment, you can see why this simple process of making liquid sunshine is getting more and more popular. I don't know about you, but I'm glad it is!

▶ The last sentence serves as an internal conclusion to the third step.

▶ The slide for the fourth main point is so simple that it really isn't needed to aid audience understanding, but it is a visual reinforcement of this step, and the audience has been conditioned to expect one slide per point, so it would seem odd if there were not a slide for this step.

▶ Louisa begins the conclusion with a summary of her main points. The sixth slide, a repetition of the first slide, visually "closes the loop" and reinforces the four steps.

▶ The conclusion includes a circular reference back to Robert Warren who was introduced at the beginning of the speech. In the conclusion, she uses statistics to drive home the point that ethanol is an important fuel source and that in the near future ethanol may be a fuel used by members of the audience.

▶ Louisa could have offered a better clincher by tying her final sentence back to her introductory comments about Henry Ford. For example, she might have said, "Almost a century later, it seems that what Henry Ford said will be coming true. Look for a green-handled pump coming soon to a gas station near you."

Quick Quiz

T F 1. Creativity is the result of hard work, not a gift that some people have and some don't.

T F 2. Productive thinking occurs when you are presented with a new idea explained in a way that sparks curiosity and interest.

T F 3. Narrations are presented only in the first- or second-person voice.

T F 4. The goal of an expository speech is to demonstrate how something is done or made, or how it works.

T F 5. Lengthy expository speeches are better known as *lectures*.

6. The characteristics of effective informative speaking include all but the following:

a. relevant
b. sensitive
c. stimulating
d. creative
e. memorable

7. _____ thinking occurs when we contemplate something from many different perspectives.

a. Creative
b. Productive
c. Informative
d. Intellectually stimulating
e. Outside-the-box

8. You can use visual aids, repetition, transitions, humor, and memory aids to

a. highlight important information that you want your audience to remember.
b. encourage productive thinking.
c. create an informative speech.
d. describe the specific goal of the speech.
e. ensure that your main points are stated in parallel language.

9. Of the four ways to define a word or idea, which does your text quote as the quickest?

a. classifying it
b. explaining its history
c. using a synonym
d. using a comparison
e. explaining its use or function

10. All of the following are required of an expository speech except

a. acquiring information from reputable sources.
b. using a variety of methods to keep the audience's attention.
c. choosing an organizational pattern that is best suited to the material being presented.
d. understanding what you are presenting.
e. believing in what you are presenting.

Answers: 1. T, 2. F, 3. F, 4. F, 5. T, 6. B, 7. B, 8. A, 9. C, 10. E

Persuasive Speaking

What do you think?
It is OK to use a shaky
argument if it will get
you what you want.

1 2 3 4 5 6 7 8 9 10
STRONGLY DISAGREE   STRONGLY AGREE

Learning Outcomes

17-1 Understand the nature of
persuasive messages and how
people listen to and evaluate
them

17-2 Write your persuasive speech
goals as propositions

17-3 Develop logical arguments to
support a proposition

17-4 Develop credibility to support a
proposition

17-5 Develop emotional arguments
to support a proposition

17-6 Identify organizational patterns
for persuasive speeches

Whether we are attempting to
influence others or others are attempting to influence us, we are
constantly involved in persuasion.
For example, friends might convince us to see a particular
movie or to eat at a certain restaurant. We are bombarded with
advertisements to buy different products whenever we turn on the radio
or television or surf the Internet. **Persuasion** is the word we use to label
this process of influencing people's attitudes, beliefs, values, or behaviors.
Persuasive speaking is the process of doing so in a public speech.

In this chapter, we begin by describing the nature of persuasive messages
and how people process them. Then we explain how to form an effective
persuasive speech goal and develop it with logos, ethos, and pathos. Finally,
we discuss several persuasive speech patterns you can use to organize your
speech.

17-1 The Nature of Persuasion

Persuasive messages are fundamentally different
from informative messages. Whereas the goal of
an informative message is to teach, the goal of a
persuasive message is to lead. So persuasive speakers
are successful only when their audience members are
convinced to agree, change their behavior, or take action. Persuasive speaking can actually be traced to its
roots in ancient Greece, where men used it to debate
public issues and make important decisions. Thinkers

persuasion
the process of
influencing people's
attitudes, beliefs,
values, or behaviors

persuasive speech
a speech attempting to
influence the attitudes,
values, beliefs, or
behavior of others

like Aristotle and Plato used the word **rhetoric** to mean using any and all "available means of persuasion" in public speeches (Solmsen, 1954). Persuasive speakers do so by developing solid arguments. An argument, in this context, is not synonymous with "quarrel" as we sometimes define it today. Rather, **argument** means articulating a position with the support of logos, ethos, and pathos (Perloff, 2010). **Logos** is a persuasive strategy of constructing logical arguments that support your position. **Ethos** is a persuasive strategy of highlighting your competence, credibility, and good character as a means to convince others to support your position (Kennedy, 1999). And **pathos** is a persuasive strategy of appealing to emotions in order to convince others to support your position.

17-1a Processing Persuasive Messages

Do you remember times when you listened carefully and thoughtfully about something someone was trying to convince you to agree with before making a deliberate decision? Do you remember other times when you only half-listened and made up your mind quickly based on your gut feeling? What determines how closely we listen to and how carefully we evaluate the hundreds of persuasive messages we hear each day? Richard Petty and John Cacioppo (1996) developed the elaboration likelihood model (ELM) to explain how likely people are to spend more or less time critically evaluating information before making their decisions.

The dual processing model that we introduced in chapter 2 suggests that people process information in one of two ways. Sometimes we use the "central route," when we listen

carefully, reflect thoughtfully, and maybe even mentally elaborate on the message before making a decision. When we use the central route, we base our decision primarily on appeals to logic and reasoning (logos). The second way, called the "peripheral route," is a shortcut that relies on simple cues, such as a quick evaluation of the speaker's competence, credibility, and character (ethos), or a gut check about what we feel (pathos) about the message.

We choose a route based on how important we perceive the issue to be for us. When we believe the issue is important, we will expend the energy necessary to process it using the central route. When we don't, we take the peripheral route. For example, if you have a serious chronic illness that is expensive to treat, you are more likely to pay attention to and evaluate carefully any proposals to change health care benefits. If you are healthy, you are more likely to quickly agree with suggestions from someone you perceive to be credible or with a proposal that seems compassionate. The ELM also suggests that when we form attitudes as a result of central processing, we are less likely to change our minds than when we base our decisions on peripheral cues.

When you prepare a persuasive speech, you will want to use strategies that address both the central and peripheral routes. You can address the central route by using rhetorical strategies that appeal to logos (logic and reasoning). And you can address the peripheral route by using rhetorical strategies that appeal to both ethos (competence, credibility, and good character) and pathos (emotions). Before doing so, however, you need to form your speech goal as a proposition.

17-2 Persuasive Speech Goals

Persuasive speech goals are stated as propositions. A **proposition** is a declarative sentence that clearly indicates the position you advocate. For example, "I want to convince my audience that pirating copyrighted media (downloading music and movies without paying for it) is wrong." Notice how a persuasive proposition differs from an

Peripheral

Direct

© viewgene/Shutterstock.com

information speech goal on the same subject: "I want to inform my audience about the practice of pirating copyrighted media." In the informative speech, you will achieve your goal if the audience understands and remembers what you talk about. In the persuasive speech, however, they must not only understand and remember, but also agree with your position and possibly even take action. The three types of propositions are fact, value, and policy.

17-2a Types of Propositions

A **proposition of fact** is a statement designed to convince your audience that something: (1) did, probably did, probably did not, or did not exist or occur; (2) is, probably is, probably is not, or is not true; or (3) will, probably will, probably will not, or will not occur. Although propositions of fact may or may not be true—both positions are arguable—they are stated as though they are, in fact, true. For example, whether or not Princess Diana's death was an unfortunate car accident or an assassination is debatable. So you could argue a proposition of fact in two ways: "Princess Diana's death was nothing more than a tragic car accident" or "Princess Diana's death was, in fact, a successful assassination attempt." Examples of propositions of fact concerning the present include "God exists" or "There is no God"; and "Mobile phone use causes brain cancer" or "Mobile phone use does not cause brain cancer." Propositions of fact concerning the future are predictions. For example, "Thanks to the Internet, iPads, and Kindles, paperbound books will eventually cease to exist" and "The New York Yankees will surely win the World Series next year" are propositions of fact concerning the future.

A **proposition of value** is a statement designed to convince your audience that something is good, bad, desirable, undesirable, fair, unfair, moral, immoral, sound, unsound, beneficial, harmful, important, or unimportant (Hill & Leeman, 1997). You can attempt to convince your audience that something has more value than something else, or you can attempt to convince them that something meets valued standards. "Running is a better form of exercise than bicycling" is an example of the former, and "The real value of a college education is that it creates an informed citizenry" is an example of the latter.

A **proposition of policy** is a statement designed to convince your audience that a particular rule, plan, or course of action should be taken. Propositions of policy implore listeners using phrases such as *do it/don't do it*, *should/shouldn't*, and *must/must not*. "All college students should be required to take an oral communication skills course in order to graduate," "The U.S. must stop deep-sea oil drilling," and "We must not text while driving" are propositions of policy. Figure 17.1 provides several examples of how propositions of fact, value, and policy can be developed from the same topic idea.

proposition of fact
a statement designed to convince the audience that something did or did not occur, is or is not true, or will or will not occur

proposition of value
a statement designed to convince the audience that something is good, fair, moral, sound, etc., or its opposite

proposition of policy
a statement designed to convince the audience that a specific course of action should be taken

FIGURE 17.1
Examples of Persuasive Speech Propositions

Propositions of Fact	Propositions of Value	Propositions of Policy
Mahatma Gandhi was the father of passive resistance.	Mahatma Gandhi was a moral leader.	Mahatma Gandhi should be given a special award for his views on and practices of passive resistance.
Pharmaceutical advertising to consumers increases prescription drug prices.	Advertising of new prescription drugs on TV is better than marketing new drugs directly to doctors.	Pharmaceutical companies should be prohibited from advertising prescription drugs on TV.
Using paper ballots is a reliable method for voting in U.S. elections.	Paper ballots are better than electronic voting machines.	Using paper ballots should be required for U.S. elections.

© Cengage Learning

17-2b **Tailoring Propositions to Your Target Audience**

Because it is very difficult to convince people to change their minds, what you can hope to accomplish in one speech depends on where your audience stands on your topic. So you'll want to analyze your audience and tailor your proposition based on their initial attitude toward the topic. An **attitude** is "a general or enduring positive or negative feeling about some person, object or issue" (Petty & Cacioppo, 1996).

Audience members' attitudes can range from highly favorable to strongly opposed and can be visualized on a continuum like the one in Figure 17.2. Even though your audience will include individuals with opinions at nearly every point along the continuum, generally audience members' opinions tend to cluster in one area of it. For instance, most of the audience members represented in Figure 17.2 are "mildly opposed," even though a few people are more highly opposed and a few have favorable opinions. This cluster point represents your **target audience**, the group of people you most want to persuade. Based on your target audience, you can classify your audience's initial attitude toward your topic as "in favor" (already supportive), "no opinion" (uninformed, neutral, or apathetic), or "opposed" (against a particular belief).

Opposed

It is unrealistic to believe that you will change your target audience's attitude from "opposed" to "in favor" in only one short speech. Instead, seek **incremental change**, that is, attempt to move them only a small degree in your direction, hoping for additional movement later. For example, if your target audience is opposed to the goal "I want to convince my audience that gay marriage should be legalized," you might rephrase it to "I want to convince my audience that committed gay couples should be afforded the same legal protection as committed heterosexual couples through state-recognized civil unions." Then brainstorm potential objections, questions, and criticisms that might arise and shape your speech to address them.

No Opinion

If your target audience has no opinion for or against your topic, you should consider whether they are uninformed, neutral, or apathetic about your topic. If they are **uninformed**, that is, they do not know enough about a topic to have formed an opinion, you will need to provide the basic arguments and information needed for them to become informed. For example, if your target audience is uninformed about the topic of gay marriage, you might need to begin by highlighting the legal benefits of marriage in general. If your target audience is **neutral**, that is, they know the basics about your topic but not enough to have formed an opinion, you will want to provide evidence and reasoning illustrating why your position is superior to others. Perhaps your audience knows the legal benefits of marriage in general but needs to understand how committed gay couples who do not have these benefits are disadvantaged. When target audience members have no opinion because they are **apathetic**, that is, indifferent to the topic, you will need to find ways to show how it relates to them or their needs. In other words, you need to provide answers to a question such as, "I'm not gay, so why should I care?" You can do this by including strong listener relevance links for each main point in your speech.

---

attitude
a general or enduring positive or negative feeling about some person, object, or issue

target audience
the group of people a speaker most wants to persuade

incremental change
an attempt to move an audience only a small degree in the speaker's direction

uninformed
not knowing enough about a topic to have formed an opinion

neutral
knowing the basics about a topic but still having no opinion about it

apathetic
having no opinion because one is uninterested, unconcerned, or indifferent to a topic

---

FIGURE 17.2

Sample Opinion Continuum

Highly opposed	Opposed	Mildly opposed	Neither in favor nor opposed	Mildly in favor	In favor	Highly in favor
2	2	11	1	2	2	0

© Cengage Learning

© Andre Bonn/Shutterstock.com

In Favor

If your target audience is only mildly in favor of your proposal, your task is to reinforce and strengthen their beliefs. Audience members who favor your topic may become further committed to the belief by hearing new reasons and more recent evidence that support it. When your target audience strongly agrees with your position, then you can consider a proposition that moves them to act on it. For example, if the topic is gay marriage and your target audience is in favor of the idea, then your goal may be "I want my audience members to e-mail or write letters to their state representatives urging them to support legislation extending the right to marry to gay couples."

Once you have identified your topic and tailored your proposition to your target audience, you are ready to develop content that addresses both the central and peripheral persuasive processing routes. You do so by using rhetorical strategies appealing to logos, ethos, and pathos.

17-3 Rhetorical Appeals to Logos

Audience members who process on the central route will evaluate the logic and reasoning of your arguments. Stephen Toulmin (1958) developed a model to explain the form of everyday arguments that has stood the test of time. His model has three major elements: the claim, the support, and the warrant.

The **claim** is the conclusion the speaker wants the audience to agree with. For example, you might *claim:* "Jim's car needs a tune-up." The **support** is the evidence offered as grounds for accepting the claim. You can support a claim with facts, opinions, experiences, and observations. In our car example, we might support our claim with observations that the engine is "missing at slow speeds" and "stalling at stoplights." The **warrant** is the reasoning process that connects the support to the claim. Sometimes, the warrant is verbalized and sometimes it is implied. For instance, if you claim that "the car needs a tune-up" on the basis of "missing" and "stalling at stoplights," you might also say "Missing at slow speeds and stalling at lights *are common indications*

that a car needs a tune-up." Or you might assume that others see these as signs that a car needs a tune-up.

Using C for claim (conclusion) S for support (reasons and evidence), and W for warrant (explanation of the reasoning process), we can write the reasoning for the proposition in our example in outline form as follows:

> **C:** I want Jim to believe that the car needs a tune-up.
> **S:** I. The engine misses at slow speeds.
> **S:** II. The car stalls at stoplights.
> **W:** (I believe this reasoning is sound because missing and stalling are *major indicators—signs—*of the need for a tune-up.) (The warrant is written in parentheses because it may not be verbalized when the speech is given.)

You can use inductive or deductive reasoning in your warrant. **Inductive reasoning** is arriving at a general conclusion based on several pieces of specific evidence. When we reason inductively, how much our audience agrees with our conclusion depends on the number, quality, and typicality of each piece of evidence you offer. For Jim's car, an inductive argument might look like this:

> **Evidence:** Jim's car is missing at slow speeds.
> **Evidence:** Jim's car is stalling at stoplights.
> **Logical Conclusion:** Jim's car needs a tune-up.

Deductive reasoning is arguing that if something is true for everything that belongs to a certain class (major premise) and a specific instance is part of that class (minor premise), then we must conclude that what

claim
the conclusion the speaker wants the audience to agree with

support
evidence offered as grounds to accept the claim

warrant
the reasoning process that connects the support to the claim

inductive reasoning
arriving at a general conclusion based on several pieces of evidence

deductive reasoning
arguing that if something is true for everything in a certain class, then it is true for a given item in that class

is true for all members of the class must be true in the specific instance (logical conclusion). This three-part form of deductive reasoning is called a **syllogism**. For Jim's car, a syllogism might look like this:

Major Premise: Cars need a tune-up when the engine misses consistently at slow speeds.
Minor Premise: Jim's car is missing at slow speeds.
Conclusion: Jim's car needs a tune-up.

With this introduction in mind, let's look at some different types of logical arguments.

17-3a Types of Logical Arguments

Although a logical argument *always* includes a claim and support, different types of warrants can be used to illustrate the relationship between the claim and the support on which it is based. Four common types of logical arguments are sign, example, analogy, and causation.

Arguing from Sign

If certain events, characteristics, or situations usually or always accompany something, those events, characteristics, or situations are signs. You **argue from sign** when you support a claim by providing evidence that the events that signal the claim have occurred.

The general warrant for reasoning from sign can be stated as follows: When phenomena that usually or always accompany a specific situation occur, then we can expect that specific situation is occurring (or will occur). For example: "Hives and a slight fever are indicators (signs) of an allergic reaction."

Signs should not be confused with causes; signs accompany a phenomenon but do not bring about, lead to, or create the claim. In fact, signs may actually be the effects of the phenomenon. In the allergy example, a rash and fever don't *cause* an allergic reaction; they are indications, or effects, of a reaction.

When arguing from sign, you can make sure that your argument is valid by answering the following questions.

1. Do the signs cited always or usually indicate the conclusion drawn?

2. Are a sufficient number of signs present?

3. Are contradictory signs in evidence?

If your answer to the first two questions is "no" or your answer to the third is "yes," then your reasoning is not sound.

Arguing from Example

You **argue from example** when the evidence you use as support are examples of the claim you are making. For almost any topic, it is easy to find examples. So you are likely to use arguing from example quite frequently. The warrant for an argument from example—its underlying logic—is, "What is true in the examples provided is (or will be) true in general or in other instances."

Suppose you are supporting Juanita Martinez for president of the local neighborhood council. One of the reasons you suggest is the claim that "Juanita is electable." In examining her résumé to find support for this claim, you find several examples of her previous victories. She was elected treasurer of her high school junior class, chairperson of her church youth group, and president of her college sorority. Each of these is an example that gives support to the claim. What would the warrant statement for this argument look like? "What was true in several instances (Juanita has been elected in three previous races) is true or will be true in general or in other instances (she will be electable in this situation)."

When arguing from example, you can make sure your argument is valid by answering the following questions.

1. Are enough instances or examples cited so that listeners understand they are not isolated or handpicked examples?

2. Are the examples typical and representative?

3. Are negative examples really atypical?

If the answer to any of these questions is "no," then your reasoning is not sound.

Arguing from Analogy

You **argue from analogy** when you support a claim with a single comparable example that is so significantly

© gokhan ilgaz/iStockphoto.com

syllogism
the three-part form of deductive reasoning

arguing from sign
supports a claim by citing information that signals the claim

arguing from example
supports a claim by providing one or more individual examples

arguing from analogy
supports a claim with a single comparable example that is significantly similar to the subject of the claim

similar to the subject of the claim as to be strong proof. The general statement of a warrant for an argument from analogy is, "What is true for situation A will also be true in situation B, which is similar to situation A" or "What is true for situation A will be true in all similar situations."

Suppose you wanted to argue that the Cherry Fork Volunteer Fire Department should conduct a raffle to raise money for three portable defibrillator units (claim). You could support the claim with an analogy to a single comparable example like this: The Jefferson City Fire Department, which is very similar to that of Cherry Fork, conducted a raffle and raised enough money to purchase four units.

When arguing from analogy, you can make sure that your argument is valid by answering the following questions.

1. Are the subjects being compared similar in every important way? If they are not, then your reasoning is not sound.

2. Are any of the ways in which the subjects are dissimilar important to the conclusion? If so, then your reasoning is not sound.

Arguing from Causation

You **argue from causation** when you support a claim by citing events that have occurred that result in the claim. Reasoning from causation says that one or more of the events cited always (or almost always) brings about, leads to, or creates or prevents a predictable effect or set of effects.

The general warrant for arguments from cause can be stated as follows: If an event comes before another event and is associated with that event, then we can say that it is the cause of the event. "If A, which is known to bring about B, has been observed, then we can expect B to occur." Let's return to Juanita's election campaign for an example.

In researching Juanita's election campaign, you might discover that (1) she has campaigned intelligently and (2) she has won the endorsement of key community leaders. If these two events are usually associated with victory, then you can form the argument that Juanita has engaged in key behaviors that lead to campaign victories. So

your causal argument supports your claim that she is electable.

When arguing from causation, you can make sure that your argument is valid by answering the following questions.

1. Are the events alone sufficient to cause the stated effect?

2. Do other events accompanying the cited events actually cause the effect?

3. Is the relationship between the causal events and the effect consistent?

If the answer to any of these questions is "no," then your reasoning is not sound.

17-3b Reasoning Fallacies

As you develop your arguments, you will want to be sure to avoid **fallacies**, or errors in reasoning. Five common fallacies are hasty generalization, false cause, either/or, straw man, and ad hominem arguments.

1. A **hasty generalization** occurs when a claim is either not supported with evidence or is supported with only one weak example. Because the supporting material that is cited should represent all the supporting material that could be cited, enough supporting material must be presented to satisfy the audience that the instances are not isolated or handpicked. For example, someone who argued, "All Akitas are vicious dogs," whose sole piece of evidence was, "My neighbor had an Akita and it bit my best friend's sister," would be guilty of a hasty generalization. It is hasty to generalize about the temperament of a whole breed of dogs based on a single action of one dog.

2. A **false cause** occurs when the alleged cause fails to be related to, or to produce, the effect. The Latin term for this fallacy is *post hoc, ergo propter hoc,* meaning "after this, therefore because of this." Just because two things happen one after the other does not mean

© Eric Isselee/Shutterstock.com

arguing from causation
supports a claim by citing evidence that shows one or more events always or almost always brings about, leads to, creates, or prevents another event or effect

fallacies
flawed reasoning

hasty generalization
a fallacy that presents a generalization that is either not supported with evidence or is supported with only one weak example

false cause
a fallacy that occurs when the alleged cause fails to be related to, or to produce, the effect

either/or
a fallacy that occurs when a speaker supports a claim by suggesting there are only two alternatives when, in fact, others exist

straw man
a fallacy that occurs when a speaker weakens the opposing position by misrepresenting it in some way and then attacks that weaker (straw person) position

ad hominem
a fallacy that occurs when one attacks the person making the argument, rather than the argument itself

that the first necessarily caused the second. Unlike people who blame monetary setbacks and illness on black cats or broken mirrors, be careful that you don't present a co-incidental event as a cause unless you can prove the causal relationship. An example of a false cause fallacy is when a speaker claims that school violence is caused only by television violence, the Internet, a certain song or musical group, or lack of parental involvement. When one event follows another, there may be no connection at all, or the first event might be just one of many causes that contribute to the second.

3. An **either/or** fallacy occurs by suggesting there are only two alternatives when, in fact, others exist. Many such cases are an oversimplification of a complex issue. For example, when Robert argued that "we'll either have to raise taxes or close the library," he committed an either/or fallacy. He reduced a complex issue to one oversimplified solution when there were many other possible solutions.

4. A **straw man** fallacy occurs when a speaker weakens the opposing position by misrepresenting it in some way and then attacks that weaker (straw man) position. For example, in her speech advocating a seven-day waiting period to purchase handguns, Colleen favored regulation, not prohibition, of gun ownership. Bob argued against that by claiming "It is our constitutional right to bear arms." However, Colleen did not advocate abolishing the right to bear arms. Hence, Bob distorted Colleen's position, making it easier for him to refute.

5. An **ad hominem** fallacy attacks or praises the person making the argument rather than addressing the argument itself. *Ad hominem* literally means "to

You Too Can Have Six-Pack Abs in Only Three Weeks!

© James Steidl/Shutterstock.com

Infomercials (the long, often parodied, television advertisements) permeate U.S. culture today. For example, in 2008 Barack Obama used the infomercial format extensively, culminating in his 30-minute advertisement, which played on seven networks and was watched by 33.55 million viewers (Carter, 2008). Infomercials are television and online programs designed to look like 30- or 60-minute talk shows, but they're actually extended advertisements that focus on a product's extraordinary features and offer testimonials of its effectiveness.

Those extraordinary features have caused infomercials to become sources of entertainment. In 2008 and 2009, the Snuggie— "A blanket with sleeves!"—and a similar product, the Slanket, were frequently referenced in popular culture, from YouTube parodies ("The Cult of Snuggie") to *30 Rock* storylines (with Liz Lemon asserting, "It's not product placement; I just like it!"). When "infomercial king" Billy Mays passed away unexpectedly in June 2009, many were inspired to affectionately celebrate his influence.

Despite the fun we like to have with infomercials, some have come under criticism for making false claims and for encouraging people to purchase items they cannot afford and do not need. For example, in 2002 Guthy-Renker, the largest producer of television infomercials, became the subject of a class-action lawsuit, which claimed Guthy-Renker made exaggerated claims of profitability and promoted an Internet "shopping mall" that was simply a scam ("Timothy D. Naegele & Associates," 2002).

Because advertisements are inherently persuasive, it's important to view them with a critical eye, although certainly not all ads and infomercials make false claims. If you suspect that an infomercial is making questionable claims, be careful before you buy.

the man." For example, if Jamal's support for his claim that his audience should buy an Apple computer is that Steve Jobs, the founder and former president of Apple Computer, was a genius, he is making an ad hominem argument. Jobs's intelligence isn't really a reason to buy a particular brand of computer. Unfortunately, politicians sometimes resort to ad hominem arguments when they attack their opponent's character rather than their platforms while campaigning for office. Bullying in person, over the Internet, and via text messaging is another example of ad hominem attacks that can have dire consequences. TV commercials that feature celebrities using a particular product are often guilty of ad hominem reasoning. For example, Robert De Niro and Jerry Seinfeld have both appeared in American Express commercials, and Gwyneth Paltrow has done ads for Estée Lauder. What makes any of these celebrities experts about the products they are endorsing?

17-4 Rhetorical Appeals to Ethos

Not everyone will choose the central processing route to make his or her decision about your proposition. One important cue people use when they process information by the peripheral route is ethos. So, you will also want to demonstrate good character, as well as say and do things to convey competence and credibility.

17-4a Conveying Good Character

We turn again to the ancient Greek philosopher Aristotle (384–322 B.C.E.) who first observed that perceived credibility is dependent on the audience's perception of the speaker's goodwill. Today, we define **goodwill** as a perception the audience forms of a speaker who they believe (1) understands them, (2) empathizes with them, and (3) is responsive to them. When audience members believe in the speaker's goodwill, they are more willing to believe what the speaker says.

One way to demonstrate that you understand your audience is by personalizing your information. For example, in his speech at the annual conference of the Property Casualty Insurers Association of America (PCI), Julian James, director of Worldwide Markets for Lloyds, demonstrated understanding by referencing membership facts from the previous year.

I would certainly contend that, following two consecutive record hurricane seasons, we have passed a key financial test. Debate after Katrina was largely about the detail of how we can do things better, and not about whether the industry could survive—as it was after 9/11. Not bad progress for an industry that faced almost double the value of claims from catastrophes in 2005 as it did for 9/11. . . . If we come out of this year intact, U.S. insurance industry profits in 2006 are forecast to be the best in a generation at $55 to 460 billion. (James, 2007)

goodwill
the audience perception that the speaker understands, empathizes with, and is responsive to them

You can also demonstrate goodwill by empathizing with your audience. Empathy is the ability to see the world through the eyes of someone else. Empathizing with the views of the audience doesn't necessarily mean that you accept their views as your own. It does mean that you acknowledge them as valid. Although your speech may be designed to change audience members' views, the sensitivity you show to audience members' feelings will demonstrate goodwill. Julian James demonstrates empathy for the reputation of business and industry today:

So far the industry's finances have rarely looked better. But not everyone is celebrating. With success in business comes greater scrutiny—just ask the oil industry.

In recent weeks we have seen a growing vilification of insurers that is unprecedented and, I believe, wholly unwarranted. Take these recent headlines I came across:

From USA Today: "Insurance rates pummel Florida homeowners"

From Dow Jones Market Watch: "Sweet are the uses of adversity: Are insurers reeling from disaster or reeling in the profits?" (No prizes for guessing which side the authors came down on in that one.)

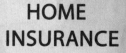

responsive
showing that you care about the audience by acknowledging feedback

terminal credibility
perception of a speaker's expertise at the end of the speech

initial credibility
perception of a speaker's expertise at the beginning of the speech

derived credibility
perception of a speaker's expertise during the speech

And from the Niagara Falls Reporter: *"Insurance companies real villains in Hurricane Katrina's aftermath"*

If that is the kind of press the industry is getting in Niagara Falls, in upstate New York, you might wonder how we are being portrayed in the Gulf States. (James, 2007)

Finally, you can demonstrate goodwill by being responsive. Speakers who are **responsive** show that they care about the audience by acknowledging feedback, especially subtle negative cues. This feedback may occur during the presentation, but it also may have occurred prior to the speech. Let's turn again to Julian James's speech as an example:

When I spoke to you at this conference, I posed a challenge and asked, "Do you want to take control of the insurance cycle. . . . or do you want to stay a passenger?" The reaction was very interesting. One group said, "That's so obvious, why hasn't anyone said that before?" Others said, "Ah, but you're very young, you don't understand, insurance cycles are a fact of life, and you can't do anything about them." . . . Ladies and gentlemen, four years ago, it may have felt like we were standing at the cliff edge, looking into the abyss.

The good news is that, in the intervening period, we have made important progress. . . . But we put our future in grave danger if we stop here. . . . The challenges we face today may be different, but the message from 2002 remains the same: "Our thinking and behaviour must change if the insurance industry is to be a stable, secure industry for our policy holders and shareholders of the future." Let's not mess it up again. (James, 2007)

17-4b Conveying Competence and Credibility

Not surprisingly, we are more likely to be persuaded when we perceive a speaker to be competent and credible. We propose the following strategies so that your **terminal credibility**, the audience's perception of your expertise at the end of your speech, is greater than your **initial credibility**, their perception of your expertise at the beginning of your speech.

1. Explain your competence. Unless someone has formally introduced you and your qualifications to your audience, your initial credibility will be low, and as you speak, you will need to tell your audience about your expertise. Sending these types of messages during the speech results in your achieving a level of **derived credibility** with your audience. You can interweave comments about your expertise into introductory comments and at appropriate places within the body of the speech.

2. Use evidence from respected sources. You can also increase your derived credibility by using supporting material from well-recognized and respected sources. So, if you have a choice between using a statistic from a known partisan organization or from a dispassionate professional association, choose the professional association. Likewise, if you can quote a local expert who is well known and respected by your audience or an international scholar with limited name recognition with your audience, use the local expert's opinion.

3. Use nonverbal delivery to enhance your credibility. Your audience assesses your credibility not only from what it hears about you before you begin speaking but also from what it observes by looking at you. Although professional attire enhances credibility in any speaking situation, it is particularly important for persuasive speeches. Persuasive speakers dressed more formally are perceived as more credible than those dressed casually or sloppily (Sellnow & Treinen, 2004).

The audience will also notice how confident you appear as you prepare to address them. From the moment you rise to speak, you will want to convey through your nonverbal behavior that you are competent. Plant your feet firmly, glance at your notes, then make eye contact or audience contact with one person or group before taking a breath and beginning to speak. Likewise, pause and establish eye contact upon finishing the speech. Just as pausing and establishing eye contact or audience contact before the speech enhances credibility, doing so upon delivering the closing lines has the same result.

4. Use vocal expression to enhance your credibility. Research shows that credibility is strongly influenced by how you sound. Speaking fluently, using a moderately fast rate, and expressing yourself with conviction makes you appear more intelligent and competent.

17-5 Rhetorical Appeals to Pathos

We are more likely to be involved with a topic when we have an emotional stake in it. **Emotions** are the buildup of action-specific energy (Petri & Govern, 2012). You can increase audience involvement by evoking negative or positive emotions during your speech (Nabi, 2002).

17-5a Evoking Negative Emotions

Negative emotions are disquieting, so when people experience them, they look for ways to eliminate them. Although you can tap numerous negative emotions, we describe five of the most common and how you might use them in a persuasive speech.

Fear

We experience *fear* when we perceive ourselves to have no control over a situation that threatens us. We may fear physical harm or psychological harm. If you use examples, stories, and statistics that evoke fear in your audience, they will be more motivated to hear how your proposal can eliminate the source of their fear or allow them to escape from it.

Guilt

We feel *guilt* when we personally violate a moral, ethical, or religious code that we hold dear. We experience guilt as a gnawing sensation that we have done something wrong. When we feel guilty, we are motivated to "make things right" or to atone for our transgression.

Shame

We feel *shame* when a moral code we violate is revealed to someone we think highly of. The more egregious our behavior or the more we admire the person who finds out, the more shame we experience. When we feel shame, we are motivated to "redeem" ourselves in the eyes of that person. Likewise, we can be convinced to refrain from doing something to avoid feelings of shame. If in your speech you can evoke feelings of shame and then demonstrate how your proposal can either redeem someone after a violation has occurred

© Robnroll/Shutterstock.com

or prevent feelings of shame, then you can motivate the audience to carefully consider your arguments.

emotions
buildup of action-specific energy

Anger

When we are faced with an obstacle that stands in the way of something we want, we experience *anger*. We may also experience anger when someone demeans us or someone we love. But be cautious: Speakers who choose to evoke anger must not incite listeners to the degree that their reasoning processes are short-circuited.

In your speeches, if you can rouse your audience's anger and then show how your proposal will enable them to achieve their goals or stop or prevent the demeaning that has occurred, you can motivate them to listen to and really consider your arguments. For example, suppose you want to convince the audience to support a law requiring the active community notification when a convicted sex offender moves into the neighborhood. You might arouse the audience's anger to get their attention by personalizing the story of Megan Kanka.

She was your little girl, just seven years old, and the light of your world. She had a smile that could bring you to your knees. And she loved puppies. So when that nice man who had moved in down the street invited her in to see his new puppy, she didn't hesitate. But she didn't get to see the puppy, and you didn't ever see her alive again. He beat her, he raped her, and then he strangled her. He packaged her body in an old toy chest and dumped it in a park. Your seven-year-old princess would never dig in a toy chest again or slip down the slide in that park. And that hurts. But what makes you really angry is that she wasn't his first. But you didn't know that. Because no one bothered to tell you that the guy down the street was likely to kill little girls. The cops knew it. But they couldn't tell you. You, the one who was supposed to keep her safe, didn't know. Angry? You bet. Yeah, he's behind bars again, but you still don't know who's living down the street from you. But you can. There is a law before Congress right now that will require active notification of the community when a known sex offender takes up residence, and today I'm going to tell how you can help to get this passed. ("Megan's Law," n.d.)

Sadness

When we fail to achieve a goal or experience a loss, we feel *sadness*. Unlike other negative emotions, we tend to withdraw and become isolated when we feel sad. Because sadness is an unpleasant feeling, we look for ways to end it. Speeches that help us understand and find answers for what has happened can comfort us and help relieve this unpleasant feeling.

17-5b Evoking Positive Emotions

Just as evoking negative emotions can cause audience members to internalize your arguments, so too can you tap *positive emotions*, which are feelings that people enjoy experiencing. We discuss five of them here.

Happiness or Joy

Happiness or *joy* is the buildup of positive energy we experience when we accomplish something, when we have a satisfying interaction or relationship, or when we see or possess objects that appeal to us. Think of how you felt when you won that ribbon in grade school or when you found out that you got an "A" on that volcano project in fourth grade. Think of how you felt when you heard that special someone say "I love you" for the very first time. Or think about the birthday when you received a toy you had been dreaming about. In each of these cases, you were happy, maybe even so happy that you were joyous. As a speaker, if you can show how your proposal will lead your audience members to be happy or joyful, then they are likely to listen and to think about your proposal.

Pride

When we experience satisfaction about something we or someone we care about accomplishes, we feel *pride*. "We're number one! We're number one!" is the chant of the crowd feeling pride in the accomplishment of "their" team. Whereas happiness is related to feelings of pleasure, pride is related to feelings of self-worth. So, if you can demonstrate how your proposal will help audience members feel good about themselves, they will be more motivated to support your proposition.

Relief

When a threatening situation has been alleviated, we feel the positive emotion of *relief*. We relax and put down our guard. As a speaker, you use relief to motivate audience members by combining it with the negative emotion of fear.

Hope

The emotional energy that stems from believing something desirable is likely to happen is called *hope*. Whereas relief causes you to relax and let down your guard, hope energizes you to take action to overcome the situation. Hope empowers. As with relief, hope appeals are usually accompanied by fear appeals. So you can motivate audience members to listen by showing them how your proposal provides a plan for overcoming a difficult situation. For example, if you propose adopting a low-fat diet to reduce the risk of high blood pressure, you can use the same personalization of statistics cited in the example of fear but change the ending to state: "Today, I'm going to convince you to beat the odds by adopting a low-fat diet."

Compassion

When we feel selfless concern for the suffering of another person and that concern energizes us to try to relieve that suffering, we feel *compassion.* Speakers can evoke audience members' feelings of compassion by vividly describing the suffering endured by someone. The audience will then be motivated to listen to see how the speaker's proposal can end that suffering.

You can evoke negative emotions, positive emotions, or both as a way to encourage listeners to internalize your message. You can do so by telling vivid stories and testimonials, offering startling statistics, using striking presentational aids and provocative language, as well as through an animated and expressive delivery style.

17-6 Persuasive Speech Patterns

The most common patterns for organizing persuasive speeches include statement of reasons, comparative advantages, criteria satisfaction, refutative, problem–solution, problem–cause–solution, and motivated sequence. In this section, we describe and illustrate each pattern by examining the same topic with slightly different propositions.

17-6a Statement of Reasons

The **statement of reasons pattern** is used to confirm propositions of fact by presenting the best-supported reasons in a meaningful order. For a speech with three reasons or more, place the strongest reason last because this is the reason you believe the audience will find most persuasive. Place the second strongest reason first because you want to start with a significant point. Place the other reasons in between.

Proposition: *I want my audience to believe that passing the proposed school tax levy is necessary.*

I. The income will enable the schools to restore vital programs. [second strongest]

II. The income will enable the schools to give teachers the raises they need to keep up with the cost of living.

III. The income will allow the community to maintain local control and will save the district from state intervention. [strongest]

17-6b Comparative Advantages

The **comparative advantages pattern** attempts to convince others that something has more value than something else. A comparative advantages approach to a school tax proposition would look like this:

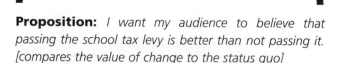

Proposition: *I want my audience to believe that passing the school tax levy is better than not passing it. [compares the value of change to the status quo]*

I. Income from a tax levy will enable schools to reintroduce important programs that had to be cut. [advantage 1]

II. Income from a tax levy will enable schools to avoid a tentative strike by teachers who are underpaid. [advantage 2]

III. Income from a tax levy will enable us to retain local control of our schools, which will be lost to the state if additional local funding is not provided. [advantage 3]

17-6c Criteria Satisfaction

The **criteria satisfaction pattern** seeks agreement on criteria that should be considered when evaluating a particular proposition and then shows how the proposition satisfies the criteria. A criteria satisfaction pattern is especially useful when your audience is opposed to your proposition, because it approaches the proposition indirectly by first focusing on the criteria that the audience should agree with before introducing the specific solution. A criteria satisfaction organization for the school levy would look like this:

Proposition: *I want my audience to believe that passing a school levy is a good way to fund our schools.*

I. We can all agree that a good school funding method must meet three criteria:

   A. A good funding method results in the reestablishment of programs that have been dropped due to budget constraints.

   B. A good funding method results in fair pay for teachers.

   C. A good funding method generates enough income to maintain local control, avoiding state intervention.

II. Passage of a local school tax levy is a good way to fund our schools.

   A. A local levy will allow us to re-fund important programs.

   B. A local levy will allow us to give teachers a raise.

   C. A local levy will generate enough income to maintain local control and avoid state intervention.

17-6d Refutative

The **refutative pattern** arranges main points according to opposing arguments and then both challenges them and bolsters your own. This pattern is particularly useful when the target audience opposes your position. Begin by acknowledging the merit of opposing arguments and then provide evidence of their flaws. Once listeners understand the flaws, they will be more receptive to the arguments you present to support your proposition. A refutative pattern for the school tax proposition might look like this:

Proposition: *I want my audience to agree that a school levy is the best way to fund our schools.*

I. *Opponents of the tax levy argue that the tax increase will fall only on property owners.*

   A. *Landlords will recoup property taxes in the form of higher rents.*

   B. *Thus, all people will be affected.*

II. *Opponents of the tax levy argue that there are fewer students in the school district, so schools should be able to function on the same amount of revenue.*

   A. *Although there are fewer pupils, costs continue to rise.*

     1. *Salary costs are increasing.*

     2. *Energy costs are increasing.*

     3. *Maintenance costs are increasing.*

     4. *Costs from unfunded federal and state government mandates are rising.*

   B. *Although there are fewer pupils, there are many aging school buildings that need replacing or retrofitting.*

III. *Opponents of the tax levy argue that parents should be responsible for the excessive cost of educating their children.*

   A. *Historically, our nation has flourished under a publicly funded educational system.*

   B. *Parents today are already paying more than previous generations.*

     1. *Activity fees*

     2. *Lab fees*

     3. *Book fees*

     4. *Transportation fees*

   C. *Of school-age children today in this district, 42 percent live in families that are below the poverty line and have limited resources.*

17-6e Problem–Solution

The **problem–solution pattern** explains the nature of a problem and proposes a solution. This organization is particularly effective when the audience is neutral or agrees only that there is a problem but has no opinion about a particular solution. A problem–solution organization for the school tax proposition might look like this:

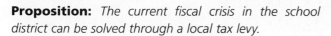

Proposition: *The current fiscal crisis in the school district can be solved through a local tax levy.*

I. *The current funding is insufficient and has resulted in program cuts, labor problems resulting from stagnant wages, and a threatened state takeover of local schools.* [statement of problem]

II. *The proposed local tax levy is large enough to solve these problems.* [solution]

17-6f Problem–Cause–Solution

The **problem–cause–solution pattern** is similar to the problem–solution pattern, but differs from it by adding a main point that reveals the causes of the problem and a solution designed to alleviate those causes. This pattern is particularly useful for addressing seemingly intractable problems that have been dealt with unsuccessfully in the past as a result of treating symptoms rather than underlying causes. A problem–cause–solution organization for the school tax proposition might look like this:

Proposition: *The current fiscal crisis in the school district can be solved through a local tax levy.*

I. *The current funding is insufficient and has resulted in program cuts, labor problems, and a threatened state takeover of local schools.* [statement of problem]

II. *These problems exist due to dwindling government support and increasing costs for operating expenses.* [causes]

III. *The proposed local tax levy will solve these problems by supplementing government support and enhancing operating budgets.* [solution]

17-6g Motivated Sequence

The **motivated sequence pattern** combines a problem–solution pattern with explicit appeals designed to motivate the audience to act. The motivated sequence pattern is a unified five-point sequence that replaces the normal introduction-body-conclusion model with (1) an attention step, (2) a need step that fully explains the nature of the problem, (3) a satisfaction step that explains how the proposal solves the problem in a satisfactory manner, (4) a visualization step that provides a personal application of the proposal, and (5) an action appeal step that emphasizes the direction that audience action should take. A motivated sequence pattern for the school tax levy proposition would look like this:

problem–cause–solution pattern demonstrates that there is a problem caused by specific things that can be alleviated with the proposed solution that addresses the causes

motivated sequence pattern a form of organization that combines the problem–solution pattern with explicit appeals designed to motivate the audience to act

Proposition: *I want my audience to vote in favor of the school tax levy on the November ballot.*

I. *Comparisons of worldwide test scores in math and science have refocused our attention on education.* [attention]

II. *The shortage of money is resulting in cost-cutting measures that compromise our ability to teach basic academic subjects well.* [need, statement of problem]

III. *The proposed increase is large enough to solve those problems in ways that allow for increased emphasis on academic need areas.* [satisfaction, how the proposal solves the problem]

IV. *Think of the contribution you will be making to the education of your children and also to efforts to return our educational system to the world-class level it once held.* [visualization of personal application]

V. *Here are "Vote Yes" buttons that you can wear to show you are willing to support this much-needed tax levy.* [action appeal showing specific direction]

Because motivational patterns are variations of problem–solution patterns, the underlying assumption is similar: When the current means are not solving the problem, a new solution that does solve the problem should be adopted. Figure 17.3 is a checklist that you can use to analyze any persuasive speech you rehearse or to critique the speeches of others.

FIGURE 17.3

Persuasive Speech Evaluation Checklist

You can use this form to critique a persuasive speech to convince that you hear in class. As you listen to the speaker, outline the speech, paying close attention to the reasoning process the speaker uses. Also note the claims and support used in the arguments and identify the types of warrants being used. Then answer the questions that follow.

General Criteria

____ 1. Was the proposition clear? Could you tell the speaker's position on the issue?

____ 2. Was the introduction effective in creating interest and involving the audience in the speech?

____ 3. Was the speech organized using an appropriate persuasive pattern?

____ 4. Was the language clear, vivid, inclusive, and appropriate?

____ 5. Was the conclusion effective in summarizing what had been said and mobilizing the audience to act?

____ 6. Was the speech delivered conversationally and expressively?

____ 7. Did the speaker establish credibility by demonstrating:
  ____ expertise?
  ____ personableness?
  ____ trustworthiness?

Primary Criteria

____ 1. Was the specific goal phrased as a proposition (were you clear about the speaker's position on the issue)?

____ 2. Did the proposition appear to be adapted to the initial attitude of the target audience?

____ 3. Were emotional appeals used to involve the audience with the topic?

____ 4. Were the reasons used in the speech
  ____ directly related to the proposition?
  ____ supported by strong evidence?
  ____ persuasive for the particular audience?

____ 5. Was the evidence [support] used to back the reasons [claims]
  ____ from well-respected sources?
  ____ recent and/or still valid?
  ____ persuasive for this audience?
  ____ typical of all evidence that might have been used?
  ____ sufficient [enough evidence cited]?

____ 6. Could you identify the types of arguments that were used?
  ____ Did the speaker argue from example?
  ____ If so, was it valid?
  ____ Did the speaker argue from analogy?
  ____ If so, was it valid?
  ____ Did the speaker argue from causation?
  ____ If so, was it valid?
  ____ Did the speaker argue from sign?
  ____ If so, was it valid?

____ 7. Could you identify any fallacies of reasoning in the speech?
  ____ hasty generalizations
  ____ arguing from false cause
  ____ ad hominem attacks
  ____ straw person
  ____ either-or

____ 8. Did the speaker demonstrate goodwill?

____ 9. If the speech called for the audience to take action,
  ____ did the speaker describe incentives and relate them to audience needs?
  ____ did the speaker acknowledge any costs associated with the action?

____ 10. Did the speaker use an appropriate persuasive organizational pattern?
  ____ statement of reasons
  ____ comparative advantages
  ____ criteria satisfaction
  ____ refutative
  ____ problem-solution
  ____ problem-cause-solution
  ____ motivated sequence

Overall evaluation of the speech (check one):
____ excellent
____ good
____ average
____ fair
____ poor

Use the information from this checklist to support your evaluation.

Sample Persuasive Speech

Read the speech adaptation plan developed by Adam Parrish in preparing his speech on cyber-bullying. Then read the transcript of Adam's speech, using the speech critique checklist from Figure 17.3 to help you evaluate his speech. You can access a video clip of Adam's speech on CourseMate.

Adaptation Plan

1. **Target audience initial attitude and background knowledge:** My audience is composed of traditional-aged college students with varying majors and classes. Most are from middle-class backgrounds. The initial attitude about bullying for most will be to agree with me already that it's a bad thing. So I will try to get them to take action. My perception is that my audience knows about cyber-bullying but not the nuances of it.

2. **Organizational framework:** I will organize my speech using a problem-cause-solution framework because my audience already agrees that bullying is bad but may not know what they can and should do to help stop it.

3. **Arguments (logos):** I will demonstrate how widespread (breadth) and harmful (depth of effects) cyber-bullying is and why it persists (causes). Once I've convinced my audience, I will propose solutions that must be taken and cite specifically what we must do to help stop this horrible practice.

4. **Building competence, credibility, and good character (ethos):** I will use credible sources to support my claims and cite them using oral footnotes. I will also offer personal stories to create goodwill.

5. **Creating and maintaining interest (pathos):** I will involve my audience by appealing to several emotions, including guilt, sadness, relief, hope, and compassion.

Speech Outline
Together, We Can Stop Cyber-Bullying

by Adam Parrish

General goal:
To persuade

Specific goal:
To convince my audience to take action to help stop cyber-bullying.

Introduction

I. "I'll miss just being around her." "I didn't want to believe it." "It's such a sad thing." These quotes are from the friends and family of 15-year-old Phoebe Prince, who, on January 14, 2010, committed suicide by hanging herself. Why did this senseless act occur? The answer is simple: Phoebe Prince was bullied to death. *Attention getter*

II. Many of us know someone who has been bullied in school. Perhaps they were teased in the parking lot or in the locker room. In the past, bullying occurred primarily in and around schools. However, with the advent of new communication technologies such as cell phones with text messaging capability, instant messaging, e-mails, blogs, and social networking sites, bullies can now follow their victims anywhere, even into their own bedrooms. Using electronic communications to tease, harass, threaten, and intimidate another person is called cyber-bullying.

▶ *Listener relevance link*

III. As a tutor and mentor to young students, I have witnessed cyber-bullying firsthand, and by examining current research, I believe I understand the problem, its causes, and how we can help end cyber-bullying.

▶ *Speaker credibility*

IV. Cyber-bullying is a devastating form of abuse that must be confronted and stopped.

V. Today, we will examine the widespread and harmful nature of cyber-bullying, discover how and why it persists, and propose some simple solutions that we must engage in to thwart cyber-bullies and comfort their victims.

▶ *Thesis statement (stated as a proposition)*

▶ *Preview*

Let's begin by tackling the problem head on.

▶ *Transition*

Body

I. Cyber-bullying is a pervasive and dangerous behavior.

▶ *The problem*

Many of us have read rude, insensitive, or nasty statements posted about us or someone we care about on social networking sites like Myspace and Facebook. Whether or not those comments were actually intended to hurt another person's feelings, they are perfect examples of cyber-bullying.

▶ *Listener relevance link*

A. Cyber-bullying takes place all over the world through a wide array of electronic media.

1. According to an article in the winter 2005 edition of *Reclaiming Children and Youth*, 57 percent of American middle-school students have experienced instances of cyber-bullying ranging from hurtful comments to threats of physical violence (Keith & Martin, 2005).

2. Females are just as likely as males to engage in cyber-bullying, although women are 10 percent more likely to be victimized (Li, 2007).

3. While the number of students who are targets of cyber-bullies decreases as students age, data from the Youth Internet Safety Survey indicate that the instances of American high school students being cyber-bullied increased nearly 50 percent from 2000 to 2005 (Ybarra, Mitchell, Wolak, & Finkelhor, 2006).

4. Quing Li (2007), a researcher of computer-mediated communication, noted that Internet and cell phone technologies have been used by bullies to harass, torment, and threaten young people in North America, Europe, and Asia.

5. A particularly disturbing incident occurred in Dallas, Texas, where an overweight student with multiple sclerosis was targeted on a school's social networking page. One message read, "I guess I'll have to wait until you kill yourself, which I hope is not long from now, or I'll have to wait until your disease kills you" (Keith & Martin, 2005, p. 226).

Clearly, cyber-bullying is a widespread problem. What is most disturbing about cyber-bullying, however, is its effects upon victims, bystanders, and perhaps even upon the bullies themselves.

▶ Transition

B. Cyber-bullying can lead to traumatic physical psychological injuries upon its victims.

1. According to a 2007 article in the *Journal of Adolescent Health*, 36 percent of the victims of cyber-bullies are also harassed by their attackers in school (Ybarra, Diener-West, & Leaf, 2007).

2. For example, the Dallas student with MS had eggs thrown at her car and a bottle of acid thrown at her house (Keith & Martin, 2005).

3. Ybarra et al. (2007) reported that victims of cyber-bullying experience such severe emotional distress that they often exhibit behavioral problems such as poor grades, skipping school, and receiving detentions and suspensions.

4. Smith et al. (2008) suggested that even a few instances of cyber-bullying can have these long-lasting and heartbreaking results.

5. What is even more alarming is that victims of cyber-bullying are significantly more likely to carry weapons to school as a result of feeling threatened (Ybarra et al., 2007). Obviously, this could lead to violent, and perhaps even deadly, outcomes for bullies, victims, and even bystanders.

Now that we realize the devastating nature, scope, and effects of cyber-bullying, let's look at its causes.

▶ Transition

II. Cyber-bullying is perpetuated because victims and bystanders do not report their abusers to authorities.

▶ The cause

Think back to a time when you may have seen a friend or loved one being harassed online. Did you report the bully to the network administrator or other authorities? Did you console the victim? I know I didn't. If you are like me, we may unknowingly be enabling future instances of cyber-bullying.

▶ Listener relevance link

A. Cyber-bullies are cowards who attack their victims anonymously.

1. Ybarra et al. (2007) discovered that 13 percent of cyber-bullying victims did not know who was tormenting them.

2. This is an important statistic because, as Keith and Martin (2005) point out, traditional bullying takes place face to face and often ends when students leave school. However, today, students are subjected to bullying in their own homes.

3. Perhaps the anonymous nature of cyber-attacks partially explains why Li (2007) found that nearly 76 percent of victims of cyber-bullying and 75 percent of bystanders never reported instances of bullying to adults.

B. Victims and bystanders who do not report attacks from cyber-bullies can unintentionally enable bullies.

1. According to De Nies, Donaldson, and Netter of *ABCNews.com* (2010) several of Phoebe Prince's classmates were aware that she was being harassed but did not inform the school's administration.

2. Li (2007) suggested that victims and bystanders often do not believe that adults will actually intervene to stop cyber-bullying.

3. However, *ABCNews.com* (2010) reports that 41 states have laws against bullying in schools, and 23 of those states target cyber-bullying specifically.

Now that we realize that victims of cyber-bullies desperately need the help of witnesses and bystanders to report their attacks, we should arm ourselves with the information necessary to provide that assistance.

▶ Transition

III. Cyber-bullying must be confronted on national, local, and personal levels.

▶ The solution

Think about the next time you see a friend or loved one being tormented or harassed online. What would you be willing to do to help?

▶ Listener relevance link

A. There should be a comprehensive national law confronting cyber-bullying in schools. Certain statutes currently in state laws should be amalgamated to create the strongest protections for victims and the most effective punishments for bullies as possible.

1. According to Limber and Small's (2003) article titled "State Laws and Policies to Address Bullying in Schools," Georgia law requires faculty and staff to be trained on the nature of bullying and what actions to take if they see students being bullied.

2. Furthermore, Connecticut law *requires* school employees to report bullying as part of their hiring contract (Limber & Small, 2003). Washington takes this a step further by protecting employees from any legal action if a reported bully is proven to be innocent (Limber & Small, 2003).

3. When it comes to protecting victims, West Virginia law demands that schools must ensure that a bullied student does not receive additional abuse at the hands of his or her bully (Limber & Small, 2003).

4. Legislating punishment for bullies is difficult. As Limber and Small (2003) noted, zero-tolerance polices often perpetuate violence because at-risk youth (bullies) are removed from all of the benefits of school, which might help make them less abusive.

5. A comprehensive anti-cyber-bullying law should incorporate the best aspects of these state laws and find a way to punish bullies that is both punitive and has the ability to rehabilitate abusers.

B. Local communities must organize and mobilize to attack the problem of cyber-bullying.

1. According to Greene (2006), communities need to support bullying prevention programs by conducting a school-based bullying survey for individual school districts. We can't know how to best protect victims in our community without knowing how they are affected by the problem.

2. It is critical to know this information. As Greene noted, only 3 percent of teachers in the United States perceive bullying to be a problem in their schools (Greene, 2006).

3. Local school districts should create a Coordinating Committee made up of "administrators, teachers, students, parents, school staff, and

community partners" to gather bullying data and rally support to confront the problem (Greene, 2006, p. 73).

    4. Even if your local school district is unable or unwilling to mobilize behind this dire cause, there are some important actions you can take personally to safeguard those you love against cyber-bullying.

C. Take note of these warning signs that might indicate a friend or loved one is a victim of a cyber-bully.

    1. Victims of cyber-bullies often use electronic communication more frequently than do people who are not being bullied.

    2. Victims of cyber-bullies have mood swings and difficulty sleeping (Keith & Martin, 2005).

    3. Victims of cyber-bullies seem depressed and/or become anxious (Keith & Martin, 2005).

    4. Victims of cyber-bullies become withdrawn from social activities and fall behind in scholastic responsibilities (Keith & Martin, 2005).

D. If you see a friend or loved one exhibiting any of these signs, I implore you not to ignore them. Rather, take action. Get involved. Do something to stop it.

    1. According to Raskauskas and Stoltz (2007), witnesses of cyber-bullying should inform victims to take the attacks seriously, especially if the bullies threaten violence.

    2. Tell victims to report their attacks to police or other authority figures (Raskauskas & Stoltz, 2007).

    3. Tell victims to block harmful messages by blocking e-mail accounts and cell phone numbers (Raskauskas & Stoltz, 2007).

    4. Tell victims to save copies of attacks and provide them to authorities (Raskauskas & Stoltz, 2007).

    5. If you personally know the bully and feel safe confronting him or her, do so! As Raskauskas and Stoltz (2007) noted, bullies will often back down when confronted by peers.

    6. By being a good friend and by giving good advice, you can help a victim report his or her attacks from cyber-bullies and take a major step toward eliminating this horrendous problem.

So, you see, we are not helpless to stop the cyber-bulling problem as long as we make the choice NOT to ignore it.

▶ Transition

Conclusion

I. Cyber-bullying is a devastating form of abuse that must be reported to authorities.

▶ Thesis restatement

II. Cyber-bullying is a worldwide problem perpetuated by the silence of both victims and bystanders. By paying attention to certain warning signs, we can empower ourselves to console victims and report their abusers.

▶ Main point summary

III. Today, I implore you to do your part to help stop cyber-bullying. I know that you agree that stopping cyber-bullying must be a priority. First, although other states have cyber-bullying laws in place, ours does not. So I'm asking

▶ Call to action and clincher

you to sign this petition that I will forward to our district's state legislators. We need to make our voices heard that we want specific laws passed to stop this horrific practice and to punish those caught doing it. Second, I'm also asking you to be vigilant in noticing signs of cyber-bullying and then taking action. Look for signs that your friend, brother, sister, cousin, boyfriend, girlfriend, or loved one might be a victim of cyber-bullying and then get involved to help stop it! Phoebe Prince showed the warning signs, and she did not deserve to die so senselessly. None of us would ever want to say, "I'll miss just being around her," "I didn't want to believe it," "It's such a sad thing" about our own friends or family members. We must work to ensure that victims are supported and bullies are confronted nationally, locally, and personally. I know that, if we stand together and refuse to be silent, we can and will stop cyber-bullying.

References

De Nies, Y., Donaldson, S., & Netter, S. (2010, January 28). Mean girls: Cyber-bullying blamed for teen suicides. ABCNews.com. Retrieved from http://abcnews.go.com/GMA/Parenting/girls-teen-suicide-calls-attention-cyberbullying/story?id=9685026

Greene, M. B. (2006). Bullying in schools: A plea for measure of human rights. *Journal of Social Issues, 62*(1), 63–79.

Keith, S., & Martin, M. (2005). Cyber-bullying: Creating a culture of respect in the cyber world. *Reclaiming Children and Youth, 13*(4), 224–228.

Li, Q. (2007). New bottle of old wine: A research of cyberbullying in schools. *Computers in Human Behavior, 23,* 1777–1791.

Limber, S. P., & Small, M. A. (2003). State laws and policies to address bullying in schools. *School Psychology Review, 32*(3), 445–455.

Raskauskas, J., & Stoltz, A. D. (2007). Involvement in traditional and electronic bullying among adolescents. *Developmental Psychology, 43*(3), 564–575.

Smith, P. K., Mahdavi, J., Carvalho, M., Fisher, S. Russel, S., & Tippett, N. (2008). Cyberbullying: Its nature and impact in secondary school pupils. *Journal of Child Psychology and Psychiatry, 49*(4), 374–385.

Ybarra, M. L., Diener-West, M., & Leaf, P. J. (2007). Examining the overlap in Internet harassment and school bullying: Implications for school intervention. *Journal of Adolescent Health, 41,* S42–S50.

Ybarra, M. L., Mitchell, K. J., Wolak, J., & Finkelhor, D. (2006). Examining characteristics and associated distress related to Internet harassment: Findings from the second Youth Internet Safety Survey. *Pediatrics, 118,* 1169–1177.

Speech and Analysis

"I'll miss just being around her." "I didn't want to believe it." "It's such a sad thing." These quotes are from the friends and family of 15-year-old Phoebe Prince, who, on January 14, 2010, committed suicide by hanging herself. Why did this senseless act occur? The answer is simple. . . . Phoebe Prince was bullied to death.

Many of us know someone who has been bullied in school. Perhaps they were teased in the parking lot or in the locker room. In the past, bullying occurred primarily in school. However, with the advent of new communication

Analysis

Adam uses quotes from family and friends of cyber-bullying victim Phoebe Prince to get attention and lead into his proposition.

Here, Adam further entices his listeners to pay attention by offering listener relevance that we all can relate to.

technologies such as cell phones, text messaging, instant messaging, blogs, and social networking sites, bullies can now follow and terrorize their victims anywhere, even into their own bedrooms. Using electronic communications to tease, harass, threaten, and intimidate another person is called cyber-bullying.

As a tutor and mentor to young students, I have witnessed cyber-bullying firsthand, and by examining current research, I believe I understand the problem, its causes, and how we can help end cyber-bullying. What I know for sure is that cyber-bullying is a devastating form of abuse that must be confronted on national, local, and personal levels.

Today, we will examine the widespread and harmful nature of cyber-bulling, uncover how and why it persists, and pinpoint some simple solutions we must begin to enact in order to thwart cyber-bullies and comfort their victims. Let's begin by tackling the problem head on.

Many of us have read rude, insensitive, or nasty statements posted about us or someone we care about on social networking sites like Myspace and Facebook. Well, whether or not those comments were actually intended to hurt another person's feelings, if they did hurt their feelings, then they are perfect examples of cyber-bullying.

Cyber-bullying is a pervasive and dangerous behavior. It takes place all over the world and through a wide array of electronic media. According to Keith and Martin's article in the winter 2005 edition of *Reclaiming Children and Youth,* 57 percent of American middle-school students had experienced instances of cyber-bullying ranging from hurtful comments to threats of physical violence. Quing Li's article published in the journal *Computers in Human Behavior* noted that cyber-bullying is not gender biased. According to Li, females are just as likely as males to engage in cyber-bullying, although women are 10 percent more likely to be victimized.

While the number of students who are targets of cyber-bullies decreases as students age, data from the *Youth Internet Safety Survey* indicates that the instances of American high school students being cyber-bullied had increased nearly 50 percent from 2000 to 2005. The problem does not exist in the United States alone.

Li noted that Internet and cell phone technologies have been used by bullies to harass, torment, and threaten young people in North America, Europe, and Asia. However, some of the most horrific attacks happen right here at home.

According to Keith and Martin, a particularly disturbing incident occurred in Dallas, Texas, where an overweight student with multiple sclerosis was targeted on a school's social networking page. One message read, "I guess I'll have to wait until you kill yourself which I hope is not long from now, or I'll have to wait until your disease kills you." Clearly, cyber-bullying is a worldwide and perverse phenomenon. What is most disturbing about cyber-bullying is its effects upon victims, bystanders, and perhaps even upon bullies themselves.

Cyber-bullying can lead to physical and psychological injuries upon its victims. According to a 2007 article in the *Journal of Adolescent Health,* Ybarra and colleagues noted that 36 percent of the victims of cyber-bullies are also harassed by their attackers in school. For example, the Dallas student with MS had eggs thrown at her car and a bottle of acid thrown at her house.

Ybarra et al. reported that victims of cyber-bullying experience such severe emotional distress that they often exhibit behavioral problems such

▷ Using the vivid term "terrorize," Adam appeals to negative emotions (pathos).

▷ Adam begins to establish ethos by mentioning why he has credibility about this topic. Mentioning that he is a tutor and mentor also conveys goodwill. Listeners are likely to think he must have good character if he volunteers as a tutor and mentor.

▷ Adam does a nice job of previewing his problem-cause-solution organizational framework, but his thesis statement phrased as a proposition is somewhat lost and could be made more overtly here.

▷ Again, Adam's use of a listener relevance link helps keep listeners tuned in and interested in hearing more.

▷ Here Adam bolsters his ethos (and avoids plagiarism) by citing an oral footnote for his statistics.

▷ Although this trend is interesting, it would have been more compelling to use a contemporary statistic.

▷ Notice Adam's word choices (harass, torment, threaten, horrific) to enhance pathos.

▷ The use of a real victim in this example creates an emotional appeal.

▷ This vivid example enhances pathos.

as poor grades, skipping school, and receiving detentions and suspensions. Furthermore, Smith et al. suggested that even a few instances of cyber-bullying can have these long-lasting negative effects.

What is even more alarming is that, according to Ybarra and colleagues, victims of cyber-bullying are significantly more likely to carry weapons to school as a result of feeling threatened. Obviously, this could lead to violent outcomes for bullies, victims, and even bystanders.

Now that we have heard about the nature, scope, and effects of cyber-bullying, let's see if we can discover its causes. Let's think back to a time when we may have seen a friend or loved one being harassed online. Did we report the bully to the network administrator or other authorities? Did we console the victim? I know I didn't. If you are like me, we may unknowingly be enabling future instances of cyber-bullying.

Cyber-bullying occurs because of the anonymity offered to bullies by cell phone and Internet technologies, as well as the failure of victims and bystanders to report incidents of cyber-bullying. You see, unlike schoolyard bullies, cyber-bullies can attack their victims anonymously.

Ybarra and colleagues discovered that 13 percent of cyber-bullying victims did not know who was tormenting them. This devastating statistic is important because, as Keith and Martin noted, traditional bullying takes place face to face and often ends when students leave school. However, today, students are subjected to nonstop bullying, even when they are alone in their own homes.

Perhaps the anonymous nature of cyber-attacks partially explains why Li found that nearly 76 percent of victims of cyber-bullying and 75 percent of bystanders never reported instances of bullying to adults. Victims and bystanders who do not report attacks from cyber-bullies can unintentionally enable bullies.

According to De Nies, Donaldson, and Netter of *ABCNews.com* (2010), several of Phoebe Prince's classmates were aware that she was being harassed but did not inform the school's administration. Li suggested that victims and bystanders often do not believe that adults will actually intervene to stop cyber-bullying. However, *ABCNews.com* reports that 41 states have laws against bullying in schools, and 23 of those states target cyber-bullying specifically.

Now that we know that victims of cyber-bullies desperately need the help of witnesses and bystanders to report their attacks, we should arm ourselves with the information necessary to provide that assistance. Think about the next time you see a friend or loved one being tormented or harassed online. What would you be willing to do to help?

Cyber-bullying must be confronted on national, local, and personal levels. There should be a comprehensive national law confronting cyber-bullying in schools. Certain statutes currently in state laws should be amalgamated to create the strongest protections for victims and the most effective punishments for bullies as possible.

According to Limber and Small's article titled "State Laws and Policies to Address Bullying in Schools," Georgia law requires faculty and staff to be trained on the nature of bullying and what actions to take if they see students being bullied.

Furthermore, Connecticut law *requires* school employees to report bullying as part of their hiring contract. Washington takes this a step further by

▶ Now that Adam has established the widespread breadth of the problem, he moves into a discussion about the depth of the effects it can have on victims.

▶ Here Adam helps pique listener interest by pointing out that bystanders can also be hurt if they don't do something to stop this form of terrorism.

▶ Notice how Adam's transition ties the point he is finishing (problem) to the next point (causes) using inclusive "we" language. This, too, bolsters a sense of goodwill and uses a conversational style that keeps listeners engaged.

▶ Again, Adam does a nice job with his transition.

▶ Notice how Adam gets right to the point about needing to take action on a variety of levels to stop this practice.

▶ Adam gives credence to his policy statement by pointing to several states that have already succeeded in creating such laws.

protecting employees from any legal action if a reported bully is proven to be innocent. When it comes to protecting victims, West Virginia law demands that schools must ensure that a bullied student does not receive additional abuse at the hands of his or her bully.

Legislating punishment for bullies is difficult. As Limber and Small noted, zero-tolerance polices often perpetuate violence because at-risk youth, i.e., bullies, are removed from all of the benefits of school, which might help make them less abusive. A comprehensive anti-cyber-bullying law should incorporate the best aspects of these state laws and find a way to punish bullies that is both punitive and has the ability to rehabilitate abusers. However, for national laws to be effective, local communities need to be supportive.

Here, Adam points to the need for consequences when bullying behavior is exposed.

Local communities must organize and mobilize to attack the problem of cyber-bullying. According to Greene's 2006 article published in the *Journal of Social Issues,* communities need to support bullying prevention programs by conducting a school-based bullying survey for individual school districts. We can't know how to best protect victims in our community without knowing how they are affected by the problem. It is critical to know this information. As Greene noted, only 3 percent of teachers in the United States perceive bullying to be a problem in their schools.

Adam offers specific action steps that communities ought to take to help stop cyber-bullying.

Local school districts should create a Coordinating Committee made up of administrators, teachers, students, parents, school staff, and community partners to gather bullying data and rally support to confront the problem. Even if your local school district is unable or unwilling to mobilize behind this dire cause, there are some important actions you can take personally to safeguard those you love against cyber-bullying.

There are several warning signs that might indicate a friend or loved one is a victim of a cyber-bully. If you see a friend or loved one exhibiting these signs, the decision to get involved can be the difference between life and death.

Here, Adam gets personal, pointing out that each person in the room has an ethical responsibility to help stop cyber-bullying.

According to Keith and Martin's article "Cyber-Bullying: Creating a Culture of Respect in a Cyber World," victims of cyber-bullies often use electronic communication more frequently than do people who are not being bullied. Victims of cyber-bullies have mood swings and difficulty sleeping. They seem depressed and/or become anxious. Victims can also become withdrawn from social activities and fall behind in scholastic responsibilities. If you witness your friends or family members exhibiting these symptoms, there are several ways you can help.

According to Raskauskas and Stoltz's 2007 article in *Developmental Psychology,* witnesses of cyber-bullying should inform victims to take the attacks seriously, especially if the bullies threaten violence. You should tell victims to report their attacks to police or other authorities, to block harmful messages by blocking e-mail accounts and cell phone numbers, and to save copies of attacks and provide them to authorities.

Adam could make this statement more compelling by offering a specific example of what one might tell the police, as well as how to install blockers on e-mail and mobile phones.

If you personally know the bully and feel safe confronting him or her, do so! As Raskauskas and Stoltz noted, bullies will often back down when confronted by peers. By being a good friend and by giving good advice, you can help a victim report his or her attacks from cyber-bullies and take a major step toward eliminating this horrendous problem. So, you see, we are not helpless to stop the cyber-bulling problem as long as we make the choice NOT to ignore it.

To conclude, cyber-bullying is a devastating form of abuse that must be reported to authorities. Cyber-bullying is a worldwide problem perpetuated by the silence of both victims and bystanders. By paying attention to certain warning signs, we can empower ourselves to console victims and report their abusers.

Today, I'm imploring you to do your part to help stop cyber-bullying. I know that you agree that stopping cyber-bullying must be a priority. First, although other states have cyber-bullying laws in place, ours does not. So I'm asking you to sign this petition that I will forward to our district's state legislators. We need to make our voices heard that we want specific laws passed to stop this horrific practice and to punish those caught doing it.

Second, I'm also asking you to be vigilant in noticing signs of cyber-bullying and then taking action. Look for signs that your friend, brother, sister, cousin, boyfriend, girlfriend, or loved one might be a victim of cyber-bullying, and then get involved to help stop it! Phoebe Prince showed the warning signs, and she did not deserve to die so senselessly. None of us would ever want to say, "I'll miss just being around her," "I didn't want to believe it," "It's such a sad thing" about our own friends or family members. We must work to ensure that victims are supported and bullies are confronted nationally, locally, and personally.

I know that, if we stand together and refuse to be silent, we can and will stop cyber-bullying.

▶ Here, Adam restates his proposition, but his argument could be more comprehensive (beyond just our need to report bullying to the authorities).

▶ Adam reminds listeners of his specific call to action and even asks them to sign a petition. His approach encourages listeners to follow through on his goal—that is—to actuate.

▶ Adam does a nice job with his clincher in terms of tying back to the Phoebe story from his attention getter. Doing so appeals to emotions (pathos) in a way that should make his speech very memorable.

©iStockphoto/Thinkstock.com

Quick Quiz

T F   1. If your audience is very much opposed to your goal, you should aim to change their attitude from "opposed" to "in favor" by the end of your speech.

T F   2. A proposition of value is a statement designed to convince your audience that they should take a specific course of action.

T F   3. A straw man is a fallacy that occurs when a speaker weakens the opposing position by misrepresenting it in some way, and then attacks that weaker position.

T F   4. An argument is an articulation of a position with the support of logos, ethos, and pathos.

T F   5. The statement of reasons pattern attempts to prove propositions of fact by presenting the best-supported reasons in a meaningful order, placing the strongest reason first because the audience will find it most persuasive.

6. You are arguing by _____ when you cite evidence that one or more events always or almost always brings about, leads to, creates, or prevents a predictable event or set of effects.
   a. examples
   b. analogy
   c. causation
   d. sign
   e. reasoning

7. Which of the following five common errors in reasoning occurs when the alleged cause fails to be related to or to produce the effect?
   a. hasty generalization
   b. ad hominem
   c. either-or
   d. false cause
   e. straw man

8. Speakers demonstrate _____ by showing the audience that they understand and empathize with them.
   a. goodwill
   b. credibility
   c. positive emotions
   d. emotional appeals
   e. responsiveness

9. The _____ pattern is a form of persuasive organization used for arguing a proposition of value when the goal is to prove that something has more value than something else.
   a. statement of reasons
   b. problem solution
   c. comparative advantages
   d. criteria satisfaction
   e. motivated sequence

10. Which of the following patterns for organizing persuasive speeches helps you organize your main points so that you persuade by both challenging opposing arguments and bolstering your own?
    a. statement of reasons
    b. problem-cause-solution
    c. criteria satisfaction
    d. comparative advantages
    e. refutative

Answers: 1. F, 2. F, 3. T, 4. T, 5. F, 6. C, 7. D, 8. A, 9. C, 10. E

Interviewing

Because interviewing is a powerful method of collecting or presenting first-hand information that may be unavailable elsewhere, it is an important communication skill to master. An **interview** is a highly structured conversation in which one person asks questions and another person answers them. By *highly structured*, we mean that the purpose and the questions to be asked are determined ahead of time. Because interviews are highly structured, they can be used to make comparisons. For example, an interviewer may ask two potential employees the same set of questions, compare the answers, and hire the person whose answers fit best with the needs of the organization and responsibilities of the position. Although we have all taken part in interviews, few have learned how to do so effectively—either as the interviewer or the interviewee.

Because the heart of effective interviewing is developing a series of good questions, we begin by describing how to do so. Then we propose some guidelines to follow when engaged in information-gathering, employment, and media interviews.

A-1 The Interview Protocol

The **interview protocol** is the list of questions used to elicit desired information from the interviewee. An effective interviewer always prepares a protocol in advance. How many questions you plan to ask depends on how much time you will have for the interview. Begin by listing the topics you want to cover. Then prioritize them.

Just as the topics in a well-developed speech are structured in an outline with main points, subpoints, and supporting material, an effective interview protocol is structured into primary and secondary questions. The questions should be a mix of open-ended and closed-ended questions, as well as neutral and leading questions. Let's briefly examine each type.

A-1a Primary and Secondary Questions

Primary questions are introductory questions about each major interview topic.

Secondary questions are follow-up questions that probe the interviewee to expand on the answers given to primary questions. The interviewee may not realize how much detail you want or may be purposely evasive. Some follow-up questions probe by simply encouraging the interviewee to continue ("And then?" or "Is there more?"); some probe into a specific detail the person mentioned or failed to mention ("What does 'regionally popular' mean?" and "You didn't mention genre. What role might that play in your decision to offer a contract?"); and some probe into their feelings ("How did it feel when her first record went platinum?").

A-1b Open-ended and Closed-ended Questions

Open-ended questions are broad-based queries that give the interviewee freedom about the specific information, opinions, or feelings that can be divulged. Open-ended questions encourage the interviewee to talk and allow the interviewer an opportunity to listen and observe. Since open-ended questions give respondents more control, interviewers need to intentionally redirect the interviewee to focus on the original purpose (Tengler & Jablin, 1983). For example, in a job interview you might be asked, "What one accomplishment has best prepared

interview
a highly structured conversation in which one person asks questions and another person answers them

interview protocol
the list of questions used to elicit desired information from the interviewee

primary questions
introductory questions about each major interview topic

secondary questions
follow-up questions that probe the interviewee to expand on the answers given to primary questions

open-ended questions
broad-based queries that give the interviewee freedom about the specific information, opinions, or feelings that can be divulged

you for this job?" In a customer service interview, a representative might ask, "What seems to be the problem?" or "Can you tell me the steps you took when you first set up this product?"

By contrast, **closed-ended questions** are narrowly focused and require very brief (one- or two-word) answers. Closed-ended questions range from those that can be answered yes or no, such as "Have you taken a course in marketing?" to those that require only a short answer, such as "Which of the artists that you have signed have won Grammys?" By asking closed-ended questions, interviewers can control the interview and obtain specific information quickly. But the answers to closed-ended questions cannot reveal the nuances behind responses, nor are they likely to capture the complexity of the story.

A-1c Neutral and Leading Questions

Open-ended and closed-ended questions may also be either neutral or leading. **Neutral questions** do not direct a person's answer. "What can you tell me about your work with Habitat for Humanity?" and "What criteria do you use in deciding whether to offer an artist a contract?" are neutral questions. The neutral question gives the respondent free rein to answer the question without any knowledge of what the interviewer thinks or believes.

By contrast, **leading questions** guide respondents toward providing certain types of information and imply that the interviewer prefers one answer over another. "What do you like about working for Habitat for Humanity?" steers respondents to describe only the positive aspects of their volunteer work. "Having a 'commercial sound' is an important criteria, isn't it?" directs the answer by providing the standard for comparison. In most types of interviews, neutral questions are preferable because they are less likely to create defensiveness in the interviewee.

A good interview protocol will use a combination of open-ended, closed-ended, neutral, and leading questions.

A-2 Information-Gathering Interviews

Interviewing is a valuable method for obtaining information on nearly any topic. Lawyers and police interview witnesses to establish facts; health care providers interview patients to obtain medical histories before making diagnoses; reporters interview sources for their stories; managers interview employees to receive updates on projects; and students interview experts to obtain information for research projects. Once you have prepared a good interview protocol, you need to choose an appropriate person to interview, conduct the interview effectively, and follow up respectfully.

A-2a Choosing the Interviewee

Sometimes the choice of interviewee is obvious, but other times you will need to do research to identify the right person to interview. Suppose your purpose is to learn about how to get a recording contract. You might begin by asking a professor in the music department for the name of a music production agency in the area. Or you could find the name of an agency by searching online. Once you find a Web site, you can usually find an "About Us" or "Contact Us" link, which will offer names, titles, e-mail addresses, and phone numbers. You should be able to identify someone appropriate to your purpose from this list.

Once you have identified the person or people to be interviewed, you should make contact to schedule an appointment. Today, it is generally best to do so by both e-mail and telephone. When you contact the interviewee, be sure to clearly state the purpose of the interview, how the interview information will be used, and how long you expect the interview to take. When setting a date and time, suggest several dates and time ranges and ask which would be most convenient for the interviewee. As you conclude, thank the person for agreeing to be interviewed and confirm the date, time, and location you have agreed to for the interview. If you make the appointment more than a few days in advance, call or e-mail the day before the interview to confirm the appointment.

You don't want to bother your interviewee with information you can get elsewhere. So to prepare appropriate protocol questions, do some research on the topic in advance. This includes learning about what the interviewee may have written about the topic and his or her credentials. Interviewees will be more responsive if you appear informed, and being informed will ensure that you ask good questions. For instance, if you are going to interview a music producer, you will want to do preliminary research about what a music producer is and does, whether any general "best practices" exist for signing artists, and whether this particular producer has published

closed-ended questions narrowly focused questions that require very brief (one- or two-word) answers

neutral questions questions that do not direct a person's answer

leading questions questions that guide respondents toward providing certain types of information and imply that the interviewer prefers one answer over another

transcribe

translate oral interview responses word for word into written form

any criteria. You can usually do so by carefully reading the information posted on their Web site. Then, during the interview, you can ask about additional criteria, about different criteria, or to expand on how the criteria is used in making judgments.

A-2b Conducting the Interview

To guide you in the process of conducting effective and ethical interviews, we offer this list of best practices.

1. Dress professionally. Dressing professionally conveys that you are serious about the interview and that you respect the interviewee and his or her time.

2. Be prompt. You also demonstrate respect by showing up prepared to begin at the time you have agreed to. Remember to allow enough time for potential traffic and parking problems.

3. Be courteous. Begin by introducing yourself and the purpose of the interview and by thanking the person for taking the time to talk to you. Remember that, although interviewees may enjoy talking about the subject, may be flattered, and may wish to share their knowledge, they most likely have nothing to gain from the interview. So you should let them know you are grateful for their time. Most of all, respect what the interviewee says regardless of what you may think of his or her responses.

4. Ask permission to record. If the interviewee says no, respect his or her wishes and take careful notes instead.

5. Listen carefully. At key points in the interview, paraphrase what the interviewee has said to be sure that you really understand. This will assure the interviewee that you will report the answers truthfully and fairly in your paper, project, or speech.

6. Keep the interview moving. You do not want to rush the person, but you do want to behave responsibly by getting your questions answered during the allotted time.

7. Monitor your nonverbal reactions. Maintain good eye contact with the person. Nod to show understanding, and smile occasionally to maintain the friendliness of the interview. How you look and act is likely to determine whether the person will warm up to you and give you an informative interview.

8. Get permission to quote. Be sure to get permission for exact quotes. Doing so demonstrates that you respect the interviewee and want to report his or her ideas honestly and fairly. Doing so also communicates that you have integrity and strive to act responsibly. You

might even offer to let the person see a copy of what you prepare before you share it with others. That way, he or she can double-check the accuracy of direct quotations.

9. Confirm credentials. Before you leave, be sure to confirm your interviewee's professional title and the company or organization he or she represents. To do so is to act responsibly because you will need these details when explaining why you chose to interview this person.

10. End on time. As with arriving promptly, ending the interview when you said you would demonstrates respect for the interviewee and that you act responsibly and with integrity.

11. Thank the interviewee. Thanking the interviewee leads to positive rapport, should you need to follow up later, and demonstrates that you appreciate his or her valuable time. You may even follow up with a short thank-you note after you leave.

A-2c Following Up

Because your interview notes were probably taken in outline or shorthand form, the longer you wait to translate them the more difficult this task will be. So you'll need to sit down with your notes as soon as possible after the interview to make more extensive notes of the information you may want to use later. If you recorded the interview, take some time to **transcribe** the responses by translating them word for word into written form. If at any point you are not sure whether you have accurately transcribed what the person said or meant, telephone or e-mail the interviewee to double-check. When you have completed a draft of your paper, project, or speech outline, you can demonstrate respect for the interviewee and integrity as a reporter by providing him or her with a copy of the product if it is a written paper or report, a link to it if it is an online document, or an invitation to attend if it is a public speech or performance.

A-3 Employment Interviews

Believe it or not, over the past 50 years, the average amount of time an employee stays with one company or organization has gone from over 23 years to about 4 years (Employee Tenure, 2010; Taylor & Hardy, 2004)! Not only that, but between 15 to 20 million Americans change jobs each year (Bashara, 2006). This means that we spend more time doing employment interviews—both as interviewers and interviewees—than ever before.

Employment interviews help interviewers assess which applicants have the knowledge, experience, and skills that best fit the responsibilities of the position and culture of the organization—characteristics and skills that cannot be judged from a résumé. And employment interviews help job-seekers determine whether they would enjoy working for the organization. So let's look at some best practices for both employment interviewers and job-seekers.

A-3a Employment Interviewers

Historically, human resource professionals have conducted most employment interviews on behalf of a firm, but today more and more workplaces are using employees as interviewers. You may have already helped conduct employment interviews, or you may be asked to do so in the near future. As with any interview, you will need to follow some guidelines as you both prepare for and conduct the interview.

Preparing for the Interview

As with information interviews, you begin employment interviews by doing research—in this case, by familiarizing yourself with the knowledge, skills, and aptitudes someone must have to be successful in the job. It also means studying applicants' résumés, reference letters, and other application materials to narrow the pool of applicants you will actually interview. Before interviewing each applicant, prepare by reviewing their materials again, making notes about topics to address with probing secondary questions.

In most employment interviewing situations, you will see several candidates. It's important to make an interview protocol to make sure that all applicants are asked the same (or very similar) questions about characteristics and skills. Be sure to identify primary questions and secondary questions that will probe knowledge, skills, characteristics, and experiences relevant to the position and the culture of your organization. Using a protocol will also help you avoid questions that violate fair employment practice legislation. The Equal Opportunity Commission has detailed guidelines that spell out which questions are unlawful.

Conducting the Interview

As with an information-gathering interview, begin with introductions and a question or two designed to establish rapport and to help the interviewee relax. Be sure to greet the applicant warmly, consider your verbal and nonverbal cues, and conclude with a clarification of next steps.

Following Up

Once you have hired one of the interviewees, be sure to follow up with a short e-mail or letter informing each of the other candidates that the position has been filled. You can do so *respectfully* by thanking each candidate for their interest in the position and taking the time to participate in the interview, reminding them that they were a strong candidate in a strong applicant pool, and wishing them well in their future employment-seeking endeavors.

A-4 Job-seekers

A **job-seeker** is anyone who is looking for a job or considering a job change. Some may be unemployed and dedicating 100 percent of their time to finding a job. Others may be happily employed and recruited to apply for another position. Still others could be employed, but seeking a more rewarding position. As many employment experts will tell you, "As a rule, the best jobs do *not* go to the best-qualified individuals—they go to the best job seekers" (Graber, 2000). Successful job-seekers are obviously the ones who get the job. To be successful, you need to follow guidelines searching for job openings, as well as when applying and interviewing.

A-4a Locating Job Openings

You have probably been through the hiring process at least once, and perhaps many times. So you know how stressful it can be. You also probably know that sometimes the most difficult part of a job search is simply finding out about job openings. Sometimes openings are easily accessible by searching the Internet, newspaper, career fairs, and career centers. We call this the **visible job market.** Other times, however, job openings are not readily apparent and require you to use other methods to locate and apply for them. We call this the **hidden job market** (Yena, 2011). We focus here on locating jobs in both the visible and hidden job markets by searching published resources (in print and online), using referral services, and networking.

Published Resources

When employers want to cast a wide net for applicants, they will publish in a variety of outlets that are read most widely by job-seekers. These range from Web sites such as CareerBuilder.com, Monster.com, HotJobs.com, USAJOBS .gov (dedicated to government jobs), and CollegeJobBank .com (dedicated to recent college graduates), as well as classified sections of online newspapers and newsletters. Some sites allow you to post your résumé online and will

job-seeker
anyone who is looking for a job or considering a job change

visible job market
easily accessible job opening announcements

hidden job market
job openings that are not readily apparent and require alternative methods to locate

career fairs
events that bring potential employers and applicants together to foster networking and create awareness about employment opportunities

employee referral programs
in-house reward programs for employees who refer strong candidates to the company

networking
the process of using developing or established relationships to make contacts regarding job openings

network
the people you know, people you meet, and people who are known to the people you know

elevator speech
a 60-second oral summary of the type of job you are seeking and your qualifications for it

résumé
a summary sheet highlighting your related experience, educational background, skills, and accomplishments

cover letter
a short, well-written letter or e-mail expressing your interest in a particular job and piquing curiosity about you as an applicant

forward it to potential employers when your credentials fit their needs. Although employers often use these sites, they also very often publish openings on their own Web sites. So even if you find an announcement posted on another site, you can improve your chances of landing an interview if you actually apply through the company's own Web site (Light, 2011).

Referral Services

Some employers like to use referral services to do the initial screening of applicants. Most colleges and universities have an on-site career center that serves this purpose. Your tuition dollars pay for this service, so it's one of the first places you should look. They post and publish local, regional, national, and international openings in a variety of for-profit, nonprofit, and government organizations. In addition to doing initial screenings for employers, career service officers also provide applicants helpful advice about writing cover letters, preparing résumés, selecting references, and doing interviews. Finally, they often facilitate on-campus **career fairs** to help bring potential employers and applicants together to learn about the company and make contacts.

Some employers also have in-house **employee referral programs** that reward current employees for referring strong candidates to the company. If you are interested in working for a particular company, you might seek an opportunity to ask a current employee to recommend you.

Networking

Networking is the process of using developing or established relationships to make contacts regarding job openings (in both the visible and hidden job markets). Some research suggests that the majority of jobs are filled via networking (Betty, 2010). Your **network** consists of the people you know, people you meet, and

the people who are known to the people you know. These people may include teachers, counselors, your friends, family friends, relatives, service club members, mentors, classmates, colleagues, and even people you meet at sporting events, country clubs, and health clubs. The following two guidelines can help make networking work for you.

1. Reach out to people you know and tell them you are in the job market. Speak up and tell the people you know that you are looking for a job. Bring it up during conversation or intentionally seek them out to let them know. Prepare business cards with your contact information and give them to the people you talk to. In addition to business cards, be prepared to provide people in your network with an **elevator speech**— a 60-second oral summary of the type of job you're seeking and your qualifications for it. Ask people in your network if they know of (1) any job opportunities that might be appropriate and (2) anyone you might contact to help you find such opportunities. Finally, ask them to keep their eyes and ears open about anything that might be of interest to you and to share such information with you.

2. Grow your network. Attend networking events in your area that may be hosted by your college or university career center, the local chamber of commerce, and your alumni association. Join professional and civic organizations. Volunteer. The more people you know, the more people you will have to ask about potential opportunities on the *hidden job market*. You should also join online networking groups such as LinkedIn, Facebook, and Twitter. Remember that the key here is to develop and nurture relationships. People will make a special effort to help you if they believe you are a friend and a good person.

A-4b Preparing Application Materials

Because interviewing is time consuming, most organizations do not interview all the people who apply for a job. Rather, they use a variety of screening devices to eliminate people who don't meet their qualifications. Chief among them are evaluating the qualifications you highlight on your résumé and in your cover letter (Kaplan, 2002). A **résumé** is a summary sheet highlighting your related experience, educational background, skills, and accomplishments. A **cover letter** is a short well-written letter or e-mail expressing your interest in the position and piquing curiosity about why your application materials deserve a closer look. The goal of your cover letter and résumé is to land an interview (Farr, 2009).

Whether you send your application materials electronically or through regular postal mail, the guidelines for preparing them effectively are the same. Before you can begin, you need to know something about the company and about the job requirements so that you can tailor your application materials to highlight how and why you are the best candidate. Today you can learn a lot about an organization by visiting its Web site and reading online material thoroughly. You can also talk to people you know who work or worked there, or acquaintances of employees.

Tailoring Your Résumé

You should tailor your résumé to highlight your skills and experiences related to the position and its responsibilities. There are two types of résumés. In both, you begin by supplying basic contact information (name, address, e-mail, phone number), educational degrees or certificates earned, and career objective. In a **chronological résumé**, you list your job positions and accomplishments in reverse chronological order. Chronological résumés are most appropriate if you have held jobs in the past that are clearly related to the position you are applying for. In a **functional résumé,** you focus on highlighting the skills and experiences you have that qualify you for the position. You may find a functional résumé best for highlighting your skills and accomplishments if you are changing careers, have a gap in your work history, or have limited formal job experience but have acquired job-related skills in other ways (courses you have taken, clubs you have belonged to, service-learning and volunteer work, etc.).

Tailoring Your Cover Letter

Just as you need to tailor your résumé to the position, you should also tailor your cover letter appropriately. Be sure to highlight your qualifications for *a specific job and its responsibilities*. You can learn some of this information in the job description, but you may also need to make inferences about it by visiting the company's Web site and talking to people who are associated with the organization or who are familiar with the type of position described in the advertisement.

Your cover letter should be short—no more than four or five paragraphs. If you prepare your cover letter in the body of an e-mail message, it should be even shorter. These paragraphs should highlight your job-related skills and experiences *using key words that appeared in the posting*. Many employers use software programs that scan e-mails and résumés for job-relevant key words. Using them in your cover letter will increase the likelihood that someone will actually look at your application materials. Use a spell-checker and carefully proofread for errors such

programs don't catch. Your cover letter must be 100 percent error free to serve as a catalyst for getting an interview.

Tailoring Materials for Online Submissions

You must also tailor your application materials for a variety of online submission programs. Because you will apply for most jobs online, make sure your materials can be submitted in several formats.

A-4c Conducting the Employment Interview

An **employment interview** is a conversation or set of conversations between a job candidate and a representative or representatives of a hiring organization. Your goal is to convince the interviewer that you are the best qualified candidate and the best fit for the position and company. Successful interviewing begins with thorough preparation, then with the actual interview, and finally with appropriate follow up.

Preparing

Once you submit your application materials, you need to prepare for the interview you hope to get. In this section, we offer four suggestions to prepare for a job interview.

1. Do your homework. Although you should have already done extensive research on the position and the organization to prepare your application materials, you should review what you've learned before going to the interview. Be sure you know the organization's products and services, areas of operation, ownership, and financial health. Nothing puts off interviewers more than applicants who arrive at an interview knowing little about the organization. Be sure to look beyond the "Work for Us" or "Frequently Asked Questions" links on the company's Web site. Find more specific information such as pages that target potential investors, report company stock performance, and describe the organization's mission (Slayter, 2006). Likewise, pictures can suggest the type of organizational culture you can expect—formal or informal dress, collaborative or individual work spaces, diversity, and so on. Researching these details will help you decide whether the organization is right for you, as well as help you form questions to ask during the interview.

chronological résumé
a résumé that lists your job positions and accomplishments in reverse chronological order

functional résumé
a résumé that focuses on highlighting the skills and experiences that qualify you for the position

employment interview
a conversation or set of conversations between a job candidate and a representative or representatives of a hiring organization

2. Prepare a self-summary. You should not need to hesitate when an interviewer asks you why you are interested in the job. You should also be prepared to describe your previous accomplishments. Form these statements as personal stories with specific examples that people will remember (Beshara, 2006). Robin Ryan (2000), one of the nation's foremost career authorities, advises job-seekers to prepare a 60-second general statement they can share with a potential employer. She advises job-seekers to identify which aspects of their training and experience would be most valued by a potential employer. She suggests making a five-point agenda that can (1) summarize your most relevant experience and (2) "build a solid picture emphasizing how you *can* do the job" (p. 10). Once you have your points identified, practice communicating them fluently in 60 seconds or less.

3. Prepare a list of questions about the organization and the job. The employment interview should be a two-way street, where you size up the company the same way they are sizing you up. So you will probably have a number of specific questions to ask the interviewer. For example, "Can you describe a typical workday for the person in this position?" or "What is the biggest challenge in this job?" Make a list of your questions and take it with you to the interview. It can be difficult to come up with good questions on the spur of the moment, so you should prepare several questions in advance. One question we do not advise asking during the interview, however, is "How much money will I make?" Save salary, benefits, and vacation-time negotiations until after you have been offered the job.

4. Rehearse the interview. Several days before the interview, spend time outlining the job requirements and how your knowledge, skills, and experiences meet those requirements. Practice answering questions commonly asked in interviews.

Interviewing

The actual interview is your opportunity to sell yourself to the organization. Although interviews can be stressful, your preparation should give you the confidence you need to relax and communicate effectively. Believe it or not, the job interview is somewhat stressful for the interviewer as well. Most companies do not interview potential employees every day. Moreover, the majority of interviewers have little or no formal training in the interview process. Your goal is to make the interview a comfortable conversation for both of you.

Use these guidelines to help you have a successful interview.

1. Dress appropriately. You want to make a good first impression, so it is important to be well groomed and neatly dressed. Although "casual" or "business casual" is common in many workplaces, some organizations still expect employees to be more formally dressed. If you don't know the dress code for the organization, call the human resources department and ask.

2. Arrive on time. The interview is the organization's first exposure to your work behavior, so you don't want to be late. Find out how long it will take you to travel by making a dry run at least a day before. Plan to arrive 10 or 15 minutes before your appointment.

3. Bring supplies. Bring extra copies of your résumé, cover letter, business cards, and references, as well as the list of questions you plan to ask. You might also bring a portfolio of previous work you have done. You will also want to have paper and a pen so that you can make notes.

4. Use active listening. When we are anxious, we sometimes have trouble listening well. Work on paying attention to, understanding, and remembering what is asked. Remember that the interviewer will be aware of your nonverbal behavior, so be sure to make and keep eye contact as you listen.

5. Think before answering. If you have prepared for the interview, make sure that as you answer the interviewer's questions, you also tell your story. Take a moment to consider how your answers portray your skills and experiences.

6. Be enthusiastic. If you come across as bored or disinterested, the interviewer is likely to conclude that you would be an unmotivated employee.

7. Ask questions. As the interview is winding down, be sure to ask any questions you prepared that have not already been answered. You may also want to ask how well the interviewer believes your qualifications match the position, and what your strengths are.

8. Thank the interviewer and restate your interest in the position. As the interview comes to a close, shake the interviewer's hand and thank him or her for the opportunity. Finally, restate your interest in the position and desire to work on the company team.

Following Up

Once the interview is over, you can set yourself apart from the other applicants by following these important steps:

1. Send a thank-you note. It is appropriate to write a short note thanking the interviewer for the experience and again expressing your interest in the job.

2. Self-assess your performance. Take time to critique your performance. How well did you do? What can you do better next time?

3. Contact the interviewer for feedback. If you don't get the job, you might call the interviewer and ask for feedback. Be polite and indicate that you are only calling to get some help on your interviewing skills. Actively listen to the feedback, using questions and paraphrases to clarify what is being said. Be sure to thank the interviewer for helping you.

A-5 Media Interviews

Today we live in a media-saturated environment in which any individual may be approached by a newsperson and asked to participate in an on-air interview. For example, the authors have a friend who became the object of media interest when the city council refused to grant him a zoning variance so that he could complete building a new home on his property. In the course of three days, his story became front-page news in his town, and reports about his situation made the local radio and TV news shows. You might be asked for an interview at public meetings, at the mall, or within the context of your work or community service. For example, you may be asked to share your knowledge of your organization's programs, events, or activities. Because media interviews are likely to be edited in some way before they are aired and because they reach a wide audience, there are specific strategies you should use to prepare for and participate in them.

A-5a Before the Interview

The members of the media work under very tight deadlines, so it is crucial that you respond immediately to media requests for an interview. When people are insensitive to media deadlines, they can end up looking like they have purposefully evaded the interview and have something to hide. When you speak with the media representative, clarify what the focus of the interview will be and how the information will be presented. At times, the entire interview will be presented; however, it is more likely that the interview will be edited or paraphrased and not all of your comments will be reported.

As you prepare for the interview, identify three or four **talking points**, that is, the central ideas you want to present as you answer questions during a media interview. For example, before our friend was interviewed by the local TV news anchor, he knew that he wanted to emphasize that he was a victim of others' mistakes: (1) he had

hired a licensed architect to draw the plans; (2) the city inspectors had repeatedly approved earlier stages of the building process; (3) the city planning commission had voted unanimously to grant him the variance; and (4) he would be out half the cost of the house if he were forced to tear it down and rebuild. Consider how you will tailor your information to the specific audience in terms they can understand. Consider how you will respond to tough or hostile questions.

talking points
the three or four central ideas you will present as you answer the questions asked during a media interview

bridge
the transition you create in a media interview so that you can move from the interviewer's subject to the message you want to communicate

A-5b During the Interview

Media interviews call for a combination of interviewing, nonverbal communication, and public speaking skills (Boyd, 1999). Follow these strategies during a media interview:

1. Present appropriate nonverbal cues. Inexperienced interviewees can often look or sound tense or stiff. By standing up during a phone interview, your voice will sound more energetic and authoritative. With on-camera interviews, when checking your notes, move your eyes but not your head. Keep a small smile when listening. Look at the interviewer, not into the camera.

2. Make clear and concise statements. It is important to speak slowly, to articulate clearly, and to avoid technical terms or jargon. Remember that the audience is not familiar with your area of expertise.

3. Realize that you are always "on the record." Say nothing as an aside or confidentially to a reporter. Do not say anything that you would not want quoted. If you do not know an answer, do not speculate, but indicate that the question is outside of your area of expertise. Do not ramble during the interviewer's periods of silence. Do not allow yourself to be rushed into an answer.

4. Learn how to bridge. Media consultant Joanna Krotz (2006) defines a **bridge** as a transition you create so that you can move from the interviewer's subject to the message you want to communicate. To do this, you first answer the direct question and then use a phrase such as "What's important to remember, however . . . ," "Let me put that in perspective . . . ," or "It's also important to know . . ." With careful preparation, specific communication strategies during the interview, and practice, one can skillfully deliver a message in any media interview format.

References

Chapter 1

Beebe, S., & Masterson, J. (2006). *Communicating in groups: Principles and practices* (8th ed.). Boston, MA: Pearson.

Berger, C. (1997). *Planning strategic interaction: Attaining goals through communicative action.* Mahwah, NJ: Lawrence Erlbaum.

Burgoon, J. K., Bonito, J. A., Ramirez, A., Jr., Dunbar, N. E., Kam, K., & Fisher, J. (2002). Testing the interactivity principle: Effects of mediation, propinquity, and verbal and nonverbal modalities in interpersonal interaction. *Journal of Communication, 52,* 657–677.

Burleson, B. R. (2009). Understanding the outcomes of supportive communication: A dual-process approach. *Journal of Social and Personal Relationships, 26*(1), 21–38.

College learning for the new global century. (2007). *A Report from the National Leadership Council for Liberal Education and America's Promise.* Washington, DC: Association of American Colleges and Universities.

Condon, S. L. & Čech, C. G. (2010). Discourse management in three modalities. *Language@ Internet, 7*(6). Retrieved from http://www.languageatinternet.org/articles/2010/2770

Cupach, W. R. & Spitzberg, B. H. (Eds.). (2011). *The dark side of close relationships II.* New York, NY: Routledge.

Darling, A.L., & Dannels, D. P. (2003). Practicing engineers talk about the importance of talk: A report on the role of oral communication in the workplace. *Communication Education, 52*(1), 1–16.

Hansen, R. S., & Hansen, K. (n.d.). Top skills and values employers seek from job-seekers. Retrieved from Quintessential Careers Web site: http://www.quintcareers.com/job_skills_values.html

Hart Research Associates. (2010). Raising the bar: Employers' views on college learning in the wake of the economic downturn. Washington, DC: Association of American Colleges and Universities.

Hart Research Associates. (2006). How should colleges prepare students to succeed in today's global economy? Washington, DC: Association of American Colleges and Universities.

Hirokawa, R. Y., Cathcart, R. S., Samovar, L. A., & Henman, L. D. (Eds.). (2003). *Small group communication: Theory and practice: An Anthology* (8th ed.). New York, NY: Oxford University Press, USA.

Kellerman, K. (1992). Communication: Inherently strategic and primarily automatic. *Communication Monographs, 59*(3), 288–300.

Kiesler, S., Zubrow, D., Moses, A., & Geller, V. (1985). Affect in computer-mediated communication: An experiment in synchronous terminal-to-terminal discussion. *Human-Computer Interaction, 1*(1), 77–104.

Knapp, M. L., & Daly, J. A. (2002). *Handbook of interpersonal communication.* Thousand Oaks, CA: Sage.

Littlejohn, S. W., & Foss, K. A. (2008). *Theories of human communication* (9th ed.). Belmont, CA: Thomson Wadsworth.

Littlejohn, S. W., & Foss, K. A. (2011). *Theories of human communication* (10th ed.). Long Grove, IL: Waveland Press.

McCroskey, J. C. (1977). Oral communication apprehension: A review of recent theory and research. *Human Communication Research, 4*(1), 78–96.

Millar, F. E. & Rogers, L. E. (1987). Relational dimensions of interpersonal dynamics. In M. E. Roloff & G. E. Miller (Eds.), *Interpersonal processes: New directions in communication research.* (pp. 117–139). Newbury Park, CA: Sage.

Pajares, F., Prestin, A., Chen, J., & Nabi, R. L. (2009). Social cognitive theory and media effects. In R. L. Nabi and M. B. Oliver (Eds.) *The SAGE handbook of media processes and effects* (pp. 283–297). Los Angeles, CA: Sage.

Richmond, V. P., & McCroskey, J. C. (1997). *Communication: Apprehension, avoidance, and effectiveness* (5th ed.). Scottsdale, AZ: Gorsuch Scarisbrick.

Samovar, L. A., Porter, R. E., & McDaniel, E. R. (2007). *Communication between cultures* (6th ed.). Belmont, CA: Thomson Wadsworth.

Samovar, L. A., Porter, R. E., & McDaniel, E. R. (2010). *Communication between cultures* (7th ed.). Belmont, CA: Thomson Wadsworth.

Spitzberg, B. H. (2000). A model of intercultural communication competence. In L. A. Samovar & R. E. Porter (Eds.), *Intercultural communication: A reader* (9th ed., pp. 375–387). Belmont, CA: Wadsworth.

Spitzberg, B. H. & Cupach, W. R. (Eds.). (2011). *The dark side of close relationships II.* New York, NY: Routledge.

Spitzer, M. (1986, January). Writing style in computer conferences. *IEEE Transactions on Professional Communications, 29*(1), 19–22.

Terkel, S. N., & Duval, R. S. (Eds.). (1999). *Encyclopedia of ethics.* New York, NY: Facts on File.

Humes, K. R., Jones, N. A., Ramirez, R.R. (2011, March). *Overview of Race and Hispanic Origin: 2010.* U. S. Census Bureau. Retrieved from http://www.census.gov/population/race/publications/

Young, M. (2003). Integrating communication skills into the marketing curriculum: A case study. *Journal of Marketing Education, 25*(1), 57–70.

Chapter 2

Aron, A. P., Mashek, D. J., & Aron, E. N. (2004). Closeness as including other in the self. In D. Mashek & A. Aron (Eds.), *Handbook of closeness and intimacy* (pp. 27–41). Mahwah, NJ: Lawrence Erlbaum.

Bandura, A. (1977). Self-efficacy: Toward a unifying theory of behavioral change. *Psychological Review, 84*(2), 191–215.

Baron, R. A., Byrne, D. R., & Branscombe, N. R. (2006). *Social psychology* (11th ed.). Boston, MA: Allyn & Bacon.

Baumeister, R. F. (2005). *The cultural animal: Human nature, meaning, and social life.* New York: Oxford University Press.

Becker, A. E. (2004). Television, disordered eating, and young women in Fiji: Negotiating body image and identity during rapid social change. *Culture, Medicine and Psychiatry, 28*(4), 533–559.

Benet-Martinez, V., & Haritatos, J. (2005). Bicultural identity integration (BII): Components and psychosocial antecedents. *Journal of Personality, 73*(4), 1015–1049.

Berger, C.R., & Bradac, J.J. (1982). *Language and social knowledge.* London, England: Edward Arnold Publishers Ltd.

Biocca, F., & Harms, C. (2002). Defining and measuring social presence: Contribution to the Networked Minds theory and measure. In F.R. Gouveia & F. Biocca (Eds.), *Proceedings of the 5th International Workshop of Presence* (7–36).

Centi, P. J. (1981). *Up with the positive—out with the negative.* Upper Saddle River, NJ: Prentice Hall.

Chen, G., & Starosta, W. (1998). *Foundations of intercultural communication.* Boston, MA: Allyn & Bacon.

Demo, D. H., Small, S. A., Savin-Williams, R. C. (1987). Family relations and the self-esteem of adolescents and their parents. *Journal of Marriage and the Family, 49*(4), 705–715.

Downey, G., Freitas, A. L., Michaelis, B., & Khouri, H. (2004). The self-fulfilling prophecy in close relationships: Rejection sensitivity and rejection by romantic partners. In H. T. Reis & C. E. Rusbult (Eds.), *Close relationships* (pp. 153–174). New York, NY: Psychology Press.

Engel, B. (2005). *Breaking the cycle of abuse: How to move beyond your past to create an abuse-free future.* Hoboken, NJ: John Wiley and Sons.

Gangestad, S. W., & Snyder, M. (2000). Self-monitoring: Appraisal and reappraisal. *Psychological Bulletin, 126*(4), 530–555.

Gibson, J. J. (1966). *The senses considered as perceptual systems.* Boston, MA: Houghton Mifflin.

Guerrero, L. K., Anderson, P. A., & Afifi, W. A. (2007). *Close encounters: Communication in relationships* (2nd ed.). Los Angeles: Sage Publications.

Haiken, M. (2012, September 26). Lady Gaga puts bulimia and body image on the table in a big way. *Forbes.* Retrieved from http://www.forbes.com/sites/melaniehaiken/2012/09/26/lady-gaga-puts-bulimia-and-body-image-on-the-table-in-a-big-way.

Hinduja, S., & Patchin, J. W. (2010). Bullying, cyberbullying, and suicide. *Archives of Suicide Research, 14*(3), 206–221.

Jones, M. (2002*). Social psychology of prejudice.* Upper Saddle River, NJ: Prentice-Hall.

Leary, M. R. (2002). When selves collide: The nature of the self and the dynamics of interpersonal relationships. In A. Tesser, D. A. Stapel, & J. V. Wood (Eds.), *Self and motivation: Emerging psychological perspectives* (pp. 119–145). Washington, DC: American Psychological Association.

Littlejohn, S. W., & Foss, K. A. (2011). *Theories of human communication* (10th ed.). Long Grove, IL: Waveland Press.

Markus, H. R., & Kitayama, S. (1991). Culture and the self: Implications for cognition, emotion, and motivation. *Psychological Review, 98*(2), 224–253.

Merton, R. K. (1968). *Social theory and social structure.* New York, NY: Free Press.

Mruk, C. (1999). *Self-esteem: Research, theory, and practice* (2nd ed.). New York, NY: Springer.

Mruk, C. J. (2006). *Self-esteem research, theory, and practice: Toward a positive psychology of self-esteem.* New York NY: Springer.

Rayner, S. G. (2001). Aspects of the self as learner: Perception, concept, and esteem. In R. J. Riding & S. G. Rayner (Eds.), *Self-perception: International perspectives on individual differences* (Vol. 2). Westport, CT: Ablex.

Sampson, E. E. (1999). *Dealing with differences: An introduction to the social psychology of prejudice.* Fort Worth, TX: Harcourt Brace.

Shedletsky, L. J., & Aitken, J. E. (2004). *Human communication on the Internet.* Boston: Pearson.

Weiten, W. (1998). *Psychology: Themes and variations* (4th ed.). Pacific Grove, CA: Brooks/Cole.

Willis, J. and Todorov, A (2006). First impressions: making up your mind after a 100-ms exposure to a face. *Psych Sci. 17*(7), 592–598.

Wood, J. T. (2007). *Gendered lives: Communication, gender, and culture* (7th ed.). Belmont, CA: Wadsworth.

Chapter 3

Anderson, P. A., Hecht, M. L., Hoobler, G. D., & Smallwood, M. (2003). Nonverbal communication across cultures. In W. B. Gudykunst (Ed.), *Cross-cultural and intercultural communication.* Thousand Oaks, CA: Sage.

Bornstein, M. H., & Bradley, R. H. (Eds.). (2003). *Socioeconomic status, parenting, and child development.* Mahwah, NJ: Lawrence Erlbaum Associates.

Bonvillain, N. (2003). *Language, culture and communication: The meaning of messages* (4th ed.). Upper Saddle River, NJ: Prentice-Hall.

Chen, G., & Starosta, W. (1998). *Foundations of intercultural communication.* Boston, MA: Allyn and Bacon.

Ellis, R. (1999). *Learning a second language through interaction.* Amsterdam: John Benjamins.

Hall, E. T. (1976). *Beyond culture.* New York, NY: Random House.

Haviland, W. A. (1993). *Cultural anthropology.* Fort Worth, TX: Harcourt, Brace, Jovanovich.

Hofstede, G. (1998). *Masculinity and femininity: The taboo.* Thousand Oaks, CA: Sage.

Hofstede, G. (2000). Masculine and feminine cultures. In A. E. Kazdin (Ed.), *Encyclopedia of psychology* (vol. 5). Washington, DC: American Psychological Association.

Hotz, R. L. (1995, April 15). Official racial definitions have shifted sharply and often. *Los Angeles Times,* p. A14.

Jackson, M. (Director). (2010). *Temple Grandin* [Motion picture]. USA: Home Box Office.

Jackson, R. L., II (Ed.). (2004). *African American communication and identities.* Thousand Oaks, CA: Sage.

Kim, M. (2005). Culture-based conversational constraints theory: Individual- and culture-level analyses. In W. B. Gudykunst (Ed.), *Theorizing about intercultural communication,* (pp. 93–117). Thousand Oaks, CA: Sage.

Kim, Y. Y. (2001). *Becoming intercultural: An integrative theory of communication and cross-cultural adaptation.* Thousand Oaks, CA: Sage.

Klyukanov, I. E. (2005). *Principles of intercultural communication.* New York, NY: Pearson.

Kraus, M. W., & Keltner, D. (2009). Signs of socioeconomic status: A thin-slicing approach. *Psychological Science, 20*(1), 99–106.

Leonhardt, D. (2005, May 24). Class matters: The college dropout doom. *New York Times.* Retrieved from http://www.nytimes.com /2005/05/24/national/class/EDUCATION -FINAL.html

Luckmann, J. (1999). *Transcultural communication in nursing.* New York, NY: Delmar.

Lugo, L., Cooperman, A., O'Connell, E., Stencel, S. (2001, Jan). *The future of the global muslim population: Projections for 2010–2030.* Washington, D.C.: Pew Research Center. Retrieved from http://www.pewforum.org/The-Future-of-the -Global-Muslim-Population.aspx

Mantilla, J. R. (2008, Oct 6). Más "speak Spanish" que en España. *El País.* Retrieved from http://elpais.com/diario/2008/10/06/cultura /1223244001_850215.html

Neuliep, J. W. (2006). *Intercultural communication: A contextual approach* (3rd ed.). Thousand Oaks, CA: Sage.

Pew Research Center. (2007). *A portrait of "Generation Next": How young people view their lives, futures, and politics* (survey report). Retrieved from http://people-press.org/ report/300/a-portrait-of-generation-next

Prensky, M. (2001). Digital natives, digital immigrants. *On the Horizon, 9*(5).

Samovar, L., Porter, R. E., & McDaniel, E. R. (2009). *Communication between cultures.* Boston, MA: Wadsworth Cengage.

Ting-Toomey, S., Yee-Jung, K. K., Shapiro, R. B., Garcia, W., Wright, T. J., & Oetzel, J. G. (2000). Ethnic/cultural identity salience and conflict styles in four U.S. ethnic groups. *International Journal of Intercultural Relations, 23*(1), 47–81.

Wallis, C. (2006, March 27). The multitasking generation. *Time, 167*(13), pp. 48–55.

Wood, J. T. (2007). *Gendered lives: Communication, gender, and culture* (7th ed.). Belmont, CA: Wadsworth.

Zemke, R., Raines, C., & Filipczak (2000). *Generations at work.* New York, NY: AMACOM Books.

Chapter 4

Aronoff, M. and Rees-Miller, J. (Eds.). (2001). *The handbook of linguistics.* Oxford, UK: Blackwell.

Chaika, E. (2008). *Language: The social mirror* (4th ed.). Boston, MA: Heinle ELT/Cengage.

Cvetkovic, L. (2009, February 21) Serbian, Croatian, Bosnian, or Montanegrin, or "Just our language." *Radio Free Europe/Radio Liberty.* Retrieved from http://www.rferl.org/content /Serbian_Croatian_Bosnian_or_Montenegrin _Many_In_Balkans_Just_Call_It_Our _Language_/1497105.html

Grice, H. P. (1975). Logic and conversation. In P. Cole & J. L. Morgan (Eds.), *Syntax and Semantics (Vol. 3).* New York, NY: Academic Press.

Higginbotham, J. (2006). Languages and idiolects: Their language and ours. In E. Lepore & B.C. Smith (Eds.), *The Oxford handbook of philosophy of language.* Oxford, UK: Oxford University Press.

Korta, K. and Perry, J. (2008). Pragmatics. In E. N. Zalta (Ed.), *Stanford Encyclopedia of Philosophy (Fall 2008 Edition).* Retrieved from http://plato .stanford.edu/archives/fall2008/entries /pragmatics/

Langer, E. J. & Moldoveanu, M. (2000). The construct of mindfulness. *Journal of Social Issues, 56*(1), 1–9.

Lewis, M. P. (Ed.). (2009). *Ethnologue: Languages of the world* (16th ed.). Dallas, TX: SIL International.

O'Grady, W., Archibald, J., Aronoff, M., & Rees-Miller, J. (2001). *Contemporary linguistics* (4th ed.). Boston, MA: Bedford/St. Martin's.

Saeid, J. I. (2003). *Semantics* (2nd ed.). Malden, MA: Blackwell.

Slattery, K., Doremus, M., & Marcus, L. (2001). Shifts in public affairs reporting on the network evening news: A move toward the sensational. *Journal of Broadcasting & Electronic Media 45*(2), 295–298.

Stewart, L. P., Cooper, P. J., Stewart, A. D., & Friedley, S. A. (1998). *Communication and gender* (3rd ed.). Boston, MA: Allyn & Bacon.

Ting-Toomey, S., & Chung, L. C. (2005). *Understanding Intercultural Communication.* Los Angeles, CA: Roxbury Publishing.

Wright, R. (2010). Chinese language facts. Retrieved from http://www.languagehelpers.com /languagefacts/chinese.html

Chapter 5

American Museum of Natural History. (1999). Exhibition highlights. *Body art: Marks of identity.* Retrieved from http://www.amnh .org/exhibitions/bodyart/exhibition_ highlights.html

Australian Museum. (2009). Shaping. *Body art.* Retrieved from http://amonline.net.au/bodyart /shaping/

Axtell, R. E. (1998). *Gestures: The do's and taboos of body language around the world.* Hoboken, NJ: John Wiley and Sons.

Birdwhistell, R. (1970). *Kinesics and context.* Philadelphia, PA: University of Pennsylvania Press.

Burgoon, J. K., & Bacue, A. E. (2003). Nonverbal communication skills. In J. O. Greene & B. R. Burleson (Eds.), *Handbook of communication and social interaction skills* (pp. 179–220). Mahwah, NJ: Erlbaum.

Burgoon, J. K., Blair, J. P., & Strom, R. E. (2008). Cognitive biases and nonverbal cue availability in detecting deception. *Human Communication Research, 34*(4), 572–599.

Daft, R. L. & Lengel, R. H. (1984). Information richness: a new approach to managerial behavior and organizational design. In: Cummings, L.L. & Staw, B.M. (Eds.), *Research in organizational behavior 6*, (pp. 191–233). Homewood, IL: JAI Press.

Gudykunst, W. B., & Kim, Y. Y. (1997). *Communicating with strangers: An approach to intercultural communication.* New York, NY: McGraw-Hill.

Hall, E. T. (1968). Proxemics. *Current Anthropology, 9*(2,3), 83–108.

Jacobs, B. (2005, June). *Adolescents and self-cutting (self-harm): Information for parents* (Bringing Science to Your Life, Guide I-104). Retrieved from http://aces.nmsu.edu/pubs/_i/I-104.pdf

Knapp, M. L., & Hall, J. A. (2006). *Nonverbal communication in human interaction* (5th ed.). Belmont, CA: Thomson Wadsworth.

Martin, J. N., & Nakayama, T. K. (2012). *Intercultural communication in contexts* (6th ed.). New York, NY: McGraw-Hill Ryerson.

Mehrabian, A. (1972). *Nonverbal communication.* Chicago, IL: Aldine.

Neuliep, J. W. (2006). *Intercultural communication: A contextual approach* (3rd ed.). Thousand Oaks, CA: Sage.

Olaniran, B. (2002–2003). Computer-mediated communication: A test of the impact of social cues on the choice of medium for resolving misunderstandings. *Journal of Educational Technology Systems, 31*(2), 205–222.

Pearson, J. C., West, R. L., & Turner, L. H. (1995). *Gender & communication* (3rd ed.). Dubuque, IA: Brown & Benchmark.

Samovar, L. A., Porter, R. E., & McDaniel, E. R. (Eds.). (2009). *Intercultural communication: A reader* (12th ed.). Belmont, CA: Cengage.

Schurman, A. (n.d.). A brief and rich body piercing history. *Life 123.* Retrieved from http://www.life123.com/beauty/style/piercings/body-piercing-history.shtml

Walther, J. B., & Parks, M. R. (2002). Cues filtered out, cues filtered in: Computer-mediated communication and relationships. In M. C. Knapp & J. A. Daly (Eds.), *Handbook of interpersonal communication* (3rd ed.; pp. 529–563). Thousand Oaks, CA: Sage.

Watzlawick, P., Bavelas, J. B., & Jackson, D. D. (1967). *Pragmatics of human communication.* New York, NY: Norton.

Wood, J. T. (2007). *Gendered lives: Communication, gender, and culture* (7th ed.). Belmont, CA: Wadsworth.

Chapter 6

Brownell, J. (2006). *Listening: Attitudes, principles, and skills* (3rd ed.). Boston, MA: Allyn & Bacon.

Burleson, B. R. (2003). Emotional support skills. In J. O. Green & B. R. Burleson (Eds.), *Handbook of communication and social interaction skills* (pp. 551–594). Mahwah, NJ: Erlbaum.

Donoghue, P. J., & Siegel, M. E. (2005). *Are you really listening?: Keys to successful communication.* Notre Dame, IN: Sorin Books.

Estes, W. K. (1989). Learning theory. In A. Lesgold & R. Glaser (Eds.), *Foundations for a psychology of education* (pp. 1–49). Hillsdale, NJ: Erlbaum.

Greenwald, G. (2011, Sept 8). Cheering for state-imposed death. *Salon.* Retrieved from http://www.salon.com/2011/09/08/death_17/

Halone, K. K. & Pecchioni, L. L. (2001). Relational listening: A grounded theoretical model. *Communication Reports, 14*(1), 59–71.

Harris, J. A. (2003). Learning to listen across cultural divides. *Listening Professional, 2*(1), 4–21.

International Listening Association. (1996). Retrieved from http://www.listen.org/

Janusik, L. A., & Wolvin, A. D. (2006). *24 hours in a day: A listening update to the time studies.* Paper presented at the meeting of the International Listening Association, Salem, OR.

Kiewitz, C., Weaver, J. B., Brosius, H. B., & Weimann, G. (1997). Cultural differences in listening style preferences. *International Journal of Public Opinion Research, 9*(3), 233–247.

Listening factoid. (2003). International Listening Association. Retrieved from http://www.listen.org/pages/factoids.html

Mutz, D., Reeves, B., & Wise, C. (2003, May 27). *Exposure to mediated political conflict: Effects of civility of interaction on arousal and memory.* Paper presented at the annual meeting of the International Communication Association, San Diego, CA. Retrieved from http://www.allacademic.com/meta/p111574_index.html

Omdahl, B. L. (1995). *Cognitive appraisal, emotion, and empathy.* Mahwah, NJ: Erlbaum.

O'Shaughnessey, B. (2003). Active attending or a theory of mental action. *Consciousness and the world* (pp. 379–407). Oxford, UK: Oxford University Press.

Salisbury, J. R. & Chen, G. M. (2007). An examination of the relationship between conversational sensitivity and listening styles. *Intercultural Communication Studies, 16*(1) 251–262.

Stiff, J. B., Dillard, J. P., Somera, L., Kim, H., & Sleight, C. (1988). Empathy, communication and prosocial behavior. *Communication Monographs, 55*(2), 198–213.

Watson, K. W., Barker, L. L., & Weaver, J. B., III (1995). The listening styles profile (LSP-16): Development and validation of an instrument to assess four listening styles. *International Journal of Listening, 9*(1), 1–13.

Weaver, J. B. III, & Kirtley, M. D. (1995). Listening styles and empathy. *The Southern Communication Journal, 60*(2): 131–140.

Wolvin, A. D., & Coakley, C. G. (1996). *Listening.* Dubuque, IA: Wm. C. Brown.

Chapter 7

Alsever, J. (2007, March 11). In the computer dating game, room for a coach. *New York Times.* Retrieved from http://www.nytimes.com/2007/03/11/business/yourmoney/11dating.html

Altman, I., & Taylor, D. (1973). *Social penetration: The development of interpersonal relationships.* New York, NY: Holt.

Aron, A., Aron, E. N., Tudor, M., & Nelson, G. (2004). Close relationships as including other in the self. In H. T. Reis & C. E. Rusbult (Eds.), *Close relationships* (pp. 365–379). New York, NY: Psychology Press.

Baxter, L. (1982). Strategies for ending relationships: Two studies. *Western Journal of Speech Communication, 46*(3), 223–241.

Baxter, L. A., & Montgomery, B. M. (1996). *Relating: Dialogues and dialectics.* New York, NY: Guilford.

Baxter, L. A., & West, L. (2003). Couple perceptions of their similarities and differences: A dialectical perspective. *Journal of Social and Personal Relationships, 20*(4), 491–514.

Baym, N. K. & Ledbetter, A. (2009). Tunes that bind? Predicting friendship strength in music-based social networks. *Information, Community, and Society, 12*(3) 408–427.

Berger, C. (1987). Communicating under uncertainty. In M. Roloff & G. Miller (Eds.), *Interpersonal processes: New directions in communication research* (pp. 39–62). Newbury Park, CA: Sage.

Boon, S. D. (1994). Dispelling doubt and uncertainty: Trust in romantic relationships. In S. Duck (Ed.), *Dynamics of relationships* (pp. 86–111). Thousand Oaks, CA: Sage.

Bowman, J. M. (2008). Gender role orientation and relational closeness: Self-disclosive behavior in same-sex male friendships. *Journal of Men's Studies, 16*(3), 316–330.

Brooks, M. (2011, February 14). How has Internet dating changed society? An insider's look. *Courtland Brooks.* Retrieved from http://internetdating.typepad.com/courtland_brooks/2011/02/how-has-internet-dating-changed-society.html

Bryner, J. (2011, November 4). You gotta have friends? Most have just 2 true pals. *Live Science.* Retrieved from http://vitals.msnbc.msn.com/_news/2011/11/04/8637894-you-gotta-have-friends-most-have-just-2-true-pals?lite

Buber, M. (1970). *I and thou* (W. Kaufman, Trans.). New York, NY: Scribner.

Burleson, B. R. (2003). Emotional support skills. In J. O. Green & B. R. Burleson (Eds.), *Handbook of communication and social interaction skills* (pp. 551–594). Mahwah, NJ: Erlbaum.

Burleson, B. R., & Goldsmith, D. J. (1998). How the comforting process works: Alleviating emotional distress through conversationally induced reappraisals. In P. A. Andersen & L. K. Guerrero (Eds.), *Handbook of communication and emotion: Research, theory, applications, and contexts* (pp. 248–280). San Diego, CA: Academic Press.

Clark, L.S. (1998). Dating on the net: Teens and the rise of "pure" relationships. In S. Jones (Ed.), *Cybersociety 2.0: Revisiting computer-mediated communication and community* (pp. 159–183). Thousand Oaks, CA: Sage.

Cupach, W. R., & Metts, S. (1986). Accounts of relational disclosure: A comparison of marital and non-marital relationships. *Communication Monographs, 53*(4), 319–321.

Dindia, K. (2000). Sex differences in self-disclosure, reciprocity of self-disclosure, and self-disclosure and liking: Three meta-analyses reviewed. In S. Petronio (Ed.), *Balancing disclosure, privacy, and secrecy.* Mahwah, NJ: Erlbaum.

Dindia, K. (2003). Definitions and perspectives on relational maintenance communication. In D. J. Canary and M. Dainton (Eds.), *Maintaining relationships through communication.* Mahwah, NJ: Erlbaum.

Dindia, K., & Timmerman, L. (2003). Accomplishing romantic relationships. In J. O. Greene & B. R. Burleson (Eds.), *Handbook of communication and social interaction* (pp. 685–722). Mahwah, NJ: Erlbaum.

Duck, S. (1982). A topography of relationship disengagement and dissolution. In S. Duck (Ed.), *Personal relationships 4: Dissolving personal relationships* (pp. 1–30). New York, NY: Academic Press.

Duck, S. (1999). *Relating to others*. Philadelphia, PA: Open University Press.

Duck, S. (2007). *Human relationships* (4th ed.). Thousand Oaks, CA: Sage.

Fiske, S. T., Gilbert, D. T., & Lindzey, G. (Eds.). (2010). *Handbook of social psychology* (5th ed.). Hoboken, NJ: John Wiley and Sons.

Gershon, I. (2010). *The Breakup 2.0: Disconnecting over new media*. Ithaca, NY: Cornell University Press.

Giddens, A. (1993). *The transformation of intimacy*. Palo Alto, CA: Stanford University Press.

Gilbert, E., Karahalois, K. & Sandvig, C. (2008). The network in the garden: An empirical analysis of social media in rural life. Paper presented at the Computer Human Interaction Conference. Florence, Italy. Retrieved from http://social.cs .uiuc.edu/papers/pdfs/chi08-rural-gilbert.pdf

Golder, S.A., Wilkinson, D., & Huberman, B.A. (2007). Rhythms of social interactions: Messaging within a massive online network. In C. Steinfield, B. Pentland, M. Ackerman, & N. Contractor (Eds.), *Proceedings of the third International Conference on Communities and Technologies* (pp. 41–66). London, UK: Springer.

Hatfield, E., & Rapson, R. L. (2006). Passionate love, sexual desire, and mate selection: Cross-cultural and historical perspectives. In P. Noller & J. A. Feeney (Eds.), *Close relationships: Functions, forms and processes* (pp. 227–243). Hove, UK: Psychology Press/Taylor & Francis.

Haythornthwaite, C. (2005). Strong, weak, and latent ties and the impact of new media. *Information Society, 8*(2) 385–401.

King, A. E., Austin-Oden, D., & Lohr, J. M. (2009). Browsing for love in all the wrong places: Does research show that Internet matchmaking is more successful than traditional dating? *Skeptic, 15*(1), 48–55. Retrieved from Infotrac.

Knapp, M. L., & Vangelisti, A. L. (2009). *Interpersonal communication and human relationships* (6th ed.). Upper Saddle River, NJ: Pearson.

Littlejohn, S. W., & Foss, K. A. (2011). *Theories of human communication* (10th ed.). Long Grove, IL: Waveland Press.

Luft, J. (1970). *Of human interaction*. Palo Alto, CA: National Press.

McKenna, K. Y. A., Green, A. S., & Gleason, M. E. J. (2002). Relationship formation on the Internet: What's the big attraction. *Journal of Social Issues, 58*(1) 9–31.

McPherson, M., Smith-Lovin, L., & Brashears, M. E. (2006). Social isolation in America: Changes in core discussion networks over two decades. *American Sociological Review, 71*(3): 353–375.

Mesch G. & Talmud, I. (2006). The quality of online and offline relationships. *The Information Society, 22*(3), 137–148.

Moore, D. W. (2003, January 3). Family, health most important aspects of life. *Gallup*. Retrieved from http://www.gallup.com/poll/7504/family-health -most-important-aspects-life.aspx

Morman, M. T., & Floyd, K. (1999). Affection communication between fathers and young adult sons: Individual and relational level correlates. *Communication Studies, 50*(4), 294–309.

Morman, M. T., & Floyd, K. (2002). A "changing culture of fatherhood:" Effects of affectionate communication, closeness, and satisfaction in men's relationships with their fathers and their sons. *Western Journal of Communication, 66*(4), 395–411.

Parks, M. R. (2007). *Personal relationships and personal networks*. Mahwah, NJ: Erlbaum.

Patterson, B. R., Bettini, L., & Nussbaum, J. F. (1993). The meaning of friendship across the life-span: Two studies. *Communication Quarterly, 41*(2), 145–160.

Peterson, C. (2006). *A primer in positive psychology*. New York, NY: Oxford.

Petronio, S. (2002). *Boundaries of privacy: Dialectics of disclosure*. Albany, NY: State University of New York Press.

Prager, K. J., & Buhrmester, D. (1998). Intimacy and need fulfillment in couple relationships. *Journal of Social and Personal Relationships, 15*(4), 435–469.

Rabby, M., & Walther, J. B. (2003). Computer mediated communication effects in relationship formation and maintenance. In D. J. Canary & M. Dainton (Eds.), *Maintaining relationships through communication* (pp. 141–162). Mahwah, NJ: Erlbaum.

Rainie, L., Lenhart, A., Fox, S., Spooner, T. & Horrigan, J. (2000). Tracking online life: How women use the Internet to cultivate relationships with family and friends. Pew Internet and American Life Project. Retrieved from www.pewinternet.org/Reports/2000 /Tracking-Online-Life.aspx

Rawlins, W. K. (1992). *Friendship matters: Communication, dialectics and the life course*. New York, NY: Aldine de Gruyter.

Rusbult, C. E., Olsen, N., Davis, J. L., & Hannon, P. A. (2004). Commitment and relationship maintenance mechanisms. In H. T. Reis & C. E. Rusbult (Eds.), *Key readings on close relationships* (pp. 287–304). Washington, DC: Taylor & Francis.

Sampter, W. (2003). Friendship interaction skills across the lifespan. In J. O. Greene & B. R. Burleson (Eds.), *Handbook of communication and social interaction skills* (pp. 637–684). Mahwah, NJ: Erlbaum.

Stafford, L., Dainton, M., & Haas, S. (2000). Measuring routine and strategic relational maintenance: Scale revision, sex versus gender roles, and the prediction of relational characteristics. *Communication Monographs, 67*(3), 306–323.

Swain, S. (1989). Covert intimacy in men's friendships: Closeness in men's friendships. In B. J. Risman & P. Schwartz (Eds.), *Gender in intimate relationships: A microstructural approach*. Belmont, CA: Wadsworth.

Taylor, D., & Altman, I. (1987). Communication in interpersonal relationships: Social penetration processes. In M. E. Roloff, & G. R. Miller (Eds.), *Interpersonal processes: New directions in communication research* (pp. 257–277). Newbury Park, CA: Sage.

Ting-Toomey, S. (2004). The matrix of face: An updated face-negotiation theory. In W. Gudykunst (Ed.), *Theorizing about intercultural communication* (pp. 71–92). Thousand Oaks, CA: Sage.

Triandis, H. C. (1994). *Culture and social behavior*. New York, NY: McGraw-Hill.

Walther, J. B. (1996). Computer-mediated communication: Impersonal, interpersonal, and hyperpersonal interaction. *Communication Research, 23*(1), 3–43.

Walther, J. B., & Parks, M. R. (2002). Cues filtered out, cues filtered in: Computer-mediated communication and relationships. In M. C. Knapp & J. A. Daly (Eds.), *Handbook of interpersonal communication* (3rd ed.; pp. 529–563). Thousand Oaks, CA: Sage.

Ward, C. C., & Tracy, T. J. G. (2004). Relation of shyness with aspects of online relationship involvement. *Journal of Social and Personal Relationships, 21*(5), 611–623.

Wood, J.T. (2000). *Relational communication: Continuity and change in personal relationships* (2nd ed.). Belmont, CA: Wadsworth.

Chapter 8

Alberti, R. E., & Emmons, M. L. (2008). *Your perfect right: Assertiveness and equality in your life and relationships* (9th ed.). Atascadero, CA: Impact Publishers.

Altman I. (1993). Dialectics, physical environments, and personal relationships. *Communication Monographs, 60*(1), 26–34.

Bilton. N. (2012, February 28). Apple loophole gives developers access to photos. *New York Times*. Retrieved from http://bits.blogs.nytimes .com/2012/02/28/tk-ios-gives-developers -access-to-photos-videos-location/

Brake, T., Walker, D. M., & Walker, T. (1995*). Doing business internationally: The guide to cross-cultural success*. New York, NY: Irwin.

Burleson, B. R. (2003). Emotional support skills. In J. O. Greene & B. R. Burleson (Eds.), *Handbook of communication and social interaction skills* (pp. 551–594). Mahwah, NJ: Erlbaum.

Cissna, K., & Seiberg, E. (1995). Patterns of interactional confirmation and disconfirmation. In M. V. Redmond (Ed.), *Interpersonal communication: Readings in theory and research*. Fort Worth, TX: Harcourt Brace.

Cupach, W. R., & Canary, D. J. (1997). *Competence in interpersonal conflict*. New York, NY: McGraw-Hill.

Dailey, R. M. (2006). Confirmation in parent-adolescent relationship and adolescent openness: Toward extending confirmation theory. *Communication Monographs, 73*(4), 434–458.

Dindia, K. (2000). Sex differences in self-disclosure, reciprocity of self-disclosure, and self-disclosure and liking: Three metaanalyses reviewed. In S. Petronio (Ed.), *Balancing the secrets of private disclosures* (pp. 21–36). Mahwah, NJ: Erlbaum.

Dindia, K., Fitzpatrick, M. A., & Kenny, D. A. (1997). Self-disclosure in spouse and stranger interaction: A social relations analysis. *Human Communication Research, 23*(3), 388–412.

Hample. D. (2003). Arguing skill. In J.O. Greene & B. R. Burleson (Eds.) *Handbook of communication and social interaction skills* (pp. 439–479). Mahwah, NJ: Lawrence Erlbaum.

Hendrick, S. S. (1981). Self-disclosure and marital satisfaction. *Journal of Personality and Social Psychology, 40*(6), 1150–1159.

Hess, N. H., & Hagen, E. H. (2006). Psychological adaptations for assessing gossip veracity. *Human Nature, 17*(3), 337–354.

Holt, J. L., & DeVore, C. J. (2005). Culture, gender, organizational role, and styles of conflict resolution: A meta-analysis. *International Journal of Intercultural Relations, 29*(2), 165–196.

Kleinman, S. (2007). *Displacing place: Mobile communication in the twenty-first century*. New York, NY: Peter Lang Publishing.

Margulis, S. T. (1977). Concepts of privacy: Current status and next steps. *Journal of Social Issues 33*(3), 5–21.

Petronio, S. (2002). *Boundaries of privacy: Dialectics of disclosure*. Albany, NY: State University of New York Press.

Rancer, A. S., & Avtgis, T. A. (2006). *Argumentative and aggressive communication: Theory, research, and application.* Thousand Oaks, CA: Sage.

Roloff, M.E., & Ifert, D.E. (2000). Conflict management through avoidance: Withholding complaints, suppressing arguments, and declaring topics taboo. In S. Petronio (Ed.), *Balancing the secrets of private disclosures* (pp. 151–163). Mahwah, NJ: LEA.

Samovar, L. A., Porter, R. E., & McDaniel, E. R. (Eds.). (2012). *Intercultural communication: A reader* (13th ed.). Belmont, CA: Cengage.

Thomas, K. W. (1976). Conflict and conflict management. In M. D. Dunnette (Ed.). *Handbook of industrial and organizational psychology* (pp. 889–935). Chicago, IL: Rand McNally.

Thomas, K. W. (1992). Conflict and conflict management: Reflections and update. *Journal of Organizational Behavior, 13*(3), 265–274.

Thomas, K. W., & Kilmann, R. H. (1978). Comparison of four instruments measuring conflict behavior. *Psychological Reports, 42,* 1139–1145.

Ting-Toomey, S. (2006). Managing intercultural conflicts effectively. In L. A. Samovar & R. E. Porter (Eds.), *Intercultural communication: A reader* (11th ed.; pp. 366–377). Belmont, CA: Wadsworth.

Ting-Toomey, S., & Chung, L. C. (2005). *Understanding intercultural communication.* Los Angeles, CA: Roxbury.

Ukashah, A., Arboleda-Flórez, J., & Sartorius, N. (2000). *Ethics, culture, and society: International perspectives.* Arlington, VA: American Psychiatric Publishing.

Warren, C. (2011, June 16). 10 people who lost jobs over social media mistakes. *Mashable.* Retrieved from http://mashable.com/2011/06/16/weinergate-social-media-job-loss/

Wilmot, W., & Hocker, J. L. (2010). *Interpersonal conflict* (8th ed.). New York, NY: McGraw-Hill.

Chapter 9

Anderson, J. (1988). Communication competency in the small group. In R. Cathcart & L. Samovar (Eds.), *Small group communication: A reader.* Dubuque, IA: Brown.

Andres, H. P. (2002) A comparison of face-to-face and virtual software development teams. *Team Performance Management: An International Journal, 8*(1/2), 39–48.

Balgopal, P. R., Ephross, P. H., & Vassil, T. V. (1986). Self-help groups and professional helpers. *Small Group Research, 17*(2), 123–137.

Becker-Beck, U., Wintermantel, M., & Borg, A. (2005). Principles regulating interaction in teams practicing face-to-face communication versus teams practicing computer-mediated communication. *Small Group Research, 36,* 499–536.

Bonito, J. (2000). The effect of contributing substantively on perceptions of participation. *Small Group Research, 31*(4), 528–553.

Bordia, P., DiFonzo, N., & Chang, A. (1999). Rumor as group problem-solving: Development patterns in informal computer-mediated groups. *Small Group Research, 30*(1), 8–28.

Eisenberg, J. (2007). Group cohesiveness. In R. F. Baumeister & K. D. Vohs (Eds.), *Encyclopaedia of social psychology* (pp. 386–388). Thousand Oaks, CA: Sage.

Evans, C., & Dion, K. (1991). Group cohesion and performance: A meta-analysis. *Small Group Research, 22*(2), 175–186.

Galvin, K. M., Byland, C. L., & Brommel, B. J. (2007). *Family communication: Cohesion and change* (7th ed.). Boston, MA: Allyn & Bacon.

Gregoire, C. (2012, June 7). The hunger blogs: A secret world of teenage "thinspiration." *Huffington Post.* Retrieved from http://www.huffingtonpost.com/2012/02/08/thinspiration-blogs_n_1264459.html

Henley, A. B., & Price, K. H. (2002). Want a better team? Foster a climate of fairness. *Academy of Management Executive, 16*(3), 153–154.

Henman, L. D. (2003). Groups as systems: A functional perspective. In R. Y. Hirokawa, R. S. Cathcart, L. A. Samovar, & L. D. Henman (Eds.), *Small group communication theory and practice: An anthology* (8th ed., pp. 3–7). Los Angeles, CA: Roxbury.

Huang, W. W., Wei, K.-K., Watson, R. T. & Tan, B. C. Y. (2003). Supporting virtual team-building with a GSS: An empirical investigation. *Decision Support Systems, 34*(4), 359–367.

Janis, I. L. (1982). *Groupthink: Psychological studies of policy decisions and fiascoes.* Boston, MA: Houghton Mifflin.

Jiang, L., Bazarova, N. N., & Hancock, J. T. (2011). The disclosure-intimacy link in computer-mediated communication: An attributional extension of the hyperpersonal model. *Human Communication Research, 37*(1), 58–77.

Johnson, D., & Johnson, F. (2003). *Joining together: Group theory and group skills* (8th ed.). Boston, MA: Allyn & Bacon.

Katz, N., & Koenig, G. (2001). Sports teams as a model for workplace teams: Lessons and liabilities. *Academy of Management Executive, 15*(3), 56–67.

Katzenbach, J. R., & Smith, D. K. (2003). *The wisdom of teams: Creating the high-performance organization.* New York, NY: Harper Business Essentials.

Koerner, A. F., & Fitzpatrick, M. A. (2002). Understanding family communication patterns and family functioning: The roles of conversation orientation and conformity orientation. In W. B. Gudykunst (Ed.), *Communication yearbook 26* (pp. 36–68). Mahwah, NJ: Erlbaum.

Kraus, G. (1997). The psychodynamics of constructive aggression in small groups. *Small Group Research, 28*(1), 122–145.

LaFasto, F. M., & Larson, C. E. (2001). *When teams work best: 6,000 team members and leaders tell what it takes to succeed.* Thousand Oaks, CA: Sage.

Li, J., & Hambrick, D. C. (2005). Factional groups: A new vantage on demographic faultlines, conflict, and disintegration in work teams. *Academy of Management Journal, 48*(5), 794–813.

Midura, D. W., & Glover, D. R. (2005). *Essentials of team-building.* Champaign, IL: Human Kinetics.

Nussbaum, M., Singer, M., Rosas, R., Castillo, M., Flies, E., Lara, R., & Sommers, R. (1999). Decisions support system for conflict diagnosis in personnel selection. *Information and Management, 36*(1), 55–62.

Olson, J., & Teasley, S. (1996) Groupware in the wild: Lessons learned from a year of virtual collocation. In *Proceedings of the ACM Conference* (pp. 419–427). Denver, CO: Association for Computing Machinery.

Pascoe, C. J. (2008, January 22). Interview in Growing up online [Television series episode].

In D. Fanning. (Executive producer) *Frontline.* Boston, MA: WGBH. Retrieved from http://www.pbs.org/wgbh/pages/frontline/kidsonline/interviews/pascoe.html

Renz, M. A., & Greg, J. B. (2000). *Effective small group communication in theory and practice.* Boston, MA: Allyn & Bacon.

Sell, J., Lovaglia, M. J., Mannix, E. A., Samuelson, C. D., & Wilson, R. K. (2004). Investigating conflict, power, and status within and among groups. *Small Group Research, 35*(1), 44–72.

Shaw, M. E. (1981). *Group dynamics: The psychology of small group behavior* (3rd ed.). New York, NY: McGraw-Hill.

Shimanoff, M. (1992). Group interaction and communication rules. In R. Cathcart & L. Samovar (Eds.), *Small group communication: A reader.* Dubuque, IA: William C. Brown.

Shoemaker-Galloway, J. (2007, August 6). Top 10 netiquette guidelines. *Suite 101.* Retrieved from http://jace-shoemaker-galloway.suite101.com/netiquette-guidelines-a26615#ixzz1HIIlhsZn

Sundstrom, E., DeMeuse, K. P., & Futrell, D. (1990, February). Work teams: Applications and effectiveness. *American Psychologist, 45*(2), 120–133.

Thompson, L. L. (2003). *The social psychology of organizational behavior: Key readings.* New York, NY: Taylor & Francis.

Timmerman, C. E., & Scott, C. R. (2006). Virtually working: Communicative and structural predictors of media use and key outcomes in virtual work teams. *Communication Monographs, 73*(1), 108–136.

Ting-Toomey, S., & Oetzel, J. (2003). Cross-cultural face concerns and conflict styles: Current status and future directions. In W. B. Gudykunst and W. B. Mody (Eds.). *Handbook of international and intercultural communication* (2nd ed.; pp. 143–163). Thousand Oaks, CA: Sage.

Tuckman, B. W. (1965). Developmental sequence in small groups. *Psychological Bulletin, 63*(6), 384–399.

Valacich, J. S., George, J. F., Nonamaker, J. F., Jr., & Vogel, D. R. (1994). Idea generation in computer based groups: A new ending to an old story. *Organizational Behavior and Human Decision Processes, 57*(3), 448–467.

Wang, Z., Walther, J. B., & Hancock, J. T. (2009). Social identification and interpersonal communication in computer mediated communication: What you do versus who you are in virtual groups. *Human Communication Research, 35*(1), 59–85.

Warkentin, M. E., Sayeed, L., & Hightower, R. (1997) Virtual teams versus face-to-face teams: An exploratory study of a Web-based conference system. *Decision Sciences 28*(4), 957–996.

Widmer, W. N., & Williams, J. M. (1991). Predicting cohesion in a coacting sport. *Small Group Research, 22*(4), 548–570.

Wilmot, W. W., & Hocker, J. L. (2007). *Interpersonal conflict.* New York, NY: McGraw-Hill.

Wilson, G. L. (2005). *Groups in context: Leadership and participation in small groups* (7th ed.). New York, NY: McGraw-Hill.

Chapter 10

Drummond, M. (2004). *Miracle meetings* [e-book]. Retrieved from http://www.superteams.com.

Duch, B. J., Groh, S. E., & Allen, D. E. (Eds.). (2001). *The power of problem-based learning.* Sterling, VA: Stylus.

Edens, K. M. (2000). Preparing problem solvers for the 21st century through problem-based learning. *College Teaching, 48*(2), 55–60.

Fairhurst, G. T. (2001). Dualism in leadership. In F. M. Jablin & L. M. Putnam (Eds.), *The new handbook of organizational communication* (pp. 379–439). Thousand Oaks, CA: Sage.

Frey, L., & Sunwulf. (2005). The communication perspective on group life. In S. A. Wheelen (Ed.)., *The handbook of group research and practice* (pp. 159–186). Thousand Oaks, CA: Sage.

Gardner, H. (2011). *Leading minds: An anatomy of leadership.* New York, NY: Basic Books.

Jensen, A. D., & Chilberg, J. C. (1991). *Small group communication: Theory and application.* Belmont, CA: Wadsworth.

Katzenbach, J. R., & Smith, D. K. (2003). *The wisdom of teams: Creating the high-performance organization.* New York, NY: Harper Collins.

Levin, B. B. (Ed.). (2001). *Energizing teacher education and professional development with problem-based learning.* Alexandria, MN: Association for Supervision and Curriculum Development.

Martin, R. A., Kuiper, N. A., Olinger, J. L., & Dance, K. A. (1993). Humor, coping with stress, self-concept, and psychological well-being. *International Journal of Humor Research, 6*(1), 89–104.

Newman, H. (2007). "World of Warcraft" players: Let's slay together. *Detroit Free Press.* Retrieved from InfoTrac.

Northouse, G. (2007). *Leadership theory and practice* (4th ed.). Thousand Oaks, CA: Sage.

O'Hair, D., O'Rourke, J., & O'Hair, M. (2001). *Business communication: A framework for success.* Cincinnati, OH: South-Western.

Rahim, M. A. (2001). *Managing conflict in organizations* (4th ed.). Westport, CT: Greenwood Press.

Seely Brown, J., & Hagel, J. (2009). How "World of War-craft" promotes innovation. *Businessweek Online.* Retrieved from Infotrac.

Snyder, B. (2004). Differing views cultivate better decisions. *Stanford Business.* Retrieved from http://www.gsb.stanford.edu/NEWS/bmag/sbsm0405/feature_workteams_gruenfeld.shtml

Teams that succeed (2004). *Harvard Business Review.* Boston, MA: Harvard Business School Press.

Tullar, W., & Kaiser, P. (2000). The effect of process training on process and outcomes in virtual groups. *Journal of Business Communication, 37*(4), 408–427.

Weiten, W., Dunn, D. S., & Hammer, E. Y. (2011). *Psychology applied to modern life: Adjustment in the 21st century.* Boston, MA: Cengage Learning.

Young, K. S., Wood, J. T., Phillips, G. M., & Pedersen, D. J. (2007). *Group discussion: A practical guide to participation and leadership* (4th ed.). Long Grove, IL: Waveland Press.

Chapter 11

Berger, C. R., & Calabrese, R. J. (1975). Some exploration in initial interaction and beyond: Toward a developmental theory of communication. *Human Communication Research, 1*(2), 99–112.

Bitzer, L. F. (1968). The rhetorical situation. *Philosophy and Rhetoric, 1*(1), 1–14.

Callison, D. (2001). Concept mapping. *School Library Media Activities Monthly, 17*(10) 30–32.

Cohen, N. (2011, May 23) Wikipedia. *The New York Times.* Retrieved from http://topics.nytimes.com/top/news/business/companies/wikipedia/index.html

Durst, G. M. (1989, March 1). The manager as a developer. *Vital Speeches of the Day* (pp. 309–314).

Frances, P. (1994). Lies, damned lies . . . *American Demographics, 16,* 2.

Helm, B. (2005, December 14). Wikipedia: "A work in progress." *Business Week.* Retrieved from http://www.businessweek.com/technology/content/dec2005/tc20051214_441708.htm?chan=db

Kirkpatrick, M. (2011, November 2). Wikipedia is a mess, wikipedians say: 1 in 20 articles bare of references. *ReadWriteWeb.* Retrieved from http://www.readwriteweb.com/archives/wikipedia_is_a_mess_wikipedians_say_1_in_20_articl.php

Manguard, S. (2011, October 31). The monster under the rug. *The Signpost.* Retrieved from http://en.wikipedia.org/wiki/Wikipedia:Wikipedia_Signpost/2011-10-31/Opinion_essay

Nelson J. C. (2006). *Leadership.* Utah School Boards Association 83rd Annual Conference, Salt LakeCity, Utah. Retrieved from http://www.ama-assn.org/ama/pub/category/15860.html

Chapter 12

Cossolotto, M. (2009, December). An urgent call to action for study abroad alumni to help reduce our global awareness deficit. *Vital Speeches,* pp. 564–568.

Fisher, W. (1987). *Human communication as narration: Toward a philosophy of reason, value, and action.* Columbia, SC: University of South Carolina Press.

Humes, J. C. (1988). *Standing ovation: How to be an effective speaker and communicator.* New York, NY: Harper and Row.

Jobs, S. (2005, June 15). You've got to find what you love. *Stanford University News.* Retrieved from http://news.stanford.edu/news/2005/june15/jobs-061505.html

Mackay, H. (July 2009). Changing the world: Your future is a work in progress. *Vital Speeches of the Day* (pp. 319–323).

Osteen, J. (2012). Best jokes of Joel Osteen. *Better Days TV.* Retrieved from http://www.betterdaystv.net/play.php?vid=247

Chapter 13

Ayers, J. (1991). Using visual aids to reduce speech anxiety. *Communication Research Reports, 8*(1), 73–79.

Booher, D. D. (2003). *Speak with confidence [electronic resources]: Powerful presentations that inform, inspire, and persuade.* New York, NY: McGraw-Hill.

Guzman, M. (2009, April 16). A Seattle geek fest spreads its wings. *Seattle PI.* Retrieved from http://www.seattlepi.com/business/405192_IGNITE16.html

Hanke, J. (1998). The psychology of presentation visuals. *Presentations, 12*(5), 42–47.

Ignite Seattle. (n.d.). Retrieved from http://www.igniteseattle.com/

Ignite Seattle 7 is happening on 8/3. (2009). *Ignite.* Retrieved from http://ignite.oreilly.com/2009/07/ignite-seattle-7-is-happening-on-83.html

Kolb, D. (1984). *Experiential learning: Experience as the source of learning and development.* Englewood Cliffs, NJ: Prentice Hall.

Long, K. (1997, August 12). *Visual aids and learning.* Retrieved from http://www.mech.port.ac.uk/av/AVALearn.htm

Tversky, B. (1997). Memory for pictures, maps, environments, and graphs. In D. G. Payne & F. G. Conrad (Eds.), *Intersections in basic and applied memory research* (pp. 257–277). Hillsdale, NJ: Erlbaum.

"What is Ignite?" (n.d.). Ignite. Retrieved from http://igniteshow.com/howto

Chapter 14

DuFrene, D. D., & Lehman, C. M. (2002). Persuasive appeal for clean language. *Business Communication Quarterly, 65*(1), 48–56.

Feldman, M. (2011, Sept 21). Report: Economists shut out of debt-ceiling debate. *Media Matters.* Retrieved from http://mediamatters.org/research/2011/09/21/report-economists-shut-out-of-debt-ceiling-deba/181620

Lanier, J. (2006). Digital Maoism: The hazards of the new online collectivism. *Edge The Third Culture.* Retrieved at: http://www.edge.org/3rd_culture/lanier06/lanier06_index.html

O'Connor, J. V. (2000). *FAQs #1.* Retrieved from http://www.cusscontrol.com/faqs.html

Rader, W. (2007). The online slang dictionary. Retrieved from http://www.ocf.berkeley.edu/~wrader/slang/b.html

Richards, I. A., & Ogden, C. K. (1923). *The meaning of meaning: A study of the influence of language upon thought and the science of symbolism.* Orlando, FL: Harcourt.

Saeid, J. I. (2003). *Semantics* (2nd ed.). Malden, MA: Blackwell Publishing Ltd.

Schertz, R. H. (1977, November 1). Deregulation: After the airlines, is trucking next? *Vital Speeches of the Day, 44*(2), p. 40.

Stewart, L. P., Cooper, P. J., Stewart, A. D., & Friedley, S. A. (2003). *Communication and gender* (3rd ed.). Boston, MA: Allyn & Bacon.

Treinen, K. P., & Warren, J. T. (2001). Anti-racist pedagogy in the basic course: Teaching cultural communication as if whiteness matters. *Basic Communication Course Annual 13,* 46–75.

Witt, P., Wheeless, L., & Allen, M. (2004). A meta-analytical review of the relationship between teacher immediacy and student learning. *Communication Monographs, 71*(2), 184–207.

Chapter 15

Ayres, J., & Hopf, T. S. (1990). The long-term effect of visualization in the classroom: A brief research report. *Communication Education, 39*(1), 75–78.

Ayres, J., Hopf, T. S., & Ayres, D. M. (1994). An examination of whether imaging ability enhances the effectiveness of an intervention designed to reduce speech anxiety. *Communication Education, 43*(3), 252–258.

Barron, J. (2011, August 26). With Hurricane Irene near, 370,000 in New York City get evacuation order. *New York Times.* Retrieved from http://www.nytimes.com/2011/08/27/nyregion/new-york-city-begins-evacuations-before-hurricane.html

Bates, B. (1992). *Communication and the sexes.* Prospect Heights, IL: Waveland Press.

Beatty, M. J., & Behnke, R. R. (1991). Effects of public speaking trait anxiety and intensity of speaking task on heart rate during performance. *Human Communication Research, 18*(2), 147–176.

Behnke, R. R., & Carlile, L. W. (1971). Heart rate as an index of speech anxiety. *Speech Monographs, 38*(1), 66.

Burgoon, J. K., Coker, D. A., & Coker, R. A. (1986). Communicative effects of gaze behavior: A test of two contrasting explanations. *Human Communication Research, 12*(4), 495–524.

Decker, B. (1992). *You've got to be believed to be heard.* New York, NY: St. Martin's Press.

Gardner, W. L. (2003). Perceptions of leader charisma, effectiveness, and integrity: Effects of exemplification, delivery, and ethical reputation. *Management Communication Quarterly, 16*(4), 502–527.

Hahner, J. C., Sokoloff, M. A., & Salisch, S. L. (2001). *Speaking clearly: Improving voice and diction* (6th ed.). New York, NY: McGraw-Hill.

Hammer, D. P. (2000). Professional attitudes and behaviors: The "A's" and "B's" of professionalism. *American Journal of Pharmaceutical Education, 64*(4), 455–464.

Kelly, L., Duran, R. L., & Stewart, J. (1990). Rhetoritherapy revisited: A test of its effectiveness as a treatment for communication problems. *Communication Education, 39*(3), 207–226.

Kelly, L., Phillips, G. M., & Keaten, J. A. (1995). *Teaching people to speak well: Training and remediation of communication reticence.* Cresskill, NJ: Hampton.

Levine, T., Asada, K. J. K., & Park, H. S. (2006). The lying chicken and the gaze avoidant egg: Eye contact, deception, and causal order. *Southern Communication Journal, 71*(4), 401–411.

Menzel, K. E., & Carrell, L. J. (1994). The relationship between preparation and performance in public speaking. *Communication Education, 43*(1), 17–26.

Morris, T. L., Gorham, J., Cohen, S. H., & Huffman, D. (1996). Fashion in the classroom: Effects of attire on student perceptions of instructors in college classes. *Communication Education, 45*(2), 135–148.

Motley, M. (1997). COM therapy. In J. A. Daly, J. C. McCroskey, J. Ayres, T. Hopf, & D. M. Ayres (Eds.) *Avoiding communication: Shyness reticence, and communication apprehension* (2nd ed.). Cresskill, NJ: Hampton Press.

Phillips, G. M. (1977). Rhetoritherapy versus the medical model: Dealing with reticence. *Communication Education, 26*(1), 34–43.

Richmond, V. P., & McCroskey, J. C. (2000). *Communication: Apprehension, avoidance, and effectiveness* (5th ed.). Scottsdale, AZ: Gorsuch Scarisbrick.

Scott, P. (1997, January–February). Mind of a champion. *Natural Health, 27,* 99.

Sellnow, D. D., & Treinen, K. P. (2004). The role of gender in perceived speaker competence: An analysis of student peer critiques. *Communication Education, 53*(3), 286–296.

Towler, A. J. (2003). Effects of charismatic influence training on attitudes, behavior, and performance. *Personnel Psychology, 56*(2), 363–381.

Chapter 16

Baerwald, D. (n.d.). Narrative. Retrieved from Northshore School District Web site: http://ccweb.nor-shore.wednet.edu/writingcorner/narrative.html.

Goldberg, B. (2011, March 14). No liberal bias at NPR—just ask NPR. [Blog post] Retrieved from http://www.bernardgoldberg.com/no-liberal-bias-at-npr-just-ask-npr/

Michalko, M. (1998). A theory about genius. *The World and I, 13*(7), 292.

Moyers, B., & Winship M. (2011, March 25). What the right means when it calls NPR "liberal." *Salon.* Retrieved from http://www.salon.com/2011/03/25/moyers_winship_npr/

Ötzi, the ice man. (n.d.). *Dig: The archaeology magazine for kids.* Retrieved from http://www.digonsite.com/drdig/mummy/22.html.

Pew Research Center for the People & The Press. (2011, September 22). Press widely criticized, but trusted more than other information sources. [Press Release] Retrieved from http://www.people-press.org/2011/09/22/press-widely-criticized-but-trusted-more-than-other-institutions/

Chapter 17

Carter, B. (2008, October 31). Infomercial for Obama is big success in ratings. *New York Times,* p. A19.

Hill, B., & Leeman, R. W. (1997). *The art and practice of argumentation and debate.* Mountain View, CA: Mayfield.

James, J. (2007, January). No time for complacency. *Vital Speeches of the Day, 73,* pp. 26–29.

Kennedy, G. A. (1999). *Classical rhetoric and its Christian and secular tradition from ancient to modern times* (2nd ed.) Chapel Hill, NC: University of North Carolina Press.

Megan's Law. (n.d.). *Parents for Megan's Law.* Retrieved from http://www.parentsformmeganslaw.com /html/questions.lasso

Nabi, R. L. (2002). Discrete emotions and persuasion. In James P. Dillard and Michael Pfau (Eds.), *The persuasion handbook: Developments in theory and practice.* (pp. 291–299). Thousand Oaks, CA: Sage.

Perloff, R. M. (2010). *The dynamics of persuasion: Communication and attitudes in the 21st century* (4th ed.). New York, NY: Taylor & Francis.

Petri, H. L., & Govern, J. M. (2012). *Motivation: Theory, research, and application* (6th ed.). Belmont, CA: Wadsworth.

Petty, R. E., & Cacioppo, J. (1996). *Attitudes and persuasion: Classic and contemporary approaches.* Boulder, CO: Westview.

Sellnow, D., & Treinen, K. (2004). The role of gender and physical attractiveness in perceived speaker competence: An analysis of student peer critiques. *Communication Education, 53*(3) 286–296.

Solmsen, F. (Ed). (1954). *The rhetoric and the poetics of Aristotle.* New York, NY: The Modern Library.

Timothy D. Naegele & Associates announces class action lawsuit against Guthy-Renker. (2002, June 26). *All Business.* Retrieved from http://www.allbusiness.com/crime-law/criminal-offenses-cybercrime/5968871-1.html

Toulmin, S. (1958). *The uses of argument.* Cambridge, UK: Cambridge University Press.

Appendix

Beshara, T. (2006). *The job search solution.* New York, NY: AMACOM.

Betty, K. (2010, July 1). The math behind the networking claim. Retrieved from http://blog.jobfully.com/2010/07/the-math-behind-the-networking-claim/

Boyd, A. (1999). *How to handle media interviews.* London, UK: Mercury.

Employee Tenure in 2010. (2012, September 14). Bureau of labor statistics economic news release. *U.S. Department of Labor,* Washington, DC. Retrieved from http://www.bls.gov/news.release/tenure.nr0.htm

Farr, J. M. (2009). *Top 100 careers without a four-year degree: Your complete guidebook to major jobs in many fields.* Indianapolis, IN: JIST.

Graber, S. (2000). *The everything get-a-job book: From résumé writing to interviewing to finding tons of job openings.* Avon, MA: Adams Media.

Kaplan, R. M. (2002). *How to say it in your job search: Choice words, phrases, sentences and paragraphs for résumés, cover letters and interviews.* Paramus, NJ: Prentice-Hall.

Krotz, J. (2006). *6 tips for taking control in media interviews.* Retrieved from http://www.microsoft.com/smallbusiness/resources/management/leadership-training/6-tips-for-taking-control-in-media-interviews.aspx

Light, J. (2011, April, 4). For job seekers, company sites beat online job boards, social media. *Wall Street Journal.* Retrieved from http://online.wsj.com/article/SB10001424052748703806304576236731318345282.html

Ryan, R. (2000). *60 seconds & you're hired.* New York, NY: Penguin Books.

Slayter, M. E. (2006, January 14). Rehearse, rehearse, repeat: Have a rock-solid plan when preparing for an interview. *The Forum,* p. E3.

Taylor, J., & Hardy D. (2004). *Monster careers: How to land the job of your life.* New York, NY: Penguin Books.

Tengler, C. D., & Jablin, F. M. (1983). Effects of question type, orientation, and sequencing in the employment screening interview. *Communication Monographs, 50*(3), 261.

Yena, D. J. (2011). *Career directions: The path to your ideal career.* New York, NY: McGraw-Hill.

Index

Key terms are **boldface.** *Italicized* page numbers indicate material in figures, graphs, or tables.

referral programs, employee, 294
referral services for locating jobs, 294
reflective thinking process paper, 146
reframing, 99
reframing the situation, 105
refutative pattern for organizing
    persuasive speeches, 276
rehearsing, 228–232
    initial, 230
relational dialects, 98–99
relationship(s), 94
    avoiding stage, 95
    beginning relationships: coming
        together, 92–93
    circumscribing stage, 95
    declining and dissolving relation-
        ships: coming apart, 95–96
    developing relationships: coming
        together, 93–95
    healthy, 85
    interpersonal, 85–103
    platonic, 88
    romantic, 88
    stages of, 92–97
    stagnating stage, 95
    terminating stage, 95, 96
    types of, 85–90
relationship cycle, technology and, 97
Relationship Filter Model, 93
relationship life cycle, 90
    disclosure in, 90–91
relationship maintenance, 94
relationship transformation, 96
relevance, 163, 206–207
    establishing, 182
relevance link, listener, *see* listener
    relevance link
relevant, 244
reliable sources, 162
relief, 274
religion, 5, 38
remembering, 78
    techniques to improve, 79
remote access report (RAR), 146
repetition, 79, 214, *247*
report,
    comprehensive, 144
    oral, 145
    progress, 139
    remote access, 146
research, 244, 245, 293, 295
    primary, 160, 163–164
    secondary, 160–163
research cards, 167
    sample, *167*
resources,
    for locating jobs, 293
    scarce, 112
respect, 13, 109, 110, 111, 124, 292
    for the speaker, 80, 81
responding, 80–82
response guidelines, 80
    critique, 81
    emotional support, 81
responses, supportive, 81
responsible, 13
responsive, 90, 272
responsiveness,
    empathic, 78
    sympathetic, 78

restructuring, cognitive, 219
résumé, 294–295
rewards, 43, 44
rhetoric, 264
rhetorical appeals to ethos, 271–272
rhetorical appeals to logos, 267–271
rhetorical appeals to pathos, 273–274
rhetorical figures of speech, 213
rhetorical question, 180, 208
rhetorical situation, 151–156
    figure, *152*
rhetorical structures of speech,
    213
Richards, I.A., 210
risk-benefit analysis, 105
ritualized touch, 65
rituals, 5, 38
role, 134
romantic relationship, 88
Romney, Mitt, 55, 76
Roosevelt, Franklin Delano, 226
Russia, 43
Ryan, Robin, 296

S

sacrifice, 94
sadness, 274
sample survey questions, *154*
saving face, 86
scaled questions, 153, *154*
Scandinavia, 41
scarce resources, perceived, 112
scarification, 69
Scotland, 50
script, 4, 12
scripted speech, 225
second language, speaking in a,
    209–210
second person, 249
secondary questions, 290
secondary research, 160–163
secret information, 92
secret pane in the Johari window, 92
section transition, 179
segmentation, topical, 99
selection and attention, 20
selective perception, 30
self-concept, 21–22, 24, 28, 88, 118
    deal, 22
self-created prophecies, 25
self-disclosure, 87, 90, 91, 99, 105
self esteem, 21, 22–23, 24, 28, 88,
    108, 118
self-fulfilling prophecy, 25
self-monitoring, 27
self-perception, 21, 25
    accuracy and distortion of, 24–26
    and communication, 26–28
    and culture, 23-26
    changing, 28
    independent, 24
    interdependent, 24
self-summary, 296
self-talk, 26
    negative, 26, 218, 219
    positive, 219
sell yourself, 296
semantic meaning, 52

semantic noise, 8
semantic triangle, *210*
semantics, 52–54
    improving, 53–54
sensationalism, 55
sensitivity, linguistic, 53, 54
sensory aids, other, 198–199
sensory language, 212–213
sequential order, 176
Serbia, 50
Serbian, 50
Serbian-Croatian, 50
service group, 120
sex, 38, 54
sexism, 30
sexual orientation, 38
Shakespeare, 183
shame, 273
shared leadership functions, 134
shared meaning, 7, 8
short-term/long-term orientation,
    43–44
short-term memory, 79
short-term oriented cultures, 43
signposts, 179, 206
silence, 50
similarity or difference, assumed, 44
simile, 213
simplicity, 20
Singapore, 42
single parent family, 118
sites, 107
situation, reframing the, 105
situational attribution, 28
situational communication apprehen-
    sion, 15
skill(s), 3, 14, 21, 74, 117
    culture-centered, 46
    knowledge, 15
skimming, 162
slang, 53, 211, 212
slices, 196
small-group communication, 6
smartphone, 5, 9, 39, *227*
social cognitive learning theory, 25
social construction of self, 27
social context, 5
social ease, 14, 15
social friendship group, 118–119
social media, 9, 29, 61, 96, 97, 106
    sites, 39
social networking, 107, 121
    online, *122*
    sites, 27, 97
social penetration theory, 90, 91
    model, *91*
social perception, 19
social presence, 29
    and mediated communication,
        29–30
social support groups online, 119
socioeconomic status (SES), 38
sociolinguistic meaning, 57
sociolinguistic understanding, improv-
    ing, 58
sociolinguistics, 52, 57–58
solution criteria, 142
    questions to guide, *142*
solutions, communicating group,
    144–146

sources, 160, 184
    accurate, 162
    citing, 167–*168*
    locating and evaluating information,
        164
    reliable, 162
    statistical, 161
    valid, 162
South America, 40, 65
space,
    acoustic, 68
    personal, 67, 207
    territorial, 67
Spanglish, 52
Spanish, 50
speaker,
    credibility, 208
    respect for, 80, 81
speaking,
    in a virtual world, guidelines for, 227
    informative, 243–262
    persuasive, 263–290
    rate, 76, 221
    vividly, 212–214
speaking appropriately, 206–210
speaking clearly, 210–212
speaking notes, 228
    preparing, 228–229
    sample, *229*
specific goal, 159, 186, 235, 256,
    279
specific language, 53, 211
speech, 26
    adapting while delivering, 231–232
    analysis, 284–288
        sample, 238
    body, 187, 235, 256, 280–283
    conclusion, 190, 237, 258, 283
    critique checklist, *233*
    critiques, effective and ineffective,
        82
    delivering through mediated tech-
        nology, 226–228
    developing the body, 172–180
    elevator, 294
    evaluating, 232–240
    evaluation response, guidelines, 82
    expository, 250–260
    extemporaneous, 226
    framework, *174*
    goal statement, writing a, 158–160
    goals, 152, 186, 235
        persuasive, 264–267
    impromptu, 225
    informative, 243
    introduction, 186, 235, 279–280,
        356
    organizing your, 171–192
    persuasive, 263
    political, 226
    process, 250
    purpose of, 155
    references, 190, 238, 258, 284
    scripted, 225
    thesis statement, 186
    time limits for classroom, 155
    timetable for preparing, *228*
    topics, identifying and selecting,
        156–158
    transition, 188, 189

PREP CARD 1

Communication Perspectives

Outline

> **Chapter at a Glance**
>
> The outline with page references gives you a quick snapshot of the content covered in the chapter.

Key Terms

> **Chapter Elements**
>
> This column contains a list of key terms with page references as well as chapter exhibits.

> **What's a Prep Card?**
>
> To help you prepare, we've developed a Prep Card for each chapter. Each card starts with a short list of key concepts covered in the chapter.

els; feedback; the communication process; channels for mediated communication; communication contexts and settings; communication principles; ethical implications; communication competence.

Learning Outcomes

1-1 Describe the nature of communication

1-2 Explain the communication process

1-3 Identify the characteristics of communication

1-4 Use the major tenets of ethical communication to create and evaluate messages

1-5 Create a plan to increase communication competence

Case Assignment: What Would You Do?

Use the following case assignment to further discuss ethical standards in communication. You might use this as a ~~~ ~~~ ~~~ ~~~ ~~~ide short answers, or you might use this to ~~~ ~~~ ~~~ ~~~ ~~~ on.

A Question of Ethics

> **Assignments**
>
> Every chapter will have an assortment of case and speech assignments and skill and communication-building exercises. These assignments will also be available through the instructor manual.

Molly has just been accepted at S~~~ ~~~ ~~~ ~~~rri to tell her the good news.

MOLLY: Hi Terri! Guess what? ~~~ ~~~ol!

TERRI: [*Surprised and disapp~~~* ~~~ ~~~te for class.

MOLLY: Oh, OK. See you.

[*The women hang up, and Terri immediately calls her friend Monica.*]

MONICA: Hey, Terri. What's up?

TERRI: I just got some terrible news—Molly got into Stanford!

MONICA: So, what's wrong with that? I think it's great. Aren't you happy for her?

TERRI: No, not at all. I didn't get in, and I have better grades and a higher LSAT score.

MONICA: Maybe Molly had a better application.

TERRI: Or maybe it was what was on her application.

MONICA: What do you mean?

TERRI: You know what I mean. Molly's black.

MONICA: You've got to be kidding me . . .

TERRI: Oh, please. You know it, and I know it. She only got in because of her race and because she's poor. Her GPA is really low and so is her LSAT.

MONICA: Did you ever stop to think that maybe she wrote an outstanding essay?

TERRI: Yes, but we've both read some of her papers, and we know she can't write. Listen, Monica, if you're black, Latino, or any other minority and poor, you've got it made. You can skate by and get into any law school you want. It's just not fair at all.

MONICA: [*Angrily*]: No, you know what isn't fair? My so-called friend insulting my intelligence and ethnic background. How dare you tell me that the only reason

Chapter Exhibits

I'll ever get into a good medical school is because I'm Latino. I'll get into med school just the same way that Molly got into law school—because of my brains, my accomplishments, and my ethical standards. And based on this conversation, it's clear that Molly and I are way ahead of you.

Describe how well each of these women followed the ethical standards for communication discussed in this chapter.

Adapted from "Racism," a case study posted on the Web site of the Ethics Connection, Markkula Center for Applied Ethics, Santa Clara University. http://www .scu.edu/ethics/practicing/focusareas/education/racism.html. Used with permission.

Experiential Assignment

Interpersonal Process Anal

Select an important interpersonal co[...]tly.
Analyze how the context, the interfe[...]on-
ship between you and the other p[...]. Be
specific and provide examples from t[...]

> **Experiential Assignments**
> Each chapter will also have a selection of shorter exercises for use in class or for students to do on their own. These assignments can also be found in the instructor manual.

What's New?

COMM2	COMM3	Section
	New section: The Nature of Communication	1-1
	New discussion of canned plans and scripts	1-1a
Section: Communication Settings	Incorporated Communications Settings section into Communication Contexts section	1-1b
LO1 The Communication Process	The Communication Process	1-2
	New focus on message production, message interpretation, and interaction coordination	1-2a
Physical interference and psychological interference	Focus on external, internal, and semantic noise	1-2c
Dot Dot Dot Dash Dash Dash (Box)	Modern Mourning (Box)	1-2d
	Mediated Communication	1-2e
LO2 Communication Principles	1-3a Communication Has Purpose	1-3a
	New section: Communication Is Irreversible	1-3c
	New section: Communication Is Situated	1-3d
Communication is Relational	Communication Is Indexical	1-3e
	Moved section Communication Is Learned	1-3f
Communication has Ethical Implications	Expanded section on Ethics	1-4
	New section: Dark Side Messages	1-4b
LO3 Increasing Competence in Communication	Increasing Your Communication Competence	1-5
Develop Goals to Improve Communication Skills	Communication Improvement Plans	1-5c
Quick Quiz (on SE Card)	Quick Quiz	End of Chapter

Outline

Key Terms

communication 4

messages 4

encoding 4

decoding 4

feedback 4

canned plan 4

script 4

In this chapter:

Communication; messages; channels; feedback; the communication process; channels for mediated communication; communication contexts and settings; communication principles; ethical implications; communication competence.

Learning Outcomes

1-1 Describe the nature of communication

1-2 Explain the communication process

1-3 Identify the characteristics of communication

1-4 Use the major tenets of ethical communication to create and evaluate messages

1-5 Create a plan to increase communication competence

Case Assignment: What Would You Do?

Use the following case assignment to further discuss ethical standards in communication. You might use this as a handout, for which students can provide short answers, or you might use this to create an opportunity for class discussion.

A Question of Ethics

Molly has just been accepted at Stanford University and calls her friend Terri to tell her the good news.

MOLLY: Hi Terri! Guess what? I just got accepted to Stanford Law School!

TERRI: [*Surprised and disappointed*]: Oh, cool. Hey, I have to go—I'm late for class.

MOLLY: Oh, OK. See you.

[*The women hang up, and Terri immediately calls her friend Monica.*]

MONICA: Hey, Terri. What's up?

TERRI: I just got some terrible news—Molly got into Stanford!

MONICA: So, what's wrong with that? I think it's great. Aren't you happy for her?

TERRI: No, not at all. I didn't get in, and I have better grades and a higher LSAT score.

MONICA: Maybe Molly had a better application.

TERRI: Or maybe it was what was on her application.

MONICA: What do you mean?

TERRI: You know what I mean. Molly's black.

MONICA: You've got to be kidding me . . .

TERRI: Oh, please. You know it, and I know it. She only got in because of her race and because she's poor. Her GPA is really low and so is her LSAT.

MONICA: Did you ever stop to think that maybe she wrote an outstanding essay?

TERRI: Yes, but we've both read some of her papers, and we know she can't write. Listen, Monica, if you're black, Latino, or any other minority and poor, you've got it made. You can skate by and get into any law school you want. It's just not fair at all.

MONICA: [*Angrily*]: No, you know what isn't fair? My so-called friend insulting my intelligence and ethnic background. How dare you tell me that the only reason

Chapter Exhibits

I'll ever get into a good medical school is because I'm Latino. I'll get into med school just the same way that Molly got into law school—because of my brains, my accomplishments, and my ethical standards. And based on this conversation, it's clear that Molly and I are way ahead of you.

Describe how well each of these women followed the ethical standards for communication discussed in this chapter.

Adapted from "Racism," a case study posted on the Web site of the Ethics Connection, Markkula Center for Applied Ethics, Santa Clara University. http://www.scu.edu/ethics/practicing/focusareas/education/racism.html. Used with permission.

Experiential Assignment

Interpersonal Process Analysis

Select an important interpersonal conversation that you have experienced recently. Analyze how the context, the interference, the people involved, and the relationship between you and the other participants affected the communication. Be specific and provide examples from the conversation.

What's New?

COMM2	COMM3	Section
	New section: The Nature of Communication	1-1
	New discussion of canned plans and scripts	1-1a
Section: Communication Settings	Incorporated Communications Settings section into Communication Contexts section	1-1b
LO1 The Communication Process	The Communication Process	1-2
	New focus on message production, message interpretation, and interaction coordination	1-2a
Physical interference and psychological interference	Focus on external, internal, and semantic noise	1-2c
Dot Dot Dot Dash Dash Dash (Box)	Modern Mourning (Box)	1-2d
	Mediated Communication	1-2e
LO2 Communication Principles	1-3a Communication Has Purpose	1-3a
	New section: Communication Is Irreversible	1-3c
	New section: Communication Is Situated	1-3d
Communication is Relational	Communication Is Indexical	1-3e
	Moved section Communication Is Learned	1-3f
Communication has Ethical Implications	Expanded section on Ethics	1-4
	New section: Dark Side Messages	1-4b
LO3 Increasing Competence in Communication	Increasing Your Communication Competence	1-5
Develop Goals to Improve Communication Skills	Communication Improvement Plans	1-5c
Quick Quiz (on SE Card)	Quick Quiz	End of Chapter

PREP CARD 2

Perception of Self and Others

Outline

Key Terms

In this chapter:

Perception; self-concept; self-esteem; perception of others; stereotyping; prejudice; discrimination; context; perception checking.

Learning Outcomes

2-1 Understand how the perception process works
2-2 Explain how self-perception is formed and maintained
2-3 Discuss how others can impact self-perception
2-4 Understand how self-perception affects communication
2-5 Discuss the ways we form perceptions of others
2-6 Know how to increase the accuracy of perceptions

Case Assignment: What Would You Do?

Use the following case assignment to further discuss social perceptions and diversity. You might use this as a handout, for which students can provide short answers, or you might use this to create an opportunity for class discussion.

A Question of Ethics

UniConCo, a multinational construction company, successfully bid to build a new minor league baseball stadium in a Midwestern city with very little ethnic diversity. Miguel Hernandez was assigned to be the assistant project manager, and he moved his family of seven to town. He quickly joined the local Chamber of Commerce, affiliated with the local Rotary group, and was feeling the first signs of acceptance in the community. One day, Mr. Hernandez was working at his desk when he accidentally overheard a group of local Anglo construction workers talking about Mexican Immigration. Mr. Hernandez was discouraged to hear the negative stereotypes that were being used. The degree of hatred expressed was clearly beyond what he was used to, and he was further upset when he recognized several of the voices as belonging to men he had fought to hire despite UniConCo's typical "in-network" hiring practices.

Mr. Hernandez was a bit shaken. He recognized his workers' prejudices, but he wasn't sure how to change them. Moreover, though he wanted to establish good work relationships with his Anglo workers for the sake of the company, he also wanted to create a good working atmosphere for the other Latino workers he was working to move to the area to work on the project. What could Mr. Hernandez do?

Devise a plan for Mr. Hernandez. How could he use his social perceptions to address the problem in a way that is within ethical, interpersonal communication guidelines?

Experiential Assignment

Who Am I?

This activity will help you assess how your self-concept aligns with how other people see you.

Chapter Exhibits

Figure 2.1
Expectations and Perception here

First, ask *How do I see myself?* List the skills, abilities, knowledge, competencies, and personality characteristics that describe how you see yourself. To generate this list, try completing these sentences: "I am skilled at . . . ," "I have the ability to . . . ," "I know things about . . . ," "I am competent at doing . . . ," and "One part of my personality is that I am . . . ." List as many characteristics in each category as you can think of. What you have developed is an inventory of your self-concept.

Second, ask *How do others see me?* List the skills, abilities, and so on that describe how you think others see you by completing sentences such as: "Other people believe I am skilled at . . . ," "Other people believe I am competent at doing . . . ," and "One part of my personality is that other people believe I am . . . ."

Compare your two lists. How are they similar? Where are they different? Do you understand why they differ? After you have thought about each, write a paragraph titled "Who I Am, and How I Know This."

What's New?

COMM2	COMM3	Section
	New Figure: 2.1 Expectations and Perception	2-1a
Organization of Stimuli	Organization	2-1b
Interpretation of Stimuli	Interpretation	2-1c
	New section: Dual Processing	2-1d
Perceptions of Self: Self-Concept and Self-Esteem	Perception of Self	2-2
Personal Experiences Reactions and Responses of Others	Combined to one section: Self-Concept	2-2a
Developing and Maintaining Self-Esteem	Self-Esteem	2-2b
The Influence of Gender and Culture on Self-Perceptions	Culture and Self-Perceptions	2-3
The Effects of Self-Perceptions on Communication Presenting Self to Others	Combined under Self-Perception and Communication	2-4
Observing Others	Forming Impressions	2-5a
Emotional State	Making Attributions	2-5a
Using Stereotypes	Inaccurate and Distorted Perceptions of Others	2-5c
Improving the Accuracy of Social Perceptions	Improving Our Perceptions of Others	2-6
	Added step 2	2-6
Quick Quiz (on SE Card)	Quick Quiz	End of Chapter

PREP CARD 3

Intercultural Communication

Outline

Key Terms

In this chapter:

Intercultural communication; dominant and co-cultures; elements of cultural identity; barriers to communication; the role of attitudes, knowledge, and skills in intercultural communication competence.

Learning Outcomes

3-1 Define culture and the role of communication in it

3-2 Explain the relationship between dominant and co-cultures

3-3 Understand the seven dimensions in which cultures differ

3-4 Describe the inherent barriers in intercultural communication and the methods to develop competent intercultural communication

Case Assignment: What Would You Do?

Use the following case assignment to further discuss ethical standards in communication. You might use this as a handout, for which students can provide short answers, or you might use this to create an opportunity for class discussion.

A Question of Ethics

Tyler, Jeannie, Margeaux, and Madhukar were sitting around Margeaux's dining room table working on a group marketing project. It was 2:00 a.m. They had been working since 6:00 p.m. and still had several hours of work remaining.

"Oh, the agony," groaned Tyler, "If I never see another photo of a veggie burger it will be too soon. Why didn't we choose a more 'appetizing' product?"

"I think it had something to do with someone wanting to promote a healthy alternative to greasy hamburgers," Jeannie replied sarcastically.

"Right," Tyler answered. "I don't know what I could have been thinking. Speaking of greasy food, anyone up for ordering a pizza?"

"Sorry, but no one will deliver up here so late," Margeaux apologized. "But I have a quiche that I could heat up."

"Sure, sounds great," Jeannie said. "I'm hungry too."

"It doesn't have any meat in it, does it?" asked Madhukar. "I don't eat meat."

"Nope, it's a cheese and spinach quiche," Margeaux answered.

Tyler and Margeaux went off to the kitchen. Tyler took the quiche, which was still in its box, from the refrigerator. "Uh-oh," he said. "Madhukar is a vegetarian, and he won't buy this brand because it has lard in the crust."

"Shhh!" said Margeaux. "I don't have anything else to offer him, and he'll never know the difference anyway. Just pretend you didn't notice."

1. What ethical principles are involved in this case?
2. What exactly are Margeaux's ethical obligations to Madhukar in this situation?
3. What should Tyler do now?

Experiential Assignments

Acquiring Accurate Cultural Knowledge

For the next week, conduct research into a distinct culture with which you have little or no familiarity. Whatever culture you choose to study, be sure you can access it locally. First, arrange to observe members of the culture engaged in a typical activity, and note as many of their individual communication behaviors as you can. Take your notes respectfully, being careful not to offend those you observe. Next, spend some time formally researching the culture and its communication behaviors at a library or over the Internet, consulting only reputable sources for your information. Finally, observe members of the culture once more and then write a paragraph in which you answer these questions: What were your impressions of the culture's communication behaviors the first time you observed its members? How were these first impressions altered, if at all, by your formal research into the culture? How did your formal research affect your second observation of the culture?

Race and Ethnicity

What is the difference between race and ethnicity? Can you think of examples of people who are ethnically different but racially the same or racially different but ethnically the same? Can you think of anyone for whom both designations might be identical or for whom the two designations might be contradictory? What does this analysis suggest about the accuracy and legitimacy of such classification systems?

What's New?

COMM2	COMM3	Section
Chapter 6 Communicating Across Cultures	Chapter 3 Intercultural Communication	
Dominant Cultures and Co-Cultures	Dominant Cultures, Co-Cultures, and Cultural Identity	3-2
Social Class	Socioeconomic Status (SES)	3-2f
Age	Age/Generation	3-2g
	New section: Disability	3-2h
Identifying Cultural Norms and Values	How Cultures Differ	3-3
	New section: Context	3-3b
	New section: Chronemics	3-3c
	New section: Long-Term/Short-Term Orientation	3-3g
Barriers to Effective Intercultural Communication	Developing Intercultural Communication Competence	3-4
Level 2 heads in Barriers to Effective Intercultural Communication	Level 3 heads under Potential Barriers	3-4a
Stereotyping a prejudice	Stereotyping	3-4a
Intercultural Communication Competence	Competent Communication Strategies	3-4b
Quick Quiz (on SE Card)	Quick Quiz	End of Chapter

PREP CARD 4

Verbal Messages

Outline

Key Terms

In this chapter:

Language; dialect; idiolect; language communities; semantics; pragmatics; socio-linguistic characteristics of language and how to use them to communicate effectively.

Learning Outcomes

4-1 Define a language, a dialect, and an idiolect

4-2 List the characteristics of language

4-3 Explain how conversational, social, and cultural contexts shape meaning and know-how to shape messages that accurately convey your meaning

Case Assignment:
What Would You Do?

Use the following case assignment to get your students to consider how different nonverbal behaviors convey different messages. You might use this as a handout, for which students can provide short answers, or you might use this to create an opportunity for class discussion.

A Question of Ethics

As Abbie was adding sweetener to her latte, she spied her friends Ethan and Nate sitting at a table in a corner of the coffee shop.

"Hi guys. What are you doing?" Abbie asked.

"Not much. How about you?"

"I'm just heading over to my philosophy class," Abbie replied. "But, I've got to say I don't know why I even bother going."

"Why not? What's up?" asked Nate.

"Well," responded Abbie, "Professor Miller is so mean. The other day, I offered my opinion and she told me I was wrong. Can you believe it? I mean, she could have praised me for offering my opinion. What makes her opinion so 'right' any-way? She is so narrow-minded and *obviously* doesn't care about her students."

Ethan asked, "Well, were you?"

"Was I what?" Abbie asked.

"Wrong."

"Well, I guess so. But that's not the point," Abbie contested.

"Actually, I think it *is*," Ethan replied. "Maybe she said you were wrong because she *does* care about her students and wants you to learn. Maybe she sets high standards and wants to help you achieve them."

"Whatever. That's *your* opinion. I bet you'd feel differently if she embarrassed *you* in front of the other students," Abbie retorted.

"Maybe you should go talk to her about it during her office hours," suggested Nate. "She probably doesn't even realize she embarrassed you."

"Oh, she knows," replied Abbie. "And there is *no way* am I going to talk to her about it. I'm just going to get through the semester and then tell her *exactly* what I think on the end-of-semester evaluations. See you later!"

1. What ethical principles, if any, are at issue in this case?
2. What do you think about the issues Abbie raises? Explain.
3. Based on what you have learned about language in this chapter, what could you say to Abbie that might help her?

Experiential Assignments

Impromptu Speech Activity

Draw a slip of paper from a container provided by your instructor. On it, you will find the name of a superhero, cartoon character, or comic strip character. Prepare and deliver a 2–3 minute impromptu speech making a case for him or her as either a positive or negative example of effective verbal communication. Be sure to draw on the principles offered in this chapter to make your case.

Evaluating Language

Pick an article from a favorite magazine. Read through it, highlighting instances in which the writer uses specific language, concrete language, and familiar language, and identify passages in which the writer might improve in each area. Then look for examples of the writer's linguistic sensitivity and find places where the writer might have done a better job. Write a 400–500-word essay identifying strengths and suggestions for improvement based on your assessment.

What's New?

COMM2	COMM3	Section
Chapter 3 Communicating Verbally	Chapter 4 Verbal Messages	
The Nature and Purposes of Language	The Nature of Language	4-1
Culture and Gender Influences on Language Use	What Is a Language?	4-1a
The Nature and Purposes of Language	Characteristics of Language	4-2
	New section: Language Is Arbitrary	4-2a
	New section: Language Is Abstract	4-2b
	New section: Language Changes over Time	4-2c
Improving Language Skills	The Relationship between Language and Meaning	4-3
Making Your Messages Meaningful	New section: Semantics	4-3a
Linguistic Sensitivity	Guidelines for Improving Semantics	4-3a
	New section: Pragmatics	4-3b
	New section: Sociolinguistics	4-3c
Quick Quiz (on SE Card)	Quick Quiz	End of Chapter

Outline

Key Terms

In this chapter:

Characteristics of nonverbal communication; nonverbal communication behaviors; vocalics; kinesics; proxemics; chronemics; self-presentation; interpreting nonverbal messages; sending nonverbal messages.

Learning Outcomes

5-1 Identify characteristics of nonverbal communication

5-2 Identify the different types of nonverbal communication

5-3 Understand guidelines for improving nonverbal communication

Case Assignment: What Would You Do?

Use the following case assignment to get your students to consider how different nonverbal behaviors convey different messages. You might use this as a handout, for which students can provide short answers, or you might use this to create an opportunity for class discussion.

A Question of Ethics

After the intramural, mixed-doubles tennis matches on Tuesday evening, most of the players adjourned to the campus grill for a drink and a chat. Marquez and Lisa sat down with Barry and Elana, the couple they had lost a match to that night—largely because of Elana's improved play. Although Marquez and Lisa were only tennis friends, Barry and Elana had been dating for much of the season.

After some general conversation about the tournament, Marquez said, "Elana, your serve today was the best I've seen it this year."

"Yeah, I was really impressed. And as you saw, I had trouble handling it," Lisa added.

"And you're getting to the net a lot better, too," Marquez added.

"Thanks, guys," Elana said in a tone of gratitude.

"Well, aren't we getting the compliments today," sneered Barry in a sarcastic tone. Then after a pause, he said, "Oh, Elana, would you get my sweater—I left it on that chair by the other table."

"Come on, Barry; you're closer than I am," Elana replied.

Barry got a cold look on his face, moved slightly closer to Elana, and said emphatically, "Get my sweater for me, Elana—now."

Elana quickly backed away from Barry as she said, "OK, Barry—it's cool," and she then quickly got the sweater for him.

"Gee, isn't she sweet," Barry said to Marquez and Lisa as he grabbed the sweater from Elana.

Lisa and Marquez both looked down at the floor. Then Lisa glanced at Marquez and said, "Well, I'm out of here—I've got a lot to do this evening."

"Let me walk you to your car," Marquez said as he stood up.

"See you next week," they both said in unison as they hurried out the door, leaving Barry and Elana alone at the table.

1. Analyze Barry's nonverbal behavior. What was he attempting to achieve?
2. How do you interpret Lisa's and Marquez's nonverbal reactions to Barry?
3. Was Barry's behavior ethically acceptable? Explain.

Chapter Exhibit

Figure 5.1
Personal Space

Experiential Assignments

Body Motions (Handout)

Go to a public place (for example, a restaurant) where you can observe two people having a conversation. You should be close enough so that you can observe their eye contact, facial expressions, and gestures, but not close enough to hear what they are saying.

Carefully observe the interaction, with the goal of answering the following questions: What is their relationship? What seems to be the nature of the conversation (social chitchat, plan making, problem solving, argument, intimate discussion)? How does each person feel about the conversation? Do feelings change over the course of the conversation? Is one person more dominant? Take note of the specific nonverbal behaviors that led you to each conclusion, and write a paragraph describing this experience and what you have learned.

Vocal Characteristics (Handout)

Spend a few hours listening to talk radio. If possible, listen to a station that broadcasts in a language with which you are unfamiliar. Attempt to block out your awareness of the speakers' words and instead focus on the meaning communicated by the pitch, volume, rate, and quality of their speech. Be sure to listen to a number of different speakers and record your results in a log. Can you detect any variations in the vocal characteristics of the different speakers? If so, what do you make of these variations and what they say about each speaker's message?

Violating Intimate Space Norms (Handout)

Enter a crowded elevator. Get on it and face the back. Make direct eye contact with the person you are standing in front of. Afterwards, record the person's reactions. Take a second ride and introduce yourself to the person who is standing next to you. Engage in an animated conversation with him or her. Record the reaction of the person and others around you. Finally, get on an empty elevator and stand in the exact center. Do not move when others board. Record their reactions. Be prepared to share what you have observed with your classmates.

What's New?

COMM2	COMM3	Section
Chapter 4 Communicating through Nonverbal Behaviors	Chapter 5 Nonverbal Messages	
	Additional information on cultural differences between facial expressions	5-2a
	Added section on the three types of touch	5-2a
Use of Voice: Vocalics	Use of Voice: Paralanguage	5-2b
Physical Space	Territorial Space Acoustic Space	5-2c
Chronemics	Moved most of this section to Chapter 3	5-2d
Self-Presentation Cues	Physical Appearance	5-2e
Quick Quiz (on SE Card)	Quick Quiz	End of Chapter

PREP CARD 6

Listening

Key Terms

listening 73
listening style 74
content-oriented listeners 74
people-oriented listeners 74
action-oriented listeners 74
time-oriented listeners 74
listening apprehension 75
passive listening 75
active listening 75
attending 75
understanding 77
question 77
paraphrasing 77
content paraphrase 77
feelings paraphrase 78
empathy 78
empathic responsiveness 78
perspective taking 78
sympathetic responsiveness 78
remembering 78
repetition 79
mnemonic device 79
evaluating 79
facts 79
inferences 79

In this chapter:

Listening; content-oriented; people-oriented; action-oriented; time-oriented; listening apprehension; passive listening; active listening; attending; understanding; remembering; evaluating; responding to the message.

Learning Outcomes

6-1 Define listening
6-2 Identify the three challenges of listening
6-3 List the steps involved in active listening

Case Assignment: What Would You Do?

Use the following case assignment to further discuss listening and attending in conversations. You might use this as a handout, for which students can provide short answers, or you might use this to create an opportunity for class discussion.

A Question of Ethics

Janeen always disliked talking on the telephone—she thought it was an impersonal form of communication. Thus, college was a wonderful respite. When friends called her, instead of staying on the phone she could quickly run over to their dorm or meet them at a coffeehouse.

One day during a reading period before exams, Janeen received a phone call from Barbara, an out-of-town friend. Before she was able to dismiss the call with her stock excuses, she found herself bombarded with information about old high school friends and their whereabouts. Not wanting to disappoint Barbara, who seemed eager to talk, Janeen tucked her phone under her chin and began straightening her room, answering Barbara with the occasional "uh-huh," "hmm," or "wow, that's cool!" As the "conversation" progressed, Janeen began reading through her mail and then her notes from class. After a few minutes, she realized there was silence on the other end of the line. Suddenly very ashamed, she said, "I'm sorry, what did you say? The phone . . . uh, there was just a lot of static."

Barbara replied, with obvious hurt in her voice, "I'm sorry I bothered you, you must be terribly busy."

Embarrassed, Janeen muttered, "I'm just really stressed, you know, with exams coming up and everything. I guess I wasn't listening very well—you didn't seem to be saying anything really important. I'm sorry. What were you saying?"

"Nothing 'important,'" Barbara answered. "I was just trying to figure out a way to tell you. I know that you were friends with my brother Billy and, you see, we just found out yesterday that he's terminal with a rare form of leukemia. But you're right—it obviously isn't really important." With that, Barbara hung up.

1. How ethical was Janeen's means of dealing with her dilemma of not wanting to talk on the phone but not wanting to hurt Barbara's feelings?
2. Identify ways in which both Janeen and Barbara could have used better and perhaps more ethical interpersonal communication skills. Rewrite the scenario incorporating these changes.

Chapter Exhibits

Experiential Assignments

Critically Analyzing the Use of Facts and Inferences in the Media (Handout)

Watch a political talk show and an infomercial on television. If possible, record the two programs so you can watch them more than once. While you are watching, note as many individual factual statements and inferences in each program as you can. Next, write a paragraph in which you answer these questions: What was the ratio of factual statements to inferences in the two programs? Did these results surprise you? If so, how? Were the ratios different for the two programs? If so, how did the results conform to or deviate from your expectations? How did evaluating the inferences used in the two programs change your perception of their messages?

Creating Mnemonics

Mnemonics are useful memory aids. Construct a mnemonic for the five phases of the listening process: attending, understanding, remembering, evaluating, and responding. Record your mnemonic.

Tomorrow, while you are getting dressed, see whether you can recall all of the mnemonic you have created. Then see whether you can recall the phases of the listening process from the cues in your mnemonic. Write a brief paragraph describing your experience.

What's New?

COMM2	COMM3	Section
Chapter 5 Listening and Responding	Chapter 6 Listening	
Types of Listening	Challenges to Effective Listening	6-2
Appreciative Listening	Listening Style	6-2a
Discriminative Listening	Listening Apprehension	6-2b
Comprehensive Listening	Processing Approach	6-2c
Steps of the Listening Process	Active Listening	6-3
Resist Interrupting Others	Make the shift fully from speaker to listener	6-3a
	Presidential Debates, Freedom of Speech, and Democratic Discourse (Box)	6-3a
	Identify the main point	6-3b
	Separate suggestions for evaluating into numbered list; added information on probing for information	6-3c
	New section on general response guidelines	6-3e
	New section on public speech evaluation guidelines	6-3e
Quick Quiz (on SE Card)	Quick Quiz	End of Chapter

Outline

Key Terms

In this chapter:

Healthy relationships; acquaintances; friends; intimates; disclosure; feedback; the Johari window; stages of relationships; dialectics in relationships.

Learning Outcomes

7-1 Identify the major types of relationships
7-2 Explain how disclosure and feedback affect relationships
7-3 Examine levels of communication at various stages in relationships
7-4 Identify the sources of tension in relationships

Case Assignment: What Would You Do?

Use the following case assignment to further discuss interpersonal relationships. You might use this as a handout, for which students can provide short answers, or you might use this to create an opportunity for class discussion.

A Question of Ethics

Jeff and Magda, seniors at a small rural college, had been dating each other since they were freshmen. Jeff loved Magda and he planned to propose to her after they graduated in spring. At the same time, though, he reluctantly recognized that their relationship had fallen into a bit of a rut over the last six months or so, and he missed the excitement and romance of their first year together. Although he was troubled by these conflicting feelings, Jeff was unsure what to do about them.

One day while he was surfing Facebook, Jeff decided, on a whim, to create a fake user profile for the person he wanted to be in his fantasies. He spent quite a bit of time researching and designing the profile of his imaginary persona, a rap singer/flamenco guitarist/snowboarder/kung fu expert who went by the user name "MoonDog13." Jeff inserted photos of an obscure young Romanian actor he found online into MoonDog13's user profile. He posted lyrics to rap songs he wrote on MoonDog13's page and joined online user groups for those interested in flamenco guitar, snowboarding, and kung fu. In very little time, MoonDog13 had made a number of online friends, many of whom were admiring young women. MoonDog13 loved to flirt with these girls.

Jeff told Magda nothing about MoonDog13, even when the time he spent online managing the fictitious life of his alter ego began to interfere with his relationship with her. He justified this decision based on the belief that MoonDog13 was an imaginary figure who existed only in cyberspace. As long as fantasy didn't cross into reality, there was no reason Jeff had to feel guilty about anything MoonDog13 said or did.

1. How is Jeff acting ethically/unethically in this situation?
2. Like Jeff, people in general have a reputation of acting differently in cyberspace than they do in the real world. Are the ethics of cyberspace any different from those of the real world? What about fantasy—are the ethics of our private desires different from the real world? Are we ethically obliged to disclose our fantasies to our loved ones?

Chapter Exhibits

Figure 7.1
Social Penetration Model
Figure 7.2
The Johari Window

Experiential Assignments

Dialectics in Your Relationships

Choose one of your current close friendships or intimate relationships. It can be with a friend or family member. Briefly explain this assignment and ask your relationship partner if she or he is willing to help you with it and to have what you discuss become part of a short paper you are doing for this class. Only if your partner consents should you proceed. Otherwise, find another friend or intimate partner.

1. Briefly explain the concept of relational dialectics to your partner. You may want to have your partner read the section of this chapter that explains this concept.
2. Once your partner understands the three specific relational dialectics discussed in the chapter, have a conversation about how each of you has experienced each of these tensions over the course of your relationship. Can you each think of specific instances when you were "out of sync"? How did this play out in the relationship? Be specific and be sure to talk about each of the three dialectical tensions.
3. Based on your conversation, write a short paper/journal entry in which you describe what you learned. How has hearing your partner talk about how he or she experienced these dialectical tensions changed your understanding?
4. Given what you have learned in this conversation, how can you use this to improve this relationship going forward?

Distinguishing between Relationship Types

List five people you have known for some time that you consider to be acquaintances. What do you talk about with each of these people? What subjects do you avoid? List five people you have known for some time whom you consider to be friends. How does your relationship with each differ from your relationships with your acquaintances? List one to three people you have known for some time whom you consider to be your best friends or intimates. Why do you consider each of these people to be best friends or intimates? Write a short essay in which you describe what you have learned about your relationships.

What's New?

COMM2	COMM3	Section
	Who Are You IRL? (Box)	7-1c
	New section: Cultural and Co-cultural Influences on Intimacy	7-1c
	New section: Social Penetration	7-2a
Figures 7.2 A, B, C, and D. Examples of Johari Windows for different relationships	Figure 7.2 The Johari Window	7-2b
Four stages of relationship development	Ten stages within three phases of coming together	7-3
Three stages of deteriorating relationships: recognition of dissatisfaction, disengaging, and ending	Four stages of deteriorating relationships: circumscribing; stagnating; avoiding; terminating	7-3c
	New section: Mediated Communication and Interpersonal Relationships	7-3d
Quick Quiz (on SE Card)	Quick Quiz	End of Chapter

PREP CARD 8

Interpersonal Communication

Outline

Key Terms

communication climate 103

positive communication climate 103

confirming communication messages 103

In this chapter:

Comforting people; privacy and disclosure; intimacy; reciprocity; information co-ownership; guidelines for disclosure; managing privacy; negotiating in relationships; managing conflict and collaboration.

Learning Outcomes

8-1 Discuss how to provide emotional support

8-2 Examine the tension between openness and privacy

8-3 Understand how to express desires and expectations

8-4 Discuss conflict management styles

Case Assignment: What Would You Do?

Use the following case assignment to further discuss interpersonal communication. You might use this as a handout, for which students can provide short answers, or you might use this to create an opportunity for class discussion.

A Question of Ethics

Ronaldo sat in the study hall cramming for a final examination when two of his classmates, Chauncey and Doug, walked up to his table.

"Studying hard, huh?" Chauncey asked.

"I'm stressing hard over this final," said Ronaldo. "What about you guys?"

"Hardly studying," said Chauncey.

Doug laughed.

Ronaldo looked at the two and saw that they both seemed relaxed and confident. "Something's not right with this picture," he said. "You're not going to tell me you guys are ready for this thing, are you?"

"Yep," said Chauncey.

Doug nodded.

"I don't get it," said Ronaldo. "You mean you've already gone back and studied everything we've covered this semester?"

"You only need to study what's actually on the test," said Chauncey.

"And how would you know that when McAllister didn't even give us a study sheet to help us know what would be on the test?" asked Ronaldo. He was beginning to put the puzzle together.

"Don't tell him anything else, man," Doug said.

"Ronaldo's cool," said Chauncey. "He knows how to keep a secret. Right?"

"I guess," Ronaldo said uneasily.

"It's like this," said Chauncey. "Doug's little brother is a super geek with computers. He hacked into McAllister's system and downloaded a copy of the final exam. You interested in getting a head start?"

1. Assuming that Ronaldo declines Chauncey's offer to cheat, what are the remaining ethical issues he faces? Which would be more ethically compromising: letting Chauncey and Doug get away with cheating, or betraying their trust by notifying the professor about their actions?

2. When, if ever, is it ethically acceptable to divulge information that you have sworn not to share with others?

disconfirming communication messages 103
comforting 104
face 104
positive face needs 104
negative face needs 104
buffering messages 104
other-centered messages 105
reframing the situation 105
giving advice 105
disclosure 105
privacy management 105
describing feelings 107
describing behavior 108
praise 108
constructive criticism 108
passive communication style 110
aggressive communication style 110
passive-aggressive communication style 111
assertive communication style 111
interpersonal conflict 112
avoiding 113
accommodating 113
competing 113
compromising 113
collaborating 114

Chapter Exhibit

Figure 8.1
Conflict Management Styles

Experiential Assignment

Praising and Criticizing

Think of someone you need to praise and someone to whom you would like to give constructive criticism. Prepare feedback for each person. In the next day or two, have a feedback conversation with at least one of these people, then write a paragraph describing what happened and how well the feedback was received. Analyze why you believe the feedback was received as it was.

What's New?

COMM2	COMM3	Section
Communication Skills in Interpersonal Relationships	Interpersonal Communication	
Comforting Messages	Providing Emotional Support	8-1
Skills for Comforting	Comforting Guidelines	8-1a
Gender and Cultural Considerations in Comforting		
Managing Privacy and Disclosure in Relationships	Managing Privacy and Disclosure	8-2
Culture, gender, motivation, context, and risk-benefit analysis	New information on media and privacy	8-2
Intimacy, Reciprocity, and Information Co-Ownership	Effects of Disclosure and Privacy on Relationships	8-2a
	Social Media Sting (Box)	8-2
Guidelines for Appropriate Disclosure	Disclosure Guidelines	8-2b
Communication Skills for Managing Privacy	Privacy Management Guidelines	8-2c
Negotiating Different Needs, Wants, and Preferences in Relationships	Expressing Desires and Expectations	8-3
Communicating Personal Needs, Wants, and Preferences: Passive, Aggressive, and Assertive Behavior	Passive Communication Style; Aggressive Communication Style; Passive-Aggressive Communication Style; and Assertive Communication Style	8-3a-d
Cultural Variations in Passive, Aggressive, and Assertive Behavior	Cultural and Co-cultural Considerations	8-3e
Managing Conflict in Relationships	Managing Interpersonal Conflict	8-4
Styles of Conflict	Avoiding (Lose-Lose); Accommodating (Lose–Win); Competing (Win–Lose); Compromising (Partial Lose–Lose); Collaborating (Win–Win)	8-4a-e
Quick Quiz (on SE Card)	Quick Quiz	End of Chapter

Outline

Key Terms

group 117

group communication 118

family 118

social friendship group 118

support group 119

In this chapter:

Work groups; group goals; group diversity; cohesiveness; norms; synergy; stages of group development; problem solving in groups; decision making.

Learning Outcomes

9-1 Identify different types of groups

9-2 Analyze the characteristics of healthy groups

9-3 Understand how groups develop

9-4 Describe the nature of conflict in groups

Case Assignment: What Would You Do?

Use the following case assignment to further discuss group communication. You might use this as a handout, for which students can provide short answers, or you might use this to create an opportunity for class discussion.

A Question of Ethics

The Community Service and Outreach committee of Students in Communication was meeting to determine what cause should benefit from their annual fund-raising talent contest.

"So," said Mark, "does anyone have any ideas about whose cause we should sponsor?"

"Well," replied Glenna, "I think we should give it to a group that's doing literacy work."

"Sounds good to me," replied Mark.

"My aunt works at the Boardman Center as the literacy coordinator, so why don't we just adopt them?" asked Glenna.

"Gee, I don't know much about the group," said Reed.

"Come on, you know, they help people learn how to read," replied Glenna sarcastically.

"Well, I was kind of hoping we'd take a look at sponsoring the local Teen Runaway Center," offered Angelo.

"Listen, if your aunt works at the Boardman Center," commented Leticia, "let's go with it."

"Right," said Pablo, "that's good enough for me."

"Yeah," replied Heather, "let's do it and get out of here."

"I hear what you're saying, Heather," Mark responded, "I've got plenty of other stuff to do."

"No disrespect meant to Glenna, but wasn't the Boardman Center in the news because of questionable use of funds?" countered Angelo. "Do we really know enough about them?"

"OK," said Mark, "enough discussion. I've got to get to class. All in favor of the literacy program at the Boardman Center indicate by saying 'aye.' I think we've got a majority. Sorry, Angelo—you can't win them all."

"I wish all meetings went this smoothly," Heather said to Glenna as they left the room. "I mean, that was really a good meeting."

1. What did the group really know about the Boardman Center? Is it good group discussion practice to rely on a passing comment of one member?

Chapter Exhibit

Figure 9.1
Types of Virtual Groups

2. Regardless of whether the meeting went smoothly, is there any ethical problem with this process? Explain.

Experiential Assignments

Cohesiveness in Homogeneous versus Heterogeneous Groups (Handout)

Identify two groups (for example, a sports team, study group, fraternal or community group, or work team) to which you belong. One group should be homogeneous and the other should be heterogeneous.

Analyze the demographic differences in each group. When you have completed this analysis, write a paragraph that discusses cohesiveness in each group. How cohesive is each group? Are both groups equally cohesive? Was it easier or more difficult to establish cohesiveness in a particular group? What real or potential pitfalls result from the level of cohesiveness in each group?

Stages of Group Development (Handout)

Think of a group to which you have belonged for less than one quarter, semester, or term (if you have an assigned group in this course, use that group). Write a paragraph that identifies the group's current stage of development and then describes how the group has transitioned through each of the previous stages. What event(s) do you recall as turning points, marking the group's movement from one stage to another? Has the group become "stuck" in a stage, or has it developed smoothly? What factors contributed to that? What can you do to help this group succeed in its current stage and transition to the next stage?

What's New?

COMM2	COMM3	Section
Characteristics of Healthy Groups	The Nature and Types of Groups	9-1
LO3	Moved sections Families; Social Friendship Groups; Support Groups; Interest Groups; Service Groups; Work Group Teams	9-1a–f
	Social Support Groups Thrive Online (Box)	9-1b
Work Groups	Work Group Teams	9-1f
	New section: Virtual Groups	9-1g
	New section: Mediated Communication and Virtual Groups	9-1h
Evaluating Group Dynamics	New section: Conflict in Groups	9-4
	New sections: Pseudo-Conflict; Issue-Related Group Conflict; Personality-Related Group Conflict; Culture and Conflict; Virtual Groups and Conflict	9-4a–e
Quick Quiz (on SE Card)	Quick Quiz	End of Chapter

Outline

Key Terms

leadership 133
formal leader 134
informal emergent leaders 134
shared leadership functions 134
role 134
task leadership roles 134
maintenance leadership roles 134

In this chapter:

Shared leadership; task roles; maintenance roles; procedural roles; meeting guidelines for leaders; meeting guidelines for participants; systematic problem solving; written formats; oral formats; virtual reports; evaluating group effectiveness.

Learning Outcomes

10-1 Understand how leadership functions in teams
10-2 Describe how to run effective meetings
10-3 List the six steps of systematic problem solving
10-4 Know the various methods for communicating group solutions
10-5 Evaluate group effectiveness using provided guidelines

Case Assignment: What Would You Do?

Use the following case assignment to further discuss group leadership practices. You might use this as a handout, for which students can provide short answers, or you might use this to create an opportunity for class discussion.

A Question of Ethics

"You know, Sue, we're going to be in deep trouble if the group doesn't support McGowan's resolution about dues reform."

"Well, we'll just have to see to it that all the arguments in favor of that resolution are heard, but in the end it's the group's decision."

"That's very democratic of you, Sue, but you know that if it doesn't pass, you're likely to be out on your tail."

"That may be, Heather, but I don't see what I can do about it."

"You don't want to see. First, right now the group respects you. If you would just apply a little pressure on a couple of the members, you'd get what you want."

"What do you mean?"

"Look, this is a good cause. You've got something on just about every member of the group. Take a couple of members aside and let them know that this is payoff time. I think you'll discover that some key folks will see it your way."

1. Should Sue follow Heather's advice? Why or why not?
2. Is it appropriate to use personal influence to affect the outcome of group decisions? If you answered yes, at what point does the use of personal influence cross the line from ethical to unethical behavior? If you answered no, explain why personal influence shouldn't be one of the many factors groups consider when making decisions.

Experiential Assignments

Stating Problems

Indicate whether each of the following is a question of fact, a question of value, or a question of policy.

1. What should we do to increase the quality of finished parts?

Chapter Exhibits

2. Do police stop African-American drivers more frequently than other drivers?
3. Should television news organizations use exit polls to call elections?
4. Is John guilty of involuntary manslaughter?
5. Is seniority the best method of handling employee layoffs?
6. What is the best vacation plan for our family?

Media Depictions of Women Leaders

Watch a television program or a film that depicts a woman in a leadership role in business, politics, or the military and evaluate what role, if any, gender plays in the depiction of the character's leadership attributes. Is the character portrayed in a positive, negative, or neutral light, and does gender factor in any way in this portrayal? Are there any gender-specific behaviors or stereotypes associated with the character? If so, what are they and what message do they send about the character's overall leadership abilities?

How Does Your Group Solve Problems?

Analyze a situation in which a group to which you belong attempted to solve a problem. Write a paragraph in which you answer the following questions: Did the group use all six of the problem-solving steps listed in the text? If not, which steps did the group overlook? Were there any steps the group should have placed more emphasis on? Was the group successful or not in its efforts to solve the problem? Explain.

What's New?

COMM2	COMM3	Section
LO2 Shared Leadership	Effective Leadership	10-1
	New section: Shared Leadership Responsibilities	10-1d
LO3 Making Meetings Effective	Effective Meetings	10-2
LO1 The Problem-Solving Process	Systematic Problem Solving	10-3
PRSSA examples	Dropped	
Step Six: Implement the Agreed-Upon Solution	Step Six: Implement the Agreed-Upon Solution and Assess It	10-3f
	WoW Problem Solving (Box)	10-3f
Virtual Reports	Virtual Formats	10-4c
Figure 10.5	Dropped	10-4c
	New section: Evaluating Group Effectiveness	10-5
	New sections: Group Dynamics; Group Presentations	10-5a-b
	New Figures: 10.5 Group Dynamics Evaluation Form; 10.6 Sample Evaluation Form for Group Presentations; 10.7 Sample Self-Critique Form for Group Presentations	10-5a-b
Quick Quiz (on SE Card)	Quick Quiz	End of Chapter

Outline

In this chapter:

The rhetorical situation; audience analysis; examining the occasion; identifying and selecting topics; brainstorming; writing a speech goal; secondary research; primary research; evaluating sources; relevant information; plagiarism; cultural perspectives; note cards; citing sources.

Learning Outcomes

11-1 Understand how the various factors that create the rhetorical situation impact topic selection

11-2 Identify and select appropriate topics for your speech

11-3 Identify the general and specific goals of your speech

11-4 List the three different types of sources you can draw from to develop your speech and explain how to evaluate them

11-5 Know how to identify and cite sources

Case Assignment: What Would You Do?

Use the following case assignment to further discuss source citation practices. You might use this as a handout, for which students can provide short answers, or you might use this to create an opportunity for class discussion.

A Question of Ethics

When Mr. Allen gave the class its final public speaking assignment, Alessandra decided that she would deliver a speech on the limited educational opportunities for women in the developing world. This topic was close to her heart, and she had already done quite a bit of reading on the topic.

As chance would have it, Alessandra came down with the flu the week before her speech was due and was flat on her back for four days before she finally recovered. Because she was so far behind in her studies, Alessandra didn't begin working on her speech until the afternoon before it was due. Still, by midnight, she had completed what she felt was a strong draft.

The next morning, she cleaned up a few typos and errors in her outline and then practiced delivering it over the next two hours. Just before leaving for school, she read the instructions one last time to double-check that she had done everything correctly. Were her eyes playing tricks on her? The speech needed to be supported by no fewer than five published sources, yet she had cited only four.

Alessandra had, of course, read other books on her topic in the past, even if she hadn't cited them in her speech. While she couldn't remember the specific details of these books, she recalled their general message well enough. That was the solution! She would write a few quotations from one of the books based on her memory, drop them into her speech, and then update her references with credit information pulled from the Internet. In less than half an hour, Alessandra completed her speech and was on her way to class.

1. While fabricating information from a source is clearly unethical, what about writing quotations based on memories of an earlier reading?
2. What ethical obligations does Alessandra have to her sources?

Key Terms

Experiential Assignment

Audience Analysis

Attend a public speech delivered outside your school. If your schedule makes going to a live speech difficult, you may watch a speech delivered on TV or cable (try C-SPAN). When watching the speech, consider how the audience and occasion might have influenced the speaker. Was the speech pitched directly at the immediate interests of the audience? If not, did the speaker attempt to draw connections between his or her topic and the audience's interests? Did the speaker use any particular words or gestures to connect better with the audience? What about the manner in which the speaker was dressed; how might this have played with the audience?

What's New?

COMM2	COMM3	Section
	New section: The Rhetorical Situation	11-1
Identify Audience Analysis Information Needs	Demographic Data; Subject-Related Data	11-1a
	New section: Ethical Use of Audience Data	11-1b
LO3 Analyze the Setting	Examine the Occasion	11-1c
LO1 Identify Topics	Identifying and Selecting Speech Topics	11-2
Identify Your General Goal	Understanding General and Specific Speech Goals	11-3a
LO6 Locate and Evaluate Information Sources	Evaluating and Selecting Information Sources	11-4
Personal Knowledge, Experience, and Observation	Personal Knowledge and Experience	11-4a
	New section: Locating Sources	11-4b
	To Wikipedia or Not to Wikipedia? (Box)	11-4b
	New section: Skim Sources	11-4b
	New sections: Fieldwork Observations; Original Artifact or Document Examinations	11-4c
LO8 Identify and Select Relevant Information	Identifying and Citing Information	11-5
LO9 Draw Information for Multiple Cultural Perspectives	Seek Information from Multiple Cultural Perspectives	11-5d
	New section: Annotated Bibliography	11-5e
Quick Quiz (on SE Card)	Quick Quiz	End of Chapter

Chapter Exhibits

PREP CARD 12   Organizing Your Speech

Outline

Key Terms

In this chapter:

Main points; thesis statement; speech outline; support material; section transitions; introduction; introduction goals; methods for getting attention; conclusion; appeal to action; sources; reviewing the outline.

Learning Outcomes

12-1 Describe methods for developing the body of your speech

12-2 Explain how to create an introduction

12-3 Explain how to prepare a conclusion

12-4 Examine guidelines for listing sources

12-5 Develop a method for reviewing the outline

Case Assignment: What Would You Do?

Use the following case assignment to get your students to consider some issues they might run into while building their speeches. You might use this as a handout, for which students can provide short answers, or you might use this to create an opportunity for class discussion.

A Question of Ethics

As Marna and Gloria were eating lunch together, Marna happened to ask Gloria, "How are you doing in Woodward's speech class?"

"Not bad," Gloria replied. "I'm working on this speech about product development. I think it will be really informative, but I'm having a little trouble with the opening. I just can't seem to get a good idea for getting started."

"Why not start with a story—that always worked for me in class."

"Thanks, Marna; I'll think on it."

The next day when Marna ran into Gloria again, she asked, "How's that introduction going?"

"Great. I've prepared a great story about Mary Kay—you know, the cosmetics woman? I'm going to tell about how she was terrible in school and no one thought she'd amount to anything. But she loved dabbling with cosmetics so much that she decided to start her own business—and the rest is history."

"That's a great story. I really like that part about being terrible in school. Was she really that bad?"

"I really don't know—the material I read didn't really focus on that part of her life. But I thought that angle would get people listening right away. And after all, I did it that way because you suggested starting with a story."

"Yes, but . . . "

"Listen, she did start the business. So what if the story isn't quite right? It makes the point I want to make—if people are creative and have a strong work ethic, they can make it big."

1. What are the ethical issues here?
2. Is anyone really hurt by Gloria opening the speech with this story?
3. What are the speaker's ethical responsibilities?

Chapter Exhibits

Experiential Assignments

Identifying Thesis Statements

Access the American Rhetoric Online Speech Bank. Select five speeches and listen to the audio recordings or read the printed transcript of each speech. As you listen to or read the speeches, identify and write down the thesis statements in each. Not all speeches necessarily have explicit thesis statements, but all speeches have an implied thesis or purpose. If you think any one of the speeches you have selected does not contain an explicit thesis, identify its implied thesis or purpose.

Identifying Main Points

Using the speeches you chose in the previous exercise, identify and write down the main points in each. What type of organizational pattern is the speaker using in each speech?

Identifying Supporting Materials

Using the speeches you chose in the first exercise, list the various types of support the speaker uses to develop each main point. Does the speaker acknowledge the sources of this information? Are there types of support that you think should have been used that are missing from this speech? Does the speaker seem to rely on one type of support to the exclusion of others? Why do you suppose the speaker chose the types of support that were used?

What's New?

COMM2	COMM3	Section
Emming's Credit Card Speech	Katie's Adderall Speech	Chapter 12
Determining Main Points	Choose Main Points	12-1a
	Raise a Glass: Giving a Toast (Box)	12-1a
Lonna's narrative speech on AIDS	Lonna's narrative speech on anorexia	12-1c
Selecting and Outlining Supporting Material	Identify Subpoints	12-1c
	Outline Subpoints	12-1c
Preparing Section Transitions and Signposts	Create Transitions	12-1d
	Separated into sections: Section Transitions; Signposts	12-1d
	Moved Stories before Jokes	12-2a
	New section: Action	12-2a
Setting a Tone; Creating a Bond of Good Will	Dropped	12-2a
	Separated into sections: Vivid Imagery; Appeal to Action	12-3b
LO4 Listing Sources	Compiling the Reference List	12-4
Does the outline include no more than one-third the total number of words anticipated in the speech?	Dropped	12-5
Figure 12.4 Sample Complete Outline	Outline: Using and Abusing Adderall: What's the Big Deal?	12-5
Quick Quiz (on SE Card)	Quick Quiz	End of Chapter

Outline

Key Terms

presentational aid **193**
visual aids **193**
audio aids **194**
audiovisual aids **194**
actual objects **195**
model **195**
diagram **195**
chart **196**
flow chart **196**
organizational chart **196**
pie chart **196**
graph **198**
bar graph **198**
line graph **198**
flip chart **202**
handout **202**

In this chapter:

Presentational aids; types of presentational aids; choosing presentational aids; displaying presentational aids

Learning Outcomes

13-1 Understand why you should incorporate presentational aids into your speech

13-2 Describe the different types of presentational aids you can choose from

13-3 Choose the appropriate visual aid for your presentation and prepare it correctly

13-4 Learn about various media you can use to display your presentational aids

Case Assignment: What Would You Do?

Use the following case assignment to further discuss presentational aids. You might use this as a handout, for which students can provide short answers, or you might use this to create an opportunity for class discussion.

A Question of Ethics

As Oscar and Max were finishing dinner, Max asked, "Have you figured out what you're going to use for presentational aids in your speech next week in Professor Gilman's class? I'm totally stumped."

Oscar replied, "Yeah, I am so ready and actually pretty pumped about mine."

"What are you going to use?" inquired Max.

"Well, you know I'm going to try to persuade the class to agree with me that the death penalty is wrong. Well, I got ahold of an audio clip of someone writhing in pain during an execution. I'm going to play it while I show several photographs of people who have been executed. THAT should really make my speech memorable and my argument convincing!"

"Yikes!" exclaimed Max. "Are you sure that's such a good idea?"

"Yeah, why not?"

1. Is it ethical to use potentially offensive presentational aids if doing so will make your speech more memorable or your argument more convincing? Why or why not?
2. Could Oscar achieve his goal using different presentational aids? If so, what might they be?

Experiential Assignment

Evaluating Visual Aids (Handout)

Analyze speeches or other public presentations such as lectures, articles, essays, newscasts, infomercials, and so on that you can find on campus, in print, online, or on television. Evaluate the use of at least one item from each of the following visuals aids: (1) objects, (2) models, (3) photographs, (4) slides, (5) film/video clips,

Chapter Exhibits

(6) drawings, (7) maps, (8) charts, and (9) graphs. How effectively does the speaker or author use each item to illustrate or support his or her speech or presentation? Are there other ways the speaker might have used the visual aid more effectively? Would a different type of visual aid have conveyed the presentation's message more clearly?

What's New?

COMM2	COMM3	Section
Adapting Verbally and Visually	Presentational Aids	
LO1 Adapting to your Audience Verbally	Much of this content is covered in chapter 12	
Information Comprehension and Retention	Dropped	
Vivid Language	Moved to Chapter 12	
LO2 Adapting to Audiences Visually	Benefits of Presentational Aids	13-1
Charts: word chart, flowchart	Charts: flow chart, organizational chart, pie chart	13-2a
Pie graph	Pie chart	13-2a
Audio Materials	Audio Aids	13-2b
Audiovisual Materials	Audiovisual Aids	13-2c
	Other Sensory Aids	13-2d
Criteria for Choosing Presentational Aids	Choosing Presentational Aids	13-3
	Simple guidelines to help choose presentational aids	13-3
Presentation Software	Moved to Benefits of Presentational Aids	13-1
LO3 Methods for Displaying Presentational Aids	Displaying Presentational Aids	13-4
CD/DVD Players and LCD Projectors; Computer Mediated Slide Shows	Computers, CD/DVD Players, and LCD Projectors	13-4f
Quick Quiz (on SE Card)	Quick Quiz	End of Chapter

PREP CARD 14 — Language

Outline

Key Terms

In this chapter:

Audience adaptation; oral style; verbal immediacy; relevance; common ground; speaker credibility; general language; speaking in a second language; speaking clearly; specific language; jargon; slang; vivid language; sensory language; rhetorical figures of speech.

Learning Outcomes

14-1 Describe the ways that oral style differs from written style

14-2 Use language strategies that allow you to speak appropriately and connect with the audience

14-3 Choose clear and specific language that helps the audience understand and remember your ideas

14-4 Choose language that helps the audience see and experience your ideas.

Case Assignment: What Would You Do?

Use the following case assignment to further discuss oral style and speaking appropriately. You might use this as a handout, for which students can provide short answers, or you might use this to create an opportunity for class discussion.

A Question of Ethics

"Kendra, I heard you telling Jim about the speech you're giving tomorrow. You think it's a winner, huh?"

"You got that right, Omar. I'm going to have Bardston eating out of the palm of my hand."

"You sound confident."

"This time I have reason to be. See, Professor Bardston's been talking about the importance of audience adaptation. These last two weeks that's all we've heard—adaptation, adaptation."

"What does she mean?"

"Talking about something in a way that really relates to people personally."

"OK—so how are you going to do that?"

"Well, you see, I'm giving this speech on abortion. Now here's the kick. Bardston let it slip that she's a supporter of Right to Life. So what I'm going to do is give this informative speech on the Right to Life movement. But I'm going to discuss the major beliefs of the movement in a way that'll get her to think that I'm a supporter. I'm going to mention aspects of the movement that I know she'll like."

"But I've heard you talk about how you're pro-choice."

"I am—all the way. But by keeping the information positive, she'll think I'm a supporter. It isn't as if I'm going to be telling any lies or anything."

1. In a speech, is it ethical to adapt in a way that resonates with your audience but isn't in keeping with what you really believe?

2 Could Kendra have achieved her goal using a different method? How?

rhetorical figures of speech 213
rhetorical structures of speech 213
simile 213
metaphor 213
analogy 213
alliteration 213
assonance 214
onomatopoeia 214
personification 214
repetition 214
antithesis 214

Chapter Exhibit

Figure 14.1
The Semantic Triangle

Experiential Assignment

Creating Common Ground

Use the Internet or the resources at your campus library to find the article "A Question of Real American Black Men," by Bailey B. Baker, Jr., *Vital Speeches*, April 15, 2002. Analyze how this speaker uses personal pronouns, rhetorical questions, common experiences, and personalized information to create common ground. Write a short essay describing the conclusions of your analysis.

What's New?

COMM2	COMM3	Section
Chapter 13 Adapting Verbally and Visually	Chapter 14: Language	
	New section: Oral Style	14-1
LO1 Adapting to Your Audience Verbally	Speaking Appropriately	14-2
Demonstrate Knowledge and Expertise	Dropped	14-2c
Establish Trustworthiness	Dropped	14-2c
Display Personableness	Dropped	14-2c
	Where Have All the Experts Gone? (Box)	14-2c
	New sections: Generic Language; Nonparallel Language; Offensive Humor; Profanity and Vulgarity	14-2d
Information Comprehension and Retention	Dropped	14-2
Figure 13.1 Kolb's Cycle of Learning	Dropped	14-2
Appeal to Diverse Learning Styles	Dropped	
Orient the Audience with Internal Reviews	Dropped	
Choose Non-Offensive Language	Moved to section Linguistic Sensitivity	14-2d
Adapting to Cultural Differences	Speaking in a Second Language	14-2e
Choose Culturally Appropriate Supporting Material	Moved *quinceañera* example to chapter 3, Intercultural Communication	
Choose Specific and Familiar Language	Moved to section Speaking Clearly	14-3a
Compare Unknown Ideas with Familiar Ones	Dropped	
	Figure 14.1 The Semantic Triangle	14-3
	New section: Familiar Terms	14-3b
Use Vivid Language and Examples	Moved to section Speaking Vividly	14-4
	Expanded sections on vivid language	14-4
Quick Quiz (on SE Card)	Quick Quiz	End of Chapter

PREP CARD 15

Delivery

Outline

In this chapter:

Public speaking apprehension; managing apprehension; elements of delivery; conversational style; impromptu speeches, scripted speeches; extemporaneous speeches; rehearsing; preparing notes; using presentation aids; practicing speeches; criteria for evaluating speeches.

Learning Outcomes

15-1 Describe symptoms and causes of public speaking apprehension and some methods for managing it

15-2 Identify the characteristics of an effective delivery style

15-3 Discuss the characteristics of the effective use of voice

15-4 Discuss the characteristics of the effective use of the body

15-5 Identify the characteristics of different delivery methods

15-6 Analyze what makes a rehearsal effective

15-7 Identify criteria for evaluating speeches

Case Assignment: What Would You Do?

Use the following case assignment to further discuss delivery. You might use this as a handout for which students can provide short answers, or you might use this to create an opportunity for class discussion.

A Question of Ethics

Nalini sighed loudly as the club members of Toastmasters International took their seats. It was her first time meeting with the public speaking group and she didn't want to be there, but her mom had insisted that she join the club in the hopes that it would help Nalini transfer from her community college to the state university. It wasn't that the idea of public speaking scared Nalini. She had already spent time in front of an audience as the lead singer of the defunct emo band, Deathstar. To Nalini's mind, public speaking was just another type of performance, like singing or acting, albeit a stuffy form better suited to middle-aged men and women than people her own age, a sentiment that explained why she wanted to be elsewhere at the moment.

After the club leader called the meeting to order, he asked each of the new members to stand; introduce themselves; and give a brief speech describing their background, aspirations, and reasons for joining the club. "Spare me," Nalini muttered loud enough for those next to her to hear. The club leader then called on a young woman to Nalini's left, who rose and began to speak about her dream of becoming a lawyer and doing public advocacy work for the poor. After the young woman sat down, the club members applauded politely. Nalini whistled and clapped loudly and kept on clapping after the others had stopped.

The club leader, somewhat taken aback, called on Nalini next. She rose from her seat and introduced herself as the secret love child of a former president and a famous actress. Nalini then strung together a series of other fantastic lies about her past and her ambitions. She concluded her speech by saying that she had joined the club in the hopes that she could learn how to hypnotize audiences into obeying her commands. After Nalini sat, a few of the club members applauded quietly, while others cast glances at each other and the club leader.

Key Terms

Chapter Exhibits

1. Is mocking behavior in a formal public speaking setting, either by an audience member or a speaker, an ethical matter? Explain your answer.
2. What ethical obligations does an audience member have to a speaker? What about a speaker to his or her audience?

Experiential Assignments

Articulation Practice

The goal of this activity is to practice articulating difficult word combinations. Go to www.jimpowell.com/ArticulationEx.htm to find a list of sentences that are difficult to articulate. Practice saying each of these sentences until you can do so without error.

Controlling Nervousness

Interview one or two people who give frequent speeches (such as a minister, a politician, a lawyer, a businessperson, or a teacher). Ask what is likely to make them more or less nervous about giving the speech. Find out how they cope with their nervousness. Write a short paragraph summarizing what you have learned from the interviews. Then identify the behaviors used by those people that you believe might work for you.

Evaluating a Speaker's Vocal and Body Action Behaviors

Attend a public speech event on campus or in your community. Watch and evaluate the speaker's use of vocal characteristics (voice and articulation), body action (facial expressions, gestures, movement, poise, and posture), animation, spontaneity, and eye contact. Which vocal or body action behaviors stood out and why? How did the speaker's use of voice, body actions, animation, spontaneity, and eye contact contribute to or detract from the speaker's message? What three things could the speaker have done to improve the delivery of the speech?

What's New?

COMM2	COMM3	Section
Chapter 14 Overcoming Speech Apprehension by Practicing Speech Delivery	Chapter 15 Delivery	
Managing Your Apprehension	Management Techniques	15-1b
Communication Orientation	Communication Orientation Motivation	15-1b
LO2 Characteristics of an Effective Delivery Style	Effective Delivery Style	15-2
	Rearranged sections; see outline.	15-4
Recording, Analyzing, and Refining Speech Delivery	Rehearsing and Refining Delivery	15-6c
	New section: Adapting while Delivering the Speech	15-6d
Sample Informative Speech: Understanding Hurricanes	Sample Informative Speech: College Student Volunteering and Civic Engagement	15-7
Quick Quiz (on SE Card)	Quick Quiz	End of Chapter

Outline

Key Terms

In this chapter:

Informative speeches; intellectual stimulation; creativity; emphasis; description; definition; comparison and contrast; narration; demonstration; process speeches; expository speeches.

Learning Outcomes

16-1   Identify the characteristics of effective informative speaking
16-2   Describe methods for conveying information
16-3   Discuss common patterns for informative speeches

Case Assignment: What Would You Do?

Use the following case assignment to further discuss expository speeches. You might use this as a handout, for which students can provide short answers, or you might use this to create an opportunity for class discussion.

A Question of Ethics

After class, as Gina and Paul were discussing what they intended to talk about in their process speeches, Paul said, "I think I'm going to talk about how to make a synthetic diamond."

Gina was impressed. "That sounds interesting. I didn't know you had expertise with that."

"I don't. But the way I see it, Professor Henderson will really be impressed with my speech because my topic will be so novel."

"Well, yeah," Gina replied, "but didn't he stress that for this speech we should choose a topic that was important to us and that we knew a lot about?"

"Sure," Paul said sarcastically, "he's going to be impressed if I talk about how to maintain a blog? Forget it. Just watch—everyone's going to think I make diamonds in my basement and I'm going to get a good grade."

1. Is Paul's plan unethical? Why?
2. What should Gina say to challenge Paul's last statement?

Speech Assignment

A Process Speech

1. Follow the speech plan Action Steps to prepare a process speech. Your instructor will announce the time limit and other parameters for this assignment.
2. Criteria for evaluation include all the general criteria of topic and purpose, content, organization, and presentation, but special emphasis will be placed on how intellectually stimulating the topic is made for the audience, how creatively ideas are presented, and how clearly the important information is emphasized.
3. Prior to presenting your speech, prepare a complete sentence outline and source list (bibliography) as well as a written plan for adapting your speech to the audience. Your adaptation plan should describe how you plan to verbally and visually adapt your material to the audience. It should also describe how you

Chapter Exhibits

will address the issues listed in Step 3 of the speech assignment for an expository speech.

An Expository Speech

1. Follow the speech plan Action Steps to prepare a five- to eight-minute informative speech in which you present carefully researched, in-depth information about a complex topic. Your instructor will announce other parameters for this assignment.
2. Criteria for evaluation include all the general criteria of topic and purpose, content, organization, and presentation, but special emphasis will be placed on how intellectually stimulating the topic is made for the audience, how creatively ideas are presented, and how clearly the important information is emphasized. Use the Informative Speech Evaluation Checklist in Figure 16.7 to critique yourself as you practice your speech.
3. Prior to presenting your speech, prepare a complete-sentence outline, a source list (bibliography), and a written plan for adapting your speech to the audience.

Experiential Assignment

Evaluating Demonstrations

Watch an informative speech involving a demonstration and evaluate how effectively the speaker performs the demonstration. (Do-it-yourself and home improvement TV programs, like those on the cable channels DIY and HGTV, often feature demonstrations. Demonstrations are also features on programs on the Food Network.) Did the speaker perform a complete or modified demonstration? Did the speaker use only the tools and equipment needed to perform the demonstrated task, or did he or she also use other items, such as visual aids? How effective was the demonstration overall? Could the speaker have improved any areas of the demonstration? Explain.

What's New?

COMM2	COMM3	Section
Chapter 15	Chapter 16	
Climatic Variation in the United States	Figure 16.1 Volunteering Rates across the United States	16-1c
Common Informative Speech Frameworks	Common Informative Patterns	16-3
Process Speech Frameworks	Process Speeches	16-3a
Flower arrangement example	Dropped	16-3a
Expository Speech Frameworks	Expository Speeches	16-3b
Quick Quiz (on SE Card)	Quick Quiz	End of Chapter

PREP CARD 17   Persuasive Speaking

Outline

In this chapter:

Persuasive speech; the elaboration likelihood model; propositions; reasons; arguments; fallacies of reasoning; emotional appeals; goodwill; credibility; incentives; organizational patterns for speeches.

Learning Outcomes

17-1 Understand the nature of persuasive messages and how people listen to and evaluate them

17-2 Write your persuasive speech goals as propositions

17-3 Develop logical arguments to support a proposition

17-4 Develop credibility to support a proposition

17-5 Develop emotional arguments to support a proposition

17-6 Identify organizational patterns for persuasive speeches

Experiential Assignments

For the following assignments, read the speech "Terrorism and Islam: Maintaining Our Faith" by Mahathir Bin Mohamad, Prime Minister of Malaysia, given at the OIC Conference of Ministers of Endowments and Islamic Affairs, May 7, 2002. Access the speech at http://www.accessmylibrary.com/coms2/summary_0286-25525765_ITM.

A Specific Goal Statement in a Persuasive Speech

The goal of this activity is to find and analyze a specific goal statement.
1. Identify the specific goal statement.
2. Given the composition of the audience, what do you think their initial attitude was toward the speaker's position?
3. Write a paragraph in which you analyze the speaker's goal statement. What type of specific speech goal is this? Does this goal seem appropriate for this audience? Explain your reasoning.

Giving Good Reasons and Evidence

The goal of this activity is to analyze reasons and evidence.

1. Identify each of the main points or reasons the speaker offers in support of his thesis.
2. Are his reasons good? Are they supported? Relevant? Adapted to the audience?
3. Analyze his supporting evidence. Assess the quality, currency, and relevance of his reasons.
4. Identify two kinds of reasoning links that he uses and then test them using the appropriate questions. Are the links you tested logical? Explain.
5. Can you detect any fallacies in his argument? Explain.

Persuasive Organizational Methods

The goal of this activity is to analyze organizational patterns.

1. Analyze the organizational methods that Mahathir uses.
2. How well does his pattern fit the attitudes you believe his audience holds toward his position? Are there other patterns that might have served him better?

Key Terms

What's New?

COMM2	COMM3	Section
Chapter 16	Chapter 17	
	New section: The Nature of Persuasion	17-1
How We Process Persuasive Messages: The Elaboration Likelihood Model (ELM)	Processing Persuasive Messages	17-1a
Writing Persuasive Speech Goals as Propositions	Persuasive Speech Goals	17-2
Types of Persuasive Goals	Types of Propositions	17-2a
Developing Arguments (Logos) That Support Your Proposition	Rhetorical Appeals to Logos	17-3
Finding Reasons to Use as Main Points Seeking Evidence to Support Reasons	Discussion of the basic form of logical arguments	17-3
Types and Tests of Arguments	Types of Logical Arguments	17-3a
Avoiding Fallacies in Your Reasons and Argument	Reasoning Fallacies	17-3b
LO5 Cueing Your Audience through Credibility (Ethos): Demonstrating Goodwill	Conveying Good Character	17-4a
	New section: Conveying Competence and Credibility	17-4b
LO4 Increasing Audience Involvement through Emotional Appeal (Pathos)	Evoking Negative Emotions Evoking Positive Emotions	17-5a-b
LO6 Motivating Your Audience to Act through Incentives	Dropped	
Organizational Patterns for Persuasive Speeches	Persuasive Speech Patterns	17-6
Sample Persuasive Speech: Sexual Assault Policy a Must	Sample Persuasive Speech: Together, We Can Stop Cyber-Bullying	
Quick Quiz (on SE Card)	Quick Quiz	End of Chapter

Chapter Exhibits

PREP CARD A

Appendix: Interviewing

Key Terms

In this chapter:

Interviewing; questions used in interviewing; interview protocol; information-gathering interviews; employment interviews; interviewing to get a job; résumé; cover letter; media interviews.

Learning Outcomes

A-1 Discuss how to form and order a series of questions for an interview

A-2 Discuss how to conduct information-gathering interviews

A-3 Examine how to conduct employment interviews

A-4 Discuss interview strategies for job-seekers

A-5 Identify strategies for dealing with news media

Case Assignment: What Would You Do?

Use the following case assignment to further discuss interviewing and résumé building. You might use this as a handout, for which students can provide short answers, or you might use this to create an opportunity for class discussion.

A Question of Ethics

Ken shifted in his chair as Ms. Goldsmith, his interviewer, looked over his résumé.

"I have to tell you that you have considerably more experience than the average applicant we usually get coming straight out of college," Ms. Goldsmith said. "Let's see, you've managed a hardware store, been a bookkeeper for a chain of three restaurants, and were the number one salesman for six straight months at a cell phone store."

"That's right," Ken said. "My family has always stressed the value of hard work, so I have worked a full-time job every summer since I entered junior high school, right through my last year of college. During the school year, I usually worked four to six hours a day after class."

"Very impressive," Ms. Goldsmith said. "And still you managed to get excellent grades and do a considerable amount of volunteer work in your spare time. What's your secret?"

"Secret?" said Ken nervously. "There's no secret—just a lot of hard work."

"Yes, I see that," said Ms. Goldsmith. "What I mean is that there are only 24 hours in a day and you obviously had a lot on your plate each day, especially for someone so young. How did you manage to do it?"

Ken thought for a moment before answering. "I only need five hours of sleep a day." He could feel Ms. Goldsmith's eyes scrutinizing his face. He hadn't exactly lied on his résumé—just exaggerated a little bit. He had, in fact, helped his father run the family hardware store for a number of years. He had helped his aunt, from time to time, keep track of her restaurant's receipts. He had also spent one summer selling cell phones for his cousin. Of course, his family always required him to do his schoolwork first before they let him help at the store, so Ken often had little time to help at all, but there was no reason Ms. Goldsmith needed to know that.

"And you can provide references for these jobs?" Ms. Goldsmith asked.

"I have them with me right here," said Ken, pulling a typed page from his briefcase and handing it across the desk.

1. Are the exaggerated claims Ken made in his résumé ethical? Do the ethics of his actions change if he has references who will vouch for his claims?
2. If the consequences of acting ethically diminish your economic prospects, are you justified in bending the rules? Explain your answer. If you think bending the rules is acceptable in such circumstances, how far can you bend them before you cross the line?

Experiential Assignments

Open and Closed Questions

Indicate which of the following questions are open ended and which are closed ended. If the question is open ended, write a closed-ended question seeking similar information. If the question is closed ended, write an open-ended question. Make sure your questions are neutral rather than leading.

1. What leads you to believe that Sheldon will be appointed?
2. How many steps are there in getting a book into print?
3. Will you try out for the Shakespeare play this year?
4. When are you getting married?
5. Have you participated in the Garden Project?

Résumé and Cover Letter

Read the help-wanted ads in your local newspaper or on an online job search service until you find a job that you think you would enjoy. Write a résumé and cover letter applying for this position.

What's New?

COMM2	COMM3	Section
Appendix to Chapter 8	Appendix	
LO1 Structuring Interviews	The Interview Protocol	A-1
Effective Questions	Primary and Secondary Questions	A-1a
Order and Time Constraints in Interview Protocols	Dropped	
Guidelines for Conducting Information Interviews	Information-Gathering Interviews	A-2
Doing Research	Choosing the Interviewee	A-2a
	New section: Following Up	A-2c
Conducting Employment Interviews	Employment Interviews	A-3
	New section: Following Up	A-3a
The Steps in Getting a Job	Job-seekers	A-4
Applying for the Job	Locating Job Openings	A-4a
It All Begins with Research	Preparing Application Materials	A-4b
Preparing to be Interviewed	Conducting the Employment Interview	A-4c
Strategies for Interviews with the Media	Media Interviews	A-5

Communicating Emotions Non-Verbally: Encoding and Decoding Skill and Practice

The Assignment

Your instructor will write a simple sentence on the board that you will recite to your classmates while attempting to convey a particular emotion non-verbally. First, you will use only your voice; then you will use your voice and face; and finally you will use your voice, face, and body. The sentence could be as simple as "I had bacon and eggs for breakfast this morning."

© Steve Devenport/iStockphoto.com

1. To find out the emotion you will convey, draw a card from a stack offered by your instructor. Without letting your classmates see, turn the card over to read what emotion is written on the front. Some possible emotions include *anger, excitement, fear, joy, worry,* and *sadness.* Consider how you will use vocalics and kinesics to convey that emotion.
2. When your instructor calls on you, go to the front of the classroom and face the wall (so your classmates cannot see your face). Try to convey that emotion with only your voice while saying the sentence with your back to the class.
3. The class might make some guesses about the emotion you are conveying and give some reasons for their guesses. You should not tell them whether they are correct at this point.
4. Turn around to face your classmates and say the sentence again, this time trying to reinforce the emotion with your face and eyes.
5. The class might again make some guesses.
6. Repeat the sentence once more, this time using your voice, face, and body to convey the emotion.
7. The class might again make some guesses.
8. Tell them the emotion that was on the card and what you did with your voice, face, and body to convey it.
9. Your instructor may lead a discussion about what worked and didn't as well as how you could have made the emotional message more clear.

Critical Listening

The Assignment

Find and attend a formal public presentation that is being given on campus or in your community. Your goal is to listen so that you remember and can critically evaluate what you have heard. Be sure to take notes and record the main ideas the speaker presents. After you have heard the speech, analyze what you heard. You can use the following questions to guide your initial thinking:

- What was the purpose of the speech? What was the speaker trying to explain to you or convince you about?
- Was it easy or difficult to identify the speaker's main ideas? What did you notice about how the speaker developed each point she or he made?
- Did the speaker use examples or tell stories to develop a point? If so, were these typical examples, or did the speaker choose examples that were unusual but seemed to prove the point?
- Did the speaker use statistics to back up what was said? If so, did the speaker tell you where the statistics came from? Did the statistics surprise you? If so, what would you have needed to hear that would have helped you accept them as accurate?
- Did the speaker do a good job? If so, why? If not, what should the speaker have done differently?

When you have finished your analysis, follow your instructor's directions. You may be asked to write a short essay about the speech or to present what you learned to the class.

Panel Discussion

The Assignment

Form a small group with three to five classmates. As a group, decide on a social issue or problem you would like to study in depth. Then select one group member to serve as moderator and the others as expert panelists. Members should do research to find out all they can about the issue, why it is a problem, and how it affects people and to what degree as well as potential ideas for solving it. The moderator's role is to come up with four to six good questions to ask the panelists. The panelists should prepare notes about the research they discovered.

On the day determined by the instructor, you will engage in a 15- to 20-minute panel discussion in front of your classmates. The moderator will guide the discussion by asking questions of the panelists as well as asking for questions from the class.

Suggested Format

1. Moderator thanks audience for coming and introduces the panelists and the topic.
2. Moderator asks panelists a series of questions, letting a different panelist respond first each time.
3. Moderator asks follow-up questions when appropriate.
4. Moderator asks for questions from the audience.
5. Moderator thanks the panelists and the audience members for participating.

A Persuasive Speech

The Assignment

1. Follow the speech plan Action Steps to prepare a speech in which you change audience belief. Your instructor will announce the time limit and other parameters for this assignment.
2. Criteria for evaluation include all the general criteria of topic and purpose, content, organization, and presentation, but special emphasis will be placed on the primary persuasive criteria of how well the speech's specific goal was adapted to the audience's initial attitude toward the topic, the soundness of the reasons, the evidence cited in support of them, and the credibility of the arguments.
3. Use the Persuasive Speech Evaluation Checklist in Figure 16.4 to critique yourself as you practice your speech.
4. Prior to presenting your speech, prepare a complete sentence outline and source list (bibliography). If you have used Speech Builder Express to complete the Action Step activities online, you will be able to print out a copy of your completed outline and source list. Also prepare a written plan for adapting your speech to the audience. Your adaptation plan should address the following issues:

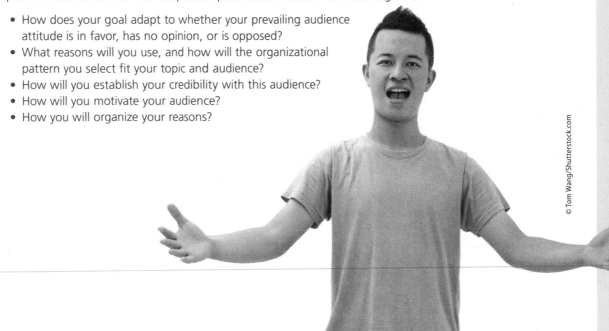

- How does your goal adapt to whether your prevailing audience attitude is in favor, has no opinion, or is opposed?
- What reasons will you use, and how will the organizational pattern you select fit your topic and audience?
- How will you establish your credibility with this audience?
- How will you motivate your audience?
- How you will organize your reasons?